# Selected
# Subaltern Studies

Edited by

Ranajit Guha
and
Gayatri Chakravorty Spivak

New York   Oxford
OXFORD UNIVERSITY PRESS
1988

Oxford University Press

Oxford   New York   Toronto
Delhi   Bombay   Calcutta   Madras   Karachi
Petaling Jaya   Singapore   Hong Kong   Tokyo
Nairobi   Dar es Salaam   Cape Town
Melbourne   Auckland

and associated companies in
Beirut   Berlin   Ibadan   Nicosia

The articles in this volume were first published in 1982, 1983, 1984, 1985, 1987
by Oxford University Press, India.

Published by Oxford University Press, Inc.
200 Madison Avenue, New York, New York 10016

First paperback edition published in 1988 by Oxford University Press, Inc., New York

Oxford is a registered trademark of Oxford University Press

Library of Congress Cataloging in Publication Data

Selected Subaltern studies / edited by Ranajit Guha and Gayatri Chakravorty Spivak.

p.   cm.
Selection of essays from five published collections of Subaltern studies between 1982 and 1987.
1. India—History—British occupation, 1765-1947.
I. Guha, Ranajit.   II. Spivak, Gayatri Chakravorty.   III. Subaltern studies.
DS463.S426 1988      954.03—dc19      87-34875
ISBN 0-19-505289-7 (PPBK.)

Printing (last digit): 9 8 7 6 5 4 3 2
Printed in the United States of America

# Selected Subaltern Studies

# Foreword

The first volume of *Sulbaltern Studies: Writings on South Asian History and Society* appeared in Delhi in 1982. Edited by Ranajit Guha, an extraordinarily brilliant Indian historian and political economist resident in Australia, it comprised six substantial essays — five of them massively detailed and frankly revisionist, one of them, Guha's, fiercely theoretical and intellectually insurrectionary. Guha's claim for the group of scholars his editorship had gathered together was relatively simple—that hitherto Indian history had been written from a colonialist and elitist point of view, whereas a large part of Indian history had been made by the subaltern classes, and hence the need for a new historiography which these scholars were now going to write—but its enactment and implementation would turn out to be complex and difficult. For not only was a great deal of new and otherwise neglected or ignored material to be excavated; there was also to be an appreciably greater heightening of the theoretical and methodological element. The point was that if a new, or at least more authentic, history of India was to be written, its authors had better bring forth new material and carefully justify the importance of this material as sufficiently as it was necessary to displace previous historical work on India.

The contents of the present volume, drawn from the five published collections of *Subaltern Studies* between 1982 and 1987, testify to the robustness of these ventures so far as Indian history is concerned. To the Western reader, however, *Subaltern Studies* does in fact also have a less specialized, more general importance, which it may be useful to speak about here. The word "subaltern," first of all, has both political and intellectual connotations. Its implied opposite is of course "dominant" or "elite," that is, groups in power, and in the Indian case, classes allied either with the British who held India for 300 years, or with a select number of disciples, students or epigones who in a sense collaborated with the British. The resonances of the word *subaltern* derive from Gramsci's usage in the *Prison Notebooks* in which, ever the astute political analyst and theoretical genius, he shows how wherever there is history, there is class, and that the essence of the historical is the long and extraordinarily varied socio-cultural interplay between ruler and ruled, between the elite, dominant, or hegemonic class and the subaltern and, as Gramsci calls it, the emergent class of the much greater mass of people ruled by coercive or sometimes mainly ideological domination from above.

Yet for the student of Indian history it is not so easy a matter as dividing India into British overlord, on the one hand, Indian nationalist on the other. There is the further distinction amongst Indians themselves, between those whose view of history essentially sees Indian independence as the result of stimulus by and reaction to British imperialism, or those who believe that guidance in the independence struggle was maintained by a small association of leaders, the Gandhis, Nehrus, Jinnas, et al. According to Guha, there is a major insufficiency in all these formulations. What is missing is the constitutive role of an enormous mass of subaltern Indians, the urban poor and the peasants, who throughout the nineteenth century and earlier, resisted British rule in terms and modes that were quite distinct from those employed by the elite. So one important historiographical prerogative of the Subaltern Studies group is to rewrite the history of colonial India from the distinct and separate point of view of the masses, using unconventional or neglected sources in popular memory, oral discourse, previously unexamined colonial administrative documents. This new history—an excellent example of which is Pandey's essay on peasant revolt—then provides an *alternative* history to the official one provided both by historians and by post-liberation Indian historians who adopt the formulae, the narratives and above all the ideology of history-writing from their own elite class alliances and from the British *raj*.

As an alternative discourse then, the work of the Subaltern scholars can be seen as an analogue of all those recent attempts in the West and throughout the rest of the world to articulate the hidden or suppressed accounts of numerous groups—women, minorities, disadvantaged or dispossessed groups, refugees, exiles, etc. And like all the authors of those other histories the Subaltern group in its work necessarily entails an examination of why, given numerical advantage, the justice of their cause, the great duration of their struggle, the Indian people *were* subaltern, why they were suppressed. As Guha puts it in his methodological opening statement, why the nation (the mass of India's people as distinct from the elite) did not come into its own is not just the *failure* of the people, "the study of this failure, . . .constitutes the central problematic of the historiography of colonial India."

I do not think it is an exaggeration to say therefore that rewriting Indian history today is an extension of the struggle between subaltern and elite, and between the Indian masses and the British *raj*. This is another way of underlining the concern with politics and power in *Subaltern Studies*. Theirs is no history of ideas, no calmly olympian narrative of events, no disengaged objective recital of facts. It is rather sharply contestary, an attempt to wrest control of the Indian past from its scribes and curators in the present, since, as we shall see, much of the past continues into the present. And if there can be no actual taking of power in the writing of history, there can at least be a demystifying exposure of what material interests are at stake, what ideology and method are employed, what parties advanced, which deferred, displaced, defeated. It is these types of strictly verbal and discursive tactics of which Gayatri Spivak speaks when she describes the "deconstruction" of historiography in *Subaltern Studies*.

The other side of this combative aspect of these scholars' work is its self-reflective, theoretically self-conscious dimension, which is remarkably different in tone and, I think, intent. Nearly every essay in the collection makes direct reference or alludes to the sheer difficulty of gaining access to the sources of subaltern history. Thus we find frequent reference to such things as gaps, absences, lapses, ellipses, all of them symbolic of the truths that historical writing is after all writing and not reality, and that as subalterns their history as well as their historical documents are necessarily in the hands of others, the Indian elite and the British colonizers who ran, as well as wrote the history of, India. In other words, subaltern history in literal fact is a narrative missing from the official story of India. Somehow to supply the narrative, or to supplement the existing narrative with a new narrative—these are epistemological tasks of great difficulty. It requires, and indeed receives, what in another connection Foucault has called a "relentless erudition," a deeply engaged search for new documents, a brilliantly resourceful re-deployment and re-interpretation of old documents, so much so that what emerges in such essays as Shahid Amin's extraordinary study of "Gandhi as Mahatma" is a new knowledge, more precarious perhaps than its familiar competitors, but strikingly rigorous, intellectually demanding, forceful and novel. Much the same can be said about Chakrabarty's essay on the knowledge of working class conditions, Gyanendra Pandey's history of a North Indian Qasba, Gautam Bhadra's alternative version of the 1857 rebellion.

The purely disciplinary aspects of dealing only with language and with documents who provenance and proprietary *morte-main* com complicate the research of the subaltern historian are set forth schematically by Guha in "The Prose of Counter-Insurgency." Yet even though his analysis is explicit on all the main issues, there is something that could perhaps be added to it here. And that is that no matter how one tried to extricate subaltern from elite histories, they are different but overlapping and curiously interdependent territories. This, I believe, is a crucial point. For if subaltern history is construed to be only a separatist enterprise—much as early feminist writing was based on the notion that women had a voice or a room of their own, entirely separate from the masculine domain—then it runs the risk of just being a mirror opposite the writing whose tyranny it disputes. It is also likely to be as exclusivist, as limited, provincial, and discriminatory in its suppressions and repressions as the master discourses of colonialism and elitism. In fact, as Guha shows, the subaltern alternative is an integrative knowledge, for all the gaps, the lapses and ignorances of which it is so conscious. Its claim is that by being subaltern it can see the whole experience of Indian resistance to colonialism more fairly than the partial histories provided by a handful of dominant native leaders or colonial historians. This is a claim not dissimilar in its moral force to Lukacs's theory of "proletarian" consciousness, where in a world of impoverished and yet fantastically widespread "reification," in which everything from the human soul to the product of human labor is turned into a commodity or an inert thing, only the view point of the human *thing* itself can comprehend and then resist the enormity of what has happened.

The bigger point of course is that Indian history continues into the present. Guha and his colleagues are oppositional critics, not only in their work about the past, but also in the conclusions their work pulls into the present. In the first place they represent a whole generation of intellectuals in the formerly colonized world who have achieved intellectual maturity after independence. We must remember that until the end of World War I, Europe and America held almost 85% of the entire world in the form of colonies, dependencies, mandates and subjugated territories. After that begins the great age of de-colonization in which all across the Third World emergent nationalist and liberation forces declare insurgencies against the Western powers. These insurgencies culminate in the post-World War II years when the classical empires were dismantled, and dozens of new independent sovereign states take their place in the world of nations. In many instances, however, the new states are still often ideologically in thrall to, and practical satellites of, their former colonial masters. Above all, the great transformation of which Frantz Fanon spoke, that after liberation, nationalist consciousness must convert itself into a new social consciousness, has not often taken place. In many new countries, dictatorships, fascist parties, brazenly neo-colonial regimes take power. Those intellectuals whose immediate predecessors fought the war of decolonization awake to the reality that imperialism continues, in newer and more complex forms. They go into opposition, politically but, more interestingly for our purposes here, also culturally and intellectually.

The nationalism that fueled the struggle, and the slogans against classical European colonialism—the quit India movement, the ideology of Arab nationalism, the pan-African movement, etc.—will no longer serve, one, because mere nationalism is undifferentiated and, two, because its thinking actually ignores allies in the metropolitan centers. The rejection of indiscriminately nationalist notions like "India for the Indians"—the nativist attitude—is the second important feature of Subaltern Studies' relationship to contemporary politics. The proper form of the slogan, they suggest, ought to be a question: which India for which Indians? Moreover there is the exciting intellectual discovery that the struggle against imperialism and its derivatives and heirs in the present may very profitably include the contribution of non-Indians, and indeed of many Europeans and Americans, whose oppositional strategies can be harnessed or solicited in the Indian context.

So in reading this selection from *Subaltern Studies* one becomes aware that this group of scholars is a self-conscious part of the vast post-colonial cultural and critical effort that would also include novelists like Salman Rushdie, Garcia Marquez, George Lamming,

Sergio Ramirez, and Ngugi Wa Thiongo, poets like Faiz Ahmad
Faiz, Mahmud Darwish, Aime Cesaire, theoreticians and political
philosophers like Fanon, Cabral, Syed Hussein Alatas, C.L.R.
James, Ali Shariati, Eqbal Ahmad, Abdullah Laroui, Omar Cabezas,
and a whole host of other figures, whose province is a post-indepen
dence world (the South of the new North-South configuration) still
dependent, still unfree, still dominated by coercion, the hegemony
of dictatorial regimes, derivative and hypocritical nationalisms, insuf-
fiently critical intellectual and ideological systems.

Yet this extraordinary common effort is not, as I implied above,
an exclusively non-European phenomenon. It is in fact a hybrid,
partaking jointly of European and Western streams and of native
Asian, Caribbean, Latin American, or African strands. None of the
Subaltern Studies scholars is anything less than a critical student of
Karl Marx, for example, and all of them have been influenced by
many varieties of Western Marxism, Gramsci's most eminently. In
addition, the influence of structuralist and post-structuralist thinkers
like Derrida, Foucault, Roland Barthes and Louis Althusser is evident, along with the influence of British and American thinkers,
like E.P. Thompson, Eric Hobsbawm, and others. Some of the
Subaltern themes—the notion of surveillance and bodily control in
Arnold's essay for example—are clearly indebted to earlier demystifi-
cations in Foucault, for example, but what we have here is the
sharing of a paradigm, rather than slavish copying.

All in all the first appearance of a selection from *Subaltern Studies*
before a general Anglo-American audience is a noteworthy event.
The rigid boundaries between academic specializations has produced
a whole gamut of jargons, of self-serving attitudes, of unattractive
provincialisms. But such boundaries are an extension of the imperialism that decreed the principle of "divide-and-rule." *Subaltern
Studies* represents a crossing of boundaries, a smuggling of ideas
across lines, a stirring up of intellectual and, as always, political
complacence. As an intervention in our current intellectual situation
this volume will accomplish an important shift in our awareness of
how scholarship and intellectual commitment combine resonsibly
in an invigorated social engagement.

New York                                           Edward W. Said
June 1987

# Editor's Note

It has been difficult to make a selection out of the uniformly exciting work of the Subaltern Studies collective. We are particularly sorry to exclude David Hardiman's "The Indian 'Faction'" from Volume I and Sumit Sarkar's "The Conditions and Nature of Subaltern Militancy" from Volume III. In making our choice, we have tried to keep a presumed audience in mind: not necessarily Indianist, but interested enough in the critique of imperialism to follow through the heterogeneity of the resistance to authority, coming from what Antonio Gramsci calls "the subaltern," during the colonial period in India.

Ranajit Guha is the general editor of all five volumes of *Subaltern Studies*. His "The Prose of Counter-Insurgency" has become the classic statement of the principle of their work. A revised version of my review of Subaltern Studies serves as introduction to this book.

The analysis of the construction of Mahatma Gandhi as a signifier for subaltern mobilization is an important achievement of the group. Shahid Amin's "Gandhi as Mahatma," and Gyan Pandey's "Peasant Revolt and Indian Nationalism" are examples of this. These pieces go into meticulous detail to make visible the problem with reading Gandhi as a monolithic figure in the seamless narrative of Indian nationalism.

The difference between indigenous subaltern perception of struggle and authoritative accounts thereof is a pervasive concern of the group. Gautam Bhadra's "Four Rebels of Eighteen-Fifty-Seven" and Gyan Pandey's "Encounters and Calamities" illustrate this. The first gives us an account of four subaltern participants in the Indian Mutiny of 1857. The second offers evidence of the contrast between subaltern and elite (colonial) narrativization of the "same" history, thus supplementing Guha's point in "The Prose of Counter-Insurgency."

The somewhat intransigent question of Western methods for Third World material is often posed in the generalized area of the critique of imperialism in the United States. In that context, it is useful to observe how Marxian and Foucauldian theories are transformed, modified, and augmented in Dipesh Chakrabarty's "Conditions for Knowledge of Working-Class Conditions," Partha Chatterjee's "More on Modes of Power and the Peasantry," and David Arnold's "Touching the Body;" often in terms of alternate structures and an alternative narrative of legitimation in the subcontinental context. I have already mentioned that nearly all the work of the group is an expansion and enrichment of Antonio Gramsci's notion of the subaltern. The heterogeneity that they present can be discovered only when the subaltern is seen in the subject-position. And in the final analysis, they make us ponder the fragility of the notion of nation and democracy when the elite, foreign and indigenous alike, intervene against the emergence of a demos.

Gayatri Chakravorty Spivak

April 1987
Jawaharlal Nehru University

# Contents

xiv Contents

# Selected Subaltern Studies

# Subaltern Studies: Deconstructing Historiography

## GAYATRI CHAKRAVORTY SPIVAK

### Change and Crisis

The work of the Subaltern Studies group offers a theory of change. The insertion of India into colonialism is generally defined as a change from semi-feudalism into capitalist subjection. Such a definition theorizes the change within the great narrative of the modes of production and, by uneasy implication, within the narrative of the transition from feudalism to capitalism. Concurrently, this change is seen as the inauguration of politicization for the colonized. The colonial subject is seen as emerging from those parts of the indigenous élite which come to be loosely described as 'bourgeois nationalist'. The Subaltern Studies group seems to me to be revising this general definition and its theorization by proposing at least two things: first, that the moment(s) of change be pluralized and plotted as confrontations rather than transition (they would thus be seen in relation to histories of domination and exploitation rather than within the great modes-of-production narrative) and, secondly, that such changes are signalled or marked by a functional change in sign-systems. The most important functional change is from the religious to the militant. There are, however, many other functional changes in sign-systems indicated in these collections: from crime to insurgency, from bondsman to worker, and so on.

The most significant outcome of this revision or shift in perspective is that the agency of change is located in the insurgent or the 'subaltern'.

A functional change in a sign system is a violent event. Even when it is perceived as 'gradual', or 'failed', or yet 'reversing itself', the change itself can only be operated by the force of a crisis. Yet, if the space for a change (necessarily also an addition) had not been there in the prior function of the sign-system, the crisis could not have made the change happen. The change in signification-function supplements the previous function.[1] The Subaltern Studies collective scrupulously annotates this double movement.

They generally perceive their task as making a theory of consciousness or culture rather than specifically a theory of change. It is because of this, I think, that the force of crisis, *although never far from their argument*, is not systematically emphasized in their work, and sometimes disarmingly alluded to as 'impingement', 'combination', 'getting caught up in a general wave', 'circumstances for unification', 'reasons for change', 'ambiguity', 'unease', 'transit', 'bringing into focus'; even as it is also described as 'switch', 'catching fire and, pervasively, as 'turning upside down'—all critical concept-metaphors that would indicate force.[2] Indeed, a general sobriety of tone will not allow them to emphasize sufficiently that they are themselves bringing hegemonic historiography to crisis. This leads them to describe the clandestine operation of supplementarity as the inexorable speculative logic of the dialectic. In this they seem to me to do themselves a disservice, for, as self-professed dialecticians, they open themselves to older debates between spontaneity and consciousness or structure and history. Their actual practice, which, I will argue, is closer to deconstruction, would put these oppositions into question. A theory of change as the site of the displacement of function between sign-systems—which is what they oblige me to read in them—is a theory of reading in the strongest possible general sense. The site of displacement of

[1] For crisis, see Paul de Man, *Blindness and Insight: Essays in the Rhetoric of Contemporary Criticism* (Minneapolis: Univ. of Minnesota Press, 1983), p. 8. For supplement, see Jacques Derrida, *Writing and Difference*, tr. Alan Bass (Chicago: Univ. of Chicago Press, 1982), p. 289. All translations modified when necessary.

[2] Ranajit Guha, ed., *Subaltern Studies I: Writings on South Asian History and Society* (Delhi: Oxford Univ. Press, 1981), p. 83, 86, 186. The three volumes of *Subaltern Studies* are hereafter cited in my text as 1, 2, and 3 with page references following. 2.65, 115; 3.21, 71. Also Ranajit Guha, *Elementary Aspects of Peasant Insurgency in Colonial India* (Delhi: Oxford Univ. Press, 1983), pp. 88, 226, 30, 318; hereafter cited in my text as *EAP*, with page references following.

the function of signs is the name of reading as active transaction between past and future. This transactional reading as (the possibility of) action, even at its most dynamic, is perhaps what Antonio Gramsci meant by 'elaboration', *e-laborare*, working out.[3] If seen in this way, the work of the Subaltern Studies group repeatedly makes it possible for us to grasp that the concept-metaphor of the 'social text' is not the reduction of real life to the page of a book. My theoretical intervention is a modest attempt to remind us of this.

It can be advanced that their work presupposes that the entire socius, at least in so far as it is the object of their study, is what Nietzsche would call a *fortgesetzte Zeichenkette*—a 'continuous sign-chain'. The possibility of action lies in the dynamics of the disruption of this object, the breaking and relinking of the chain. This line of argument does not set consciousness over against the socius, but sees it as itself also constituted as and on a semiotic chain. It is thus an instrument of study which participates in the nature of the object of study. To see consciousness thus is to place the historian in a position of irreducible compromise. I believe it is because of this double bind that it is possible to unpack the aphoristic remark of Nietzsche's that follows the image of the sign-chain with reference to this double bind: 'All concepts in which an entire process is comprehended [*sich zusammenfasst*] withdraws itself from [*sich entzieht*] definition; only that which has no history is definable.'[4] At any rate these presuppositions are not, strictly speaking, consonant with a desire to find a consciousness (here of the subaltern) in a positive and pure state. My essay will also try to develop this discrepancy.

## Cognitive Failure is Irreducible

All of the accounts of attempted discursive displacements provided by the group are accounts of failures. For the subaltern displacements, the reason for failure most often given is the much greater scope, organization, and strength of the colonial authorities. In the case of the nationalist movement for independence it is clearly pointed out that the bourgeoisie's 'interested' refusal to recognize the importance of, and to ally themselves with, a politicized peasan-

[3] See Edward W. Said, *The World, the Text, and the Critic* (Cambridge: Harvard Univ. Press, 1983), pp. 170-2 for a discussion of "elaboration" in Gramsci.

[4] Friedrich Nietzsche, *On the Genealogy of Morals and Ecce Homo*, tr. Walter J. Kaufmann (New York: Vintage Books, 1969), pp. 77, 80.

try accounted for the failure of the discursive displacement that operated the peasants' politicization. Yet there is also an incipient evolutionism here which, trying perhaps to avoid a vulgar Marxist glorification of the peasant, lays the blame on 'the existing level of peasant consciousness' for the fact 'that peasant solidarity and peasant power were seldom sufficient or sustained enough' (3.52, 3.115). This contradicts the general politics of the group—which sees the élite's hegemonic access to 'consciousness' as an interpretable construct.

To examine this contradiction we must first note that discursive displacements wittingly or unwittingly operated from above are also failures. Chakrabarty, Das, and Chandra chart the failures of trade union socialism, functionalist entrepreneurialism and agrarian communism to displace a semi-feudal into a 'modern' discourse. Chatterjee shows how Gandhi's initial dynamic transaction with the discursive field of the Hindu religious Imaginary had to be travestied in order that his ethics of resistance could be displaced into the sign system of bourgeois politics.[5] My point is, simply, that failures or partial successes in discursive-field displacement do not necessarily relate, following a progressivist scale, to the 'level of consciousness' of a class.

Elite historiography itself, on the right or the left, nationalist or colonialist, is by the analysis of this group, shown to be constituted by cognitive failures. Indeed, if the theory of change as the site of the displacement of a discursive field is their most pervasive argument, this comes a close second. Here too no distinction is made, quite properly in my estimation, between witting and unwitting lapses. It is correctly suggested that the sophisticated vocabulary of much contemporary historiography *successfully* shields this cognitive *failure* and that this success-in-failure, this sanctioned ignorance, is inseparable from colonial domination.

Within this tracking of successful cognitive failure, the most interesting manoeuvre is to examine the production of 'evidence', the

---

[5] Chakrabarty, "Conditions for Knowledge," (in this volume), Arvind N. Das, "Agrarian Change from Above and Below: Bihar 1947-78," 2; N.K. Chandra, "Agricultural Workers in Burdwan," 2. I am using the word "Imaginary" loosely in the sense given to it by Jacques Lacan. For a short definition, see Jean Laplanche and J.B. Pontalis, *The Language of Psycho-Analysis*, tr. David Nicholson-Smith (New York: Norton, 1973), p. 210.

cornerstone of the edifice of historical truth (3.231–70), and to anatomize the mechanics of the construction of the self-consolidating Other—the insurgent and insurgency. In this part of the project, Guha seems to radicalize the historiography of colonial India through a combination of Soviet and Barthesian semiotic analysis. The discursivity (cognitive failure) of disinterested (successful and therefore true) historiography is revealed. The Muse of History and counter-insurgency are shown to be complicit (2.1–42 & *EAP*).

I am suggesting, of course, that an implicitly evolutionist or progressivist set of presuppositions measuring failure or success in terms of level of consciousness is too simple for the practice of the collective. If we look at the varieties of activity treated by them, subaltern, insurgent, nationalist, colonialist, historiographic, it is a general field of failures that we see. In fact the work of the collective is making the distinction between success and failure indeterminate—for the most successful historical record is disclosed by them to be crosshatched by cognitive failure. Since in the case of the subaltern they are considering consciousness (however 'negative') and culture (however determining); and in the case of the élite, culture and manipulation—the subaltern is also operating in the theatre of 'cognition'. At any rate, where does cognition begin and end? I will consider later the possible problems with such compartmentalized views of consciousness. Here suffice it to say that by the ordinary standards of coherence, and in terms of their own methodology, the possibility of failure cannot be derived from any criterion of success unless the latter is a theoretical fiction.[6]

A word on 'alienation', as used by members of this group, to mean 'a failure of *self*-cognition', is in order here.

> To overestimate . . . [the] lucidity or depth [of the subaltern consciousness] will be . . . ill-advised . . . This characteristic expression of a negative consciousness on the insurgent's part matched its other symptom, that is, his self-alienation. He was still committed to envisaging the coming war on the Raj as the project of a will independent of himself and his own role in it as no more than instrumental . . . [In their own] parwana

---

[6] As always my preferred example of a theoretical fiction remains the primary process in Freud. *The Complete Psychological Works*, tr. James Strachey et al. (London: Hogarth Press, 1961), vol. 5, p. 598f.

[proclamation] . . . the authors did not recognize even their own voice, but heard only that of God (*EAP* 28).

To be sure, within his progressivist narrative taxonomy Hegel describes the march of history in terms of a diminution in the self-alienation of the so-called world historical agent. Kojève and his followers in France distinguished between this Hegel, the narrator of (a) history, and the speculative Hegel who outlined a system of logic.[7] Within the latter, alienation is irreducible in any act of consciousness. Unless the subject separates from itself to grasp the object there is no cognition, indeed no thinking, no judgment. Being and Absolute Idea, the first and last sections of *The Science of Logic*, two accounts of simple unalienability, are not accessible to individual or personal consciousness. From the strictly philosophical point of view, then, (a) élite historiography (b) the bourgeois nationalist account, as well as (c) re-inscription by the Subaltern Studies group, are operated by alienation—*Verfremdung* as well as *Entäu Berung*. Derrida's reading of Hegel as in *Glas* would question the argument for the inalienability even of Absolute Necessity and Absolute Knowledge, but here we need not move that far. We must ask the opposite question. How shall we deal with Marx's suggestion that man must strive toward self-determination and unalienated practice and Gramsci's that 'the lower classes' must 'achieve self-awareness via a series of negations?'[8]

Formulating an answer to this question might lead to far-reaching practical effects if the risks of the irreducibility of cognitive 'failure' and of 'alienation' are accepted. The group's own practice can then be graphed on this grid of 'failures', with the concept of failure generalized and re-inscribed as I have suggested above. This subverts the inevitable vanguardism of a theory that otherwise criticizes the vanguardism of theory. This is why I hope to align them with deconstruction: 'Operating necessarily from the inside, borrowing all the strategic and economic resources of subversion from the old structure, borrowing them structurally, that is to say without being

---

[7] For an excellent discussion of this, see Judith Butler, "Geist ist Zeit: French Interpretations of Hegel's Absolute", *Berkshire Review* 20 (Summer, 1985), p. 66-80.

[8] Antonio Gramsci, cited in *EAP* 28.

able to isolate their elements and atoms, the enterprise of deconstruction always in a certain way falls prey to its own work.'[9]

This is the greatest gift of deconstruction: to question the authority of the investigating subject without paralysing him, persistently transforming conditions of impossibility into possibility.[10] Let us pursue the implications of this in our particular case.

The group, as we have seen, tracks failures in attempts to displace discursive fields. A deconstructive approach would bring into focus the fact that they are themselves engaged in an attempt at displacing discursive fields, that they themselves 'fail' (in the general sense) for reasons as 'historical' as those they adduce for the heterogeneous agents they study; and would attempt to forge a practice that would take this into account. Otherwise, refusing to acknowledge the implications of their own line of work because that would be politically incorrect, they would, willy-nilly, 'insidiously objectify' the subaltern (2.262), control him through knowledge even as they restore versions of causality and self-determination to him (2.30), become complicit, in their desire for totality (and therefore totalization) (3.317), with a 'law [that] assign[s] a[n] undifferentiated [proper] name' (*EAP* 159) to 'the subaltern as such'.

### Subaltern Studies and the European Critique of Humanism

A 'religious idiom gave the hillmen [of the Eastern Ghats] a framework, within which to conceptualize their predicament and to seek solutions to it' (1.140–1). The idiom of recent European theories of interpretation seem to offer this collective a similar framework. As they work their displacement, they are, as I suggest above, expanding the semantic range of 'reading' and 'text', words that are, incidentally, not prominent in their vocabularly. It is appropriately marked by attempts to find local parallels, as in the concept of *atideśa* in Guha's work, and to insert the local into the general, as in the pervasive invocation of English, French, German, and occasionally Italian insurgency in *EAP*, and in the invocation of the

---

[9] Derrida, *Of Grammatology*, tr. Spivak (Baltimore: Johns Hopkins Univ. Press, 1976), p. 24.

[10] Since the historian is gender-specific in the work of the collective (see pp. 33-43), I have consistently used "he".

anthropology of Africa in Partha Chatterjee's work on modes of power.

It is the force of a crisis that operates functional displacements in discursive fields. In my reading of the volumes of *Subaltern Studies*, this critical force or bringing-to-crisis can be located in the energy of the questioning of humanism in the post-Nietzschean sector of Western European structuralism, for our group Michel Foucault, Roland Barthes, and a certain Lévi-Strauss. These structuralists question humanism by exposing its hero—the sovereign subject as author, the subject of authority, legitimacy, and power. There is an affinity between the imperialist subject and the subject of humanism. Yet the crisis of anti-humanism—*like all crises*—does not move our collective 'fully'. The rupture shows itself to be also a repetition. They fall back upon notions of consciousness-as-agent, totality, and upon a culturalism, that are discontinuous with the critique of humanism. They seem unaware of the historico-political provenance of their various Western 'collaborators'. Vygotsky and Lotman, Victor Turner and Lévi-Strauss, Evans-Pritchard and Hindess and Hirst can, for them, fuel the same fire as Foucault and Barthes. Since one cannot accuse this group of the eclecticism of the supermarket consumer, one must see in their practice a repetition of as well as a rupture from the colonial predicament: the transactional quality of inter-conflicting metropolitan sources often eludes the (post)colonial intellectual.

## The Problem of Subaltern Consciousness

To investigate, discover, and establish a subaltern or peasant consciousness seems at first to be a positivistic project—a project which assumes that, if properly prosecuted, it will lead to firm ground, to some *thing* that can be disclosed. This is all the more significant in the case of recovering a consciousness because, within the post-Enlightenment tradition that the collective participates in as interventionist historians, consciousness is *the* ground that makes all disclosures possible.

And, indeed, the group is susceptible to this interpretation. There *is* a certain univocal reflection or signification-theory presupposed here by which 'peasant action in famine as in rebellion' is taken to 'reflect . . a single underlying consciousness' (3.112); and 'solidarity' is seen as a 'signifier of consciousness', where signification is representation, figuration, propriation (stringent de-limitation within a unique and self-adequate outline), and imprinting (*EAP* 169).

Yet even as 'consciousness' is thus entertained as an indivisible self-proximate signified or ground, there is a force at work here which would contradict such a metaphysics. For consciousness here is not consciousness-in-general, but a historicized political species thereof, subaltern consciousness. In a passage where 'transcendental' is used as 'transcending, because informing a hegemonic narrative' rather than in a strictly philosophical sense, Guha puts this admirably: 'Once a peasant rebellion has been assimilated to the career of the Raj, the Nation or the people [the hegemonic narratives], it becomes easy for the historian to abdicate the responsibility he has of exploring and describing the consciousness specific to that rebellion and be content to ascribe to it a transcendental consciousness . . . representing them merely as instruments of some other will' (2.38).

Because of this bestowal of a historical specificity to consciousness in the narrow sense, even as it implicitly operates as a metaphysical methodological presupposition in the general sense, there is always a counterpointing suggestion in the work of the group that subaltern consciousness is subject to the cathexis of the élite, that it is never fully recoverable, that it is always askew from its received signifiers, indeed that it is effaced even as it is disclosed, that it is irreducibly discursive. It is, for example, chiefly a matter of 'negative consciousness' in the more theoretical of these essays. Although 'negative consciousness' is conceived of here as an historical stage peculiar to the subaltern, there is no logical reason why, given that the argument is inevitably historicized, this 'negative', rather than the grounding positive view of consciousness, should not be generalized as the group's methodological presupposition. One view of 'negative consciousness', for instance, sees it as the consciousness not of the being of the subaltern, but of that of the oppressors (*EAP* chap. 2, 3.183). Here, in vague Hegelian limnings, is the anti-humanist and anti-positivist position that it is always the desire for/ of (the power of the Other) that produces an image of the self. If this is generalized, as in my reading of the 'cognitive failure' argument, it is the subaltern who provides the model for a general theory of consciousness. And yet, since the 'subaltern' cannot

appear without the thought of the 'élite', the generalization is by definition incomplete—in philosophical language 'non-originary'.

Another note in the counterpoint deconstructing the metaphysics
of consciousness in these texts is provided by the reiterated fact that
it is only the texts of counter-insurgency or élite documentation
that give us the news of the consciousness of the subaltern. 'The
peasants' view of the struggle will probably never be recovered, and
whatever we say about it at this stage must be very tentative' (1.50);
'Given the problems of documenting the consciousness of the jute
mill workers, their will to resist and question the authority of their
employers can be read only in terms of the sense of crisis it produced among the people in authority' (3.121); 'It should be possible
to read the presence of a rebel consciousness as a necessary and
pervasive element within that body of evidence' (*EAP* 15). To be
sure, it is the vocabulary of 'this stage', 'will to resist', and 'presence'. Yet the language seems also to be straining to acknowledge
that the subaltern's view, will, presence, can be no more than a
theoretical fiction to entitle the project of reading. It cannot be recovered, 'it will probably never be recovered'. If I shifted to the
slightly esoteric register of the language of French post-
structuralism, I could put it thus: 'Thought [here the thought of
subaltern consciousness] is here for me a perfectly neutral name, the
blank part of the text, the necessarily indeterminate index of a future
epoch of difference.[11]

Once again, in the work of this group, what had seemed the historical predicament of the colonial subaltern can be made to become
the allegory of the predicament of *all* thought, *all* deliberative consciousness, though the élite profess otherwise. This might seem pre-
posterous at first glance. A double take is in order. I will propose it
in closing this section of my paper.

I am progressively inclined, then, to read the retrieval of subaltern
consciousness as the charting of what in post-structuralist language
would be called the subaltern subject-effect.[12] A subject-effect can
be briefly plotted as follows: that which seems to operate as a sub-

---

[11] Derrida, *Of Grammatology*, p. 93. Since my intention here is simply to offer a
moment of transcoding, I have not undertaken to "explain" the Derridean passage.

[12] The most, perhaps too, spectacular deployment of the argument is in Gilles
Deleuze and Felix Guattari, *Anti-Oedipus: Capitalism and Schizophrenia*, tr. Robert
Hurley et al. (New York: Viking Press, 1977).

ject may be part of an immense discontinuous network ('text' in the general sense) of strands that may be termed politics, ideology, economics, history, sexuality, language, and so on. (Each of these strands, if they are isolated, can also be seen as woven of many strands.) Different knottings and configurations of these strands, determined by heterogeneous determinations which are themselves dependent upon myriad circumstances, produce the effect of an operating subject. Yet the continuist and homogenist deliberative consciousness symptomatically requires a continuous and homogeneous cause for this effect and thus posits a sovereign and determining subject. This latter is, then, the effect of an effect, and its positing a metalepsis, or the substitution of an effect for a cause. Thus do the texts of counter-insurgency locate, in the following description, a 'will' as the sovereign cause when it is no more than an effect of the subaltern subject-effect, itself produced by the particular conjunctures called forth by the crises meticulously described in the various *Subaltern Studies*:

> It is of course true that the reports, despatches, minutes, judgements, laws, letters, etc. in which policemen, soldiers, bureaucrats, landlords, usurers and others hostile to insurgency register their sentiments, amount to a representation of their will. But these documents do not get their content from that will alone, for the latter is predicated on another will—that of the insurgent. It should be possible therefore to read the presence of a rebel consciousness as a necessary and pervasive element within that body of evidence (*EAP* 15).

From within but against the grain, elements in their text would warrant a reading of the project to retrieve the subaltern consciousness as the attempt to undo a massive historiographic metalepsis and 'situate' the effect of the subject as subaltern. I would read it, then as a *strategic* use of positivist essentialism in a scrupulously visible political interest. This would put them in line with the Marx who locates fetishization, the ideological determination of the 'concrete', and spins the narrative of the development of the money-form; with the Nietzsche who offers us genealogy in place of historiography, and the Derrida of 'affirmative deconstruction'. This would allow them to use the critical force of anti-humanism, in other words, even as they share its constitutive paradox: that the essentializing moment, the object of their criticism, is irreducible.

The strategy becomes most useful when 'consciousness' is being

used in the narrow sense, as *self*-consciousness. When 'consciousness' is being used in that way, Marx's notion of un-alienated practice
or Gramsci's notion of an 'ideologically *coherent*', 'spontaneous
philosophy of the multitude' are plausible and powerful.[13] For
class-consciousness does not engage the ground-level of
consciousness—consciousness in general. 'Class' is not, after all, an
inalienable description of a human reality. Class-consciousness on
the *descriptive* level is itself a strategic and artificial rallying awareness which, on the *transformative* level, seeks to destroy the mechanics which come to construct the outlines of the very class of which
a collective consciousness has been situationally developed. 'Any
member of the insurgent community'—Guha spends an entire
chapter showing how that collective consciousness of community
develops—'who chooses to continue in such subalternity is regarded as hostile towards the inversive process initiated by the
struggle and hence as being on the enemy's side' (*EAP* 202). The
task of the 'consciousness' of class or collectivity within a social
field of exploitation and domination is thus necessarily self-
alienating.[14]

It is within the framework of a strategic interest in the
self-alienating displacing move of and by a consciousness of
collectivity, then, that self-determination and an unalienated
self-consciousness can be broached. In the definitions of 'consciousness' offered by the Subaltern Studies group there are
plenty of indications that they are in fact concerned with
consciousness not in the general, but in this crucial narrow sense.

Subaltern consciousness as emergent *collective* consciousness is
one of the main themes of these books. The group places this theory
of the emergent collective subaltern consciousness squarely in the
context of that tendency within Western Marxism which would refuse
class-consciousness to the pre-capitalist subaltern, especially in the
theatres of Imperialism. Chakrabarty's analysis of how historically

[13] Gramsci, *Prison Notebooks*, tr. Quintin Hoare and Geoffrey Noel-Smith (New
York: International Publishers, 1971), p. 421.

[14] The tradition of the English translations of Marx often obliterates this. Consider,
for example, the fate of *Aufhebung* in Karl Marx and Friedrick Engels, "The Manifesto
of the Communist Party," *Selected Works* (Moscow: Foreign Languages Publishing
House, 1951), p. 51 in the light of Hegel's explanation of the term in *The Science of
Logic*, tr. A.V. Miller (New York: Humanities Press, 1976), p. 107.

unsound it is simply to reverse the gesture and try to impose a Marxian *working*-class consciousness upon the urban proletariat in a colonial context and, by implication, as Guha shows, upon the rural subaltern, takes its place within this confrontation.

For readers who notice the points of contact between the Subaltern Studies group and critics of humanism such as Barthes and Foucault, the confusion arises because of the use of the word 'consciousness', unavoidably a post-phenomenological and post-psychoanalytic issue with such writers. I am not trying to clear the confusion by revealing through analysis that the Subaltern Studies group is not entertaining 'consciousness' within that configuration at all, but is rather working exclusively with the second-level collective consciousness to be encountered in Marx and the classical Marxist tradition. I am suggesting, rather, that although the group does not wittingly engage with the post-structuralist understanding of 'consciousness', our own transactional reading of them is enhanced if we see them as *strategically* adhering to the essentialist notion of consciousness, that would fall prey to an anti-humanist critique, within a historiographic practice that draws many of its strengths from that very critique.

## Historiography as Strategy

Can a strategy be unwitting? Of course not fully so. Consider, however, statements such as the following: '[a] discrepancy . . . is necessarily there at certain stages of the class struggle between the level of its objective articulation and that of the consciousness of its subjects'; or, 'with all their practical involvement in a rebellion the masses could still be tricked by a false consciousness into trusting the magical faculties of warrior heroes . . .'; or yet, 'the peasant rebel of colonial India could do so [learn his very first lesson in power] only by translating it backwards into the semi-feudal language of politics to which he was born' (*EAP* 173, 270, 76). A theory which allows a partial lack of fit in the fabrication of any strategy cannot consider itself immune from its own system. It must remain caught within the possibility of that predicament in its own case. If in translating bits and pieces of discourse theory and the critique of humanism back into an essentialist historiography the historian of subalternity aligns himself to the pattern of conduct of the subaltern himself, it is only a progressivist view, that diagnoses the subaltern as necessarily inferior, that will see such an alignment to be without interventionist value. Indeed it is in their very insistence upon the subaltern as the subject of history that the group acts out such a translating back, an interventionist strategy that is only partially unwitting.

If it were embraced as a strategy, then the emphasis upon the 'sovereignty, . . . consistency and . . . logic' of 'rebel consciousness' (*EAP* 13) can be seen as 'affirmative deconstruction': knowing that such an emphasis is theoretically non-viable, the historian then breaks his theory in a scrupulously delineated 'political interest'.[15] If, on the other hand, the restoration of the subaltern's subject-position in history is seen by the historian as the establishment of an inalienable and final truth of things, then any emphasis on sovereignty, consistency, and logic will, as I have suggested above, inevitably objectify the subaltern and be caught in the game of knowledge as power. Even if the discursivity of history is seen as a *fortgesetzte Zeichenkette*, a restorative genealogy cannot be undertaken without the strategic blindness that will entangle the genealogist in the chain. It is in this spirit that I read *Subaltern Studies* against its grain and suggest that its own subalternity in claiming a *positive* subject-position for the subaltern might be reinscribed as a strategy for our times.

What good does such a re-inscription do? It acknowledges that the arena of the subaltern's persistent emergence into hegemony must always and by definition remain heterogenous to the efforts of the disciplinary historian. The historian must persist in *his* efforts in this awareness, that the subaltern is necessarily the absolute limit of the place where history is narrativized into logic. It is a hard lesson to learn, but not to learn it is merely to nominate elegant solutions to be correct theoretical practice. When has history ever contradicted that practice norms theory, as subaltern practice norms official historiography in this case? If that assumption, rather than the dissonant thesis of the subaltern's infantility were to inhabit *Subaltern Studies*, then their project would be proper to itself in recognizing that it can never be proper to 'subaltern consciousness'; that

---

[15] This concept-metaphor of "interest" is orchestrated by Derrida in *Spurs*, tr. Barbara Harlow (Chicago: Univ. of Chicago Press, 1978) with notions of "affirmative deconstruction", which would acknowledge that no example of deconstruction can match its discourse.

it can never be continuous with the subaltern's situational and uneven entry into political (not merely disciplinary, as in the case of
the collective) hegemony as the content of an after-the-fact description. This is the always asymmetrical relationship between the interpretation and transformation of the world which Marx marks in the
eleventh thesis on Feuerbach. There the contrast is between the
words *haben interpretiert* (present participle—a completed action—
of *interpretieren*—the Romance verb which emphasizes the establishment of a meaning that is commensurate with a phenomenon
through the metaphor of the fair exchange of prices) and *zu ver-
ändern* (infinitive—always open to the future—of the German verb
which 'means' strictly speaking, 'to make other'). The latter expression matches *haben interpretiert* neither in its Latinate philosophical weight nor in its signification of propriety and completion,
as *transformieren* would have done. Although not an unusual word,
it is not the most common word for 'change' in German—
*verwandeln*. In the open-ended 'making-other'—*ver-änderung*—of
the properly self-identical—adequately *interpretiert*—lies an allegory of the theorist's relationship to his subject-matter. (There is no
room here to comment on the richness of 'es kommt darauf an', the
syntactical phrase that joins the two parts of the Eleventh Thesis.) It
is not only '*bad*' theory but *all* theory that is susceptible to this
open-endedness.

Theoretical descriptions cannot produce universals. They can
only ever produce provisional generalizations, even as the theorist
realizes the crucial importance of their persistent production.
Otherwise, because they desire perhaps to claim some unspecified
direct hand in subaltern practice, the conclusions to the essays become abrupt, inconclusive, sometimes a series of postponements in
some empirical project. One striking example of this foreclosed desire is where Das, in an otherwise brilliant essay, repudiates *formal-
ization* as thwarting for practice, even as he deplores the lack of
sufficient *generalization* that might have allowed subaltern practice
to flourish (2.227).

The radical intellectual in the West is either caught in a deliberate
choice of subalternity, granting to the oppressed either that very expressive subjectivity which s/he criticizes or, instead, a total unrep-
resentability. The logical negation of this position is produced by
the discourse of post-modernism, where the 'mass is only the mass

because its social energy has already frozen. It is a cold reservoir, capable of absorbing and neutralizing any hot energy. It resembles those half-dead systems into which more energy is injected than is withdrawn, those paid-out deposits exorbitantly maintained in a state of artificial exploitation.' This negation leads to an emptying of the subject-position: "Not to arrive at the point where one no longer says I, but at the point where it's no longer of any importance whether one says I or not.'[16] Although some of these Western intellectuals express genuine concern about the ravages of contemporary neo-colonialism is their own nation-states, they are not knowledgeable in the history of imperialism, in the epistemic violence that constituted/effaced a subject that was obliged to cathect (occupy in response to a desire) the space of the Imperialists' self-consolidating other. It is almost as if the force generated by their crisis is separated from its appropriate field by a sanctioned ignorance of that history.

It is my contention that, if the Subaltern Studies group saw their own work of subject-restoration as crucially strategic, they would not miss this symptomatic blank in contemporary Western anti-humanism. In his innovative essay on modes of power, Partha Chatterjee quotes Foucault on the eighteenth century and writes:

> Foucault has sought to demonstrate the complexities of this novel regime of power in his studies of the history of mental illness, of clinical practice, of the prison, of sexuality and of the rise of the human sciences. When one looks at regimes of power in the so-called backward countries of the world today, not only does the dominance of the characteristically 'modern' modes of exercise of power seem limited and qualified by the persistence of older modes, but by the fact of their combination in a particular state and formation, it seems to open up at the same time an entirely new range of possibilities for the ruling classes to exercise their domination (3.348–9).

I have written earlier that the force of crisis is not systematically emphasized in the work of the group. The Foucauldian example being considered here, for instance, can be seen as marking a crisis *within* European consciousness. A few months before I had read Chatterjee's essay, I wrote a few sentences uncannily similar in

---

[16] Jean Baudrillard, *In the Shadow of the Silent Majorities or the End of the Social and Other Essays,* tr. Paul Foss et al. (New York; Semiotext(e), 1983), p. 26: and Deleuze and Guattari, *On the Line,* tr. John Johnston (New York: Semiotext(e), 1983), p. 1.

sentiment upon the very same passage in Foucault. I write, of course, within a workplace engaged in the ideological production of neo-colonialism even through the influence of such thinkers as Foucault. It is not therefore necessarily a mark of extraordinary acumen that what I am calling the crisis in European consciousness is much more strongly marked in my paragraph, which I take the liberty of quoting here. My contention below is that the relationship between First World anti-humanist post-Marxism and the history of imperialism is not merely a question of 'enlarging the range of possibilities', as Chatterjee soberly suggests above.

> Although Foucault is a brilliant thinker of power-in-spacing, the awareness of the topographic reinscription of imperialism does not inform his presuppositions. He is taken in by the restricted version of the West produced by that reinscription and thus helps to consolidate its effects. Notice, for example, the omission of the fact, in the following passage, that the new mechanism of power in the seventeenth and eighteenth centuries (the extraction of surplus-value without extra-economic coercion is its Marxist description) is secured *by means of* territorial imperialism—the Earth and its products—'elsewhere'. The representation of sovereignty is crucial in those theatres: 'In the seventeenth and eighteenth centuries, we have the production of an important phenomenon, the emergence, or rather the invention, of a new mechanism of power possessed of highly specific procedural techniques . . . which is also, I believe, absolutely incompatible with the relations of sovereignty . . . '. I am suggesting that to buy a self-contained version of the West is symptomatically to ignore its production by the spacing-timing of the imperialist project. Sometimes it seems as if the very brilliance of Foucault's analysis of the centuries of European imperialism produces a miniature version of that heterogeneous phenomenon: management of space—but by doctors, development of administrations—but in asylums, considerations of the periphery—but in terms of the insane, prisoners, and children. The clinic, the asylum, the prison, the university, seem screen-allegories that foreclose a reading of the broader narratives of imperialism.[17]

Thus the discourse of the unified consciousness of the subaltern *must* inhabit the strategy of these historians, even as the discourse of the micrologized or 'situated' subject must mark that of anti-humanists on the other side of the international division of labour. The two following remarks by Ranajit Guha and Louis Althusser

[17] Spivak, "Can the Subaltern Speak?".

can then be seen as marking not a contradiction but the fracture of a discontinuity of philosophic levels, *as well as* a strategic asymmetry: 'Yet we propose', writes Guha in the eighties, 'to focus on this consciousness as our central theme, because it is not possible to make sense of the experience of insurgency merely as a history of events without a subject' (4.11). Precisely, 'it is not possible'. And Althusser, writing in 1967:

> Undeniably, for it has passed into his works, and *Capital* demonstrates it, Marx owes to Hegel the decisive philosophical category of process. He owes him yet more, that Feuerbach himself did not suspect. He owes him the concept of the process *without subject* . . . . The origin, indispensable to the teleological nature of the process . . . must be *denied* from the start, so that the process of alienation may be a process without subject . . . . Hegel's logic is of the affirmed-denied Origin: first form of a concept that Derrida has introduced into philosophical reflection, the *erasure*.[18]

As Chakrabarty has rightly stated, 'Marx thought that the logic of capital could be best deciphered only in a society where "the notion of human equality has already acquired the fixity of a popular prejudice" ' (2.263). The first lesson of ideology is that a 'popular prejudice' mistakes itself for 'human nature', the original mother-tongue of history. Marxist historiography can be caught within the mother-tongue of a history and a culture that had graduated to bourgeois individualism. As groups such as the Subaltern Studies collective attempt to open up the texts of Marx beyond his European provenance, beyond a homogeneous internationalism, to the persistent recognition of heterogeneity, the very goal of 'forget-[ting] his original [or "rooted"—*die ihm angestammte Sprache*] language while using the new one' must be reinscribed.[19] A repeated acknowledgement of the complicity of the new and the 'original' is now on the agenda. I have tried to indicate this by deconstructing the opposition between the collective and their object of investigation—the subaltern—on the one hand; and by deconstructing the seeming continuity between them and their anti-humanist models on the other.

---

[18] Althusser, "Sur le rapport de Marx à Hegel" in *Hegel et la pensée moderne*, ed. Jacques d'Hondt (Paris: Presses universitaires, 1970), pp. 108-9.

[19] Karl Marx, "The Eighteenth Brumaire of Louis Bonaparte", in *Surveys from Exile*, ed. David Fernbach (New York: Vintage Books, 1974), p. 147.

You can only read against the grain if misfits in the text signal the way. (These are sometimes called 'moments of transgression' or 'critical moments'.) I should like to bring the body of my argument to a close by discussing two such moments in the work of this group. First, the discussion of rumour; and, second, the place of woman in their argument.

## Rumour

The most extensive discussion of rumour, to be found in *EAP*, is not, strictly speaking, part of the work of the group. I think I am correct, however, in maintaining that Guha's pages make explicit an implicit set of assumptions about the nature and role of subaltern means of communication, such as rumour, in the mobilization of insurgency, present in the work of the entire group. It also points up the contradiction inherent in their general practice, which leans toward post-structuralism, and their espousal of the early semiological Barthes, Levi-Strauss, Greimas, and taxonomic Soviet structuralists such as Vygotsky, Lotman, and Propp.[20]

One of the enterprises made problematic by the critique of the subject of knowledge identified with post-structuralist anti-humanism is the desire to produce exhaustive taxonomies, 'to assign names by a metalinguistic operation' (2.10). I have already discussed this issue lengthily in another part of my essay. All of the figures listed above would be susceptible to this charge. Here I want to point at their common phonocentrism, the conviction that speech is a direct and immediate representation of voice-consciousness and writing an indirect transcript of speech. Or, as Guha quotes Vygotsky, ' "The speed of oral speech is unfavourable to a complicated process of formulation—it does not leave time for deliberation and choice. Dialogue implies immediate unpremeditated utterance" ' (*EAP* 261).

By this reckoning the history of writing is coincident with the inauguration and development of exploitation. Now there is no reason to question this well-documented story of what one might call writing in the 'narrow' or 'restricted' sense. However, over

---

[20] In Barthes's case, for example, one would have to take into account his own reputation and rejection of his early positions. See Steven Ungar, *Roland Barthes: the Professor of Desire*, (Lincoln: The Univ. of Nebraska Press, 1983).

against this restricted model of writing one must not set up a model of speech to which is assigned a total self-identity based on a psychological model so crude as to imply that the space of 'pre-meditation' is confined to the deliberative consciousness, and on empirical 'evidence' so impressionistic as 'the speed of oral speech'.

By contrast, post-structuralist theories of consciousness and language suggest that all possibility of expression, spoken or written, shares a common distancing from a self so that meaning can arise— not only meaning for others but also the meaning of the self to the self. I have advanced this idea in my discussion of 'alienation'. These theories suggest further that the 'self' is itself always production rather than ground, an idea I have broached in my discussion of the 'subject-effect'. If writing is seen in terms of its historical predication, the production of our sense of self as ground would seem to be structured like writing.

> The essential predicates in a minimal determination of the classical concept of writing . . . [are that] a written sign . . . is a mark that remains [_reste_], . . . [that] carries with it a force that breaks with its context, . . . [and that] this force of rupture is tied to the spacing . . . which separates it from other elements of the internal contextual chain . . . Are these three predicates, together with the entire system they entail, limited, as is often believed, strictly to 'written' communication in the narrow sense of the word? Are they not to be found in all language, in spoken language for instance, and ultimately in the totality of 'experience' insofar as it is inseparable from this field of the mark, which is to say, from the network of effacement and of difference, of units of iterability, which are separable from their internal and external context and also from themselves, inasmuch as the very iterability which constituted their identity does not permit them ever to be a unit of self-identity?[21]

For the burden of the extended consideration of how the exigencies of theory forbid an ideological manipulation of _naive_ psychologism and empiricism, we should turn to Derrida's 'Signature Event Context', from where the long passage above is taken. By this line of argument it would not only appear that to 'describe speech as the immediate expression of the self' marks the site of a desire that is obliged to overlook the complexity of the production of (a) sense(s) of self. One would, by this, also have to acknowledge that no speech, no 'natural language' (an unwitting oxy-

---

[21] Derrida, "Signature Event Context", in _Margins of Philosophy_, tr. Alan Bass (Chicago: Univ. of Chicago Press, 1981), p. 146.

moron), not even a 'language' of gesture, can signify, indicate, or express without the mediation of a pre-existing code. One would further begin to suspect that the most authoritative and potentially exploitative manifestations of writing in the narrow sense—the codes of law—operate on an implicit phonocentrism, the presupposition that speech is the immediate expression of the self.

I would submit that it is more appropriate to think of the power of rumour in the subaltern context as deriving from its participation in the structure of illegitimate writing rather than the authoritative writing of the law—itself sanctioned by the phonocentric model of the spirit of the law. 'Writing, the outlaw, the lost son. It must be recalled here that Plato always associates speech and law, *logos* and *nomos*. Laws speak. In the personification of *Crito*, they speak to Socrates directly'.[22]

Let us now consider *EAP* 259–64, where the analysis of rumour is performed. (These pages are cited in 3.112, n. 157.) Let us also remember that the mind-set of the peasants is as much affected by the phonocentrism of a tradition where *śruti*—that which is heard—has the greatest authority, as is the mind-set of the historian by the phonocentrism of Western linguistics. Once again, it is a question of complicity rather than the distance of knowledge.

If, then, 'rumour is spoken utterance *par excellence*' (*EAP* 256), it must be seen that its 'functional immediacy' is its non-belonging to any *one* voice-consciousness. This is supposed to be the signal characteristic of writing. Any reader can 'fill' it with her 'consciousness'. Rumour evokes comradeship because it belongs to every 'reader' or 'transmitter'. No one is its origin or source. Thus rumour is not error but primordially (originarily) errant, always in circulation with no assignable source. This illegitimacy makes it accessible to insurgency. Its 'absolute' (we would say 'indefinite', since 'fictive source[s] may be assigned to it') 'transitivity', collapsed at origin and end (a clear picture of writing) can be described as the received model of *speech* in the narrow sense ('the collaterality of word and deed issuing from a common will') only under the influence of phonocentrism. In fact the author himself comes closer to the case about fifteen pages later, when he notices the open verbality of

[22] Derrida, "Plato's Pharmacy", in *Dissemination*, tr. Barbara Johnson (Chicago: Univ. of Chicago Press, 1981), p. 146.

rumour being restricted by the insurgents—who are also under the influence of phonocentrism—by an apocalyptic horizon. Subaltern, élite authority, and critic of historiography become complicit here. Yet the description of rumour in its 'distinctive features [of] . . . anonymity and transitivity' (*EAP* 260) signal a contradiction that allows us to read the text of *Subaltern Studies* against its grain.

The odd coupling of Soviet structuralism and French anti-humanism sometimes produces a misleading effect. For example, the applicability to rumour of Barthes' suggestion that ascription of an author closes up *writing*, should alert us to rumour's writing-like (*scriptible*) character rather than oblige us to displace Barthes' remark to speech via Vygotsky. Dialogue for Vygotsky is the privileged example of the so-called communication of direct verbality, of two immediately self-present sources or 'authors'. Dialogue is supposed to be 'unpremeditated' (although theories of subject-effect or the abstract determination of the concrete would find this a dubious claim). Rumour is a relay of something always assumed to be pre-existent. In fact the mistake of the colonial authorities was to take rumour for speech, to impose the requirements of speech in the narrow sense upon something that draws its strength from participation in writing in the general sense.

The Subaltern Studies group has here led us to a theme of great richness. The crosshatching of the revolutionary non-possessive possibilities in the structure of writing in general and its control by subaltern phonocentrism gives us access to the micrology or minute-scale functioning of the subaltern's philosophical world.

The matter of the role of 'the reading aloud of newspapers' in the construction of Gandhi as a signifier is perhaps too quickly put to rest as a reliance on 'spoken language', when, through such an act, 'a story acquires its authentication from its motif and the name of its place of origin rather than the authority of the correspondent' (3.48–9). I have dwelt on this point so long that it might now do to say no more than that the newspaper is exploitative writing in the narrow sense, 'spoken language' is a phonocentric concept where authority is supposed to spring directly from the voice-consciousness of the self-present speaker, and the reading out of someone else's text as 'an actor does on the stage' is a setting-in-motion of writing in the general sense. To find corroboration of this, one can see the contrast made between speaker and rhetor in the Western tradi-

tion from the Platonic Socrates through Hobbes and Rousseau to
J.L. Austin.[23] When newspapers start reporting rumours (3.88),
the range of speculative possibilities becomes even more seductive.
The investigator seems herself beckoned by the circuit of 'absolute
transitivity'.

Without yielding to that seduction, the following question can be
asked: what is the use of noticing this misfit between the suggested
structure of writing-in-general and the declared interest in phonocentrism? What is the use of pointing out that a common phonocentrism binds subaltern, élite authority, and disciplinary-critical
historian together, and only a reading against the grain discloses the
espousal of illegitimacy by the first and the third? Or, to quote
Terry Eagleton:

> Marx is a metaphysician, and so is Schopenhauer, and so is Ronald
> Reagan. Has anything been gained by this manoeuvre? If it is true, is it
> informative? What is ideologically at stake in such homogenizing? What
> differences does it exist to suppress? Would it make Reagan feel uncom-
> fortable or depressed? If what is in question for deconstructionism is
> metaphysical discourse, and if this is all-pervasive, then there is a sense
> in which in reading against the grain we are subverting everything and
> nothing.[24]

Not all ways of understanding the world and acting upon it are
*equally* metaphysical or phonocentric. If, on the other hand, there *is*
something shared by élite (Reagan), colonial authority, subaltern
and mediator (Eagleton/Subaltern Studies) that we would rather not
acknowledge, any elegant solution devised by means of such a refusal would merely mark a site of desire. It is best to attempt to
forge a practice that can bear the weight of that acknowledgement.
And, using the buried operation of the structure of writing as a lev-
er, the strategic reader can reveal the asymmetry between the three
groups above. Yet, since a 'reading against the grain' must forever
remain strategic, it can never claim to have established the authoritative truth of a text, it must forever remain dependent upon practical

[23] Hobbes's discussion of authority in the *Leviathan* and Kant's discussion of the
genius in *The Critique of Judgment* are two of the many *loci classici*. There are lengthy
discussions of this thematic—as found in the Platonic Socrates, in Rousseau, and in
J.L. Austin—in Derrida's "Plato's Pharmacy", *Of Grammatology*, and "Signature
Event Context", respectively.

[24] Terry Eagleton, *Walter Benjamin: or Towards a Revolutionary Criticism* (London:
Verso Press, 1981), p. 140.

exigencies, never legitimately lead to a theoretical orthodoxy. In the case of the Subaltern Studies group, it would get the group off the dangerous hook of claiming to establish the truth-knowledge of the subaltern and his consciousness.

## Woman

The group is scrupulous in its consideration towards women. They record moments when men and women are joined in struggle (1.178, *EAP* 130), when their conditions of work or education suffer from gender or class discrimination (2.71, 2.241, 243, 257, 275). But I think they overlook how important the concept-metaphor woman is to the functioning of their discourse.[25] This consideration will bring to an end the body of my argument.

In a certain reading, the figure of woman is pervasively instrumental in the shifting of the function of discursive systems, as in insurgent mobilization. Questions of the mechanics of this instrumentality are seldom raised by our group. 'Femininity' is as important a discursive field for the predominantly male insurgents as 'religion'. When cow-protection becomes a volatile signified in the re-inscription of the social position of various kinds of subaltern, semi-subaltern, and indigenous élite groups, the cow is turned into a female figure of one kind or another. Considering that in the British nineteenth century the female access to 'possessive individualism' is one of the most important social forces, what does it mean to imply that 'femininity' has the same discursive sense and force for all the heterogeneous groups meticulously documented by Pandey? Analogous research into the figure of the 'worker' is performed by Chakrabarty. No such luck for the 'female'.

On the most 'ancient and indigenous' religious level, a level that 'perhaps gave [the rebellious hillmen] an extra potency [*sic*] in times of collective distress and outside oppression' (1.98), all the deities are man-eating goddesses. As this pre-insurgent level of collectivity begins to graduate into revolt, the sacrifices continue to be made to

[25] The work of the collective is now including more overtly feminist material. Most significant is Ranajit Guha's "Chandra's Death" in the forthcoming volume V, where he takes that particular feminist position which suggests that there is a woman's separate domain which is centered on childbirth and its vicissitudes under subaltern patriarchy. My point, about woman as the syntagm of the socius, is, of course, somewhat different.

goddesses rather than gods. And, even as this level of subaltern-led revolt is contrasted to the 'élite struggles of the earlier period' (1.124), we notice that in that earlier period the struggles began on two occasions because men would not accept female leadership (1.102).

In terms of social semiosis, what is the difference between man-eating goddesses, objects of reverence and generators of solidarity on the one hand, and secular daughters and widows, unacceptable as leaders, on the other? On the occasion of the 'culture of sugarcane' in Eastern UP, Shahid Amin speaks of the deliberate non-coincidence created between natural inscription (script as used when referring to a play) of the harvest calendar and the artificial inscription of the circuit of colonial monopoly capital. It is of course of great interest to wonder in what ways the composition of the peasantry and landownership would have developed had the two been allowed to coincide. Yet I think it should also be noticed that it is dowry that is the invariably mentioned *social* demand that allowed the demands of nature to devastate the peasant via the demands of empire. Should one trouble about the constitution of the subaltern as (sexed) subject when the exploitation of sexual difference seems to have so crucial a role on so many fronts? Should one notice that the proverb on 1.53 is sung by a young daughter who will deny her lover's demands in order to preserve her father's fields? Should one notice this metaphoric division of sexuality (in the woman's case, sex is of course identical with selfhood or consciousness) as property to be passed on or not from father to lover? Indeed, in a collective where so much attention is rightly paid to the subjectivity or subject-positioning of the subaltern, it should be surprising to encounter such indifference to the subjectivity, not to mention the indispensable presence, of the woman as crucial instrument. These four sentences should illustrate my argument:

> It was not uncommon for a 'superior' Patidar to spend his dowry money and return his wife to her father so that he could marry for a new dowry. Amongst Patidars, it was considered very shameful to have to take back a daughter [!] . . . *Gols* were formed to prevent ruinous hypergamous marriages with 'superior' Patidar lineages. . . . Here, therefore, we discover a strong form of subaltern organization within the Patidar caste which provided a check on the power of the Patidar élite. . . . Even Mahatma Gandhi was unable to break the solidarity of the Patidar *gol* of twenty-one villages.

I do not see how the crucial instrumentality of woman as symbolic object of exchange can be overlooked here. Yet the conclusion is: 'the solidarity of the *Gols* was a form of *class* solidarity' (1.202, 203, 207). As in the case of the insurgent under colonial power, the condition of the woman gets 'bettered' as a bye-product, but what's the difference? Male subaltern and historian are here united in the common assumption that the procreative sex is a species apart, scarcely if at all to be considered a part of civil society.

These are not unimportant questions in the context of contemporary India. Just as the *ulgulan* of 1899–1901 dehegemonized millennarian Christianity in the Indian context, so also did the Adivasis seem to have tapped the emergent possibilities of a goddess-centred religion in the Devi movement of 1922–3, a movement that actively contested the re-inscription of land into private property.[26] In the current Indian context, neither religion nor femininity shows emergent potential of this kind.

I have left till last the two broad areas where the instrumentality of woman seems most striking: notions of territoriality and of the communal mode of power.

## Concept-metaphors of Territoriality and of Woman

The concept of territoriality is implicit in most of the essays of the three volumes of *Subaltern Studies*. Here again the explicit theoretical statement is to be found in *EAP*. Territoriality is the combined 'pull of the primordial ties of kinship, community' which is part 'of the actual mechanics of . . . autonomous mobilization' (*EAP* 118). On the simplest possible level, it is evident that notions of kinship are anchored and consolidated by the exchange of women. This consolidation, according to Guha, cuts across the religious division of Hindu and Muslim.[27] In all these examples woman is the neglected syntagm of the semiosis of subalternity or insurgency.

Throughout these pages it has been my purpose to show the complicity between subject and object of investigation—the Subaltern Studies group and subalternity. Here too, the historians' tendency, not to ignore, but to re-name the semiosis of sexual difference 'class'

---

[26] See Hardiman, "Adivasi Assertion in South Gujarat: The Devi Movement of 1922-3", in 3.

[27] See, for examples, *EAP* 229, 316.

or 'caste-solidarity' (*EAP* 316), bears something like a relationship with the peasants' general attempt to undo the distinction between consanguinity and co-residence. Here, as in the case of the brutal marriage customs of the Patidars, the historian mentions, but does not pause to reflect upon, the significance of the simple exclusion of the subaltern as female (sexed) subject: 'In each of these [rebel villages] nearly all the population, *barring females acquired by marriage*, claimed descent from a common patrilineage, consanguinal or mythical, and regarded themselves as members of the same clan or gotra. This belief in a shared ancestry made the village assert itself positively by acting as a solidarity unit and negatively by operating an elaborate code of discrimination against aliens' (*EAP* 314; italics mine).

Although it was unemphatically and trivially accepted by everyone that it was the woman, without proper identity, who operated this consanguinal or mythic patrilineage; and although, in the historian's estimation, 'these village-based primordial ties were the principal means of rebel mobilization, mauza by mauza, throughout northern and central India in 1857' (*EAP* 315), it seems that we may not stop to investigate the subject-deprivation of the female in the operation of this mobilization and this solidarity. It seems clear to me that, if the question of female subaltern consciousness, whose instrumentality is so often seen to be crucial, is a red herring, the question of subaltern consciousness as such must be judged a red herring as well.

If the peasant insurgent was the victim and the unsung hero of the first wave of resistance against territorial imperialism in India, it is well known that, for reasons of collusion between pre-existing structures of patriarchy and transnational capitalism, it is the urban sub-proletarian female who is the paradigmatic subject of the current configuration of the International Division of Labour. As we investigate the pattern of resistance among these 'permanent casual'-s, questions of the heterogeneous subject-constitution of the subaltern female gain a certain importance.

## The Communal Mode of Power and the Concept of Woman

Although Partha Chatterjee's concept of the communal mode of power is not as pervasively implicit in all the work of the group, it is an important and sustaining argument for the enterprise of Subaltern Studies. Here the importance of communal power structures, based largely on kin and clan, are shown to embrace far-flung parts of the pre-capitalist world. And, once again, the crucial syntagmatic and micrologically prior defining importance of sexual difference in the deployment of such power is foreclosed so that sexuality is seen only as one element among the many that drive this 'social organization of production' (2.322). The making-visible of the figure of woman is perhaps not a task that the group should fairly be asked to perform. It seems to this reader, however, that a feminist historian of the subaltern must raise the question of woman as a structural rather than marginal issue in each of the many different types and cultures that Chatterjee invokes in 'More on Modes of Power and the Peasantry'.

If in the explanation of territoriality I notice a tension between consanguinal and spatial accounts shared by subaltern and historian alike, in the case of 'the communal mode of power' we are shown a clash between explanations from kinship and 'political' perceptions. This is a version of the same battle—the apparent gender-neutralizing of the world finally explained through reason, domestic society sublated and subsumed in the civil.

The clash between kinship and politics is one of Chatterjee's main points. What role does the figure of woman play here? In the dispersal of the field of power, the sexual division of labour is progressively defined from above as power-sharing. That story is the underside of the taxonomy of power that Chatterjee unfolds.

Chatterjee quotes Victor Turner, who suggests that the resurgence of communal modes of power often generates ways to fight feudal structures: 'resistance or revolt often takes on the form of . . . *communitas*' (2.339). This is particularly provocative in the case of the dehegemonization of monarchy. In this fast-paced fable of the progress of modes of power, it can be seen that the idea of one kind of a king may have supplemented a built-in gap in the ideology of community-as-a-whole: 'a new kind of chief whom Tacitus calls "king" (*rex*) who was elected from within a "royal clan" ' (2.323). The figure of the exchanged woman still produces the cohesive unity of a 'clan', even as what emerges is a 'king'. And thus, when the insurgent *community* invokes monarch against *feudal* authority, the explanation that they are re-cathecting or re-filling the king with the old patriarchal ideology of consanguinity, never far from the metaphor of the King as Father, seems even less surprising (3.344).

My point is, of course, that through all of these heterogeneous examples of territoriality and the communal mode of power, the figure of the woman, moving from clan to clan, and family to family as daughter/sister and wife/mother, syntaxes patriarchal continuity even as she is herself drained of proper identity. In this particular area, the continuity of community or history, for subaltern and historian alike, is produced on (I intend the copulative metaphor— philosophically and sexually) the dissimulation of her discontinuity, on the repeated emptying of her meaning as instrument.

If I seem to be intransigent here, perhaps the distance travelled between high structuralism and current anti-humanism can best be measured by two celebrated passages by two famous men. First the Olympian dismissal, ignoring the role of representation in subject-constitution:

> These results can be achieved only on one condition: considering marriage regulations and kinship systems as a kind of language. . . . That the 'message' ['*message*'] should be constituted by the *women of the group*, which are circulated between class, lineages, or families, in place of the *words of the group*, which are *circulated* between individuals, does not at all change the identity of the phenomenon considered in the two cases . . . This ambiguity [between values and signs] is clearly manifested in the critique sometimes addressed to the *Elementary Structures of Kinship* as an 'anti-feminist' book by some, because women are there treated as objects. . . . [But] words do not speak, while women do. The latter are signs and producers of signs; as such, they cannot be reduced to the status of symbols or tokens.[28]

And, second, the recognition of a limit:

> The significations or conceptual values which apparently form the stakes or means of all Nietzschean analyses on sexual difference, on the 'unceasing war between the sexes', on the 'mortal hatred of the sexes' on 'love', eroticism, etc., are all on the vector of what might be called the process of *propriation* (appropriation, expropriation, taking, taking possession, gift and exchange, mastery, servitude, etc.). Through numerous analyses, that I cannot follow here, it appears, by the law already formalized, that sometimes the woman is woman by giving, *giving herself*, while the man takes, possesses, takes possession, and sometimes by contrast the woman by giving herself, gives-herself-as, and thus simulates and assures for herself possessive mastery. . . . As a sexual operation propriation is more powerful, because undecideable, than the question *ti esti* [what is it], than the question of the veil of truth or the meaning of

[28] Claude Lévi-Strauss, *Structural Anthropology*, tr. Claire Jacobson and Brooke Grundfest Schoepf (Garden City, N.Y.: Anchor Books, 1967), p. 60.

Being. All the more—and this argument is neither secondary nor supplementary—because the process of propriation organizes the totality of the process of language and symbolic exchange in general, including, therefore, all ontological statements [*enonćes*].[29]

I quote these passages, by Lévi-Strauss and Derrida, and separated by twenty years, as a sign of the times. But I need not add that, in the latter case, the question of being and the ontological statement would relate to the phenomenality of subaltern consciousness itself.

[29] Derrida, *Spurs*, pp. 109-11.

# I Methodology

# Preface

The aim of the present collection of essays, the first of a series, is to promote a systematic and informed discussion of subaltern themes in the field of South Asian studies, and thus help to rectify the elitist bias characteristic of much research and academic work in this particular area.

The word 'subaltern' in the title stands for the meaning as given in the *Concise Oxford Dictionary,* that is, 'of inferior rank'. It will be used in these pages as a name for the general attribute of subordination in South Asian society whether this is expressed in terms of class, caste, age, gender and office or in any other way.

The words 'history and society' in the subtitle are meant to serve as a shorthand for all that is involved in the subaltern condition. As such there is nothing in the material and spiritual aspects of that condition, past or present, which does not interest us. It will be idle of us, of course, to hope that the range of contributions to this series may even remotely match the six-point project envisaged by Antonio Gramsci in his 'Notes on Italian History'. However, within the limitations of the present state of research and our own resources we expect to publish well-written essays on subaltern themes from scholars working in the humanities and social sciences. There will be much in these pages which should relate to the history, politics, economics and sociology of subalternity as well as to the attitudes, ideologies and belief systems—in short, the culture informing that condition.

We recognize of course that subordination cannot be understood except as one of the constitutive terms in a binary relationship of which the other is dominance, for 'subaltern groups are always subject to the activity of ruling groups, even when they rebel and rise up'. The dominant groups will therefore receive in these volumes the consideration they deserve without, however, being endowed with that spurious primacy assigned to them by the long-standing tradition of elitism in South Asian studies. Indeed, it will be very much a part of our endeavour to make sure that our emphasis on the subaltern functions both as a measure of objective assessment of the role of the elite and as a critique of elitist interpretations of that role.

We believe that we are not alone in our concern about such elitism and the need to combat it. Others too have been equally unhappy about the distortions and imbalances generated by this trend in academic work on South Asian questions. We therefore hope that other scholars will join us in this venture by publishing on their own or with us their researches on subaltern themes, their critique of elitism in their respective disciplines and generally by helping us with their advice on the contents of this and subsequent volumes of *Subaltern Studies*.

Canberra                                                                 Ranajit Guha
August 1981

# On Some Aspects of the Historiography of Colonial India[1]

RANAJIT GUHA

1.   The historiography of Indian nationalism has for a long time been dominated by elitism—colonialist elitism and bourgeois-nationalist elitism.[2] Both originated as the ideological product of British rule in India, but have survived the transfer of power and been assimilated to neo-colonialist and neo-nationalist forms of discourse in Britain and India respectively. Elitist historiography of the colonialist or neo-colonialist type counts British writers and institutions among its principal protagonists, but has its imitators in India and other countries too. Elitist historiography of the nationalist or neo-nationalist type is primarily an Indian practice but not without imitators in the ranks of liberal historians in Britain and elsewhere.

2.   Both these varieties of elitism share the prejudice that the making of the Indian nation and the development of the consciousness—nationalism—which informed this process were exclusively or predominantly elite achievements. In the colonialist and neo-colonialist historiographies these achievements are credited to British colonial rulers, administrators, policies, institutions and culture; in the nationalist and neo-nationalist writings—to Indian elite personalities, institutions, activities and ideas.

3.   The first of these two historiographies defines Indian nationalism primarily as a function of stimulus and response. Based on a

[1]The author is grateful to all the other contributors to this volume as well as to Gautam Bhadra, Dipesh Chakrabarty and Raghabendra Chattopadhyay for their comments on an earlier version of this statement.

[2]For a definition of the terms 'elite', 'people', 'subaltern', etc. as used in these paragraphs the reader may kindly turn to the note printed at the end of this statement.

narrowly behaviouristic approach this represents nationalism as
the sum of the activities and ideas by which the Indian elite
responded to the institutions, opportunities, resources, etc. generated by colonialism. There are several versions of this historiography, but the central modality common to them is to describe
Indian nationalism as a sort of 'learning process' through which the
native elite became involved in politics by trying to negotiate the
maze of institutions and the corresponding cultural complex introduced by the colonial authorities in order to govern the country.
What made the elite go through this process was, according to this
historiography, no lofty idealism addressed to the general good of
the nation but simply the expectation of rewards in the form of a
share in the wealth, power and prestige created by and associated
with colonial rule; and it was the drive for such rewards with all its
concomitant play of collaboration and competition between the
ruling power and the native elite as well as between various
elements among the latter themselves, which, we are told, was
what constituted Indian nationalism.

4.   The general orientation of the other kind of elitist historiography is to represent Indian nationalism as primarily an idealist
venture in which the indigenous elite led the people from subjugation to freedom. There are several versions of this historiography
which differ from each other in the degree of their emphasis on the
role of individual leaders or elite organizations and institutions as
the main or motivating force in this venture. However, the modality common to them all is to uphold Indian nationalism as a
phenomenal expression of the goodness of the native elite with the
antagonistic aspect of their relation to the colonial regime made,
against all evidence, to look larger than its collaborationist aspect,
their role as promoters of the cause of the people than that as
exploiters and oppressors, their altruism and self-abnegation than
their scramble for the modicum of power and privilege granted by
the rulers in order to make sure of their support for the Raj. The
history of Indian nationalism is thus written up as a sort of spiritual
biography of the Indian elite.

5.   Elitist historiography is of course not without its uses. It
helps us to know more of the structure of the colonial state, the
operation of its various organs in certain historical circumstances,
the nature of the alignment of classes which sustained it; of some
aspects of the ideology of the elite as the dominant ideology of the

period; of the contradictions between the two elites and the complexities of their mutual oppositions and coalitions; of the role of some of the more important British and Indian personalities and elite organizations. Above all it helps us to understand the ideological character of historiography itself.

6. What, however, historical writing of this kind cannot do is to explain Indian nationalism for us. For it fails to acknowledge, far less interpret, the contribution made by the people *on their own*, that is, *independently of the elite* to the making and development of this nationalism. In this particular respect the poverty of this historiography is demonstrated beyond doubt by its failure to understand and assess the mass articulation of this nationalism except, negatively, as a law and order problem, and positively, if at all, either as a response to the charisma of certain elite leaders or in the currently more fashionable terms of vertical mobilization by the manipulation of factions. The involvement of the Indian people in vast numbers, sometimes in hundreds of thousands or even millions, in nationalist activities and ideas is thus represented as a diversion from a supposedly 'real' political process, that is, the grinding away of the wheels of the state apparatus and of elite institutions geared to it, or it is simply credited, as an act of ideological appropriation, to the influence and initiative of the elite themselves. The bankruptcy of this historiography is clearly exposed when it is called upon to explain such phenomena as the anti-Rowlatt upsurge of 1919 and the Quit India movement of 1942—to name only two of numerous instances of popular initiative asserting itself in the course of nationalist campaigns in defiance or absence of elite control. How can such one-sided and blinkered historiography help us to understand the profound displacements, well below the surface of elite politics, which made Chauri-Chaura or the militant demonstrations of solidarity with the RIN mutineers possible ?

7. This inadequacy of elitist historiography follows directly from the narrow and partial view of politics to which it is committed by virtue of its class outlook. In all writings of this kind the parameters of Indian politics are assumed to be or enunciated as exclusively or primarily those of the institutions introduced by the British for the government of the country and the corresponding sets of laws, policies, attitudes and other elements of the superstructure. Inevitably, therefore, a historiography hamstrung by

such a definition can do no more than to equate politics with the aggregation of activities and ideas of those who were directly involved in operating these institutions, that is, the colonial rulers and their *élèves* — the dominant groups in native society. To the extent that their mutual transactions were thought to be all there was to Indian nationalism, the domain of the latter is regarded as coincident with that of politics.

8.   What clearly is left out of this un-historical historiography is the *politics of the people*. For parallel to the domain of elite politics there existed throughout the colonial period another domain of Indian politics in which the principal actors were not the dominant groups of the indigenous society or the colonial authorities but the subaltern classes and groups constituting the mass of the labouring population and the intermediate strata in town and country—that is, the people. This was an *autonomous* domain, for it neither originated from elite politics nor did its existence depend on the latter. It was traditional only in so far as its roots could be traced back to pre-colonial times, but it was by no means archaic in the sense of being outmoded. Far from being destroyed or rendered virtually ineffective, as was elite politics of the traditional type by the intrusion of colonialism, it continued to operate vigorously in spite of the latter, adjusting itself to the conditions prevailing under the Raj and in many respects developing entirely new strains in both form and content. As modern as indigenous elite politics, it was distinguished by its relatively greater depth in time as well as in structure.

9.   One of the more important features of this politics related precisely to those aspects of mobilization which are so little explained by elitist historiography. Mobilization in the domain of elite politics was achieved vertically whereas in that of subaltern politics this was achieved horizontally. The instrumentation of the former was characterized by a relatively greater reliance on the colonial adaptations of British parliamentary institutions and the residua of semi-feudal political institutions of the pre-colonial period; that of the latter relied rather more on the traditional organization of kinship and territoriality or on class associations depending on the level of the consciousness of the people involved. Elite mobilization tended to be relatively more legalistic and constitutionalist in orientation, subaltern mobilization relatively more violent. The former was, on the whole, more cautious and

controlled, the latter more spontaneous. Popular mobilization in
the colonial period was realized in its most comprehensive form in
peasant uprisings. However, in many historic instances involving
large masses of the working people and petty bourgeoisie in the
urban areas too the figure of mobilization derived directly from
the paradigm of peasant insurgency.

10. The ideology operative in this domain, taken as a whole,
reflected the diversity of its social composition with the outlook of
its leading elements dominating that of the others at any particular
time and within any particular event. However, in spite of such
diversity one of its invariant features was a notion of resistance to
elite domination. This followed from the subalternity common to
all the social constituents of this domain and as such distinguished
it sharply from that of elite politics. This ideological element was
of course not uniform in quality or density in all instances. In the
best of cases it enhanced the concreteness, focus and tension of
subaltern political action. However, there were occasions when
its emphasis on sectional interests disequilibrated popular movements in such a way as to create economistic diversions and
sectarian splits, and generally to undermine horizontal alliances.

11. Yet another set of the distinctive features of this politics
derived from the conditions of exploitation to which the subaltern
classes were subjected in varying degrees as well as from its
relation to the productive labour of the majority of its protagonists, that is, workers and peasants, and to the manual and intellectual labour respectively of the non-industrial urban poor and the
lower sections of the petty bourgeoisie. The experience of exploitation and labour endowed this politics with many idioms, norms
and values which put it in a category apart from elite politics.

12. These and other distinctive features (the list is by no means
exhaustive) of the politics of the people did not of course appear
always in the pure state described in the last three paragraphs. The
impact of living contradictions modified them in the course of
their actualization in history. However, with all such modifications they still helped to demarcate the domain of subaltern politics from that of elite politics. The co-existence of these two
domains or streams, which can be sensed by intuition and proved
by demonstration as well, was the index of an important historical
truth, that is, the *failure of the Indian bourgeoisie to speak for the nation*.
There were vast areas in the life and consciousness of the people

which were never integrated into their hegemony. The *structural dichotomy* that arose from this is a datum of Indian history of the colonial period, which no one who sets out to interpret it can ignore without falling into error.

13.   Such dichotomy did not, however, mean that these two domains were hermetically sealed off from each other and there was no contact between them. On the contrary, there was a great deal of overlap arising precisely from the effort made from time to time by the more advanced elements among the indigenous elite, especially the bourgeoisie, to integrate them. Such effort when linked to struggles which had more or less clearly defined anti-imperialist objectives and were consistently waged, produced some splendid results. Linked, on other occasions, to movements which either had no firm anti-imperialist objectives at all or had lost them in the course of their development and deviated into legalist, constitutionalist or some other kind of compromise with the colonial government, they produced some spectacular retreats and nasty reversions in the form of sectarian strife. In either case the braiding together of the two strands of elite and subaltern politics led invariably to explosive situations indicating that the masses mobilized by the elite to fight for their own objectives managed to break away from their control and put the characteristic imprint of popular politics on campaigns initiated by the upper classes.

14.   However, the initiatives which originated from the domain of subaltern politics were not, on their part, powerful enough to develop the nationalist movement into a full-fledged struggle for national liberation. The working class was still not sufficiently mature in the objective conditions of its social being and in its consciousness as a class-for-itself, nor was it firmly allied yet with the peasantry. As a result it could do nothing to take over and complete the mission which the bourgeoisie had failed to realize. The outcome of it all was that the numerous peasant uprisings of the period, some of them massive in scope and rich in anti-colonialist consciousness, waited in vain for a leadership to raise them above localism and generalize them into a nationwide anti-imperialist campaign. In the event, much of the sectional struggle of workers, peasants and the urban petty bourgeoisie either got entangled in economism or, wherever politicized, remained, for want of a revolutionary leadership, far too fragmented to form

effectively into anything like a national liberation movement.

15.   It is the study of this *historic failure of the nation to come to its own,* a failure due to the inadequacy of the bourgeoisie as well as of the working class to lead it into a decisive victory over colonialism and a bourgeois-democratic revolution of either the classic nineteenth-century type under the hegemony of the bourgeoisie or a more modern type under the hegemony of workers and peasants, that is, a 'new democracy'— *it is the study of this failure which constitutes the central problematic of the historiography of colonial India.* There is no one given way of investigating this problematic. Let a hundred flowers blossom and we don't mind even the weeds. Indeed we believe that in the practice of historiography even the elitists have a part to play if only by way of teaching by negative examples. But we are also convinced that elitist historiography should be resolutely fought by developing an alternative discourse based on the rejection of the spurious and un-historical monism characteristic of its view of Indian nationalism and on the recognition of the co-existence and interaction of the elite and subaltern domains of politics.

16.   We are sure that we are not alone in our concern about the present state of the political historiography of colonial India and in seeking a way out. The elitism of modern Indian historiography is an oppressive fact resented by many others, students, teachers and writers like ourselves. They may not all subscribe to what has been said above on this subject in exactly the way in which we have said it. However, we have no doubt that many other historiographical points of view and practices are likely to converge close to where we stand. Our purpose in making our own views known is to promote such a convergence. We claim no more than to try and indicate an orientation and hope to demonstrate in practice that this is feasible. In any discussion which may ensue we expect to learn a great deal not only from the agreement of those who think like us but also from the criticism of those who don't.

## A note on the terms 'elite', 'people', 'subaltern', etc. as used above

The term 'elite' has been used in this statement to signify *dominant* groups, foreign as well as indigenous. The *dominant foreign* groups included all the non-Indian, that is, mainly British officials of the colonial state and foreign industrialists, merchants, financiers, planters, landlords and missionaries.

The *dominant indigenous* groups included classes and interests operating at two levels. At the *all-India level* they included the biggest feudal magnates, the most important representatives of the industrial and mercantile bourgeoisie and native recruits to the uppermost levels of the bureaucracy.

At the *regional and local levels* they represented such classes and other elements as were *either* members of the dominant all-India groups included in the previous category *or* if belonging to social strata hierarchically inferior to those of the dominant all-India groups still *acted in the interests of the latter and not in conformity to interests corresponding truly to their own social being.*

Taken as a whole and in the abstract this last category of the elite was *heterogeneous* in its composition and thanks to the uneven character of regional economic and social developments, *differed from area to area.* The same class or element which was dominant in one area according to the definition given above, could be among the dominated in another. This could and did create many ambiguities and contradictions in attitudes and alliances, especially among the lowest strata of the rural gentry, impoverished landlords, rich peasants and upper-middle peasants all of whom belonged, *ideally speaking,* to the category of 'people' or 'subaltern classes', as defined below. It is the task of research to investigate, identify and measure the *specific* nature and degree of the *deviation* of these elements from the ideal and situate it historically.

The terms 'people' and 'subaltern classes' have been used as synonymous throughout this note. The social groups and elements included in this category represent *the demographic difference between the total Indian population and all those whom we have described as the 'elite'.* Some of these classes and groups such as the lesser rural gentry, impoverished landlords, rich peasants and upper-middle peasants who 'naturally' ranked among the 'people' and the 'subaltern', could under certain circumstances act for the 'elite', as explained above, and therefore be classified as such in some local or regional situations—an ambiguity which it is up to the historian to sort out on the basis of a close and judicious reading of his evidence.

# The Prose of Counter-Insurgency[1]

## RANAJIT GUHA

### I

When a peasant rose in revolt at any time or place under the Raj, he
did so necessarily and explicitly in violation of a series of codes which
defined his very existence as a member of that colonial, and still
largely semi-feudal society. For his subalternity was materialized by
the structure of property, institutionalized by law, sanctified by
religion and made tolerable—and even desirable—by tradition. To
rebel was indeed to destroy many of those familiar signs which he had
learned to read and manipulate in order to extract a meaning out of
the harsh world around him and live with it. The risk in 'turning
things upside down' under these conditions was indeed so great that
he could hardly afford to engage in such a project in a state of
absent-mindedness.

There is nothing in the primary sources of historical evidence to
suggest anything other than this. These give the lie to the myth,
retailed so often by careless and impressionistic writing on the subject,
of peasant insurrections being purely spontaneous and unpremeditated affairs. The truth is quite to the contrary. It would be difficult
to cite an uprising on any significant scale that was not in fact
preceded either by less militant types of mobilization when other
means had been tried and found wanting or by parley among its
principals seriously to weigh the pros and cons of any recourse to
arms. In events so very different from each other in context, character
and the composition of participants such as the Rangpur *dhing*
against Debi Sinha (1783), the Barasat *bidroha* led by Titu Mir
(1831), the Santal *hool* (1855) and the 'blue mutiny' of 1860 the

---

[1] I am grateful to my colleagues of the editorial team for their comments on an initial
draft of this essay.

*Note*: For a list of Abbreviations used in the footnotes of this chapter, see p. 40.

protagonists in each case had tried out petitions, deputations or other forms of supplication before actually declaring war on their oppressors.[2] Again, the revolts of the Kol (1832), the Santal and the Munda (1899-1900) as well as the Rangpur *dhing* and the jacqueries in Allahabad and Ghazipur districts during the Sepoy Rebellion of 1857-8 (to name only two out of many instances in that remarkable series) had all been inaugurated by planned and in some cases protracted consultation among the representatives of the local peasant masses.[3] Indeed there is hardly an instance of the peasantry, whether the cautious and earthy villagers of the plains or the supposedly more volatile *adivasis* of the upland tracts, stumbling or drifting into rebellion. They had far too much at stake and would not launch into it except as a deliberate, even if desperate, way out of an intolerable condition of existence. Insurgency, in other words, was a motivated and conscious undertaking on the part of the rural masses.

Yet this consciousness seems to have received little notice in the literature on the subject. Historiography has been content to deal with the peasant rebel merely as an empirical person or member of a class, but not as an entity whose will and reason constituted the praxis called rebellion. The omission is indeed dyed into most narratives by metaphors assimilating peasant revolts to natural phenomena: they break out like thunder storms, heave like earthquakes, spread like wildfires, infect like epidemics. In other words, when the proverbial clod of earth turns, this is a matter to be explained in terms of natural history. Even when this historiography is pushed to the point of producing an explanation in rather more human terms it will do so by assuming an identity of nature and culture, a hall-mark, presumably, of a very low state of civilization and exemplified in 'those periodical outbursts of crime and lawlessness to which all wild tribes are subject', as the first historian of the Chuar rebellion put it.[4]

[2] The instances are far too numerous to cite. For some of these see *MDS*, pp. 46-7, 48-9 on the Rangpur *dhing*; *BC* 54222: Metcalfe & Blunt to Court of Directors (10 April 1832), paras 14-15 on the Barasat uprising; W. W. Hunter, *Annals of Rural Bengal* (7th edition; London, 1897), pp. 237-8 and JP, 4 Oct. 1855: 'The Thacoor's Perwannah' for the Santal *hool* C. E. Buckland, *Bengal Under the Lieutenant-Governors*, vol. I (Calcutta, 1901), p. 192 for the 'blue mutiny'.

[3] See, for instance, *MDS*, pp. 579-80; *Freedom Struggle in Uttar Pradesh*, vol.IV (Lucknow, 1959), pp. 284-5, 549.

[4] J. C. Price, *The Chuar Rebellion of 1799*, p. cl. The edition of the work used in this essay is the one printed in A. Mitra (ed.), *District Handbooks: Midnapur* (Alipore, 1953), Appendix IV.

Alternatively, an explanation will be sought in an enumeration of causes—of, say, factors of economic and political deprivation which do not relate at all to the peasant's consciousness or do so negatively—triggering off rebellion as a sort of reflex action, that is, as an instinctive and almost mindless response to physical suffering of one kind or another (e.g. hunger, torture, forced labour, etc.) or as a passive reaction to some initiative of his superordinate enemy. Either way insurgency is regarded as *external* to the peasant's consciousness and Cause is made to stand in as a phantom surrogate for Reason, the logic of that consciousness.

## II

How did historiography come to acquire this particular blind spot and never find a cure? For an answer one could start by having a close look at its constituting elements and examine those cuts, seams and stitches—those cobbling marks—which tell us about the material it is made of and the manner of its absorption into the fabric of writing.

The corpus of historical writings on peasant insurgency in colonial India is made up of three types of discourse. These may be described as *primary*, *secondary* and *tertiary* according to the order of their appearance in time and their filiation. Each of these is differentiated from the other two by the degree of its formal and/or acknowledged (as opposed to real and/or tacit) identification with an official point of view, by the measure of its distance from the event to which it refers, and by the ratio of the distributive and integrative components in its narrative.

To begin with primary discourse, it is almost without exception official in character—official in a broad sense of the term. That is, it originated not only with bureaucrats, soldiers, sleuths and others directly employed by the government, but also with those in the non-official sector who were symbiotically related to the Raj, such as planters, missionaries, traders, technicians and so on among the whites and landlords, moneylenders, etc. among the natives. It was official also in so far as it was meant primarily for administrative use—for the information of government, for action on its part and for the determination of its policy. Even when it incorporated statements emanating from 'the other side', from the insurgents or their allies for instance, as it often did by way of direct or indirect reporting in the body of official correspondence or even more characteristically as 'enclosures' to the latter, this was done only as a part of an argument prompted by administrative concern. In other words, whatever its particular form—and there was indeed an amazing variety ranging from the exordial letter, telegram, despatch and communiqué to the terminal summary, report, judgement and proclamation—its production and circulation were both necessarily contingent on reasons of State.

Yet another of the distinctive features of this type of discourse is its immediacy. This derived from two conditions: first, that statements of this class were written either concurrently with or soon after the event, and secondly, that this was done by the participants concerned, a 'participant' being defined for this purpose in the broad sense of a contemporary involved in the event either in action or indirectly as an onlooker. This would exclude of course that genre of retrospective writing in which, as in some memoirs, an event and its recall are separated by a considerable hiatus, but would still leave a massive documentation—'primary sources' as it is known in the trade—to speak to the historian with a sort of ancestral voice and make him feel close to his subject.

The two specimens quoted below are fairly representative of this type. One of these relates to the Barasat uprising of 1831 and the other to the Santal rebellion of 1855.

## TEXT 1[5]

To the Deputy Adjutant General of the Army

Sir,

Authentic information having reached Government that a body of *Fanatic Insurgents* are now committing *the most daring and wanton atrocities on the Inhabitants* of the Country in the neighbourhood of Tippy in the Magistracy of Baraset and have set at defiance and repulsed the utmost force that the local Civil Authority could assemble for their apprehension, I am directed by the Hon'ble Vice President in Council to request that you will without delay Communicate to the General Officer Commanding the Presidency Division the orders of Government that one Complete Battalion of Native Infantry from Barrackpore and two Six Pounders manned with the necessary compliment (sic) of Golundaze from Dum Dum, the whole under the Command of a Field Officer of judgement and decision, be immediately directed to proceed

[5] *BC* 54222: *JC*, 22 Nov. 1831: 'Extract from the Proceedings of the Honorable the Vice President in Council in the Military Department under date the 10th November 1831'. Emphasis added.

and rendezvous at Baraset when they will be joined by 1 Havildar and 12 Troopers of the 3rd Regiment of Light Cavalry now forming the escort of the Hon'ble the Vice President.

2nd. The Magistrate will meet the Officer Commanding the Detachment at Barraset and will afford the necessary information for his guidance relative to the position of the Insurgents; but without having any authority to interfere in such Military operations as the Commanding Officer of the Detachments may deem expedient, for the purpose of routing or seizing or in the event of resistance destroying those who persevere in *defying the authority of the State* and *disturbing the public tranquil[l]ity.*

3rd. It is concluded that the service will not be of such a protracted nature as to require a larger supply of ammunition than may be carried in Pouch and in two Tumbrils for the Guns, and that no difficulties will occur respecting carriage. In the contrary event any aid needed will be furnished.

4th. The Magistrate will be directed to give every assistance regarding supplies and other requisites for the Troops.

Council Chamber

I am & ca

10th November 1831

(Sd.) Wm. Casement Coll.

Secy. to Govt. Mily. Dept.

## TEXT .

From W. C. Taylor Esqre.

To  F. S. Mudge Esqre.

Dated 7th July 1855

My dear Mudge,

There is a great gathering of Sontals 4 or 5000 men at a place about 8 miles off and I understand that they are all well armed with Bows and arrows, Tulwars, Spears & ca. and that *it is their intention to attack all the Europeans round and plunder and murder them. The cause of all this is that one of their Gods is supposed to have taken the Flesh and to have made his appearance at*

---

[6] *JP*, 19 July 1855: Enclosure to letter from the Magistrate of Murshidabad, dated 11 July 1855. Emphasis added.

*some place near this, and that it is his intention to reign as a King over all this part of India, and has ordered the Sontals to collect and put to death all the Europeans and influential Natives round. As this is the nearest point to the gathering I suppose it will be first attacked* and think it would be best for you to send notice to the authorities at Berhampore and ask for military aid as *it is not at all a nice look out being murdered* and as far as I can make out this is a *rather serious affair.*

Sreecond                                                                    Yours & ca

7th July 1855                                                    /Signed/ W. C. Taylor

Nothing could be more immediate than these texts. Written as soon as these events were acknowledged as rebellion by those who had the most to fear from it, they are among the very first records we have on them in the collections of the India Office Library and the West Bengal State Archives. As the evidence on the 1831 *bidroha* shows,[7] it was not until 10 November that the Calcutta authorities came to recognize the violence reported from the Barasat region for what it was—a full-blooded insurrection led by Titu Mir and his men. Colonel Casement's letter identifies for us that moment when the hitherto unknown leader of a local peasantry entered the lists against the Raj and thereby made his way into history. The date of the other document too commemorates a beginning—that of the Santal *hool*. It was on that very day, 7 July 1855, that the assassination of Mahesh daroga following an encounter between his police and peasants gathered at Bhagnadihi detonated the uprising. The report was loud enough to register in that note scribbled in obvious alarm at Sreecond by an European employee of the East India Railway for the benefit of his colleague and the *sarkar*. Again, these are words that convey as directly as possible the impact of a peasant revolt on its enemies in its first sanguinary hours.

### III

None of this instantaneousness percolates through to the next level—that of the secondary discourse. The latter draws on primary discourse as *matériel* but transforms it at the same time. To contrast the two types one could think of the first as historiography in a raw, primordial state or as an embryo yet to be articulated into an organism with

[7] Thus, *BC* 54222: *JC*, 3 Apr. 1832: Alexander to Barwell (28 Nov. 1831).

discrete limbs, and the second as the processed product, however crude the processing, a duly constituted if infant discourse.

The difference is quite obviously a function of time. In the chronology of this particular corpus the secondary follows the primary at a distance and opens up a perspective to turn an event into history in the perception not only of those outside it but of the participants as well. It was thus that Mark Thornhill, Magistrate of Mathura during the summer of 1857 when a mutiny of the Treasury Guard sparked off jacqueries all over the district, was to reflect on the altered status of his own narrative in which he figured as a protagonist himself. Introducing his well-known memoirs, *The Personal Adventures And Experiences Of A Magistrate During The Rise, Progress, And Suppression Of The Indian Mutiny* (London, 1884) twenty-seven years after the event he wrote:

> After the suppression of the Indian Mutiny, I commenced to write an account of my adventures . . . by the time my narrative was completed, the then interest of the public in the subject was exhausted. Years have since passed, and an interest of another kind has arisen. The events of that time have become history, and to that history my story may prove a contribution . . . I have therefore resolved to publish my narrative . . .

Shorn of contemporaneity a discourse is thus recovered as an element of the past and classified as history. This change, aspectual as well as categorial, sites it at the very intersection of colonialism and historiography, endowing it with a duplex character linked at the same time to a system of power and the particular manner of its representation.

Its authorship is in itself witness to this intersection and Thornhill was by no means the only administrator turned historian. He was indeed one of many officials, civilian and military, who wrote retrospectively on popular disturbances in rural India under the Raj. Their statements, taken together, fall into two classes. First, there were those which were based on the writers' own experience as participants. Memoirs of one kind or another these were written either at a considerable delay after the events narrated or almost concurrently with them but intended, unlike primary discourse, for a public readership. The latter, an important distinction, shows how the colonialist mind managed to serve Clio and counter-insurgency at the same time so that the presumed neutrality of one could have hardly been left unaffected by the passion of the other, a point to

which we shall soon return. Reminiscences of both kinds abound in
the literature on the Mutiny, which dealt with the violence of the
peasantry (especially in the North Western Provinces and central
India) no less than with that of the sepoys. Accounts such as Thornhill's written long after the event, were matched by near contemporary
ones such as Dunlop's *Service and Adventure with Khakee Ressallah;*
or *Meerut Volunteer Horse during the Mutinies of 1857-58* (London,
1858) and Edwards' *Personal Adventures during the Indian Rebellion
in Rohilcund, Futtehghur, and Oudh* (London 1858) to mention
only two out of a vast outcrop intended to cater for a public who
could not have enough of tales of horror and glory.

The other class of writings to qualify as secondary discourse is also
the work of administrators. They too addressed themselves to a
predominantly non-official readership but on themes not directly
related to their own experience. Their work includes some of the
most widely used and highly esteemed accounts of peasant uprisings
written either as monographs on particular events, such as Jamini
Mohan Ghosh's on the Sannyasi-and-Faqir disturbances and J. C.
Price's on the Chuar Rebellion, or as statements included in more
comprehensive histories like W. W. Hunter's story of the Santal *hool*
in *The Annals of Rural Bengal.* Apart from these there were those
distinguished contributions made by some of the best minds in the
Civil Service to the historical chapters of the *District Gazetteers.*
Altogether they constitute a substantial body of writing which enjoys
much authority with all students of the subject and there is hardly
any historiography at the next, that is, tertiary level of discourse that
does not rely on these for sustenance.

The prestige of this genre is to no mean extent due to the aura of
impartiality it has about it. By keeping their narrative firmly beyond
the pale of personal involvement these authors managed, if only by
implication, to confer on it a semblance of truth. As officials they
were carriers of the will of the state no doubt. But since they wrote
about a past in which they did not figure as functionaries themselves,
their statements are taken to be more authentic and less biased than
those of their opposite numbers whose accounts, based on reminiscences, were necessarily contaminated by their intervention in rural
disturbances as agents of the Raj. By contrast the former are believed
to have approached the narrated events from the outside. As observers
separated clinically from the site and subject of diagnosis they are

supposed to have found for their discourse a niche in that realm of perfect neutraility—the realm of History—over which the Aorist and the Third Person preside.

## IV

How valid is this claim to neutrality? For an answer we may not take any bias for granted in this class of historical work from the mere fact of its origin with authors committed to colonialism. To take that as self-evident would be to deny historiography the possibility of acknowledging its own inadequacies and thus defeat the purpose of the present exercise. As should be clear from what follows, it is precisely by refusing to *prove* what appears as obvious that historians of peasant insurgency remain trapped—in the obvious. Criticism must therefore start not by naming a bias but by examining the components of the discourse, vehicle of all ideology, for the manner in which these might have combined to describe any particular figure of the past.

The components of both types of discourse and their varieties discussed so far are what we shall call segments. Made up of the same linguistic material, that is strings of words of varying lengths, they are of two kinds which may be designated, according to their function, as indicative and interpretative. A gross differentiation, this is meant to assign to them, within a given text, the role respectively of reporting and explaining. This however does not imply their mutual segregation. On the contrary they are often found embedded in each other not merely as a matter of fact but of necessity.

One can see in *Texts 1* and *2* how such imbrication works. In both of them the straight print stands for the indicative segments and the italics for the interpretative. Laid out according to no particular pattern in either of these letters they interpenetrate and sustain each other in order to give the documents their meaning, and in the process endow some of the strings with an ambiguity that is inevitably lost in this particular manner of typographical representation. However, the rough outline of a division of functions between the two classes emerges even from this schema—the indicative stating (that is reporting) the actual and anticipated actions of the rebels and their enemies, and the interpretative commenting on them in order to understand (that is to explain) their significance.

The difference between them corresponds to that between the two basic components of any historical discourse which, following Roland Barthes' terminology, we shall call *functions* and *indices*.[8] The former are segments that make up the linear sequence of a narrative. Contiguous, they operate in a relation of solidarity in the sense of mutually implying each other and add up to increasingly larger strings which combine to produce the aggregative statement. The latter may thus be regarded as a sum of micro-sequences to each of which, however important or otherwise, it should be possible to assign names by a metalinguistic operation using terms that may or may not belong to the text under consideration. It is thus that the functions of a folk-tale have been named by Bremond, after Propp, as *Fraud, Betrayal, Struggle, Contract,*etc. and those of a triviality such as the offer of a cigarette in a James Bond story designated by Barthes as *offering, accepting, lighting,* and *smoking.* One may perhaps take a cue from this procedure to define a historical statement as a discourse with a name subsuming a given number of named sequences. Hence it should be possible to speak of a hypothetical narrative called 'The Insurrection of Titu Mir' made up of a number of sequences including Text 1 quoted above.

Let us give this document a name and call it, say, *Calcutta Council Acts.* (Alternatives such as *Outbreak of Violence* or *Army Called Up* should also do and be analysable in terms corresponding to, though not identical with, those which follow.) In broad terms the message *Calcutta Council Acts (C)* in our text can be read as a combination of two groups of sequences called *alarm* (a) and *intervention* (b), each of which is made up of a pair of segments—the former of *insurrection breaks out* (a') and *information received* (a'') and the latter of *decision to call up army* (b') and *order issued* (b''), one of the constituents in each pair being represented in its turn by yet another linked series—(a') by *atrocities committed* ($a_1$) and *authority defied* ($a_2$), and (b'') by *infantry to proceed* ($b_1$), *artillery to support* ($b_2$) and *magistrate to co-operate* ($b_3$). In other words the narrative in this document can be written up in three equivalent steps so that

[8] My debt to Roland Barthes for many of the analytic terms and procedures used in this section and generally throughout this essay should be far too obvious to all familiar with his 'Structural Analysis of Narratives' and 'The Struggle with the Angel' in Barthes, *Image-Music-Text* (Glasgow, 1977), pp. 79-141, and 'Historical Discourse' in M. Lane (ed.), *Structuralism, A Reader* (London, 1970), pp. 145-55, to require detailed reference except where I quote directly from this literature.

$$C \equiv (a+b) \dots\dots\dots\dots\dots\dots\dots\dots\dots I$$
$$\equiv (a'+a'') + (b'+b'') \dots\dots\dots\dots\dots II$$
$$\equiv (a_1+a_2) + a'' + b' + (b_1+b_2+b_3) \dots\dots III$$

It should be clear from this arrangement that not all the elements of step II can be expressed in micro-sequences of the same order. Hence we are left at step III with a concatenation in which segments drawn from different levels of the discourse are imbricated to constitute a roughly hewn and uneven structure. In so far as functional units of the lowest denomination like these are what a narrative has as its syntagmatic relata its course can never be smooth. The hiatus between the loosely cobbled segments is necessarily charged with uncertainty, with 'moments of risk' and every micro-sequence terminates by opening up alternative possibilities only one of which is picked up by the next sequence as it carries on with the story. 'Du Pont, Bond's future partner, offers him a light from his lighter but Bond refuses; the meaning of this bifurcation is that Bond instinctively fears a booby-trapped gadget.'[9] What Barthes identifies thus as 'bifurcation' in fiction, has its parallels in historical discourse as well. The alleged commitment of atrocities ($a_1$) in that official despatch of 1831 cancels out the belief in the peaceful propagation of Titu's new doctrine which had already been known to the authorities but ignored so far as inconsequential. The expression, *authority defied* ($a_2$), which refers to the rebels having 'set at defiance and repulsed the utmost force that the local Civil Authority could assemble for their apprehension', has as its other if unstated term his efforts to persuade the Government by petition and deputation to offer redress for the grievances of his co-religionists. And so on. Each of these elementary functional units thus implies a node which has not quite materialized into an actual development, a sort of zero sign by means of which the narrative affirms its tension. And precisely because history as the verbal representation by man of his own past is by its very nature so full of hazard, so replete indeed with the verisimilitude of sharply differentiated choices, that it never ceases to excite. The historical discourse is the world's oldest thriller.

## V

Sequential analysis thus shows a narrative to be a concatenation of

[9] Barthes, *Image-Music-Text*, p. 102.

not so closely aligned functional units. The latter are dissociative in their operation and emphasize the analytic rather than the synthetic aspect of a discourse. As such they are not what, by themselves, generate its meaning. Just as the sense of a word (e.g. 'man') is not fractionally represented in each of the letters (e.g. M, A, N) which make up its graphic image nor of a phrase (e.g. 'once upon a time') in its constituting words taken separately, so also the individual segments of a discourse cannot on their own tell us what it signifies. Meaning in each instance is the work of a process of integration which complements that of sequential articulation. As Benveniste has put it, in any language 'it is dissociation which divulges to us its formal constitution and integration its signifying units'.[10]

This is true of the language of history as well. The integrative operation is carried out in its discourse by the other class of basic narrative units, that is, *indices*. A necessary and indispensable correlate of *functions* they are distinguished from the latter in some important respects:

> Indices, because of the vertical nature of their relations are truly semantic units: unlike 'functions' . . . they refer to a signified, not to an 'operation'. The ratification of indices is 'higher up' . . . a paradigmatic ratification. That of functions, by contrast, is always 'further on', is a syntagmatic ratification. *Functions* and *indices* thus overlay another classic distinction: functions involve metonymic relata, indices metaphoric relata; the former correspond to a functionality of doing, the latter to a functionality of being.[11]

The vertical intervention of indices in a discourse is possible because of the disruption of its linearity by a process corresponding to dystaxia in the behaviour of many natural languages. Bally who has studied this phenomenon in much detail finds that one of several conditions of its occurrence in French is 'when parts of the same sign are separated' so that the expression, 'elle a pardonné' taken in the negative, is splintered and re-assembled as 'elle *ne nous a jamais plus pardonné*'.[12]

---

[10] Émile Benveniste, *Problèmes de linguistique générale, I* (Paris, 1966), p. 126. The original, 'la dissociation nous livre la constitution formelle; l'intégration nous livre des unités signifiantes', has been rendered somewhat differently and I feel, less happily, in the English translation of the work, *Problems in General Linguistics* (Florida, 1971), p. 107.

[11] Barthes, *Image-Music-Text*, p. 93.

[12] Charles Bally, *Linguistique Générale et Linguistique Française* (Berne, 1965), p. 144.

Similarly the simple predictive in Bengali 'shé jābé' can be re-written by the insertion of an interrogative or a string of negative conditionals between the two words to produce respectively 'shé *ki* jābé' and 'shé *nā hoy nā* jābé'.

In a historical narrative too it is a process of 'distension and expansion' of its syntagm which helps paradigmatic elements to infiltrate and reconstitute its discrete segments into a meaningful whole. It is precisely thus that the co-ordination of the metonymic and metaphorical axes is brought about in a statement and the necessary interaction of its functions and indices actualized. However these units are not distributed in equal proportions in all texts: some have a greater incidence of one kind than of the other. As a result a discourse could be either predominantly metonymic or metaphorical depending on whether a significantly larger number of its components are syntagmatically ratified or paradigmatically.[13] Our *Text I* is of the first type. One can see the formidable and apparently impenetrable array of its metonymic relata in step III of the sequential analysis given above. Here at last we have the perfect authentication of the idiot's view of history as one damn'd thing after another: *rising - information - decision - order*. However, a closer look at the text can detect chinks which have allowed 'comment', to worm its way through the plate armour of 'fact'. The italicized expressions are witness to this paradigmatic intervention and indeed its measure. Indices, they play the role of *adjectives* or *epithets* as opposed to verbs which, to speak in terms of homology between sentence and narrative, is the role of functions.[14] Working intimately together with the latter they make the despatch into more than a mere register of happenings and help to inscribe into it a meaning, an interpretation so that the protagonists emerge from it not as peasants but as *'Insurgents'*, not as Musalman but as *'fanatic'*; their action not as resistance to the tyranny of the rural elite but as *'the most daring and wanton atrocities on the inhabitants'*; their project not as a revolt against zamindari but as *'defying the authority of the State'*, not as a search for an alternative order in which the peace of the countryside would not be violated by the officially condoned anarchy of semi-feudal landlordism but as, *'disturbing the public tranquil[l]ity'*.

If the intervention of indices 'substitutes meaning for the straight-

[13] Barthes, *Elements of Semiology* (London, 1967), p. 60.
[14] Barthes, *Image-Music-Text*, p. 128.

forward copy of the events recounted,[15] in a text so charged with metonymy as the one discussed above, it may be trusted to do so to an even greater degree in discourses which are predominantly meta- phorical. This should be evident from *Text 2* where the element of comment, italicized by us, largely outweighs that of report. If the latter is represented as a concatenation of three functional sequences, namely, *armed Santals gathering, authorities to be alerted* and *military aid requested*, it can be seen how the first of these has been separated from the rest by the insertion of a large chunk of explanatory material and how the others too are enveloped and sealed off by comment. The latter is inspired by the fear that Sreecond being *'the nearest point to the gathering . . . will be first attacked'* and of course *'it is not at all a nice look out being murdered'*. Notice, however, that this fear justifies itself *politically*, that is, by imputing to the Santals an *'intention to attack . . . plunder . . . and put to death all the Europeans and influential Natives'* so that *'one of their Gods'* in human form may *'reign as a King over all this part of India'*. Thus, this document is not neutral in its attitude to the events witnessed and put up as 'evidence' before the court of history it can hardly be expected to testify with im- partiality. On the contrary it is the voice of committed colonialism. It has already made a choice between the prospect of Santal self-rule in Damin-i-Koh and the continuation of the British Raj and identi- fies what is allegedly good for the promotion of one as fearsome and catastrophic for the other—as *'a rather serious affair'*. In other words the indices in this discourse—as well as in the one discussed above—introduce us to a particular code so constituted that for each of its signs we have an antonym, a counter-message, in another code. To borrow a binary representation made famous by Mao Tse-tung,[16] the reading, *'It's terrible!'* for any element in one must show up in the other as *'It's fine!'* for a corresponding element and vice versa. To put this clash of codes graphically one can arrange the indices italicized below of *Texts 1* and *2* in a matrix called 'TERRIBLE' (in conformity to the adjectival attribute of units of this class) in such a way as to indicate their mapping into the implied, though unstated terms (given in straight types) of a cor- responding matrix 'FINE'.

[15] Ibid., p. 119
[16] *Selected Works of Mao Tse-tung*, vol. I (Peking, 1967), pp. 26-7.

| TERRIBLE | FINE |
|---|---|
| *Insurgents* ................................................. | peasants |
| *fanatic* ...................................................... | Islamic puritan |
| *daring and wanton atrocities on the Inhabitants*... | resistance to oppression |
| *defying the authority of the State* ...................... | revolt against zamindari |
| *disturbing the public tranquil(l)ity* .................... | struggle for a better order |
| *intention to attack, etc* .................................. | intention to punish oppressors |
| *one of their Gods to reign as a King* ................... | Santal self-rule |

What comes out of the interplay of these mutually implied but opposed matrices is that our texts are not the record of observations uncontaminated by bias, judgement and opinion. On the contrary, they speak of a total complicity. For if the expressions in the right-hand column taken together may be said to stand for insurgency, the code which contains all signifiers of the subaltern practice of 'turning things upside down' and the consciousness that informs it, then the other column must stand for its opposite, that is, counter-insurgency. The antagonism between the two is irreducible and there is nothing in this to leave room for neutrality. Hence these documents make no sense except in terms of a code of pacification which, under the Raj, was a complex of coercive intervention by the State and its protégés, the native elite, with arms and words. Representatives of the primary type of discourse in the historiography of peasant revolts, these are specimens of the prose of counter-insurgency.

## VI

How far does secondary discourse too share such commitment? Is it possible for it to speak any other prose than that of a counter-insurgency? Those narratives of this category in which their authors figure among the protagonists are of course suspect almost by definition, and the presence of the grammatical first person in these must be acknowledged as a sign of complicity. The question however is whether the loss of objectivity on this account is adequately made up by the consistent use of the aorist in such writings. For as Benveniste observes, the historical utterance admits of three variations of the past tense—that is, the aorist, the imperfect and the pluperfect, and of course the present is altogether excluded.[17] This condition is

[17] Benveniste, op. cit., p. 239.

indeed satisfied by reminiscences separated by a long enough hiatus from the events concerned. What has to be found out therefore is the extent to which the force of the preterite corrects the bias caused by the absence of the third person.

Mark Thornhill's memoirs of the Mutiny provide us with a text in which the author looks back at a series of events he had experienced twenty-seven years ago. 'The events of that time' had 'turned into history', and he intends, as he says in the extract quoted above, to make a contribution 'to that history', and thus produce what we have defined as a particular kind of secondary discourse. The difference inscribed in it by that interval is perhaps best grasped by comparing it with some samples of primary discourse we have on the same subject from the same author. Two of these[18] may be read together as a record of his perception of what happened at the Mathura sadar station and the surrounding countryside between 14 May and 3 June 1857. Written by him donning the district magistrate's topee and addressed to his superiors—one on 5 June 1857, that is, within forty-eight hours of the terminal date of the period under discussion, and the other on 10 August 1858 when the events were still within vivid recall as a very recent past—these letters coincide in scope with that of the narrative covering the same three weeks in the first ninety pages of his book written nearly three decades later donning the historian's hat.

The letters are both predominantly metonymic in character. Originating as they did almost from within the related experience itself they are necessarily foreshortened and tell the reader in breathless sequences about some of the happenings of that extraordinary summer. The syntagm thus takes on a semblance of factuality with hardly any room in it for comment. Yet here again the welding of the functional units can be seen, on close inspection, to be less solid than at first sight. Embedded in them there are indices revealing the anxieties of the local custodian of law and order ('the state of the district generally is such as to *defy all control*'; 'the *law* is at a *standstill*'), his fears ('*very alarming* rumours of the approach of the rebel army'), his moral disapproval of the activities of the armed villagers ('the disturbances in the district . . . increasing . . . in . . . *enormity*'), his appreciation by contrast of the native collaborators hostile to the

---

[18] *Freedom Struggle in Uttar Pradesh*, vol. V, pp. 685-92.

insurgents ('. . . 'the Seths' house . . . *received us most kindly*'). Indices such as these are ideological birth-marks displayed prominently on much of this type of material relating to peasant revolts. Indeed, taken together with some other relevant textual features—e.g. the abrupt mode of address in these documents so revealing of the shock and terror generated by the *émeute*—they accuse all such allegedly 'objective' evidence on the militancy of the rural masses to have been tainted at its source by the prejudice and partisan outlook of their enemies. If historians fail to take notice of these tell-tale signs branded on the staple of their trade, that is a fact which must be explained in terms of the optics of a colonialist historiography rather than construed in favour of the presumed objectivity of their 'primary sources'.

There is nothing immediate or abrupt about the corresponding secondary discourse. On the contrary it has various perspectives built into it to give it a depth in time and following from this temporal determination, its meaning. Compare for instance the narration of events in the two versions for any particular day—for, say, 14 May 1857 at the very beginning of our three-week period. Written up in a very short paragraph of fifty-seven words in Thornhill's letter of 10 August 1858 this can be represented fully in four pithy segments without any significant loss of message: *mutineers approaching; information received from Gurgaon; confirmed by Europeans north of the district; women and non-combattants sent off to Agra*. Since the account starts, for all practical purposes, with this entry, there are no exordia to serve as its context, giving this instant take-off the sense, as we have noticed, of a total surprise. In the book however that same instant is provided with a background spread over four and a half months and three pages (pp. 1-3). All of this time and space is devoted to some carefully chosen details of the author's life and experience in the period preceding the Mutiny. These are truly *significant*. As indices they prepare the reader for what is to come and help him to *understand* the happenings of 14 May and after, when these enter into the narrative at staggered stages. Thus the mysterious circulation of chapatis in January and the silent but expressive concern on the narrator's brother, a high official, over a telegram received at Agra on 12 May conveying the still unconfirmed news of the Meerut uprising, portend the developments two days later at his own district headquarters. Again the trivia about his 'large income and great authority', his house, horses, servants, 'a chest full of silver plate, which stood in the hall and . . . a great store of Cashmere shawls, pearls, and diamonds' all help to index, by contrast, the holocaust which was soon to reduce his authority to nothing, and turn his servants into rebels, his house into a shambles, his property into booty for the plundering poor of town and country. By anticipating the narrated events thus, if only by implication, secondary discourse destroys the entropy of the first, its raw material. Henceforth there will be nothing in the story that can be said to be altogether unexpected.

This effect is the work of the so-called 'organization shifters'[19] which help the author to superimpose a temporality of his own on that of his theme, that is 'to "dechronologize" the historical thread and restore, if only by way of reminiscence or nostalgia, a Time at once complex, parametric, and non-linear . . . braiding the chronology of the subject-matter with that of the language-act which reports it'. In the present instance the 'braiding' consists not only in fitting an evocative context to the bare sequence related in that short paragraph of his letter. The shifters disrupt the syntagm twice to insert in the breach, on both occasions, a moment of authorial time suspended between the two poles of 'waiting', a figure ideally constituted to allow the play of digressions, asides and parentheses forming loops and zigzags in a story-line and adding thereby to its depth. Thus, waiting for news about the movements of the mutineers he reflects on the peace of the early evening at the sadar station and strays from his account to tell us in violation of the historiographical canon of tense and person: 'The scene was simple and full of the repose of Eastern life. In the times that followed it often recurred to my memory.' And, again, waiting later on for transport to take away the evacuees gathered in his drawing room, he withdraws from that particular night for the duration of a few words to comment: 'It was a beautiful room, brightly lighted, gay with flowers. It was the last time I thus saw it, and so it remains impressed on my memory.'

How far does the operation of these shifters help to correct the bias resulting from the writer's intervention in the first person? Not much by this showing. For each of the indices wedged into the narrative represents a principled choice between the terms of a paradigmatic

---

[19] For Roman Jakobson's exposition of this key concept, see his *Selected Writings, 2: Word and Language* (The Hague and Paris, 1971), pp. 130-47. Barthes develops the notion of organization shifters in his essay 'Historical Discourse', pp. 146-8. All extracts quoted in this paragraph are taken from that essay unless otherwise mentioned.

opposition. Between the authority of the head of the district and its defiance by the armed masses, between the habitual servility of his menials and their assertion of self-respect as rebels, between the insignia of his wealth and power (e.g. gold, horses, shawls, bungalow) and their appropriation or destruction by the subaltern crowds, the author, hardly differentiated from the administrator that he was twenty-seven years ago, consistently chooses the former. Nostalgia makes the choice all the more eloquent—a recall of what is thought to be 'fine' such as a peaceful evening or an elegant room emphasizing by contrast the 'terrible' aspects of popular violence directed against the Raj. Quite clearly there is a logic to this preference. It affirms itself by negating a series of inversions which, combined with other signs of the same order, constitute a code of insurgency. The pattern of the historian's choice, identical with the magistrate's, conforms thus to a counter-code, the code of counter-insurgency.

## VII

If the neutralizing effect of the aorist fails thus to prevail over the subjectivity of the protagonist as narrator in this particular genre of secondary discourse, how does the balance of tense and person stand in the other kind of writing within the same category? One can see two distinct idioms at work here, both identified with the standpoint of colonialism but unlike each other in expressing it. The cruder variety is well exemplified in *The Chuar Rebellion of 1799* by J. C. Price. Written long after the event, in 1874, it was obviously meant by the author, Settlement Officer of Midnapur at the time, to serve as a straightforward historical account with no particular administrative end in view. He addressed it to 'the casual reader' as well as to any 'future Collector of Midnapore', hoping to share with both 'that keen interest which I have felt as I have read the old Midnapore records'.[20] But the author's 'delight . . . experienced in pouring over these papers' seems to have produced a text almost indistinguishable from the primary discourse used as its source. The latter is, for one thing, conspicuous by its sheer physical presence. Over a fifth of that half of the book which deals specifically with the events of 1799 is made up of direct quotations from those records and another large part of barely modified extracts. More important for us, however, is the evidence we have of the author's identification of his own senti-

---

[20] Price, op. cit., p. *clx*.

ments with those of that small group of whites who were reaping the whirlwind produced by the wind of a violently disruptive change the Company's Government had sown in the south-western corner of Bengal. Only the fear of the beleaguered officials at Midnapur station in 1799 turns seventy-five years later into that genocidal hatred characteristic of a genre of post-Mutiny British writing. 'The disinclination of the authorities, civil or military, to proceed in person to help to quell the disturbances is most striking', he writes shaming his compatriots and then goes on to brag:

> In these days of breech-loaders half a dozen Europeans would have been a match for twenty times their number of Chuars. Of course with the imperfect nature of the weapons of that day it could not be expected that Europeans would fruitlessly rush into danger, but I should have expected that the European officers of the station would have in some instances at least courted and met an attack in person and repulsed their assailants. I wonder that no one European officer, civilian or military, with the exception of perhaps Lieutenant Gill, owned to that sensation of joyous excitement most young men feel now-a-days in field sports, or in any pursuit where there is an element of danger. I think most of us, had we lived in 1799, would have counted it better sport had we bagged a marauding Chuar reeking with blood and spoils, than the largest bear that the Midnapore jungles can produce.[21]

Quite clearly the author's separation from his subject-matter and the difference between the time of the event and that of its narration here have done little to inspire objectivity in him. His passion is apparently of the same order as that of the British soldier who wrote on the eve of the sack of Delhi in 1857: 'I most sincerely trust that the order given when we attack Delhi will be. . ."Kill every one; no quarter is to be given" '.[22] The historian's attitude to rebels is in this instance indistinguishable from that of the State—the attitude of the hunter to his quarry. Regarded thus an insurgent is not a subject of understanding or interpretation but of extermination, and the discourse of history, far from being neutral, serves directly to instigate official violence.

There were however other writers working within the same genre who are known to have expressed themselves in a less

[21] Ibid.
[22] Reginald G. Wilberforce, *An Unrecorded Chapter of the Indian Mutiny* (2nd edition; London, 1894), pp. 76-7.

sanguinary idiom. They are perhaps best represented by W. W. Hunter and his account of the Santal insurrection of 1855 in *The Annals of Rural Bengal*. It is, in many respects, a remarkable text. Written within a decade of the Mutiny and twelve years of the *hool*,[23] it has none of that revanchist and racist overtone common to a good deal of Anglo-Indian literature of the period. Indeed the author treats the enemies of the Raj not only with consideration but with respect although they had wiped it off from three eastern districts in a matter of weeks and held out for five months against the combined power of the colonial army and its newly acquired auxiliaries—railways and the 'electric telegraph'. One of the first modern exercises in the historiography of Indian peasant revolts, it situates the uprising in a cultural and socio-economic context, analyses its causes, and draws on local records and contemporary accounts for evidence about its progress and eventual suppression. Here, to all appearances, we have that classic instance of the author's own bias and opinion dissolving under the operation of the past tense and the grammatical third person. Here, perhaps, historical discourse has come to its own and realized that ideal of an 'apersonal . . . mode of narrative . . . designed to wipe out the presence of the speaker'?[24]

This semblance of objectivity, of the want of any obviously demonstrable bias, has however nothing to do with 'facts speaking for themselves' in a state of pure metonymy unsullied by comment. On the contrary the text is packed with comment. One has to compare it with something like the near contemporary article on this subject in *Calcutta Review* (1856) or even K. K. Datta's history of the *hool* written long after its suppression to realize how little there is in it of the details of what actually happened.[25] Indeed the narration of the event occupies in the book only about 7 per cent of the chapter which builds up climactically towards it, and somewhat less than 50 per cent of the print devoted specifically to this topic within that chapter. The syntagm is broken up again and again by dystaxia and interpretation

[23] It appears from a note in this work that parts of it were written in 1866. The dedication bears the date 4 March 1868. All our references to this work in quotation or otherwise are to Chapter IV of the seventh edition (London, 1897) unless otherwise stated.

[24] Barthes, *Image-Music-Text*, p. 112.

[25] Anon., 'The Sonthal Rebellion', *Calcutta Review* (1856), pp. 223-64; K. K. Datta, 'The Santal Insurrection of 1855-57', in *Anti-British Plots and Movements before 1857* (Meerut, 1970), pp. 43-152.

filters through to assemble the segments into a meaningful whole of a primarily metaphorical character. The consequence of this operation that is most relevant for our purpose here is the way in which it distributes the paradigmatic relata along an axis of historical continuity between a 'before' and an 'after', forelengthening it with a context and extending it into a perspective. The representation of insurgency ends up thus by having its moment intercalated between its past and future so that the particular values of one and the other are rubbed into the event to give it the meaning specific to it.

## VIII

To turn first to the context, two-thirds of the chapter which culminates in the history of the insurrection is taken up with an inaugural account of what may be called the natural history of its protagonists. An essay in ethnography this deals with the physical traits, language, traditions, myths, religion, rituals, habitat, environment, hunting and agricultural practices, social organization and communal government of the Santals of the Birbhum region. There are many details here which index the coming conflict as one of contraries, as between the noble savage of the hills and mean exploiters from the plains—references to his personal dignity ('He does not abase himself to the ground like the rural Hindu'; the Santal woman is 'ignorant of the shrinking squeamishness of the Hindu female', etc.) implying the contrast his would-be reduction to servitude by Hindu moneylenders, his honesty ('Unlike the Hindu, he never thinks of making money by a stranger, scrupulously avoids all topics of business, and feels pained if payment is pressed upon him for the milk and fruit which his wife brings out'), the greed and fraud of the alien traders and landlords leading eventually to the insurrection, his aloofness ('The Santals live as much apart as possible from the Hindus'), the *diku*'s intrusion into his life and territory and the holocaust which inevitably followed.

These indices give the uprising not only a moral dimension and the values of a just war, but also a depth in time. The latter is realized by the operation of diachronic markers in the text—an imaginary past by creation myths (appropriate for an enterprise taken up on the Thakur's advice) and a real but remote past (befitting a revolt steeped in tradition) by the sherds of prehistory in ritual and speech with the Santals' ceremony of 'Purifying for the Dead' mentioned, for instance, as the trace of 'a faint remembrance of the far-off time when they dwelt beside great rivers' and their language as 'that intangible record on which a nation's past is graven more deeply than on brass tablets or rock inscriptions'.

Moving closer to the event the author provides it with a recent past covering roughly a period of sixty years of 'direct administration' in the area. The moral and temporal aspects of the narrative merge here in the figure of an irreconcilable contradiction. On the one hand there were, according to Hunter, a series of beneficial measures introduced by the government—the Decennial Settlement helping to expand the area under cultivation and induce the Santals, since 1792, to hire themselves out as agricultural labourers; the setting up, in 1832, of an enclosure ringed off by masonry pillars where they could colonize virgin land and jungle without fear of harassment from hostile tribes; the development of 'English enterprise' in Bengal in the form of indigo factories for which 'the Santal immigrants afforded a population of day-labourers'; and last but not the least of bonanzas, their absorption by thousands into labour gangs for the construction of railways across that region in 1854. But there were, on the other hand, two sets of factors which combined to undo all the good resulting from colonial rule, namely, the exploitation and oppression of the Santals by greedy and fraudulent Hindu landlords, money-lenders and traders, and the failure of the local administration, its police and the courts to protect them or redress the wrongs they suffered.

## IX

This emphasis on contradiction serves on obviously interpretative purpose for the author. It makes it possible for him to locate the cause of the uprising in a failure of the Raj to make its ameliorative aspects prevail over the still lingering defects and shortcomings in its exercise of authority. The account of the event therefore fits directly into the objective stated at the beginning of the chapter, that is, to interest not only the scholar 'in these lapsed races' but the statesman as well. 'The Indian statesman will discover', he had written there referring euphemistically to the makers of British policy in India, 'that these Children of the Forest are . . . amenable to the same reclaiming influences as other men, and that upon their capacity for civilisation the future extension of English enterprise in Bengal in a large measure depends'. It is this concern for 'reclamation' (shorthand for accelerating the transformation of the tribal peasantry into wage labour and harnessing them to characteristically colonialist projects for the exploitation of Indian resources) which explains the mixture of firmness and 'understanding' in Hunter's attitude to the rebellion. A liberal-imperalist he regarded it both as a menace to the stability of the Raj and as a useful critique of its far from perfect administration. So while he censured the government of the day for not declaring Martial Law soon enough in order to cut down the *hool* at its inception, he was careful to differentiate himself from those of his compatriots who wanted to punish the entire Santal community for the crime of its rebels and deport overseas the population of the districts involved. A genuinely far-sighted imperialist he looked forward to the day when the tribe, like many other aboriginal peoples of the subcontinent, would demonstrate its 'capacity for civilisation' by acting as an inexhaustible source of cheap labour power.

This vision is inscribed into the perspective with which the narration ends. Blaming the outbreak of the *hool* squarely on that 'cheap and practical administration' which paid no heed to the Santals' complaints and concentrated on tax collection alone it goes on to catalogue the somewhat illusory benefits of 'the more exact system that was introduced after the revolt' to keep the power of the usurers over debtors within the limits of the law, check the use of false weights and measures in retail trade, and ensure the right of bonded labourers to choose freedom by desertion or change of employers. But more than administrative reform it was 'English enterprise' again which radically contributed to the welfare of the tribe. The railways 'completely changed the relation of labour to capital' and did away with that 'natural reason for slavery—to wit, the absence of a wage-fund for free workmen'. The demand for plantation labour in the Assam tea-districts 'was destined still further to improve the position of the Santals' and so was the stimulus for indenturing coolies for the Mauritius and the Carribeans. It was thus that the tribal peasant prospered thanks to the development of a vast sub-continental and overseas labour market within the British Empire. In the Assam tea gardens 'his whole family gets employment, and every additional child, instead of being the means of increasing his poverty, becomes a source of wealth', while the coolies returned from Africa or the West Indies 'at the expiry of their contracts with savings averaging £20 sterling, a sum sufficient to set up a Santal as a considerable proprietor in his own village'.

Many of these so-called improvements were, as we know now looking back at them across a century, the result of sheer wishful thinking or so ephemeral as not to have mattered at all. The connection between usury and bonded labour continued all through British rule well into independent India. The freedom of the labour market was seriously restricted by the want of competition between British and indigenous capital. The employment of tribal families on tea plantations became a source of cynical exploitation of the labour of women and children. The advantages of mobility and contractuality were cancelled out by irregularities in the process of recruitment and the manipulation of the contrary factors of economic dependence and social differentiation by *arkatis*. The system of indenturing helped rather less to liberate servile labour than to develop a sort of second serfdom, and so on.

Yet this vision which never materialized offers an insight into the character of this type of discourse. The perspective it inspired amounted in effect to a testament of faith in colonialism. The *hool* was assimilated there to the career of the Raj and the militant enterprise of a tribal peasantry to free themselves from the triple yoke of *sarkari*, *sahukari* and *zamindari* to 'English enterprise'—the infrastructure of Empire. Hence the objective stated at the beginning of the account could be reiterated towards the end with the author saying that he had written at least 'partly for the instruction which their [the Santals'] recent history furnishes as to the proper method of dealing with the aboriginal races'. The suppression of local peasant revolts was a part of this method, but it was incorporated now in a broader strategy designed to tackle the economic problems of the British Government in India as an element of the global problems of imperial politics. 'These are the problems', says Hunter in concluding the chapter, 'which Indian statesmen during the next fifty years will be called upon to solve. Their predecessors have given civilisation to India; it will be their duty to render that civilisation at once beneficial to the natives and safe for ourselves.' In other words this historiography was assigned a role in a political process that would ensure the security of the Raj by a combination of force to crush rebellion when it occurred and reform to pre-empt it by wrenching the tribal peasantry out of their rural bases and distributing them as cheap labour power for British capital to exploit in India and abroad. The overtly aggressive and nervous prose of counter-insurgency born of the worries of the early colonial days came thus to adopt in this genre of historical writing the firm but benign, authoritarian but understanding idiom of a mature and self-assured imperialism.

## X

How is it that even the more liberal type of secondary discourse is unable thus to extricate itself from the code of counter-insurgency? With all the advantage he has of writing in the third person and addressing a distinct past the official turned historian is still far from being impartial where official interests are concerned. His sympathies for the peasants' sufferings and his understanding of what goaded them to revolt, do not, when the crunch comes, prevent him from siding with law and order and justifying the transfer of the campaign against the *hool* from civilian to military hands in order to crush it completely and quickly. And as discussed above, his partisanship over the outcome of the rebellion is matched by his commitment to the aims and interests of the regime. The discourse of history, hardly distinguished from policy, ends up by absorbing the concerns and objectives of the latter.

In this affinity with policy historiography reveals its character as a form of *colonialist knowledge*. That is, it derives directly from that knowledge which the bourgeoisie had used in the period of their ascendancy to interpret the world in order to master it and establish their hegemony over Western societies, but turned into an instrument of national oppression as they began to acquire for themselves 'a place in the sun'. It was thus that political science which had defined the ideal of citizenship for European nation-states was used in colonial India to set up institutions and frame laws designed specifically to generate a mitigated and second-class citizenship. Political economy which had developed in Europe as a critique of feudalism was made to promote a neo-feudal landlordism in India. Historiography too adapted itself to the relations of power under the Raj and was harnessed more and more to the service of the state.

It was thanks to this connection and a good deal of talent to back it up that historical writing on themes of the colonial period shaped up as a highly coded discourse. Operating within the framework of a many-sided affirmation of British rule in the subcontinent it assumed the function of representing the recent past of its people as 'England's Work in India'. A discourse of power in its own right it had each of its moments displayed as a triumph, that is, as the most favourable upshot of a number of conflicting possibilities for the regime at any particular time. In its mature form, therefore, as in Hunter's *Annals,* continuity figures as one of its necessary and cardinal aspects. Unlike primary discourse it cannot afford to be foreshortened and without a sequel. The event does not constitute its sole content, but is the middle term between a beginning which serves as a context and an end which is at the same time a perspective linked to the next sequence. The only element that is constant in this ongoing series is the Empire and the policies needed to safeguard and perpetuate it.

Functioning as he does within this code Hunter with all the good-will so solemnly announced in his dedicatory note ('These pages... have little to say touching the governing race. My business is with the people') writes up the history of a popular struggle as one in which the real subject is not the people but, indeed, 'the governing race' institutionalized as the Raj. Like any other narrative of this kind his account of the *hool* too is there to celebrate a continuity—that of British power in India. The statement of causes and reforms is no more than a structural requirement for this continuum providing it respectively with context and perspective. These serve admirably to register the event as a datum in the life-story of the Empire, but do nothing to illuminate that consciousness which is called insurgency. The rebel has no place in this history as the subject of rebellion.

## XI

There is nothing in tertiary discourse to make up for this absence. Farthest removed in time from the events which it has for its theme it always looks at them in the third person. It is the work of non-official writers in most cases or of former officials no longer under any professional obligation or constraint to represent the standpoint of the government. If it happens to carry an official view at all this is only because the author has chosen it of his own will rather than because he has been conditioned to do so by any loyalty or allegiance based on administrative involvement. There are indeed some historical works which actually show such a preference and are unable to speak in a voice other than that of the custodians of law and order—an instance of tertiary discourse reverting to that state of crude identification with the regime so characteristic of primary discourse.

But there are other and very different idioms within this genre ranging from liberal to left. The latter is particularly important as perhaps the most influential and prolific of all the many varieties of tertiary discourse. We owe to it some of the best studies on Indian peasant insurgency and more and more of these are coming out all the time as evidence both of a growing academic interest in the subject and the relevance that the subaltern movements of the past have to contemporary tensions in our part of the world. This literature is distinguished by its effort to break away from the code of counter-insurgency. It adopts the insurgent's point of view and regards, with him, as 'fine' what the other side calls 'terrible', and vice versa. It leaves the reader in no doubt that it wants the rebels and not their enemies to win. Here unlike in secondary discourse of the liberal-imperialist type recognition of the wrongs done to the peasants leads directly to support for their struggle to seek redress by arms.

Yet these two types, so very different from and contrary to each other in ideological orientation, have much else that is common between them. Take for instance that remarkable contribution of radical scholarship, Suprakash Ray's *Bharater Krishak-bidroha O Ganatantrik Samgram*[26] and compare its account of the Santal up-rising of 1855 with Hunter's. The texts echo each other as narratives. Ray's being the later work has all the advantage of drawing on more recent research such as Datta's, and thus being more informed. But much of what it has to say about the inauguration and development of the *hool* is taken—in fact, quoted directly—from Hunter's *Annals*.[27] And both the authors rely on the *Calcutta Review* (1856) article for much of their evidence. There is thus little in the description of this particular event which differs significantly between the secondary and the tertiary types of discourse.

Nor is there much to distinguish between the two in terms of their admiration for the courage of the rebels and their abhorrence of the genocidal operations mounted by the counter-insurgency forces. In fact, on both these points Ray reproduces *in extenso* Hunter's testimony, gathered first-hand from officers directly involved in the campaign, that the Santals 'did not understand yielding', while for the army, 'it was not war . . . it was execution'.[28] The sympathy expressed for the enemies of the Raj in the radical tertiary discourse is

[26] Vol.I (Calcutta, 1966), Ch.13.
[27] For these see ibid.,pp. 323, 325, 327, 328.
[28] Ibid., p. 337; Hunter, op. cit., pp. 247-9.

matched fully by that in the colonialist secondary discourse. Indeed, for both, the *hool* was an eminently just struggle—an evaluation derived from their mutual concurrence about the factors which had provoked it. Wicked landlords, extortionate usurers, dishonest traders, venal police, irresponsible officials and partisan processes of law—all figure with equal prominence in both the accounts. Both the historians draw on the evidence recorded on this subject in the *Calcutta Review* essay, and for much of his information about Santal indebtedness and bond slavery, about moneylenders' and landlords' oppression and administrative connivance at all this Ray relies heavily again on Hunter, as witness the extracts quoted liberally from the latter's work.[29]

However, causality is used by the two writers to develop entirely different perspectives. The statement of causes has the same part to play in Hunter's account as in any other narrative of the secondary type—that is, as an essential aspect of the discourse of counter-insurgency. In this respect his *Annals* belongs to a tradition of colonialist historiography which, for this particular event, is typically exemplified by that racist and vindicative essay, 'The Sonthal Rebellion'. There the obviously knowledgeable but tough-minded official ascribes the uprising, as Hunter does, to banias' fraud, mahajani transaction, zamindari despotism and sarkari inefficiency. In much the same vein Thornhill's *Personal Adventures* accounts for the rural uprisings of the period of the Mutiny in Uttar Pradesh quite clearly by the breakdown in traditional agrarian relations consequent on the advent of British rule. O'Malley identifies the root of the Pabna *bidroha* of 1873 in rack-renting by landlords, and the Deccan Riots Commission that of the disturbances of 1875 in the exploitation of the Kunbi peasantry by alien moneylenders in Poona and Ahmednagar districts.[30] One could go on adding many other events and texts to this list. The spirit of all these is well represented in the following extract from the *Judicial Department Resolutions* of 22 November 1831 on the subject of the insurrection led by Titu Mir:

[29] Ray, op. cit., pp. 316-19.

[30] Anon., op. cit., pp. 238-41; Thornhill, op. cit., pp. 33-5; L.S.S. O'Malley, *Bengal District Gazetteers:Pabna* (Calcutta, 1923), p. 25; *Report of the Commission Appointed in India to Inquire into the Causes of the Riots which took place in the year 1875 in the Poona and Ahmednagar Districts of the Bombay Presidency* (London, 1878), *passim*.

The serious nature of the late disturbances in the district of Baraset renders it an object of paramount importance that the *cause* which gave rise to them should be fully *investigated* in order that the motives which activated the insurgents may be rightly *understood* and such measures adopted as may be deemed expedient *to prevent a recurrence of similar disorders*.[31]

That sums it up. To know the cause of a phenomenon is already a step taken in the direction of controlling it. To *investigate* and thereby *understand* the cause of rural disturbances is an aid to measures 'deemed expedient *to prevent a recurrence of similar disorders*'. To that end the correspondent of the *Calcutta Review* (1856) recommended 'that condign retribution', namely, 'that they [the Santals] should be surrounded and hunted up everywhere . . . that they should be compelled, by force, if need be, to return to the Damin-i-koh, and to the wasted country in Bhaugulpore and Beerbhoom, to rebuild the ruined villages, restore the desolate fields to cultivation, open roads, and advance general public works; and do this under watch and guard . . . and that this state of things should be continued, until they are completely tranquillized, and reconciled to their allegiance'.[32] The gentler alternative put forward by Hunter was, as we have seen, a combination of Martial Law to suppress an ongoing revolt and measures to follow it up by 'English enterprise' in order (as his compatriot had suggested) to absorb the unruly peasantry as a cheap labour force in agriculture and public works for the benefit respectively of the same *dikus* and railway and roadwork engineers against whom they had taken up arms. With all their variation in tone, however, both the prescriptions to 'make . . . rebellion impossible by the elevation of the Sonthals'[33]—indeed, all colonialist solutions arrived at by the casual explanation of our peasant uprisings—were grist to a historiography committed to assimilating them to the transcendental Destiny of the British Empire.

## XII

Causality serves to hitch the *hool* to a rather different kind of Destiny in Ray's account. But the latter goes through the same steps as Hunter's—that is, *context-event-perspective* ranged along a historical continuum—to arrive there. There are some obvious parallelisms in

[31] *BC* 54222: *JC*, 22 Nov. 1831 (no.91). Emphasis added.
[32] Anon., op. cit., pp. 263-4.
[33] Ibid., p. 263.

the way the event acquires a context in the two works. Both start off with prehistory (treated more briefly by Ray than Hunter) and follow it up with a survey of the more recent past since 1790 when the tribe first came into contact with the regime. It is there that the cause of the insurrection lies for both—but with a difference. For Hunter the disturbances originated in a local malignance in an otherwise healthy body—the failure of a district administration to act up to the then emerging ideal of the Raj as the *ma-baap* of the peasantry and protect them from the tyranny of wicked elements within the native society itself. For Ray it was the very presence of British power in India which had goaded the Santals to revolt, for their enemies the landlords and moneylenders owed their authority and indeed their existence to the new arrangements in landed property introduced by the colonial government and the accelerated development of a money economy under its impact. The rising constituted, therefore, a critique not only of a local administration but of colonialism itself. Indeed he uses Hunter's own evidence to arrive at that very different, indeed contrary, conclusion:

> It is clearly proved by Hunter's own statement that the responsibility for the extreme misery of the Santals lies with the English administrative system taken as a whole together with the zamindars and mahajans. For it was the English administrative system which had created zamindars and mahajans in order to satisfy its own need for exploitation and government, and helped them directly and indirectly by offering its protection and patronage.[34]

With colonialism, that is, the Raj as a system and in its entirety (rather than any of its local malfunctions) identified thus as the prime cause of rebellion, its outcome acquires radically different values in the two texts. While Hunter is explicit in his preference of a victory in favour of the regime, Ray is equally so in favour of the rebels. And corresponding to this each has a perspective which stands out in sharp contrast to that of the other. It is for Hunter the consolidation of British rule based on a reformed administration which no longer incites jacqueries by its failure to protect *adivasis* from native exploiters, but transforms them into an abundant and mobile labour force readily and profitably employed by Indian landlords and 'English enterprise'. For Ray the event is 'the precursor of the great

[34] Ray, op. cit., p. 318.

rebellion' of 1857 and a vital link in a protracted struggle of the Indian people in general and peasants and workers in particular against foreign as well as indigenous oppressors. The armed insurrection of the Santals, he says, has indicated a way to the Indian people. 'That particular way has, thanks to the great rebellion of 1857, developed into the broad highway of India's struggle for freedom. That highway extends into the twentieth century. The Indian peasantry are on their march along that very highway.'[35] In fitting the *hool* thus to a perspective of continuing struggle of the rural masses the author draws on a well-established tradition of radical historiography as witness, for instance, the following extract from a pamphlet which had a wide readership in left political circles nearly thirty years ago:

> The din of the actual battles of the insurrection has died down. But its echoes have kept on vibrating through the years, grcwing louder and louder as more peasants joined in the fight. The clarion call that summoned the Santhals to battle . . . was to be heard in other parts of the country at the time of the Indigo Strike of 1860, the Pabna and Bogra Uprising of 1872, the Maratha Peasant Rising in Poona and Ahmednagar in 1875-76. It was finally to merge in the massive demand of the peasantry all over the country for an end to zamindari and moneylending oppression . . . . Glory to the immortal Santhals who . . . showed the path to battle! The banner of militant struggle has since then passed from hand to hand over the length and breadth of India.[36]

The power of such assimilative thinking about the history of peasant insurgency is further illustrated by the concluding words of an essay written by a veteran of the peasant movement and published by the Pashchimbanga Pradeshik Krishak Sabha on the eve of the centenary of the Santal revolt. Thus,

> The flames of the fire kindled by the peasant martyrs of the Santal insurrection a hundred years ago had spread to many regions all over India. Those flames could be seen burning in the indigo cultivators' rebellion in Bengal (1860), in the uprising of the raiyats of Pabna and Bogra (1872), in that of the Maratha peasantry of the Deccan (1875-76). The same fire was kindled again and again in the course of the Moplah peasant revolts of Malabar. That fire has not been extinguished yet, it is still burning in the hearts of the Indian peasants . . .[37]

[35] Ibid., p. 340.
[36] L. Natarajan, *Peasant Uprisings in India, 1850-1900* (Bombay, 1953), pp. 31-2.
[37] Abdulla Rasul, *Saontal Bidroher Amar Kahini* (Calcutta, 1954), p. 24.

The purpose of such tertiary discourse is quite clearly to try and retrieve the history of insurgency from that continuum which is designed to assimilate every jacquerie to 'England's Work in India' and arrange it along the alternative axis of a protracted campaign for freedom and socialism. However, as with colonialist historiography this, too, amounts to an act of appropriation which excludes the rebel as the conscious subject of his own history and incorporates the latter as only a contingent element in another history with another subject. Just as it is not the rebel but the Raj which is the real subject of secondary discourse and the Indian bourgeoisie that of tertiary discourse of the History-of-the-Freedom-Struggle genre, so is an *abstraction* called Worker-and-Peasant, *an ideal rather than the real historical personality of the insurgent,* made to replace him in the type of literature discussed above.

To say this is of course not to deny the political importance of such appropriation. Since every struggle for power by the historically ascendant classes in any epoch involves a bid to acquire a tradition, it is entirely in the fitness of things that the revolutionary movements in India should lay a claim to, among others, the Santal rebellion of 1855 as a part of their heritage. But however noble the cause and instrument of such appropriation, it leads to the mediation of the insurgent's consciousness by the historian's—that is, of a past consciousness by one conditioned by the present. The distortion which follows necessarily and inevitably from this process is a function of that hiatus between event-time and discourse-time which makes the verbal representation of the past less than accurate in the best of cases. And since the discourse is, in this particular instance, one about properties of the mind—about attitudes, beliefs, ideas, etc. rather than about externalities which are easier to identify and describe, the task of representation is made even more complicated than usual.

There is nothing that historiography can do to eliminate such distortion altogether, for the latter is built into its optics. What it can do, however, is to acknowledge such distortion as parametric—as a datum which determines the form of the exercise itself, and to stop pretending that it can *fully* grasp a past consciousness and reconstitute it. Then and only then might the distance between the latter and the historian's perception of it be reduced significantly enough to amount to a close approximation which is the best one could hope for. The gap as it stands at the moment is indeed so wide that there is much more than an irreducible degree of error in the existing literature on this point. Even a brief look at some of the discourses on the 1855 insurrection should bear this out.

## XIII

Religiosity was, by all accounts, central to the *hool*. The notion of power which inspired it, was made up of such ideas and expressed in such words and acts as were explicitly religious in character. It was not that power was a content wrapped up in a form external to it called religion. It was a matter of both being inseparably collapsed as the signified and its signifier (*vāgarthāviva samprktau*) in the language of that massive violence. Hence the attribution of the rising to a divine command rather than to any particular grievance; the enactment of rituals both before (e.g. propitiatory ceremonies to ward off the apocalypse of the Primeval Serpents—Lag and Lagini, the distribution of *tel-sindur*, etc.) and during the uprising (e.g. worshipping the goddess Durga, bathing in the Ganges, etc.); the generation and circulation of myth in its characteristic vehicle—rumour (e.g. about the advent of 'the exterminating angel' incarnated as a buffalo, the birth of a prodigious hero to a virgin, etc.).[38] The evidence is both unequivocal and ample on this point. The statements we have from the leading protagonists and their followers are all emphatic and indeed insistent on this aspect of their struggle, as should be obvious even from the few extracts of source material reproduced below in the *Appendix*. In sum, it is not possible to speak of insurgency in this case except as a religious consciousness—except, that is, as a massive demonstration of self-estrangement (to borrow Marx's term for the very essence of religiosity) which made the rebels look upon their project as predicated on a will other than their own: 'Kanoo and Seedoo Manjee are not fighting. The Thacoor himself will fight.'[39]

How authentically has this been represented in historical discourse? It was identified in official correspondence at the time as a case of 'fanaticism'. The insurrection was three months old and still going strong when J. R. Ward, a Special Commissioner and one of the most important administrators in the Birbhum region, wrote in some

---

[38] The instances are far too numerous to cite in an essay of this size, but for some samples see *Mare Hapram Ko Reak Katha*, Ch.79, in A. Mitra (ed.), *District Handbooks: Bankura* (Calcutta, 1953).

[39] *Appendix*: Extract 2.

desperation to his superiors in Calcutta, 'I have been unable to trace the insurrection in Beerbhoom to any thing but *fanaticism.*' The idiom he used to describe the phenomenon was typical of the shocked and culturally arrogant response of nineteenth-century colonialism to any radical movement inspired by a non-Christian doctrine among a subject population: 'These Sonthals have been led to join in the rebellion under a persuasion which is clearly traceable to their brethren in Bhaugulpore, that an Almighty & inspired Being appeared as the redeemer of their Caste & their *ignorance & superstition* was easily worked into a *religious frenzy* which has stopped at nothing.'[40] That idiom occurs also in the *Calcutta Review* article. There the Santal is acknowledged as 'an eminently religious man' and his revolt as a parallel of other historical occasions when '*the fanatical spirit of religious superstition*' had been 'swayed to strengthen and help forward a quarrel already ready to burst and based on other grounds.'[41] However, the author gives this identification a significantly different slant from that in the report quoted above. There an incomprehending Ward, caught in the blast of the *hool*, appears to have been impressed by the spontaneity of 'a religious frenzy which...stopped at nothing'. By contrast the article written after the regime had recovered its self-confidence, thanks to the search-and-burn campaign in the disturbed tracts, interprets religiosity as a propagandist ruse used by the leaders to sustain the morale of the rebels. Referring, for instance, to the messianic rumours in circulation it says, 'All these absurdities were no doubt *devised* to keep up the courage of the numerous rabble.'[42] Nothing could be more elitist. The insurgents are regarded here as a mindless 'rabble' devoid of a will of their own and easily manipulated by their chiefs.

But elitism such as this is not a feature of colonialist historiography alone. Tertiary discourse of the radical variety, too, exhibits the same disdain for the political consciousness of the peasant masses when it is mediated by religiosity. For a sample let us turn to Ray's account of the rising again. He quotes the following lines from the *Calcutta Review* article in a somewhat inaccurate but still clearly recognizable translation:

Seedoo and Kanoo were at night seated in their home, revolving many things . . . a bit of paper fell on Seedoo's head, and suddenly the Thakoor

[40] *JP*, 8 Nov. 1855: Ward to Government of Bengal (13 Oct. 1855). Emphasis added.
[41] Anon., op. cit., p. 243. Emphasis added.
[42] Ibid., p. 246. Emphasis added.

(god) appeared before the astonished gaze of Seedoo and Kanoo; he was like a white man though dressed in the native style; on each hand he had ten fingers; he held a white book, and wrote therein; the book and with it 20 pieces of paper . . . he presented to the brothers; ascended upwards, and disappeared. Another bit of paper fell on Seedoo's head, and then came two men . . . hinted to them the purport of Thakoor's order, and they likewise vanished. But there was not merely one apparition of the sublime Thakoor; each day in the week for some short period, did he make known his presence to his favourite apostles . . . . In the silvery pages of the book, and upon the white leaves of the single scraps of paper, were words written; these were afterwards deciphered by literate Sonthals, able to read and interpret; but their meaning had already been sufficiently indicated to the two leaders.[43]

With some minor changes of detail (inevitable in a living folklore) this is indeed a fairly authentic account of the visions the two Santal leaders believed they had had. Their statements, reproduced in part in the *Appendix* (Extracts 3 and 4), bear this out. These, incidentally, were not public pronouncements meant to impress their followers. Unlike 'The Thacoor's Perwannah' (*Appendix*: Extract 2) intended to make their views known to the authorities before the uprising, these were the words of captives facing execution. Addressed to hostile interrogators in military encampments they could have little use as propaganda. Uttered by men of a tribe which, according to all accounts had not yet learnt to lie,[44] these represented the truth and nothing but the truth for their speakers. But that is not what Ray would credit them with. What figures as a mere insinuation in the *Calcutta Review* is raised to the status of an elaborate propaganda device in his introductory remarks on the passage cited above. Thus:

> Both Sidu and Kanu knew that the slogan (*dhwani*) which would have the most effect among the *backward* Santals, was one that was religious. Therefore, *in order to inspire* the Santals to struggle they *spread* the word about God's directive in favour of launching such a struggle. The story *invented (kalpita)* by them is as follows.[45]

There is little that is different here from what the colonialist writer had to say about the presumed backwardness of the Santal peasantry,

---

[43] Ibid., pp. 243-4. Ray, op. cit., pp. 321-2.

[44] This is generally accepted. See, for instance, Sherwill's observation about the truth being 'sacred' to the Santals 'offering in this respect a bright example to their lying neighbours, the Bengalis'. *Geographical and Statistical Report of the District Bhaugulpoor* (Calcutta, 1854), p. 32.

[45] Ray, op. cit., p. 321. Emphasis added.

the manipulative designs of their leaders and the uses of religion as the means of such manipulation. Indeed, on each of these points Ray does better and is by far the more explicit of the two authors in attributing a gross lie and downright deception to the rebel chiefs without any evidence at all. The invention is all his own and testifies to the failure of a shallow radicalism to conceptualize insurgent mentality except in terms of an unadulterated secularism. Unable to grasp religiosity as the central modality of peasant consciousness in colonial India he is shy to acknowledge its mediation of the peasant's idea of power and all the resultant contradictions. He is obliged therefore to rationalize the ambiguities of rebel politics by assigning a worldly consciousness to the leaders and an otherworldly one to their followers making of the latter innocent dupes of crafty men armed with all the tricks of a modern Indian politician out to solicit rural votes. Where this lands the historian can be seen even more clearly in the projection of this thesis to a study of the Birsaite *ulgulan* in Ray's subsequent work. He writes,

> In order to propagate this religious doctrine of his Birsa adopted *a new device (kaushal)*—just as Sidu, the Santal leader, had done on the eve of the Santal rebellion of 1885. Birsa knew that the Kol were a *very backward* people and were full of *religious superstition* as a result of Hindu-Brahmanical and Christian missionary propaganda amongst them over a long period. Therefore, it would not do to avoid the question of religion if the Kol people were to be liberated from those wicked religious influences and drawn into the path of rebellion. Rather, in order to overcome the evil influences of Hindu and Christian religions, it would be necessary to spread his new religious faith among them in the name of that very God of theirs, and to introduce new rules. *To this end, recourse had to be had to falsehood, if necessary, in the interests of the people.*
>
> Birsa *spread* the word that he had received this new religion of his from the chief deity of the Mundas, Sing Bonga, himself.[46]

Thus the radical historian is driven by the logic of his own incomprehension to attribute a deliberate falsehood to one of the greatest of our rebels. The ideology of that mighty *ulgulan* is nothing but pure fabrication for him. And he is not alone in his

[46] Ray, *Bharater Baiplabik Samgramer Itihas,* vol. I (Calcutta, 1970), p. 95. Emphasis added. The sentence italicized by us in the quoted passage reads as follows in the Bengali original: 'Eijanyo prayojan hoiley jatir svarthey mithyar asroy grahan karitey hoibey'.

misreading of insurgent consciousness. Baskay echoes him almost word for word in describing the Santal leader's claim to divine support for the *hool* as propaganda meant 'to inspire the Santals to rise in revolt'.[47] Formulations such as these have their foil in other writings of the same genre which solve the riddle of religious thinking among the Santal rebels by ignoring it altogether. A reader who has Natarajan's and Rasul's once influential essays as his only source of information about the insurrection of 1855, would hardly suspect any religiosity at all in that great event. It is represented there *exclusively* in its secular aspects. This attitude is of course not confined to the authors discussed in this essay. The same mixture of myopia and downright refusal to look at the evidence that is there, characterizes a great deal more of the existing literature on the subject.

## XIV

Why is tertiary discourse, even of the radical variety, so reluctant to come to terms with the religious element in rebel consciousness? Because it is still trapped in the paradigm which inspired the ideologically contrary, because colonialist, discourse of the primary and secondary types. It follows, in each case, from a refusal to acknowledge the insurgent as the subject of his own history. For once a peasant rebellion has been assimilated to the career of the Raj, the Nation or the People, it becomes easy for the historian to abdicate the responsibility he has of exploring and describing the consciousness specific to that rebellion and be content to ascribe to it a transcendental consciousness. In operative terms, this means denying a will to the mass of the rebels themselves and representing them merely as instruments of some other will. It is thus that in colonialist historiography insurgency is seen as the articulation of a pure spontaneity pitted against the will of the State as embodied in the Raj. If any consciousness is attributed at all to the rebels, it is only a few of their leaders— more often than not some individual members or small groups of the gentry—who are credited with it. Again, in bourgeois-nationalist historiography it is an elite consciousness which is read into all peasant movements as their motive force. This had led to such grotesqueries as the characterization of the Indigo Rebellion of 1860 as 'the first non-violent mass movement'[48] and generally of all the

[47] Dhirendranath Baskay, *Saontal Ganasamgramer Itihas* (Calcutta, 1976), p. 66.
[48] Jogesh Chandra Bagal (ed.), *Peasant Revolution in Bengal* (Calcutta, 1953), p. 5.

popular struggles in rural India during the first hundred and twenty-five years of British rule as the spiritual harbinger of the Indian National Congress.

In much the same way the specificity of rebel consciousness had eluded radical historiography as well. This has been so because it is impaled on a concept of peasant revolts as a succession of events ranged along a direct line of descent—as a heritage, as it is often called—in which all the constituents have the same pedigree and replicate each other in their commitment to the highest ideals of liberty, equality and fraternity. In this ahistorical view of the history of insurgency all moments of consciousness are assimilated to the ultimate and highest moment of the series—indeed to an Ideal Consciousness. A historiography devoted to its pursuit (even when that is done, regrettably, in the name of Marxism) is ill-equipped to cope with contradictions which are indeed the stuff history is made of. Since the Ideal is suppose to be one hundred per cent secular in character, the devotee tends to look away when confronted with the evidence of religiosity as if the latter did not exist or explain it away as a clever but well-intentioned fraud perpetrated by enlightened leaders on their moronic followers—all done, of course, 'in the interests of the people'! Hence, the rich material of myths, rituals, rumours, hopes for a Golden Age and fears of an imminent End of the World, all of which speaks of the self-alienation of the rebel, is wasted on this abstract and sterile discourse. It can do little to illuminate that combination of sectarianism and militancy which is so important a feature of our rural history. The ambiquity of such phenomena, witnessed during the Tebhaga movement in Dinajpur, as Muslim peasants coming to the Kisan Sabha 'sometimes inscribing a hammer or a sickle on the Muslim League flag' and young maulavis 'reciting melodious verse from the Koran' at village meetings as 'they condemned the jotedari system and the practice of charging high interest rates',[49] will be beyond its grasp. The swift transformation of class struggle into communal strife and vice versa in our countryside evokes from it either some well-contrived apology or a simple gesture of embarrassment, but no real explanation.

However, it is not only the religious element in rebel consciousness which this historiography fails to comprehend. The specificity of a rural insurrection is expressed in terms of many other contradictions

[49] Sunil Sen, *Agrarian Struggle in Bengal, 1946-47* (New Delhi, 1972), p. 49.

as well. These too are missed out. Blinded by the glare of a perfect and immaculate consciousness the historian sees nothing, for instance, but solidarity in rebel behaviour and fails to notice its Other, namely, betrayal. Committed inflexibly to the notion of insurgency as a generalized movement, he underestimates the power of the brakes put on it by localism and territoriality. Convinced that mobilization for a rural uprising flows exclusively from an overall elite authority, he tends to disregard the operation of many other authorities within the primordial relations of a rural community. A prisoner of empty abstractions tertiary discourse, even of the radical kind, has thus distanced itself from the prose of counter-insurgency only by a declaration of sentiment so far. It has still to go a long way before it can prove that the insurgent can rely on its performance to recover his place in history.

## Abbreviations

*BC:*      Board's Collections, India Office Records (London).
*JC:*      Fort William Judicial Consultations in *BC.*
*JP:*      Judicial Proceedings, West Bengal State Archives
           (Calcutta).
*MDS:*     *Maharaja Deby Sinha* (Nashipur Raj Estate, 1914).

# Appendix

## Extract 1

I came to plunder ... Sidoo and Kaloo [Kanhu] declared themselves Rajas & [said] they would plunder the whole country and take possession of it—they said also, no one can stop us for it is the order of Takoor. On this account we have all come with them.

*Source:* JP, 19 July 1855: Balai Majhi's Statement (14 July 1855).

## Extract 2

The Thacoor has descended in the house of Seedoo Manjee, Kanoo Manjee, Bhyrub and Chand, at Bhugnudihee in Pergunnah Kunjeala. The Thakoor in person is conversing with them, he has descended from Heaven, he is conversing with Kanoor and Seedoo, The Sahibs and the white Soldiers will fight. Kanoo and Seedoo Manjee are not fighting. The Thacoor himself will fight. Therefore you Sahibs and Soldiers fight with the Thacoor himself Mother Ganges will come to the Thacoor's (assistance) Fire will rain from Heaven. If you are satisfied with the Thacoor then you must go to the other side of the Ganges. The Thacoor has ordered the Sonthals that for a bulluck plough 1 anna is to be paid for revenue. Buffalo plough 2 annas The reign of Truth has begun True justice will be administered He who does not speak the truth will not be allowed to remain on the Earth. The Mahajuns have committed a great sin The Sahibs and the amlah have made everything bad, in this the Sahibs have sinned greatly.

Those who tell things to the Magistrate and those who investigate cases for him, take 70 or 80 R.s. with great oppression in this the Sahibs have sinned. On this account the Thacoor has ordered me saying that the country is not the Sahibs...

P.S. If you Sahibs agree, then you must remain on the other side of the Ganges, and if you dont agree you cant remain on that side of the river, I will rain fire and all the Sahibs will be killed by the hand of God in person and Sahibs if you fight with muskets the Sonthal will not be hit by the bullets and the Thacoor will give your Elephants and horses of his own accord to the Sonthals ... if you fight with the Sonthals two days will be as one day and two nights as one night. This is the order of the Thacoor.

*Source:* JP, 4 October 1855: 'The Thacoor's Perwannah' ('dated 10 Saon 1262').

### Extract 3

Then the Manjees & Purgunnaits assembled in my Verandah, & we consulted for 2 months, "that Pontet & Mohesh Dutt don't listen to our complaints & no one acts as our Father & Mother" then a God descended from heaven in the form of a cartwheel & said to me "Kill Pontet & the Darogah & the Mahajuns & then you will have justice & a Father & Mother"; then the Thacoor went back to the heavens; after this 2 men like Bengallees came into my Verhandah; they each had six fingers half a piece of paper fell on my head before the Thacoor came & half fell afterwards. I could not read but Chand & Seheree & a Dhome read it, they said "The Thacoor has written to you to fight the Mahajens & then you will have justice" . . .

*Source:* JP, 8 November 1855: 'Examination of Sedoo Sonthal late Thacoor'.

### Extract 4

In Bysack the God descended in my house I sent a perwannah to the Burra Sahib at Calcutta . . . I wrote that the Thacoor had come to my house & was conversing with me & had told all the Sonthals that they were to be under the charge of me & that I was to pay all the revenue to Government & was to oppress no one & the zamindars & Mahajans were committing great oppression taking 20 pice for one & that I was to place them at a distance from the sonthals & if they do not go away to fight with them.

    . . .      . . .      . . .

Ishwar was a white man with only a dootee & chudder he sat on the ground like a Sahib he wrote on this bit of paper. He gave me 4 papers but afterwards presented 16 more. The thacoor had 5 fingers on each hand. I did not see him in the day I saw him only in the night. The sonthals then assembled at my house to see the thacoor.

    . . .      . . .      . . .

[At Maheshpur] the troops came & we had a fight . . . afterwards seeing that men on our side were falling we both turned twice on them & once drove them away, then I made poojah . . . & then a great many balls came & Seedoo & I were both wounded. The thacoor had said "water will come out of the muskets" but my troops committed some crime therefore the thacoors prediction[s] were not fulfilled about 80 sonthals were killed.

    . . .      . . .      . . .

All the blank papers fell from heaven & the book in which all the pages are blank also fell from heaven.

*Source:* JP, 20 December 1855: 'Examination of Kanoo Sonthal'.

# II  From Mughal to British

# 'Encounters and Calamities':
# The History of a North Indian *Qasba*
# in the Nineteenth Century.[1]

GYANENDRA PANDEY

## The Sources

The history of colonial India has generally been written on the basis
of British official records for the simple reason that non-official
sources are neither quite so abundant nor as easily accessible. This is
especially true for the period up to the end of the nineteenth century,
i.e. before organizations like the Indian National Congress had
emerged and the memoirs of leaders, as well as newspapers and
journals in Indian languages and in English, became available in some
number. This paper seeks to re-examine a small part of this earlier
colonial history in the light of a local historical account, or more
precisely a chronicle of events entitled *Wāqeāt-ō-Hādesāt: Qasba
Mubarakpur*, written in the 1880s and preserved in an Urdu manuscript in the qasba of Mubarakpur in the district of Azamgarh,

[1] I am deeply indebted to Qazi Atahar of Muhalla Haidarabad, Mubarakpur, who
allowed me to use Sheikh Mohammad Ali Hasan's manuscript history, *Wāqeāt-ō-
Hādesāt: Qasba Mubarakpur* (which is maintained in Qazi Atahar's personal library),
spent several days translating this and two other valuable documents (referred to in
notes 47 and 58 below) that he had traced in the course of his own researches, and
helped in many other ways with his intimate knowledge of the area. I owe thanks also
to Maulvi Kamruzzaman, Babu Saroj Agrawal and others in Mubarakpur who were
unstinting with their time in answering my questions and showing me around.

'*Wāqeāt-ō-Hādesāt*': according to Platts' *Classical Urdu Dictionary*, *Wāqeāt* =
'events, occurrences; accidents; grievous calamities, battles; conflicts; casualties;
deaths'; *Hādesāt* = 'new things; accidents; incidents; events; occurrences; adventures;
casualties; mishaps; misfortunes; disasters; calamities; afflictions'. 'Events' and
'occurrences' would cover both these terms but I have translated them as 'Encounters
and Calamities' in the title of this paper as this seems to me to convey somewhat better
the rhetoric and the sense of Ali Hasan's title.

eastern UP. I hope through this re-examination to say something about the way in which the people of Mubarakpur perceived the formidable developments of the period, something of how *they* read their history.

In the past it has generally been the anthropologist rather than the historian who has undertaken this kind of task,[2] and several distinguished anthropologists have written about the experience of small towns and cities under colonialism. As we shall see, some of their observations and conclusions are not entirely inappropriate to the history which is the subject of this paper. Mubarakpur was a major textile centre in the eighteenth and early nineteenth centuries specializing in the production of silk and mixed silk-and-cotton fabrics known as *sangi* and *ghalta*, and dependent to a large extent on the patronage of the courts and the nobility of Awadh, Nepal and other places. The establishment and consolidation of a centralized colonial power, the representative of a powerful manufacturing nation, entailed considerable dislocation in Mubarakpur and its environs. The cloth trade was seriously affected, though it survived better here than in many other textile centres of the region. The rules under which land was held were altered and—with their rent-free lands being reduced, other lands fragmented and sub-divided or sold under the pressure of heavy taxation and increased dependence on cash, credit and markets—many like the Sheikh Muslim zamindars of Mubarakpur and neighbouring areas came under severe pressure. Professional moneylenders and traders apparently entered a period of increased prosperity at the turn of the nineteenth century but did not make such headway as to overthrow the existing relations of power in the qasba of Mubarakpur or the countryside around. In Mubarakpur there were other colonial innovations, among them the establishment of a police outpost, an Imperial Post Office and Middle School. Nevertheless, while the power of the panchayat and the zamindars was much reduced, these remained the major court of appeal for most local disputes; and most of those who studied still obtained a traditional religious education.

[2] This paper was completed before I was able to see C. A. Bayly's 'The Small Town and Islamic Gentry in North India: The Case of Kara' in K. Ballhatchet and J. Harrison (eds.), *The City in South Asia* (London, 1980) or the same author's *Rulers, Townsmen and Bazaars: North Indian Society in the Age of British Expansion 1770–1870* (Cambridge, 1983). Bayly's excellent account of the small town 'gentry' under pressure, based on local non-official as well as official sources, is not however directly concerned with consciousness and the perceptions of change that are central to this essay.

The 'advance towards vagueness' that Geertz writes about for Modjokuto in east central Java[3] might be a suggestive description of the nineteenth-century history of Mubarakpur too. The 'uncertainty', the 'sense of disequilibrium and disorientation' that he and others find among the population of such towns by the end of the colonial period[4] is however scarcely a satisfactory indication of the local people's perceptions and responses, or of their will to live with dignity, to carve out and preserve for themselves areas of independence and honour.

The problem remains one of finding sources adequate to our purpose. In the case of Mubarakpur, while the official colonial records provide us with a particular élite perception (necessarily biased in a certain way), what the *Wāqeāt-ō-Hādesāt* provides is an alternative élite perception, closer to the ground to be sure but not the less one-sided for that. Sheikh Mohammad Ali Hasan, its author, was a member of a local Muslim zamindari family. He wrote the chronicle at an advanced age, within a few years of his death in 1888. And the *Wāqeāt*, without ever referring to the wider politics of the emerging public associations (Muslim or other), mirrors several of the contemporary concerns and attitudes of élite Muslim groups in many different parts of northern India—of men who were in many cases from a zamindari background similar to Ali Hasan's who felt their position in political and economic affairs, as well as important areas of their erstwhile cultural domination, threatened.

We have nothing comparable to the *Wāqeāt* that emanates from the lower classes of Mubarakpur. Yet we are allowed glimpses of how the ordinary labouring people of the qasba spoke and acted—both in the official record relating to a succession of violent outbreaks in the nineteenth century and in Ali Hasan's detailed narration of these and other events. I have been fortunate enough also to gain access to two sketchy but valuable documents that come from the weavers of Mubarakpur: one a petition drawn up by the leaders of the weaving community to try and clear themselves from blame for the violent outbreak of 1813; the other the occasional 'notes' (or diary) of a weaver that dates from the end of our period.

In what follows I first summarize some of the basic information

---

[3] C. Geertz, *The Social History of an Indonesian Town* (Cambridge, Massachusetts, 1965), p. 5.

[4] R. G. Fox, *Urban Anthropology: Cities in their Cultural Settings* (New Jersey, 1977), p. 139.

regarding numbers, occupations and class differences among the
people of Mubarakpur in the nineteenth century, and then set out
side by side the alternative versions of the history of the qasba as it
appears in the official accounts and Ali Hasan's chronicle. I then use
the evidence that can be drawn out of these histories and the weavers'
own isolated statements to make a few comments regarding subaltern
consciousness in nineteenth-century Mubarakpur.

## The Qasba

The most important elements in the population of Mubarakpur were
the zamindars, the weavers and the trader-moneylenders. There was
also a sizeable body of cultivating tenants and labourers as well as
men and women belonging to various other service groups. In 1813
the population was estimated at between 10,000 and 12,000. Of these
3,000 were supposed to be 'weavers of the Mussulman cast [*sic*]', i.e.
Julahas, while some were wealthy Hindu traders.[5] In 1881, according
to the census of that year, the population was 13,157 (9,066 Muslims
and 4,091 Hindus). Among 'actual workers' the principal groups
were 143 'landholders'; 560 'cultivators and tenants'; 1,877 weavers;
43 *halwais* (makers and sellers of Indian sweets); 49 *pansaris* (condi-
ment sellers); 254 'general labourers' and 44 'beggars'.[6] By 1901 the
population had risen to 15,433 inhabitants—11,442 of them Muslims
and the remaining 3,991 Hindus.

The zamindars were the 'leaders' of the qasba in historical
memory—since their ancestors had re-established the place in the
eighteenth century and presumably induced weavers, traders and
other groups to come and settle there[7]—and by virtue of their

[5] UP Regional Archives, Allahabad (hereafter UPRAA): MG4, Judl. Series I, Acc.
169, Vol. 168, R. Martin, Magistrate Goruckpore to G. Dowdeswell, Camp
Mobarruckpore, 25 April 1813.

[6] F. H. Fisher, *Statistical, Descriptive and Historical Account of the North Western
Provinces, Vol. XIII, Pt I: Azamgarh* (Allahabad, 1883), p. 171.

[7] D. L. Drake-Brockman, *Azamgarh: A Gazetteer, being Vol. XXXIII of the
District Gazetteers of the United Provinces of Agra and Oudh* (Allahabad, 1911), notes
that little is known of the early history of Mubarakpur. It was said to have been called
Qasimabad earlier and to have fallen into decay before it was resettled under the name
of Mubarakpur in the eighteenth century (pp. 260–1). For the way in which Maunath
Bhanjan and Kopaganj, the other major weaving towns of Azamgarh district, were
established and fostered, see my 'Economic Dislocation in Nineteenth-Century Eastern
U.P.: Some Implications of the Decline of Artisanal Industry in Colonial India'
(Centre for Studies in Social Sciences, Calcutta. 'Occasional Paper' No. 37, May
1981), pp. 15 & 34.

recognition as revenue-payers and local 'representatives' by the colonial authorities. They received a small *kargahi* for every working loom (*kargah*) in the qasba, said to be no more than a few annas in the 1830s but 'highly prized by the Zemindars and cheerfully paid by the weavers'.[8] They also collected certain feudal dues from the local traders and merchants of various castes as well as other dues and services from the weavers and members of other artisanal and service castes.[9] For 'agriculturists' what the Settlement Officer, J. R. Reid, wrote for the district as a whole in 1877 applied to Mubarakpur as well. High-caste tenants, both resident and non-resident—and of these there were few in Mubarakpur—paid a fixed rent in cash or grain; and non-resident low-caste tenants did the same. But resident low-castes called *parjas* (*praja* = subjects) rendered to the landlord 'a number of petty dues and services besides rent, and . . . look[ed] upon him as a feudal superior'. In villages, or qasbas such as Mubarakpur with several proprietors, the parjas were generally distributed among them, but the distribution was not necessarily proportionate to the land held. 'A *parja* allotted to a sharer remains solely his, though the man cultivate[s] land under another sharer, and even though he cease[s] to cultivate land under his superior. The sale and mortgage of *parjas*—that is, of the dues and services they render—is not unknown'.[10]

By this time however the Sheikh zamindars of Mubarakpur held 'only a few villages' and were said to be 'in difficulties'.[11] That there were as many as 143 'landholders' listed among the inhabitants of Mubarakpur, and others living in neighbouring Sikhthi and Amlo also held parts of the qasba, indicates the extent of the sub-division of zamindaris. There is evidence too from early in the century of the impoverished state of several of these zamindars. Thus Rikhai Sahu, 'a Mahajan of considerable wealth' who was killed in the course of a major clash between Hindus and Muslims in April 1813, was reckoned to be 'the chief person' residing in the qasba; and we know that at least two of the zamindars of Mubarakpur were in debt to him. Also

[8] J. Thomason, *Report on the Settlement of Chuklah Azimgurh* (Agra, 1837), pp. 130–1.

[9] Azamgarh Collectorate Record Room: Zila Bandobast, Mauza Mubarakpur, Tappa Bihrozpur, Pargana Muhammadabad (1280 F., i.e. AD 1873), *Wajib-ul-arz*, for 'Mubarakpur-Chak Sikhthi', 'Sikhthi-Shah Mahammadpur', 'Mubarakpur Rasulpur', esp. section 6.

[10] J. R. Reid, *Report on the Settlement of the Temporarily Settled Parganas of Azamgarh District, 1877* (Allahabad, 1881), pp. 86–7.     [11] Ibid., p. 70.

prominent in the events of April 1813 (apparently instrumental in drawing into the fight Hindu zamindars and their men from a wide area around) was Devi Dube of Amlo—'second to (Rikhai Sahu) in point of wealth and influence and more intimately connected with the surrounding zamindars for his having the management of landed property to a considerable extent in the neighbourhood'.[12]

It was the traders and moneylenders who profited most in this period from the cloth trade that was the very life blood of Mubarkpur. Eight or ten years before the outbreak of 1813, Rikhai Sahu had built a grand *thakurduara* outside the south-eastern limits of the qasba which the Gorakhpur magistrate described after personal inspection as 'a beautiful building ornamented with marble images, adorned with gold and silver ornaments'. 'Such a magnificent building was not to be found anywhere else in Azamgarh', Ali Hasan records in his chronicle of events in qasba Mubarakpur.[13] Family tradition has it that under the headship of Babu Ramdas, and therefore probably not long after the events of 1813, the family had a grand *rangmahal* constructed at Ayodhya for use by any relatives who went there on pilgrimage.[14] Again, Bicchuk Kalwar, who was one of the principal targets of attack in another major outbreak of violence in 1842, had 'by great care, pecuniousness, and usury raised himself to be a dabbler in Mahajunee' and built for himself a 'fine, delicate' two-storied house not long before that event. According to the officials who undertook a detailed enquiry in the qasba following this outbreak, Bicchuk was 'a hard unrelenting creditor' who had 'several of the reckless and profligate Mussulman weavers of Mubarakpur' in his debt.[15]

That 'recklessness' and 'profligacy' alone were not responsible for this state of affairs is however made abundantly clear by other evidence. In 1881–2 there were 65 *karkhanas* (or firms) employing a total of 315 artisans for the manufacture of silk and satinette in Mubarakpur and the neighbouring (and far smaller) weaving centre of Khairabad. Together with another 2,168 artisans who worked 'independently', these weavers produced sangi and ghalta valued at approximately Rs 3.5 lakhs per annum.[16]

[12] UPRAA: MG4, Judl. Series I, Acc. 169, Vol. 168, Magistrate Gorakhpur's letter of 17 Dec. 1813, para 3.

[13] Ibid., para 4; Ali Hasan, *Wāqeāt-ō-Hādesāt*, pp. 9–10.

[14] Interview with Babu Saroj Agrawal of Mubarakpur.

[15] UPRAA: COG, Judl. Azamgarh, Vol. 68, File 47, Craigee-Morrieson, 25 March 1842.

[16] *Report on the Railway-borne Traffic of the North-Western Provinces and Oudh during the year ending 31 March 1882* (Allahabad, 1883), p. 37.

Yet, as was reported for the most important silk-weaving centre of this area, Banaras, the weavers were bound down by 'hopeless indebtedness to the firms who employ them, and their remuneration depends as little on the demand which may exist for their goods as if their condition was one of actual slavery'. 'Even those [who are] styled independent for want of a better word are in reality in the hands of mahajans, who advance them what is necessary for the support of life and absorb all the profits of their labour'.[17] In Banaras a man who produced in one month a brocade worth Rs 200 was paid a pittance of 2 annas (1/8 of a rupee per day). In Mubarakpur and Khairabad, we are told, 'the *julahas* . . . are miserably poor, but the master weavers are some of them very well off. Three of them are landholders and own indigo factories'.[18]

Such are some of the bare facts of 'economic' relations as they existed among the principal groups of inhabitants in nineteenth-century Mubarakpur. It remains to say a word about the relations of the qasba with the towns and countryside around. There is evidence of prolonged zamindari quarrels for control of land and power in this region during the eighteenth century.[19] This contest appears to have been accentuated by the uncertain conditions produced by the end of nawabi rule, and the nineteenth century is replete with instances of tension and conflict between the zamindars of Mubarakpur and those of neighbouring villages and estates.[20]

At the same time, in more everyday terms, Mubarakpur was like other qasbas something of a nodal point for the economy of the surrounding countryside. Milk and vegetable sellers brought their goods to sell here; a number of weavers came in to work from their homes in nearby villages; and of course the landholders, tenants and

[17] Loc. cit., and ibid., for year ending 31 March 1883, p. 37.

[18] Loc. cit.

[19] In the course of these struggles several of the local notables linked up with some of the greater powers beyond the district such as the Nawab of Awadh, the Raja of Banaras, and the Bangash Pathans who had at one stage extended their influence as far as Jaunpur. In an attempt to resolve the intrigues of men at a higher level the Nawab of Awadh settled the revenue of Azamgarh in 1764 with 'local farmers', among them Mir Fazl Ali of Muhammadabad. But following the Battle of Buxar, Azam Khan, the Raja of Azamgarh, appears to have regained favour at the court and his authority over the district. On his death in 1771 the district was put under a *chakladar* under whom it remained until 1801. See Drake-Brockman, *Azamgarh Gazetteer*, pp. 172–3; A. L. Srivastava, *The First Two Nawabs of Oudh* (Lucknow, 1933).

[20] Several examples will be found in the discussion below. See also Thomason, *Settlement of Chuklah Azimgurh* (1837), pp. 130–1; Reid, *Settlement of Azamgarh District 1877*, pp. 70–1.

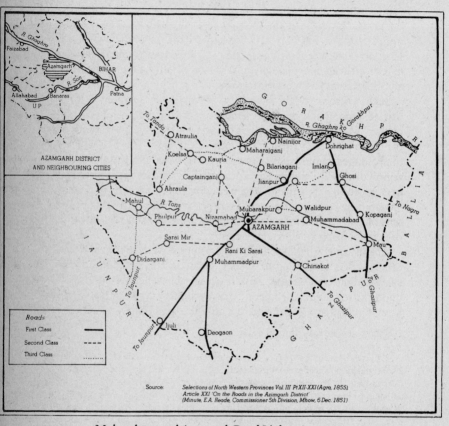

**Mubarakpur and Azamgarh Road Links,** *circa* **1850**

cultivators of the place held and worked a certain amount of land outside Mubarakpur. But in the vicinity there were other centres that vied for this position of leadership as meeting-place and reference-point.

Six miles south-east of Mubarakpur stood the substantial qasba of Muhammadabad Gohna (or simply Muhammadabad), residence of pargana officers and a *qazi* under nawabi rule and headquarters of the pargana and tahsil of Muhammadabad under British administration (see map). Eight miles west of it was Azamgarh town, founded and nurtured by the important family of the rajas of Azamgarh since the seventeenth century, enjoying fairly good road communications at least from that time and further favoured when it was adopted as the headquarters of a British district from 1832.

Consequently Mubarakpur seems never to have been very important as a commercial or administrative centre. Whereas a bazaar or retail market for the sale of sundry commodities was held here twice a week in the later nineteenth century, Muhammadabad had a similar bazaar four times a week. Significantly too the list of 'principal occupations' for Muhammadabad at the beginning of the 1880s included 'petty bankers and traders' and 'shopkeepers' as well as 'landowners', 'agriculturists', weavers and other artisans. Recall that the first two groups were not numerous enough to be mentioned in the corresponding list of 'principal occupations' for Mubarakpur.[21]

It is interesting to compare the above information with that regarding Maunath Bhanjan (or Mau), the other major cloth-producing centre of Azamgarh district in the nineteenth century. Mau, with a population that was only slightly larger than that of Mubarakpur in 1881 (14,945 against Mubarakpur's 13,157), appears to have combined in itself the roles of Mubarakpur and Muhammadabad, and added a little more besides, since it was that much further from the district headquarters (see map). A bazaar was held here daily and the 'principal occupations' included: employment under the government or municipality; 'ministers of the Hindu religion'; domestic servants; hackney-carriage keepers and drivers; palanquin keepers and bearers; 'messengers'; landholders; cultivators and tenants; agricultural

[21] Fisher, *Statistical, Descriptive and Historical Account of . . . . Azamgarh*, pp. 171, 176. I have some doubts about the accuracy of occupational details for Mubarakpur as found in this report but have unfortunately not managed to obtain the district census data for either 1881 or 1891. Nevertheless the general point made here remains valid, I think.

labourers; carpenters; weavers; cloth merchants (*bazzaz*); tailors; shoe-makers and sellers; washermen; corn and flour dealers; general labourers; and beggars.[22]

The accompanying map of road links in the mid-nineteenth century shows, too, the poor state of the long distance communications of Mubarakpur. This is one reason why Maharajganj on the Choti Sarju river, which lay some fifteen miles north-west of Azamgarh town and not far from the border of Awadh, had become the chief mart for cloths from Mubarakpur (as well as from Mau, Kopaganj and other places).

The nineteenth century brought important changes in communications, the direction of trade and Mubarakpur's general outlook on the world. The movement of traffic to and from Azamgarh seems always to have been northward towards the Ghaghra and southward towards the Ganga, not eastward and westward. This remained the case throughout the nineteenth century both for Azamgarh district as a whole and for the qasba of Mubarakpur. But soon after the uprising of 1857–9 the old road from Allahabad and Jaunpur through Azamgarh town and Jianpur to Dohrighat and (across the Ghaghra) to Gorakhpur was metalled. So was the road linking Dohrighat with Mau and Ghazipur. Within the next couple of decades metalled roads were also developed to connect Azamgarh town directly with Ghazipur and Banaras, and (through Muhammadabad) with Mau on the east. By the end of the century a branch railway line had also been laid to connect Azamgarh and Muhammadabad with Mau, from where a section of the Bengal and North-Western Railway ran to Banaras.

The opening up of the interior and the growing influx of mill-cloth from Britain led also to a reversal in the direction of the cloth trade. In the later nineteenth century the East Indian and Oudh and Rohilkhand railways, fed by the improved roads, became the main passages out of Azamgarh district for sugar exports to the south and west and indigo exports to the east, and into it for imports of not only raw cotton and grain but cloth, metal and 'other manufactured wares'.[23] After the artificial 'boom' in exports created by the East India Company's 'investments' at the beginning of the nineteenth century, the balance of trade in quality cloth had soon turned against the district. The weaving industry of Mubarakpur survived rather better than that of the other neighbouring textile centres: 'In silk fabrics, especially of

[22] Ibid., p. 169.
[23] Reid, *Settlement 1877*, p. 23.

the mixed kind manufactures in this district', one official observed, 'there is a peculiar adaptation to local conditions and prejudices, which enables the industry to hold its own, or at least to *decline less slowly than it would otherwise have done*'.[24] Thus the exports of sangi and ghalta (along with some cottons from Mau and Kopaganj) continued.[25] But the scale was much reduced, the increasing competition for raw material and its cost tended to increase dependence on moneylenders and other intermediaries; and the trade depression of the 1870s to 1890s dealt yet another crippling blow to the local industry, compelling many of the weavers of Mubarakpur to shift to the weaving of cotton handkerchiefs and turbans which were now 'more in demand than satins'.[26]

By the end of the century the chief exports of Azamgarh were refined sugar and oilseeds (and, one might add, labour in the form of migrants to the industrial belt of eastern India and colonial plantations overseas): 'with the money obtained therefrom, and from their relatives abroad, the inhabitants meet their revenue and the cost of their litigation, and pay for the cloth, metal goods and foodgrains they have to import'.[27] The situation of Mubarakpur was in essentials the same. By this time, it would be fair to say, Mubarakpur faced not, as it had done at the start of our period, north and west to Maharajganj, Nepal and the kingdom of Awadh, but south—to the road and the railway that linked the qasba with the district headquarters and with Ghazipur, Banaras and faraway Calcutta. What bearing all this had on power relations within the qasba and the consciousness of its people is a theme that should emerge out of the 'histories' that have been handed down to us.

## Two 'Histories'

If one draws up a chronology of events in nineteenth-century Mubarakpur from the official records and from Ali Hasan's *Wāqeāt*,

---

[24] A. Yusuf Ali, *A Monograph on Silk Fabrics Produced in the North-Western Provinces and Oudh* (Allahabad, 1900), p. 103. Emphasis added.

[25] Ibid., 170; Fisher, *Statistical, Descriptive and Historical Account of Azamgarh*, p. 124.

[26] Drake-Brockman, *Azamgarh Gazetteer*, p. 262. See also Gorakhpur Commissioner's Record Room, Dept. XIII, File 40/1905–9, 'Rules for the relief of distressed weavers' that became necessary (as the Chief Secretary to the Government put it in a circular to District Officers on 28 Jan. 1908) 'owing to scarcity and high prices having rendered it difficult, and in some cases impossible for them [the weavers] to find a market for their manufactured goods'.

[27] C. E. Crawford, *Final Report on the Seventh Settlement of the Azamgarh District of the United Provinces, 1908 A. D.* (Allahabad, 1908), p. 9.

one obtains very different results. I set out these chronologies in the table below, placing Ali Hasan's more detailed list of events on the left (see Table 1).

I have omitted from the right-hand column some purely administrative 'Events' such as the establishment of a Police Station in 1813 or its reduction to a smaller police outpost later on, and included in both columns certain '*Non*-Events' or '*Near* Events' (N) that were recorded by the respective sources as being of significance for one reason or another. It is plain that what makes an Event in the official reckoning is a marked positive or negative correlation with the question of 'law and order'. Everything in this account is dated from the 'accession' of 1801, which allegedly divides darkness from light, the days of 'order' and 'improvement' from the previous regime of 'anarchy' and 'misrule'. 1857 is a notable Non-Event, for in this dangerous moment when 'order', 'progress' and 'civilization' were threatened all over northern India, Mubarakpur remained peaceful. Horne, the Magistrate of Azamgarh, reported in September 1857 that the Muhammadabad tahsil was the 'best' in the district, with 'crime' low and roads safe. It was a matter for self-congratulation as 'there is great distress at present in Mubarakpur and Mhow, in each of which places there are about 5,000 Julahas, who have lost all their capital by the robbery of their stocks of manufactured goods, which had been sent out for sale at the time of the outbreak'. Moreover 'these people are generally very turbulent'. On this occasion however they had been 'excellently kept in order by the tehseeldar Mahomed Tukee, who deserves great credit every way'.[28]

Almost all the other entries in the official chronology relate to outbreaks or threatened outbreaks of violence over the desecration of religious symbols—proof in this view of the essential irrationality and fanaticism of the local people, ingredients that would ensure a return to anarchy if ever the controlling hand of the colonial power were to be withdrawn. Often there is a harking back to 1813, the year of 'the great disturbances' in Mubarakpur when 'disorder reigned for several days unchecked'.[29] Or as the Azamgarh District Gazetteer of 1911 put it in a classic summary of the history of Mubarakpur since 'accession':

[28] *Parliamentary Papers. House of Commons. Accounts and Papers. Vol. 44, Pt 3. 1857–58*, Memorandum on Azamgarh, 11 Sept. 1857 (p. 571).

[29] UPRAA: COG, Judl. Azamgarh, Vol. 68, File 47, Thomason-Currie, 23 May 1835; ibid., Letter no. 96, Sessions Judge Azamgarh to Commissioner 5th Division, 29 May 1844.

## TABLE 1: Chronology of Events in Mubarakpur in the Nineteenth Century[30]

| | According to the *Wāqeāt-ō-Hādesāt* | | | | According to the Official Records | | |
|---|---|---|---|---|---|---|---|
| Event | Date | Nature of Occurrence | Supposed Implications | Event | Date | Nature of Occurrence | Supposed Implications |
| I | Late 1790s | Shia-Sunni riot. One killed. | Pro-Shia stance of local Nawabi officials. | 1 | 1801 | 'Accession'. Establishment of direct British administration in Azamgarh and eastern UP. | Establishment of law and order. |
| II | 1810 (1226 Hijri) | 'Nakku Shahi'. Shia-Sunni quarrel; Nakku seriously wounded. | | | | | |
| III | 1813 | 'Rikhai Shahi'. Great Hindu-Muslim clash. Arson and looting for nine days. Rikhai Sahu and numerous others killed. | Growing insolence of Hindu money-lenders. Bravery of the Mubarakpur Muslims. | 2 | 1813 | Great 'disturbance', sanguinary battle and plunder for days until British magistrate and troops arrived. | Religious fanaticism. Breakdown of law and order. |
| IV | n.d. | Suicide of a Brahman. | | | | | |
| N1 | n.d. | Cow killed, head placed on platform. Riot averted by local officials. | Greatness of British rule. | | | | |

30 In this Table the words 'Supposed Implications' refer to inferences which are neither explicitly drawn or implied in the relevant records; 'N' stands for an occurrence or incident that is mentioned in the records but does not rank as a major 'Event'.

(Table 1 *continued*)

| | According to the *Waqēāt-ō-Hādesāt* | | | According to the Official Records | | | |
|---|---|---|---|---|---|---|---|
| Event | Date | Nature of Occurrence | Supposed Implications | Event | Date | Nature of Occurrence | Supposed Implications |
| V | n.d. | 'Katuaru Shahi'. Katuaru, a tailor, apprehended and killed during a burglary. | | | | | |
| VI | n.d. | 'Ali Shahi'. Quarrel between two teams of wrestlers. One killed. | | | | | |
| VII | 1832 (1247 H.) | 'Daka Zani'. Several dacoits apprehended and killed while attacking a money-lender's house. | Bravery of the townsfolk. | | | | |
| VIII | 1834 | 'Sukhlal Shahi'. Piglet killed and placed on Panj-i-Sharif. Sukhlal Singh, Hindu *barkandaz* wounded, succumbed to injuries. | | 3 | 1834 | Dead pig on Panj-i-Sharif. Hindu *barkandaz* who went to investigate received several sword-cuts. | Near breakdown of law and order. |
| N2 | 1834–41 | Successful tenure of Mirza Wali Beg as thanadar or Mubarakpur. | | N1 | 1835 | Dead pig on a *chauk*. *Thanadar* had it quickly removed. | Near breakdown of law and order. |

| | | | | | |
|---|---|---|---|---|---|
| IX | 1842 | 'Bicchuk Shahi'. Clash between Muslims and Hindu moneylenders. Several of the latter killed. | 4 | 1842 | Serious riot. Several killed. / Religious fanaticism. Breakdown of law and order. |
| X | 1849 (1265 H.) | 'Doma Shahi'. Quarrel between two teams of wrestlers. One killed. | | | |
| XI | n.d. | 'Karima-Shahi'. Murder of a girl and theft of her jewellery. | | | |
| XII | 1850 (1266 H.) | 'Daka Zani'. Dacoits attacked a moneylender's house. Chased away by townsfolk. / Solidarity and bravery of the townsfolk. | | | |
| XIII | n.d. | 'Tilanga Shahi'. Suicide of a sepoy carried away by his grief while participating in the lamentations at Muharram. | | | |

(Table 1 *continued*)

| | | According to the *Wáqeát-ô-Hádesát* | | | | According to the Official Records | |
| Event | Date | Nature of Occurrence | Supposed Implications | Event | Date | Nature of Occurrence | Supposed Implications |
| --- | --- | --- | --- | --- | --- | --- | --- |
| XIV | 1851 (1267 H.) | 'Baqridu Shahi'. Baqridu killed in a game of *kabaddi*. | | | | | |
| XV | n.d. | 'Amanullah Shahi'. Amanullah, *hajjam*, apprehended and killed during burglary. | | | | | |
| XVI | n.d. | 'Faqruddin Shahi'. Faqruddin killed a pig and placed its carcass on the Jama Masjid, nearly causing a riot. | | | | | |
| XVII | 1857 | Mubarakpur threatened repeatedly by the rebels, but preparations and warnings staved off any attack. | Renowned bravery of townsfolk. Courageous leadership of the zamindars and *sardars* of the qasba. | N2 | 1857 | No disturbance, though great distress among the weavers. | Near breakdown of law and order. Yeoman service by local officials. |

| No. | Date | | | |
|-----|------|---|---|---|
| 5 | 1860 | | Introduction of local administration under Act XX of 1856. Local revenue to pay for police and 'improvement'. | Extension of local self-government and works of 'improvement'. |
| XVIII | 1877 | 'Manohar Shahi'. Prolonged dispute over Manohar Das Agrawal's building of a temple inside the qasba. | Qasba tradition defended. | |
| N3 | 1860–80s | Repair and extension of Jama Masjid, Imambarah, etc. through contributions of all castes and communities. | Qasba tradition honoured. | |
| 6 | 1893–4 | | 'Religious disturbances'. | Religious fanaticism. Breakdown of law and order. |
| 7 | 1904 | | Riot. | Religious fanaticism. Breakdown of law and order. |

The Muhammadans [of Mubarakpur] consist for the most part of fanatical and clannish Julahas, and the fire of religious animosity between them and the Hindus of the town and neighbourhood is always smouldering. Serious conflicts have occurred between the two from time to time, notably in 1813, 1842 and 1904. The features of all these disturbances are similar, so that a description of what took place on the first occasion will suffice to indicate their character. In 1813 a petty dispute about the inclosing within the grounds of a Hindu temple of a little piece of land near a Muhammadan *takia* platform was followed first by the slaughter on the spot of a cow by the Muhammadans and then by the defiling of the platform and of a neighbouring *imambara* with pig's blood by the Hindus. The Muhammadans retaliated by cruelly murdering a wealthy Hindu merchant of the place name Rikhai Sahu, by plundering and burning his house and by defacing a handsome temple which he had erected. Hereupon the whole Hindu population of the vicinity rose and a sanguinary battle ensumed in which the Muhammadans were overpowered after many had been killed and wounded on both sides. The inhabitants of the town fled and the place was given up to plunder for some days till a magistrate arrived with troops from Gorakhpur and restored order. Similar disturbances occurred in 1893–94 and punitive police were quartered on the town for several months.[31]

The power of auto-suggestion displayed here is truly remarkable. Consider the writer's statements on the 'disturbances of 1893–94'. 1893 was a year of widespread strife between groups of Hindus and Muslims, when the agitation for cow protection led to violent demonstrations and clashes in many places in Azamgarh and other districts of this region.[32] Nowhere in the detailed official records relating to these events, however, or in contemporary newspapers is it reported that Mubarakpur was involved in these outbreaks. Nor is the qasba included in the list of villages and towns upon which a punitive police force was imposed in their wake. But riots *had* occurred at numerous spots in Banaras and Ghazipur, Shahabad and Ballia, not to mention Mau and Kopa, Azmatgarh and a host of other places close to Mubarakpur. And in Mubarakpur itself, as the compiler of the District Gazetteer saw it, 'the fire of religious animosity' between Muslims and Hindus was 'always smouldering'. There were serious conflicts between them in 1813, 1842 and 1904: or 'from time to time' in his phrase. So the 'disturbances of 1893–94' which were not mentioned at the beginning of this paragraph on the history of

[31] Drake-Brockman, *Azamgarh Gazetteer*, pp. 260–1.

[32] For an account of these, see my 'Rallying Round the Cow: Sectarian Strife in the Bhojpuri Region, *c.* 1888–1917', in R. Guha (ed.), *Subaltern Studies II* (Delhi, 1983).

Mubarakpur had become a major Event by the end of it, 'and punitive police were quartered on the town for several months'.[33]

Ali Hasan's *Wāqeāt-ō-Hādesāt* gives us a very different 'history'. First, it contains no reference to the 'accession' of 1801, that favourite date of colonial administrators of the region. There is a statement, in the discussion on Event II, that the British power was already installed. But in this narrative the Great Event, the turning-point, is Event III—the 'Rikhai Shahi' of 1813. 'British rule' it would seem was established only when an English magistrate and troops first arrived in Mubarakpur after the outbreak of violence in April that year. It was in 1813 we are told, after the 'riot', that a *thana* was established in Mubarakpur and courts in Azamgarh[34]—though the latter suggestion is clearly incorrect for it was only in 1820 that a Deputy Magistracy under the Jaunpur collectorate was established at Azamgarh, and Muhammadabad pargana (which contained Mubarakpur) was then part of Ghazipur district.

This difference in perspective is not attributable simply to the inevitable distance that separates a local from a wider—regional, national or colonial—view. If 1801 was the beginning of a new era in colonialist reckoning for obvious reasons, 1813 was for equally good reasons a watershed in the eyes of the people of Mubarakpur which became a point of reference for a long time afterwards. This was not however—as officials would have it—because of the 'delightful license' to plunder that 1813 had provided.[35] (Otherwise 1857 would have been welcomed as another great opportunity for this pastime: on the contrary, the people of Mubarakpur prepared for battle to defend the qasba's moneylenders when these were threatened by rebels in the vicinity[36]). What 1813 stood for locally was a dreadful calamity—such a blood-bath, writes Ali Hasan, that 'God save every Musalman from such a fate' (*Wāqeāt-ō-Hādesāt*, p. 18)—and what people feared was the repetition of such a massacre. So in N1 (see Table 1) the thanadar Mirza Karam Ali Beg promised that what had happened in the 'Rikhai Shahi' would not happen again (*Wāqeāt*, p. 22). Or more strikingly in Event VII, the armed dacoity of 1832, Muslim

---

[33] Yet the District Gazetteers compiled by the British are relied upon heavily by most writers on the political history of colonial India. And the argument is still readily put forward that 'the interpretation may be biased, but the facts are correct'.

[34] *Wāqeāt-ō-Hādesāt*, p. 20.

[35] COG, Judl. Azamgarh, Vol. 68, File 47, Sessions Judge Azamgarh to Commissioner 5th Division, 29 May 1844.

[36] Ali Hasan, *Wāqeāt-ō-Hādesāt*, pp. 60–73.

youth like Fateh and his comrades moved to the defence of Babu Ramdas, mahajan, with some slight hesitation because the dacoits were Hindus (mainly Rajputs) and the youths did not want to arouse Hindu fears of another 'Muslim' attack upon Hindus (*Wāqeāt*, p. 30). It is noteworthy too that Ali Hasan undertook to write this history, as he tells us in a prefatory statement, one day in the early 1880s when conversation turned to the bloodshed of 1813 and someone remarked that such a holocaust had never occurred before or since (*Wāqeāt*, p. 1).

The difference between the colonialist outlook and that of the *Wāqeāt* is revealed very clearly indeed in the criterion employed for the selection of Events. If it is the question of 'law and order', its consolidation, its breakdown or its being endangered, that made an Event in the colonialist reckoning, it seems to have been 'unnatural death' that did so in Ali Hasan's. Thirteen of the eighteen Events recorded in the *Wāqeāt*—all except II, XII, XVI, XVII and XVIII (see Table 1)—involved the violent death of one or more persons killed in the course of quarrels, riots, dacoities and, in two cases (IV and XIII), through suicide. Of the remaining five Events too, two involved casualties. In the 'Nakku Shahi', Event II, Nakku was badly beaten up and left for dead, though Ali Hasan tells us that he died a natural death shortly after the termination of the court case that arose out of this incident. (*Wāqeāt*, pp. 6–7). In Event XVII (1857) of course there was a considerable amount of violence and deaths all around; and the author takes care to note what he calls 'the only death of the Mutiny period' in Mubarakpur—that of a young lad called Magrooh, attacked one night as he was returning from the Katra bazaar by some constables from the local police outpost, possibly on account of a personal grudge (*Wāqeāt*, p. 73). The very title of Ali Hasan's chronicle, *Wāqeāt-ō-Hādesāt*, with its suggestion of disasters and calamities, perhaps reflects this concern with violent, 'unnatural' occurrences and incidents, interruptions in the normal progress of the life of the qasba.

To put it differently and perhaps more fairly, what makes an Event in the eyes of the author of the *Wāqeāt* is its 'public' character—the fact that the qasba community as a whole was interested, involved in or affected by a particular happening. It is possible to say a little more about this collective, the 'public', for with all the attention to violence and death there are certain other principles of selection at work in the compilation of this 'history'. The *Wāqeāt* is very clearly a *Muslim* account. This perhaps is one reason why N1 in the Table above, an incident in which a cow was killed and its head placed on a *chauk*, and an explosive situation developed, is mentioned but not given the status of an independent Event, whereas No. XVI which is very similar—a piglet being killed and placed on the Jama Masjid, and tension mounting—is discussed as a major Event, the 'Faqruddin Shahi'. The nature of the discussion of this Event is even more revealing. Ali Hasan begins by saying that now he has to write about a great outrage, an insult to Muslims, perpetrated by a Muslim (Faqruddin): 'but since the *wāqeāt* [occurrences, misfortunes] of the qasba are being related, it is necessary to include this incident too' (*Wāqeāt*, p. 56). 'Faqruddin' means 'the pride of religion', but this man should have been called 'Faqrushsheyatin'—'the pride of the *shaitans* (devils)', for he betrayed his religion by this base deed in the hope of profiting from the plunder that might follow. Fortunately such a calamity was averted. Faqruddin was discovered to have been the rogue responsible for the act, arrested and sentenced to three years rigorous imprisonment. On his return he was not accepted back into the community, for he was '*zalil-o-khar*' (base and disagreeable).[37] He was still alive when Ali Hasan wrote, had become a faqir, wandered from village to village and was known as Pakhurdia *badmaash*. (*Wāqeāt*, p.60).

Equally significant is the choice of other Non-Events (N2 and N3) that are included in the record, and of the remaining Event that was unaccompanied by unnatural death or grievous injury—the 'Manohar Shahi' of 1877 (Event XVIII). N2 refers to Mirza Wali Beg's 'memorable' tenure as thanadar of Mubarakpur. What made it memorable, we learn from the brief entry, was that Wali Beg, a Shia, called excellent *marsia* readers to participate in the Muharram celebrations in the qasba: this was something that people still remarked upon forty years later when Ali Hasan wrote (*Wāqeāt*, p. 35).[38] N3 relates to the repair of the *mazār* of Raja Mubarak Shah, a Sufi saint of the eighteenth century after whom Mubarakpur was named, and the

[37] According to Ali Hasan a similar punishment was meted out to those Muslims who gave evidence against Muslims involved in the attack on Hindu moneylenders and the temple in 1842. They were thrown out of the community and not re-accepted even after two of them had performed the *haj* to Mecca: '*lekin yah daag hamesha ke liye raha aur tamam Musalmanon men hamesha zalil-o-khar rahe*': *Wāqeāt-ō-Hādesāt*, pp. 45.

[38] For the central place of the Muharram celebrations in the life of other such habitations, see Rahi Masoom Raza, *Aadha Gaon* (Delhi, 1966), *passim*.

repair and extension of the Jama Masjid and Imambarah that were built adjacent to it, tasks that had gone on for twenty years and more from 1866-7 until the last pages of the *Wāqeāt* came to be written. And Event XVIII (which does not find place in the colonial 'history') was a long drawn out dispute that arose when Manohar Das, mahajan, challenged a long established custom by building a *shivalaya* (temple) within the limits of the qasba.

The last two entries lead us on to a rather different perspective. The *Wāqeāt* is the work of a Muslim who is steeped in and deeply concerned about the traditions of an isolated qasba, settled in the eighteenth century by Sheikh Muslim zamindars and made prosperous by the patronage of the nawabs of Awadh and other contemporary rulers. 'Mubarakpur', rather than 'British rule' or even the 'Muslim community', emerges as the real hero of this story. There is striking testimony to this in Ali Hasan's discussion of the defence of the qasba's Hindu moneylenders on different occasions when they were attacked by dacoits (Events VII and XII and again in 1857, Event XVII).

When the 'Daka Zani' of 1832 (Event VII) occurred a large number of townsfolk turned out as the cry went up for help from the house of Babu Ramdas, mahajan: such a crowd congregated that 'it was difficult to find standing space' inside or around the house. The dacoit gang was surrounded, engaged in battle and a number of its members killed. Later on, Ali Hasan tells us, a wounded dacoit who was arrested told the magistrate of the district that the gang included such renowned and dreaded dacoits as Bagi Singh and Chatar Singh, that they had attacked and looted all sorts of places before, including the government treasury, but no one had stood up to them until they encountered the 'warlike' (*jangi*) men of Mubarakpur (*Wāqeāt*, pp. 30-2).

In 1857 Rajab Ali, the rebel landowner of village Bamhur a couple of miles south-west of Mubarakpur, announced his intention of plundering the mahajans of the qasba in a letter addressed to Sheikh Gada Husain, zamindar, and Baksh Mehtar, '*sardar nurbaf*', the head of the weavers. 'Everyone' in Mubarakpur was enraged, writes Ali Hasan, and after consultations Gada Husain threw back the challenge to Rajab Ali with the warning that if the rebels tried to enter Mubarakpur to loot the mahajans they would have to bear all the consequences. 'Do you think that the inhabitants of Mubarakpur are dead that you have made this decision [to loot the mahajans]? If ever again such a threat [*kalma*, literally 'word'] escapes from your mouth, then you should prepare to defend your own village. Let us see who has the greater abilities in war' (*Wāqeāt*, p.63). And regarding a further message (possibly, a ruse) in which Rajab Ali expressed his desire to make offerings at the Panj-i-Sharif and Raja Sahib's mazār in Mubarakpur, the 'Mubarakpur people together' wrote in reply that four or five persons could come unarmed and fulfil this wish for prayer. But if a larger number came or any were armed, then '*tum apnon ko misl shirini-niaz ke tassawur karna* (you can think of yourselves as sweets which will be distributed and eaten). We have 1,700 guns and 9 maunds of powder and shot ready for you' (*Wāqeāt*, p. 64).

It is noteworthy too that Ali Hasan emphasizes that all castes and communities, Hindu as well as Muslim, contributed to the repair of Raja Mubarak Shah's mazār and certain extensions of the Jama Masjid. We are told that the Hindu mahajans of Mubarakpur revered the memory of Raja Sahib and lit lamps and made offerings of sweets at his mazār every Thursday. But the poor state of the walls of the Jama Masjid, which lay in the same compound as the mazār, meant that 'dogs and cats' got to these offerings and put out the lamps. Sometime in 1866-7 (1281 H.) therefore Sheikh Gada Husain, a widely respected and influential zamindar, appealed to the mahajans to help in the repair of these walls. Ali Hasan records that the latter responded very generously indeed at that time and later on, so that 'the entire wall along the length of the mazār was built through the donations of the Hindus', and work estimated to take all of six months for repairing the walls and the floors, as well as for the construction of a washroom and excavation of a well adjacent to the mosque, was completed in four (*Wāqeāt*, pp. 86, 88).[39]

Ali Hasan's description of the defence of the traditions of the qasba in the 'Manohar Shahi' of 1877—occurring as it did while the joint endeavours described above were still in progress—is again instructive. When it was discovered that Manohar Das had built a small shivalaya inside the compound of his house, anger flared up among the Muslims of Mubarakpur. It should be mentioned that there was already a history of such moneylender encroachment on the rights of the Muslims as embodied in the traditions of the place: in 1813, Angnu

---

[39] For a similar corporate identity and pride in other Muslim qasbas in the region, and the role of the Sufis in their establishment, see Bayly, *Rulers, Townsmen and Bazaars*, Ch. 9, esp. pp. 366-7.

(Aknu?) Kalwar had built a shivalaya inside the qasba and an attempted extension of its boundary was the immediate cause of the outbreak of violence on that occasion; in the years before the 1842 outbreak too there had been continuous friction between the mahajans and the Muslims after Bicchuk Kalwar and Babu Ramdas Agrawal had extended a wall onto the road and thus created an obstruction in the path of the *tazias* taken out in procession during the Muharram.[40] Now in 1877 Sheikh Gada Husain and other Muslim leaders questioned Manohar Das over this new development and, receiving no satisfactory reply, reported the matter at the police station in Muhammadabad and to the Collector in Azamgarh. The latter came to Mubarakpur to make an on-the-spot enquiry along with another English official who was, by chance, already there and some of the exchanges that Ali Hasan reports as having taken place before them are of the utmost interest.

Manohar Das argued that he had built the temple within the compound of his own house and the zamindars had nothing to do with that area. He pointed out too that the Muslims of Mubarakpur built mosques and other places of worship wherever they liked without objection from any source; that no more than five or seven months ago Faqir Kunjra erected a *masjid* close to a place that was sacred to the Hindus and 'we did not object'. Yet the Muslims wished to destroy the small shivalaya that he had built inside his own house: this was nothing but 'a show of power and tyranny'. To this Muslim leaders replied that Faqir Kunjra had built his masjid with the per-mission of 'us zamindars': all the zamindars of Mubarakpur were Muslims, none Hindu—so 'what right had the Hindus to object or allow?' (*Wāqeāt*, pp. 77–8, 81–2).

Gada Husain put the rest of the case against Manohar Das's new shivalaya as follows: Raja Mubarak was 'the guiding light of his age' and the founder of Mubarakpur. It was Raja Sahib's 'blessing' that had maintained the prosperity of Mubarakpur, and it was his *farman* (injunction) that 'when any person shall try to rise higher than me in this habitation [i.e. erect a building that rises higher than the height of Raja Sahib's mazār], he and his line will be no more'. The qasba had many great and very wealthy mahajans and many rich Muslims as well, Gada Husain said. But because of Raja Sahib's farman, 'no one has a two-storied house'. Only once was this injunction defied, when

---

[40] See Pandey, 'Rallying Round the Cow' for an analysis of the circumstances leading to these outbreaks.

Angnu Sahu had a shivalaya built inside the town. He spent a great sum of money and all the Hindus of the town worshipped there. But, Gada Husain went on, the shivalaya lasted less than ten years. In the plunder, arson and bloodshed of 1813 which raged for nine days and nights, the building was destroyed and Angnu killed while his son 'so lost his mind that he began to eat the food of the Musalmans, and perished in his madness. Now no one survives from that family'. (*Wāqeāt*, pp. 81–2). Ultimately the shivalaya was dismantled, but that is not the point of this digression.

What emerges from the evidence is a certain picture of the author of the *Wāqeāt-ō-Hādesāt*, or should we say the 'authors'. For it is necessary to stress the unusual nature of this 'history', which appears very much in the form of a collective catalogue. Quite unlike the practice of the standard 'histories' we have become used to since colonial times,[41] there is no attempt here to authenticate the chronicle that is presented. The narrative, it appears, requires no 'proof'. It is the inherited knowledge of the qasba, or at least those sections of it that for Ali Hasan represented the qasba. In the sole instance of direct authorial intervention found in the manuscript, which comes in the prefatory statement referred to above, it is stated that the idea of putting together this chronicle arose out of a conversation in the Middle School at Mubarakpur, when someone remarked that the bloodshed of 1813 had been unprecedented and unrepeated, and Gada Husain asked Ali Hasan to undertake this task as 'a labour of love' (*Wāqeāt*, p. 1). It is important to look at the construction of this narrative, then, not simply as the product of a single authorial voice, but rather to carefully consider its different constitutive aspects. For this reason it may help to dwell a little longer on the *Wāqeāt*'s perception of some of the wider changes that came with colonialism.

## The Wāqeāt *and the British*

Where the *Wāqeāt* refers directly to these changes is in the area of administrative control, and here it appears at one level to share the perspective of the colonial authorities. The importance of having good local officials is stressed (see N1 and N2 in Table 1). There is implicit recognition of the strength of British rule: thus when writing of how groups of men from Sikhthi, a village adjoining Mubarakpur, joined in the plunder of 1857 the author remarks that they had not

---

[41] Cf. the discussion regarding 'shifters' and authorial intervention in R. Barthes, 'Historical Discourse', in M. Lane (ed.), *Structuralism: A Reader* (London, 1970).

stopped to consider what would happen to them afterwards (*Wāqeāt*, p. 61).[42] Again, Ali Hasan expresses much admiration for individual British officials—'Penny',[43] who emerges as the hero of 1857–8, fighting bravely and successfully against very great odds, or Tucker, Officiating Magistrate at the time of the 1842 outbreak in Mubarakpur who was 'a very worthy (capable) Englishman' (*Wāqeāt*, p. 36). We have indeed a formal acknowledgement of 'the greatness of British rule'. In the incident listed as N1 above, when a cow's head was placed on a chauk in the qasba, the thanadar, Mirza Karam Ali Beg apparently handled the situation with efficiency and tact. He assured the inhabitants that what had happened in the 'Rikhai Shahi' of 1813 would not happen again, that no one from the countryside would be allowed to invade Mubarakpur, and that they should not panic and flee. He also sent an urgent message to the District Magistrate, who came with a troop of sepoys and camped in the qasba for several days. Thus 'a riot was averted'. 'All this was the greatness of British rule'. (*Wāqeāt*, pp. 22–3).

Yet in spite of this sympathy for the British and their administration, it is, as we observed in the last section, the differences in perception revealed by the two accounts that really stand out. We may obtain a better appreciation of this if we pursue some of the above points of similarity further. While Ali Hasan recognizes the importance of having fair-minded and experienced officials appointed by the state, he emphasizes also the wisdom and influence of local leaders which is recognized only obliquely in the colonial account. Writing about Event I, a clash between Shias and Sunnis in the qasba, he accuses the Nawab's *amil* of favouring the Shias because he was, like the Nawab himself, a Shia. But Shahab Mehtar, the head of the Mubarakpur weavers, 'wise and respected', 'the like of whom is not to be found in

---

[42] What happened afterwards is described by Ali Hasan himself in the following words: 'The people of Mubarakpur, especially the Nurbaf [weaving] community, *on behalf of the Government and at the orders of both Penny Sahib and the Tahsildar of Muhammadabad*' took a prominent and profitable part in the loot of Sikhthi; *Wāqeāt*, p.69. Emphasis added.

[43] This name refers almost certainly to Mr Pennywell, Deputy Magistrate of Azamgarh in 1857, but Ali Hasan appears to have confused his story with that of the European indigo planter, E. F. Venables. It is the latter who appears as hero and saviour in British accounts of the Mutiny in Azamgarh and it was he—not 'Penny', as Ali Hasan believed—who was fatally wounded in an encounter with the forces of Kunwar Singh in April 1858; S. A. A. Rizvi (ed.), *Freedom Struggle in Uttar Pradesh, Source Material, Volume IV* (Lucknow, 1959), pp. 5–6, 77, 85, 139–40, 466.

our times', who had had to journey to Lucknow before the nawabi officials agreed to act at all, now saved the situation and restored amity between the sects (*Wāqeāt*, p. 5). At the time of Event II, another Shia-Sunni conflict, Shahab Mehtar 'who was still alive' again intervened, unravelled a complicated court case and obtained the release of the innocent men who had been arrested by the police of the Muhammadabad thana. (*Wāqeāt*, p. 7).[44] In 1857–8, to take just one more instance, it was in Ali Hasan's view the determination and foresight of the zamindars and *sardars* (leaders) of Mubarakpur that was responsible for the maintenance of peace in the qasba. In the British official's view, we may recall, this achievement was credited to the tahsildar of Muhammadabad, Mohammad Taqi. If 'Penny Sahib Bahadur' had lived, Ali Hasan comments, the local zamindars and sardars would certainly have been rewarded and decorated (*Wāqeāt*, p. 73)—a notable example of the acceptance of colonial standards and colonial aspirations by the 1880s.

But that this was not always how the Muslims of Mubarakpur, or even their zamindars and leaders, had responded to the colonial power is amply demonstrated by local actions in the aftermath of the Hindu-Muslim fight of April 1813. Then the intervention of the colonial power had produced a quick closing of ranks and a display of considerable suspicion and hostility towards the new regime by both Hindus and Muslims of the region. Eight months after the 'riot' the Gorakhpur magistrate reported his failure to obtain the kind of evidence that was required in spite of the transfer of two sets of officials suspected of being insufficiently energetic in the pursuit of their enquiries. He felt that further delay in the commitment of the trial was pointless. In part this was because both sides, 'having been guilty of great outrage', were afraid to come forward. More significant however was his observation that 'the parties have now mutually agreed to adjust their grievances'. Further:

> The accounts existing between the Muhammadans and Hindoos which were destroyed by the fire or otherwise have been re-adjusted and new bonds and agreements have been entered into by the parties concerned, and I am of the opinion that a considerable quantity of property plundered must have been restored or that an understanding exists between the parties that it shall be when an opportunity offers . . .[45]

[44] We may note in passing that the earliest detailed report on Mubarakpur to be found in the colonial records acknowledged the influence of Shahab Mehtar: See p. 258 below.

[45] MG4, Judl. Series I, Acc. 169, Vol. 168, magistrate's letter 17 Dec. 1813, paras 7–8.

By the 1880s some of this had changed and the change is reflected in the pages of the *Wāqeāt*. A particular class of Muslims speaks to us here at (need I add?) a particular time: these are men from an impoverished zamindari background, acquainted with Arabic and Persian and Islamic theology, beginning to pick up elements of a 'modern' English education, having to reckon with the wealth of moneylender-traders and other 'upstarts', sometimes sharing a belief which was gaining ground in certain quarters that British power alone could defend their positions and their culture. Ali Hasan now emphasized the importance of 'Muslim' tradition and 'Muslim' unity, and with these the 'benefits' of British rule. He harked back to Shia-Sunni conflicts that are supposed to have plagued the qasba of Mubarakpur both before and immediately after the establishment of the colonial power (Events I and II). One wonders whether this does not have more to do with the Shia-Sunni and other sectarian differences that were coming to the fore in the later nineteenth century than with the state of affairs as it existed in the last years of nawabi administration.[46]

Shahab Mehtar, 'the like of whom is not to be found in our times', and 'the greatness of British rule' is a curious juxtaposition. Yet it is not quite so curious if one bears in mind the overall perspective of the *Wāqeāt-ō-Hādesāt*. What is honoured in Ali Hasan's chronicle is a body of traditions, customs and values that were for him the life of the qasba. There is a fundamental consistency here. British rule is saluted, as is the memory of Shahab Mehtar, for both served (or might serve) in their different ways, more or less efficaciously, to uphold these traditions and the position of the class that was above all responsible for creating them.

[46] For the later nineteenth century developments in Muslim public affairs, see F. Robinson, *Separatism Among Indian Muslims. The Politics of the United Provinces Muslims, 1860–1923* (Cambridge, 1974), Chs. 2 and 3; R. Ahmed, *The Bengal Muslims, 1871–1906. A Quest for Identity* (Delhi, 1981). The implications for the Muslim élite at the local level are spelt out in Bayly, 'The Small Town and Islamic Gentry in North India' and his *Rulers, Townsmen and Bazaars*, pp. 354–8. The 'Village Crime Register' for Mubarakpur, Pt. IV, entry for 1909 or 1910, notes that the qasba was inhabited by Muslims belonging to four sects: Sunni, Hanfi, Wahabi (which is inaccurately identified with Ahl-i-Hadis) and Shia. 'All these sects have their own separate mosques. They do not pray in one another's mosques. All take part together in the *taziadari* [at Muharram] but the Ahl-i-Hadis do not participate in this at all'. Qazi Atahar's researches also indicate that Shia-Sunni and other sectarian differences among the local Muslims became significantly more pronounced in the later nineteenth century; see his *Tazkara-i-ulema-i-Mubarakpur* (Bombay, 1974), pp. 30–3.

## A Weaver Speaks

To what extent did the other, lower-class Muslims of Mubarakpur—in particular the weavers who constituted by far the largest segment of the population—share Ali Hasan's perspective and entertain the same hopes, fears and expectations? The available records do not enable us to give a definite answer to this question. They do however indicate some of the elements of one.

There was without doubt an important area of beliefs and concerns shared by these different classes. We get some idea of this from a comparison of the *Wāqeāt* with the 'notes' (or diary) kept by Sheikh Abdul Majid (c. 1864–193?), a weaver of *muhalla* Pura Sofi in Mubarakpur. Abdul Majid writes some time after Ali Hasan, his 'notes' dating mostly from the 1910s and '20s, but he pays similar attention to disputes between Hindus and Muslims of the qasba. Thus Event XVIII in Ali Hasan's chronicle, the dispute over the temple built by Manohar Das in 1877, is remembered and described by Abdul Majid in a note headed *Mubārakpur kā wāqeā* ('An event in Mubarakpur').[47] The *'balwa'* ('riot', 'insurrection') of 1904, the latter part of which at least was witnessed in person by the diarist, is traced to its 'root'—Mian Khuda Baksh, son of Fateh Kalandar, zamindar of Mustafabad (a hamlet near Mubarakpur), who planted a pig's head in a masjid in the hope of using the commotion that would ensue to settle scores with a rival zamindar. In a reaction reminiscent of Ali Hasan's when he wrote of the baseness of Faqruddin in the 'Faqruddin Shahi' (Event XVI), Abdul Majid remarks on Khuda Baksh that this *'kam-zāt'* ('base person', 'of low origin') was behind all the trouble.[48] At a certain level 'Muslim unity' is accepted as natural and essential in this weaver's diary as in the *Wāqeāt*. Hence the Muslim police official, during whose time in 1906 Hindus of Mubarakpur were first permitted to blow *shankhs* (conch-shells) at prayer, is accused of having taken a bribe from the Hindus.[49] And as Ali Hasan had written of the Muslims who gave evidence against other Muslims after the 'riot' of 1842, so Abdul Majid comments on Muslim witnesses against Muslim 'accused' during the Non-Cooperation Movement of 1921–2: 'These Musalmans are responsible for having sent other Musalmans to jail'.[50]

[47] The diary of Sheikh Abdul Majid, c. 1864–193? is retained at the house of his descendant, Sheikh Wazir Ahmad, Muhalla Pura Sofi, Mubarakpur. The date of the above dispute is given as 1875–6 in the diary.

[48] Entry headed 19 May 1904. For details of this incident see Pandey, 'Rallying Round the Cow'. [49] Entry headed 29 June 1906. [50] Entry headed 19 June 1922.

Other evidence indicates that Abdul Majid's outlook was not a departure from the views of the local weavers in the nineteenth century. Members of the weaving community had taken a leading part in raising contributions for and supervising the work of repair and construction of the mazār, Jama Masjid and Imambarah in the 1860s and 1870s.[51] The concluding sentences of Ali Hasan's chronicle expressed the hope that the system of public subscriptions organized by the weavers would within a short time enable them to buy land to be bestowed as *waqf* (charity) on the masjid, and the prayer that God may grant the weavers of Mubarakpur such favour that they would 'with their abilities and determination forever maintain this system of subscriptions' in the service of religion.[52]

In 1842 there was a striking demonstration of local Muslim unity in the face of an insult to their faith. On the occasion of the 'Bicchuk Shahi' (Event IX in Ali Hasan's list), the 'simultaneous attack' by several thousand Muslims 'headed by old offenders' on the houses of five Hindu merchant-moneylenders was so swift—it was launched 'within fifteen minutes' of the carcass of a pig being found on the imambarah at day-break—that the Magistrate saw in it evidence of 'design, unanimity and previous arrangement . . . throughout'.[53] Yet even if the dead pig was planted on the imambarah as a pretext (a suggestion that the weavers and other Muslims of the town indignantly rejected), the evidence speaks unmistakably of a large number of angry Muslims gathering by the imambarah to discuss their course of action. Bearing in mind the obstacles deliberately thrown in the path of the tazia procession by Bicchuk Kalwar and his associates at the Muharram for several years prior to this, we may infer that the 'unanimity' observed here was one of emotion rather than of 'design' or 'conspiracy'.[54]

[51] *Wāqeāt-ò-Hādesāt*, pp. 87–9.                                   [52] Ibid., 89.
[53] COG, Judl. Azamgarh, Vol. 68, File 47, Craigee-Morrieson, 25 March 1842.
[54] Cf. India Office Library: Home Misc., Vol. 775, Report on Benares City by W. W. Bird, 20 Aug. 1814, para 12, which notes: 'The inhabitants by the most simple process imaginable can assemble in multitudes at any given spot on the shortest of notice. The method by which they do this bears a striking affinity to the practice of "gathering" in the Highlands of Scotland, and to a similar practice in Scandinavia. Swift and trusty messengers run full speed all over the City proclaiming in a single word the place of rendezvous, and invoking infamy and eternal vengeance on those who do not at the appointed hour repair to it. From the City the alarm is spread over the country. The first messenger conveys the symbol, which is a Dhurmputtree or paper containing a mystic inscription to the next village, and that to the next, till all know where, when, and wherefore they must meet. This practice is common not only among the Hindoos but the Mahomedans [here too, chiefly weavers] also, and in the disturbances of 1809 and 1810 was the means of collecting together an innumerable multitude at one spot in the space of no more than a few hours'.

In 1877 it was a general body of Muslims at prayer (*namaaz parhne wale*) who, on noticing the *trishul* at the top of Manohar Das's recently completed shivalaya went to ask of Gada Husain whether he had given permission for the building. The Hindus, they remonstrated, would sound the shankh and bells in the temple morning and evening; these and the *bhajans* would disturb the namaaz. And it was the threat of violence which weighed heavily with the Collector when he decided to order the dismantling of the shivalaya.[55]

Similarly in 1904 it was some weavers of Pura Sofi who discovered that a small unenclosed mosque which was being constructed by them in the open fields outside the qasba had been desecrated with the carcass of a piglet. They returned immediately to raise the matter in one or two mosques in their muhalla. A party went out to consult the zamindars of Sikhthi, in whose estate this section of Mubarakpur fell. An attempt was also made to get the local police to take action and then a deputation of weavers went out to Muhammadabad to report the matter at the police station there. Barring the brief consultation with the zamindars of Sikhthi, which was followed by further discussions in their own muhalla, the weavers appear to have acted on their own—gathering a large crowd at the defiled mosque by the sound of a drum, marching north to Gujarpar where the temple was defiled by the killing of a cow seized on the way, and then marching back to the town and through it (inviting 'neighbours and friends' to join them) onto the Mubarakpur temple which lay just beyond its southern extremity, where a cow belonging to the priest and a calf confiscated on the way south from Gujarpar were slaughtered and the images smashed.[56]

In 1813 too the investigating magistrate had observed that 'Shah Mahter, the Surdar of the Musulmans' (this refers to Shahab Mehtar, the head of the weavers) was at the time of the outbreak absent in Gorakhpur: 'had he been present the act [that set off the violence] would probably not have been committed'.[57] The sequence of events leading up to this outbreak is described in the *Wāqeāt-ō-Hādesāt* as also in a petition presented to the Gorakhpur court in 1813 by Shahab Mehtar and four other weavers of Mubarakpur, and a comparison of these is instructive.

[55] *Wāqeāt-ō-Hādesāt*, p. 78, records that the magistrate warned Manohar Das that he was creating the conditions for a riot.

[56] Gorakhpur Commissioner's Record Room, Dept. XIII, File 63/1902-5, 'Judgement' in Mubarakpur Riot Case, forwarded by Magistrate Azamgarh, 5–1–1905, esp. evidence of Bechu, Julaha of Pura Sofi.

[57] UPRAA: MG4, Judl. Series I, Acc. 169, Vol. 168, magistrate's letter, 17 Dec. 1813, para 3.

It is said in Ali Hasan's narrative and in the weavers' petition that
the merchant-moneylenders were becoming arrogant, 'puffed up by
their earnings' and 'drunk on their wealth'. According to the former
it was roughly around the time of the construction of Rikhai Sahu's
thakurduara that Angnu Kalwar, another prospering mahajan, also
built a shivalaya in the middle of Mubarakpur and all the Hindus of
the town began to worship there. Adjacent to the shivalaya was a
chauk (or platform) on which tazias used to be kept during the
Muharram: and the Hindus, out of consideration for their Muslim
neighbours, used to suspend the singing of bhajans and the playing of
music during prayers for the ten days of the Muharram. Thus four or
five years passed in peace. Then, writes Ali Hasan, some among the
Hindus argued that they should not have to suspend their worship
for 'ten to twelve' days: 'Islam reigns over us for that period'. So 'the
mahajans of the town, puffed up with their earnings', had a wall built
around the Muslim platform—and this was the immediate cause of
the 'famous Rikhai Shahi', the 'biggest', bloodiest and most fearful
Event of all.[58]

The petition by Shahab Mehtar and other representatives of the
weavers ('representatives of those who have suffered') puts the matter
in a slightly different and broader historical context. It observes that
Hindus and Muslims had lived together in amity until then, with
tolerance and respect for one another's religious practices and
customs; but 'since the Hindus have gained *amaldari* [from *amil*—
important government official] the killing [*sic*] of Muslims has
begun'.[59] The petitioners quote Devi Dube and Rikhai Sahu as saying
to the panchayat, when the Muslims brought the question of the
extension of the boundary wall before it, that they would spend a
lakh of rupees if necessary on the shivalaya and 'leave not a trace of
you people [the Muslims]'. In addition they explain the slaughter of a
cow on the chauk in front of Angnu Kalwar's shivalaya in terms of a
religious necessity.

Among Muslims and among 'the lower castes of other religions',
says the petition, there is a practice of doing a *minnat* (prayer for a
particular blessing) at an imambarah, masjid, Qadam Rasool or any

---

[58] *Wāqeāt-ō-Hādesāt*, p. 8.
[59] *Arzi ba Adalat Gorakhpur, ba silsila-i-jang Mubarakpur* (Sat. 17 April, AD 1813)
Signed by Sheikh Shahabuddin and four other nurbafs on 7 June 1813, Introduction
and para 2. Qazi Atahar made a copy of this petition from a copy he found in a rather
poor condition with the late Maulvi Hakim Abdul Majid, Bakhri, Mubarakpur, and
very graciously translated for me from the Persian.

*dargah*, [60] and sacrificing a cow or performing some other act of piety when the prayer is answered. Just so, 'someone' (a weaver called Boodhan, according to the Magistrate's report), had done a minnat at this chauk, and promised the sacrifice of a cow if his wish was fulfilled. Now, seeing the boundary wall of the shivalaya being extended to enclose the chauk, a step that would end his chances of making the sacrifice there, he had killed a cow at the spot 'to fulfil his minnat'. There may be no truth in this story; for a petition submitted after such destruction and murder as occurred in 1813 to a court that will determine the punishment to be meted out to the petitioners or their friends, has good cause for exaggeration and fabrication. But the fact that Boodhan, when arrested soon after the 'riot', confessed his deed and explained the killing of the cow in similar terms[61] lends some credence to it. What in any case is significant in the present discussion is the fact that such an argument was put forward at all in defence of the act.

Thus far the evidence points to substantial agreement among the Muslims of Mubarakpur. Yet it would be surprising if there were no variations in outlook. There were after all marked differences of status among both the Muslims and the Hindus of the qasba. The distinction between the *sharif* (or *ashraf*, the 'respectable' classes) and the *razil* (literally 'base', the labouring people) was well established. And Ali Hasan revealed his perception of these distinctions of community and birth in his peculiar interpretation of the Mubarakpur people's anger on receipt of Rajab Ali's letter threatening an attack on the mahajans in 1857: how could 'this Rautara ('new Muslim' zamindar)' dare to contemplate such action?[62]

In spite of all the influence of their Mehtars and sardars, there was a difference between the weavers and other lowly classes on the one hand and the 'pure' or 'noble' Muslims of the upper classes on the other, which the weavers were not easily allowed to forget. As a maulvi of the town put it to me, until well into the twentieth century 'no one was willing to give them [the weavers] the sardar's position in public prayers' or indeed to sit behind them in the congregation.[63]

[60] Cf. W. Crooke, *Religion and Folklore of Northern India* (Oxford, 1926), pp. 166–9; E. A. H. Blunt, *Caste System of Northern India* (Delhi, 1969), p. 292; H. R. Nevill, *Bahraich: A Gazetteer, being Volume XLV of the District Gazetteers of the United Provinces of Agra and Oudh* (Allahabad, 1903), pp. 149–50.

[61] UPRAA: MG4, Judl. Series I, Acc. 169, Vol. 168, magistrate's letter, 17 Dec. 1813, para 3; *Arzi ba Adalat* (17 April 1813), para 3.

[62] *Wāqeāt-ō-Hādesāt*, p. 62.

[63] Interview with Maulvi Kamruzzaman, Mubarakpur.

There is a clear recognition of this division between those with wealth and social standing and those without in Abdul Majid's comments on the 'riot' of 1904: 'It occurred at the instance of the notables [*bade log*, literally, big men]', he wrote in his diary. 'The lower classes [*chote log*, literally, small or unprivileged people]' were taken unawares. 'If the latter had known that they would in their haste commit excesses and be punished for them [in place of the bade log who had inspired the disturbance], they would certainly never have taken such action'.[64]

In the later nineteenth and early twentieth centuries the weavers struggled to close this gap between sharif and razil Muslims in a movement that gradually spread across most of northern India. Their caste appellation, Julaha, was in all probability of Persian origin (from *jula*—ball of thread), but many commentators sought to derive the word from the Arabic *juhala* ('the ignorant class'). The weavers responded with the argument that it came from *jils* (decorated), *jal* (net), or *ujla* (lighted up, or white), from which perhaps came one of the other names that the community used for itself (the one that Ali Hasan also employed) in the later nineteenth century—*nurbafs* or 'weavers of light'. By this time Muslim weavers in many places had come to reject the name Julaha altogether, and insisted that they be called Ansaris (after a claimed Arabic ancestor who practiced the art of weaving) or Momins (i.e. 'the faithful' or 'people of honour').[65] Yet it was to be a long and determined struggle before the community of weavers could overcome the marks of social inferiority and ignorance implicit in the 'impure' status, and indeed the very name, ascribed to them: and even then the label would not come completely unstuck.

The marked distinctions of caste and class noticed above were bound to make for important differences of outlook among diverse groups of Muslims in Mubarakpur, as elsewhere. One aspect of these differences is highlighted by another comparison of Ali Hasan's *Wāqeāt* with Abdul Majid's diary. What the advent of colonialism meant for the people of Mubarakpur is perhaps not unfairly summed up in the following terms: more rigorous administrative demands and control following the establishment of a centralized colonial

---

[64] Entry headed 29 May 1904.

[65] W. Crooke, *The Tribes and Castes of the North-Western Provinces and Oudh*, Vol. *III* (Calcutta, 1896), pp. 69–70; C. A. Silberrad, *A Monograph on Cotton Fabrics Produced in the North-Western Provinces and Oudh* (Allahabad, 1898), p. 1.

power; improved communications, increased traffic and a significant change in the direction of the cloth trade; and higher prices of food and of the raw materials needed for the local cloth industry, at least for important stretches of time. Of these new trends however it is only the first that finds place in Ali Hasan's 'history'.

The fortunes of the cloth trade are a notable silence. For if it was the bazaar and the palace, the 'Islamized trader' and the 'Hinduized aristocrat' who in Geertz's phrase 'stamped (their) character' on the Indonesian towns of Modjokuto and Tabanan,[66] it was the weaving of silken fabrics and the Muslim Julaha that gave to Mubarakpur its distinctive figure[67]—as the above pages should have made clear. Large stocks of finished goods were lost by the weavers in 1857–8 (as we learn from a single-line entry in the colonial records). The miserable condition of the majority of the local weavers was testified to by officials who enquired into the region's industry and trade in the early 1880s. Large numbers of these 'workers in silk' were being forced by the later nineteenth century to turn to the weaving of ordinary cottons—a far less 'honorable' vocation.

Yet these occurrences feature nowhere in Ali Hasan's chronicle. 'Processes' are of course not expressed as 'public' Events in this particular 'history'. But what of the loss of substantial stocks by the weavers in 1857? We do not get any hint of the longer-term process or this sudden loss in the not inconsiderable space devoted by the author to 'Non-Events' or 'Near Events' either.

Abdul Majid's sketchy diary offers a sharp contrast in this regard. Everyday life figures prominently here—births, deaths ('natural' as well as 'unnatural'), marriages and scandalous affairs in the qasba.[68] And while this certainly has something to do with the fact that 'diaries' and 'histories', even 'local histories', are different genres, there is no understating the concern with the cloth trade and its progress—a concern that is entirely missing from the *Wāqeāt*.

[66] C. Geertz, *Peddlers and Princes, Social Change and Economic Modernization in Two Indonesian Towns* (Chicago, 1963), p. 18.

[67] This remains true to this day; thus a young educated Kayasth contractor who gave me a lift to and from the qasba on one occasion said to me that this was only his second visit to the place because *'mujhe to in lungi walon se dar lagta hai'* ('I am afraid of these *lungi*-clad folk'). The lungi was the dress of lower-caste Muslims in this region, cf. Raza, *Aadha Gaon*, p. 65.

[68] See ibid., *passim*, for a very rich 'anthropological' account which reveals very much the same kind of everyday concerns among other Muslim inhabitants in this region in a slightly later period.

The haphazard entries in the diary contain numerous detailed statements regarding the price of different kinds of cloth and of silk
thread, as of grain and other necessities, and comments on their
implications. Thus on 10 August 1919: 'This year the trade has been
such that Mubarakpur has become prosperous [*aabaad*, literally,
'populated' or 'full of life']. Until this year there has never been such a
(prosperous) trade—nor will there be (again) . . . . And this year as
many as 142 members of our brotherhood have proceeded to Hajj-i-
Kaaba from here'. Again in July 1920: 'This year the outlook for the
trade is not so happy. Silk thread has become very expensive'.[69] Or
on a different subject, referring to the soaring prices of goat-skins in
November 1916, the price having touched Rs 3 and Rs 4 per skin by
this time: 'Many of the big and wealthy Muslims have taken to
trading in these skins'.[70]

The concern with the immediate problems of subsistence that is
reflected here may be one reason why the weavers of Mubarakpur
appeared on the whole somewhat more ambiguous in their response
to British rule than the Ali Hasans of the 1880s. In respect of the cloth
trade, colonialism had certainly not been an unmixed blessing. I have
written at some length elsewhere about the hardships suffered by the
weavers of eastern UP owing to the dislocation of their market and
supplies of raw material, and the increased dependence on intermediaries and new trails of migration that developed.[71] Whether it
was because of this experience of being buffeted about or because of
Gandhian support for handicraft industry or some other local factors,
we know that the weavers of Azamgarh were, with most of their
community throughout the rest of UP and Bihar, supporters of the
Congress struggle for independence long after the emergence of a
Hindu-Muslim schism at the level of provincial and 'national' politics.[72]

---

[69] Both these entires appear under the date, 10 Aug. 1919, but the second is clearly
an addition made in a new paragraph.              [70] Entry for Nov. 1916.
[71] See Pandey, 'Economic Dislocation in Nineteenth-Century Eastern UP', section
VII. There appears to have been a wave of migration from Mubarakpur and other such
places to Malegaon and other cloth-producing centres in western and central India
during the rising of 1857–9, Hafiz Malegumi, *Nakūsh* (Malegaon, 1979), pp. 70, 72,
116. (I owe this reference to Maulvi Kamruzzaman).
[72] National Archives of India: Govt. of India, Home Dept., Political (I) Branch,
File 31/1/41, 'D.I.B's report on the political situation in Bihar' (Memo. by D. Pilditch,
15 Jan. 1941); Rajendra Prasad Papers, File XV/37, Col. I, tlg. Hakim Wasi Ahmad,
Pres., Bihar Jamiat-al-Momineen to Rajendra Prasad, received 12 July 1937; Raza
*Aadha Gaon*, pp. 252–4; interviews Maunath Bhanjan, Mubarakpur and Banaras.

Abdul Majid's own evidence on this is somewhat paradoxical. At more than one place in his diary he refers to the death of some distinguished British personage—Lord Kitchener or the wife of the Lieutenant-Governor of UP—and expresses a feeling of deep sorrow: 'The subjects [of the Lieutenant-Governor] were deeply grieved and they mourned for four days, and whatever we could give as charity we gave'.[73] Again, referring to the boycott of the Prince of Wales on his visit to Calcutta in December 1921, he writes: '*Afsos! Sad afsos!* [Shame! Undying shame!]. As far as my understanding goes, we cannot obtain Suraj [Swaraj] by such means'.[74]

But we know from other sources that Abdul Majid was very close to the police and local offcials: 'Abdul Majid, resident of Pura Sofi, although he is an ordinary person [i.e. of no great wealth or distinction], always informs police officers of any secret—[meetings?] in the qasba that he comes to know about'.[75] It is probable that this relationship had something to do with the opinions he formed. In addition it is not entirely clear what significance one can attach to this reverence for (or fear of) distant overlords like Lord Kitchener, the Lieutenant-Governor's wife and the Prince of Wales. For not only does the diarist add to the above comment on the Prince of Wales' visit: 'Yes, if God wills it, then there can be Suraj'.[76] He also condemns those Muslims who were responsible as prosecution witnesses for sending other Muslims to jail for their part in Non-Co-operation activities.[77]

In any case the weavers of Mubarakpur seem to have taken an active part in the Non-Co-operation Movement. Abdul Majid records meetings of the 'panchayat of twenty-eight' (referring to the twenty-eight *muhallas* of Mubarakpur) and of the '*chaurasi*' (or 'eighty-four', which drew in the leaders of the weavers from a considerable number of villages and qasbas to decide on matters of

[73] Entries dated 12 July 1914 & June 1916.

[74] 'Note' on Congress, Nov–Dec. 1921.

[75] 'Village Crime Register', Mubarakpur, Pt. IV (entry dated 1909 or 1910).

[76] 'Note' on Congress, Nov–Dec. 1921. Cf. also his note on Shibli Nomani, a Muslim 'unequalled in Hindustan' who had had dealings with 'great rulers all over the world'. The 'great rulers' here would seem to be on a par with those 'omniscient' and 'just', faraway and unseen rulers who provided the inspiration for numerous peasant uprisings in Russia, India and elsewhere in the eighteenth and nineteenth centuries; D. Field, *Rebels in the Name of the Tsar* (Boston, 1976); I. J. Catanach, 'Agrarian Disturbances in Nineteenth-Century India', *Indian Economic & Social History Review*, III, 1 (1966).

[77] Entry for 19 June 1922.

importance) that were called to enforce the boycott of foreign cloth.[78] It is also clear from his evidence that the leaders of the Khilafat Committee in Mubarakpur were mostly members of the weaving community[79]: the Sheikh zamindars of the qasba appear to have maintained a low profile during this period.

We have in all this some glimpses of the Mubarakpur weavers' outlook on the nineteenth-century world. This outlook differed in certain significant respects from that of the élite Muslims of the qasba but shared with it an important area of common concern. In common with exploited classes elsewhere in pre-capitalist societies, the weavers of Mubarakpur appear to have been further removed than their economically or culturally more privileged neighbours from direct political dealings with the colonial bureaucracy, and are consequently somewhat more hazy about their relations with their rulers. They were more ambivalent too in their response to the putative 'Muslim' community; more concerned about the bare problem of survival; yet in some ways more 'independent' with their reliance on the panchayat[80] and their faith in the power of 'tradition'; and at the same time deeply concerned about the honour of the community.

[78] Entries for 12 Dec. 1919, 8 Feb. 1920 & July 1921. L. S. S. O'Malley, *Census of India, 1911, Vol. V. Bengal, Bihar & Orissa & Sikkim. Pt I. Report* (Calcutta, 1913), pp. 462–3 explains the *Chaurasi* as follows: The lowest unit of caste government was the *chatai*, i.e. the right to sit together on a mat (or chatai) at a caste council meeting. Each chatai had a headman and other functionaries, and its area depended on the strength of the caste locally: there could be several chatais in one village or one chatai for several villages. These chatais were sometimes grouped into larger unions called Baisi or Chaurasi (consisting of 22 and 84 Chatais respectively). A Baisi could cover 10–15 miles, a Chaurasi 40–50. 'The jurisdiction of the Panchayat is necessarily local, but the combination of different Chatais helps to make its sentence effective over a considerable area'.

[79] Entry for 19 June 1922.

[80] O'Malley, *Census 1911, Bengal, Bihar & Orissa, Pt I*, p. 461, notes that an organized system of caste government existed among most of the lower castes in Bihar but not among the higher castes. He comments further that 'none of the Musalman groups approach so closely to the Hindu caste system with its numerous restrictions as the Jolahas'. The Julaha panchayat, headed by a sardar assisted by a *chharidar*, covered 10–50 houses, its sphere usually being coterminous with a village but sometimes covering several villages (p. 489). (In Mubarakpur there appears to have been a panchayat, headed by a *mehtar*, for each of the muhallas of the qasba). See also F.H. Fisher, *Statistical, Descriptive and Historical Account of the North-Western Provinces, Ghazipur* (Allahabad, 1883), pp. 56–7; and n. 54 & n. 78 above.

'Ham log wahan maujud the. Yah dekhkar nihayat dil dukha'.
Translation: 'We were present there [when the Inspector of
Police, Mohan Singh, trampled a copy of the Qoran underfoot
during searches after the 'riot' of 1904]. We were deeply wounded
by this sight'.

'Bade-bade logon ka ishara tha, aur chote logon ne yah samjha ki
sarkari intazam ki vajah se kuch nahin hoga'.
Translation: 'It was at the instigation of 'big men' [that the 1904
outbreak occurred]; the 'smaller folk' thought that nothing
would happen because of official precautions'.

'Inke intakāl ka hamare badshah ko bahut bada ranj hua. Aur
hamko bhi bahut bada gam hua'.
Translation: 'His [Lord Kitchener's] death caused very great
grief to our King. It also caused us very deep sorrow'.

'In logon ne Musalman hokar Musalman ko qaid karaya'.
Translation: 'These people who are Musalmans are responsible
for having sent other Musalmans to jail'.[81]

What is indubitably represented in these extracts from Abdul
Majid's diary is a consciousness of the 'collective'—the community.
Yet this consciousness of community was an ambiguous one, straddling
as it did the religious fraternity, class, qasba and mohalla.[82] Here, as
in Ali Hasan's account, the boundaries of the collective shift all the
time. It is difficult to translate this consciousness into terms that are
readily comprehensible in today's social science—Muslim/Hindu,
working class/rentier, urban/rural—or even to argue that a particular
context would inevitably activate a particular solidarity. What is clear
is that Ali Hasan is quite untroubled by the problems that confound
the modern researcher as he moves from one notion of the collective
to another through the eighty-nine pages of his manuscript.

I have suggested above that there is nonetheless a certain basic
consistency in Ali Hasan's stand. In Abdul Majid's random notes too
it is possible to discern a similar consistency; for what they speak of is
a fight on several fronts for self-respect and human dignity.[83] Honour

[81] These quotations are taken from Abdul Majid's diary, entries headed 29 May
1904 (first two quotations), June 1916 and 19 June 1922.
[82] For the importance of muhalla loyalty in the politics of Muslim weavers elsewhere, see J. C. Masselos, 'Power in the Bombay 'Moholla', 1904–5', South Asia,
No.6 (Dec. 1976).
[83] Dipesh Chakrabarty has pointed out to me how the semiotics of insult (honour/
shame) carries over from this region to the industrial city, reproducing an identical
structure of riots in the Calcutta mills in the later nineteenth and earlier twentieth
century.

(*izzat*) was inextricably linked as we have seen with certain kinds of worship, certain ritual practices; and any insult to these was unacceptable. But honour was also tied up by the later decades of this century of dislocation with the assertion of the rights of the chote log, the shedding of the degrading label of razil, and full acceptance in the equal fraternity of Islam that the Wahabis had propagated and other 'learned' Muslims now so often talked about.[84] If the positions of all men, high and low, seemed increasingly insecure in a fateful world, these were not fates that men and women, high or low, would accept without a struggle.

---

[84] For a different but relevant example of the importance attached to izzat by the peasants of this region, see K. Mukherjee and R. S. Yadav, *Bhojpur* (Delhi, 1980).

# Four Rebels of Eighteen-Fifty-Seven[1]

## GAUTAM BHADRA

> History does nothing, it possesses 'no immense wealth', it 'wages
> no battles'. It is man, real, living man who does all that, who pos-
> sesses and fights; history is not, as it were a person apart, using
> man as a means to achieve its own aims, history is nothing but the
> activity of man pursuing his aims.
>
> Marx & Engels, *The Holy Family*

## I. *Introduction*

There is a curious complicity between all the principal modes of
historiography which have engaged so far in the study of the rebellion of 1857. According to S.B. Chaudhuri, an eminent nationalist
historian, 'it was the class of the landed chiefs who led the struggle
against the British', for they were 'the natural leaders'. R.C. Majumdar, too, is of the view that *taluqdars* and zamindars, regarded highly by the mass of the peasantry, were responsible for the 'origin and
prolongation of popular revolt'. Eric Stokes, in his otherwise admir-
able work on the local background of the popular upsurge, has also

ABBREVIATIONS ACR = Agra Commissioner's Records. BR = Board of Revenue.
*DG = District Gazetteer of the United Provinces of Agra & Oudh* compiled by
H.R. Nevill & D.L. Drake-Brockman (Allahabad, 1909–30). Relevant volumes.
F = File No. *FSUP = Freedom Struggle in Uttar Pradesh*, ed. by S.A.A. Rizvi &
M.L. Bhargava, vols. I, II & v. (Lucknow, 1957–60). JP = Judicial Proceedings,
Judicial Department. MCR = Meerut Commissioner's Records, dept. XII.
*NE = Narrative of Events Regarding the Mutiny of India of 1857–1858 and the
Restoration of Authority.* 2 vols. (Calcutta, 1881). NWP = North Western Pro-
vinces. *PP = Parliamentary Papers, House of Commons, Accounts & Papers*, vol.
44, part 4, 1857–58. Proc. = Proceedings No. RD = Revenue Department.
UPRA = Uttar Pradesh Regional Archives, Allahabad. UPSA = Uttar Pradesh
State Archives, Lucknow. WBSA = West Bengal State Archives, Calcutta.

[1] This article is dedicated to Samar Sen. I am grateful to Partha Chatterjee,
Ranajit Guha, Gyan Pandey, Bharati Roy and Tapti Roy for their comments and
editorial suggestions.

described the rural insurgency of 1857 as essentially élitist in character, for 'the mass of the population appeared to have played little part or at most tamely followed the behests of caste superiors'. The stance of radical historiography has not been fundamentally different. Promode Sengupta, a Marxist scholar, has written the history of the Great Rebellion in terms of the activities and motives of Nana Saheb, Lakshmi Bai, Bahadur Shah, etc., because these feudal chiefs were, to him, the 'natural leaders'. Even that revolutionary intellectual, Saroj Datta, a leader of the movement identified with the Naxalbari insurrection, had demanded the replacement of statues of nineteenth-century intellectuals in public places by those of Rani Lakshmi Bai and Tantia Topi. With the best of intentions, radical historiography does not appear to have opted out of the paradigm within which the bourgeois-nationalist and liberal historians operate.[2]

In all these representations what has been missed out is the ordinary rebel, *his* role and *his* perception of alien rule and contemporary crisis. By contrast, the present essay tries to rehabilitate some of the rebels of 1857 who have already been forgotten by historians or scantily treated, with no more than a nod in their direction. I study four of them—a small landlord, a cultivator belonging to a substantial peasant community, a poor tribal youth and a Maulvi. These four may be said to represent between them a fairly large number of ordinary and yet complex insurgent personalities of that time. Leaders of a type very different from the well-known landed magnates, they were among those whom a knowledgable district official of Saharanpur was to describe, soon after the revolt, as '*the few active spirits* who originated and organised the movement in various localities'.[3]

## II. *Shah Mal*

Shah Mal was a resident of Bijraul, a large village situated in the eastern portion of the *pargana* of Barout. This village was irrigated

[2] See S.B. Chaudhuri, *Civil Rebellion in the Indian Mutinies* (Calcutta, 1957); R.C. Majumdar, *The Sepoy Mutiny and the Revolt of 1857* (Calcutta, 1963); Eric Stokes, *The Peasant and the Raj* (Delhi, 1980); Promode Sengupta, *Bharatiya Mahabidroha* (Calcutta, 1981); Sasanka (Saroj Datta), 'Murti Bhangar Swapakshe' (Deshabrati Prakasan, Calcutta, n.d.). For a recent study, see Rudrangshu Mukherjee, *Awadh in Revolt, 1857–58* (Delhi, 1984).

[3] H. Dundas Robertson, *District Duties during the Revolt in the North West Provinces of India* (London, 1859), p. 192.

by the Bijwara and Kishanpur *rajbahas* of the Jumna canal.[4] He was a *malik* of a portion of the village which at the time of the mutiny was divided into two *pattis*, known as Kullo and Bholy or Ladura. The 'notorious rebel leader Shah Mal' had control only over the former. Even there he had co-sharers like Seesram and others who remained aloof from his activities, so that after the suppression of the revolt their rights were left unimpaired. The other patti, with its four *thoks*, also did not participate in the rebellion and 'was in like manner ordered to be exempted from confiscation'.[5]

The *tehsil* Barout, with its rich dark loam of considerable fertility and abundant means of irrigation,[6] was regarded as the most prosperous pargana of the district. T.C. Plowden was eloquent in his report about its prosperity. The proportion of inferior land, he calculated, was 'very small, being about ⅛ of the whole'. The area of the whole of the pargana was irrigated by the small canals from the rivers Jumna, Hindun and Krishna, which led to the cultivation of 'profitable products' such as sugarcane, cotton, *mukka* and wheat. The whole area was within the circuit of a thriving commerce. Barout, Binowlle and Sirdhana, convenient marts with linkages to Meerut, Shamlee, Kandlah, Baghpat, Tandah and Delhi, afforded 'ample facilities for the disposal of every species of produce'.[7]

The population was densely settled and composed principally of Jat cultivators who were considered to be the sole masters of Chuprowlee, Barout, Katana and the upper portion of Burwana.[8] Stokes's description of the *bhaiyachara* community is quite applicable to this area. For, as the settlement report stated, there were 'of this large agricultural population an exceptional number of petty proprietors'—indeed, only 975 zamindari mahals as opposed to 2,235 *pattadari* and *bhaiyachari* tenures.[9] Zamindars like Shah Mal

[4] *DG*: Meerut, pp. 209–10.
[5] Forbes to Williams, 24 April 1862, F18/1862, MCR, UPRA.
[6] *DG*: Meerut, p. 203.
[7] Plowden to Franco, 16 March 1840, in H.M. Elliot, *Report of the Settlement of the District of Meerut, 1835* (Benaras, 1861), p. 228. Hereafter *Meerut Settlement*.
[8] W.A. Forbes & J.S. Porter, *Settlement Report of the District of Meerut 1865–1870*, (Allahabad, 1874), p. 62.
[9] R.W. Gillan, *Final Settlement Report of the Meerut District* (Allahabad, 1901), p. 9.

were actually principal cultivators and had to 'till nearly half the land themselves'.[10]

In this area the village proprietors and cultivators rarely belonged to different castes. 'As all the four proprietory castes follow the occupation of agriculture to a greater or lesser degree', wrote Forbes, 'it is perhaps a natural consequence that the caste of cultivators should shadow those of proprietors'.[11] There was a large number of Chamars who were agricultural labourers. They were excluded from the cultivating community though they were no less numerous than the Jats. It is important to note that in the mutiny of 1857 the Chamars remained largely unnoticed.

On the eve of the English conquest Barout was under the rule of Begam Samru. It was alleged that the Jat proprietors were unfavourably treated by a high-handed Taga minister. After the year 1836, when the English authority was established in this area, Plowden tilted the balance in favour of the Jats during the settlement. Yet the assessment remained heavy. But the Jat peasants, according to a settlement officer, withstood the demand. The progress in agriculture was substantial and proprietary rights were not transferred to any significant extent.[12]

But there was a smouldering grievance against the settlement. The settlement officer faced tough opposition from the petty proprietors in Baghpat. 'They have destroyed all their best cultivation in anticipation of re-settlement', he wrote.[13] To such petty cultivators every settlement was full of uncertainty, and they therefore regarded it with suspicion and apprehension. It was ultimately the iron fist of colonial authority that made them accept the settlement with 'a decided reluctance'. The directives of the Board were categorical with regard to the recalcitrant proprietors of Baghpat and Barout:

> If the zamindars or cultivators refuse to take *pattahs* and to execute cabooleat at the established rates of rents for lands, in their occupancy, you will let such lands to any of the zamindars or ryotts who may be willing to undertake the cultivation of them or allow them to remain

[10] *DG*: Meerut, p. 205.

[11] Forbes & Porter, p. 4.

[12] Plowden, in Elliott, *Meerut Settlement*, p. 229; Gillan, p. 12; Willey to Greathead, 2 December 1854: 'Frequency of the transfer of Proprietary Titles', *Selections from the Records of the Government of the North-Western Provinces*, vol. IV, pt. XXIV. Hereafter *Selections*.

[13] Letter from Meerut Collector, 12 October 1822. BR, NWP, 2 November 1822, UPSA.

fallow; in the latter case giving the recusants to understand that in the event of their cultivation without pattahs the whole produce will be liable to be attached and brought to sale on account of the government.[14]

Thus a political threat and an assertion of the coercive power of the state was implicit in the process of settlement. Its impact on popular perception cannot, therefore, be measured solely by statistics. There is some evidence in the records of the tensions and pressures generated by this process in the Baghpat and Barout regions of Meerut district in the 1840s and 1850s involving, as it sometimes inevitably did, the threat, actual or real, of the alienation of land from the older proprietors and the intrusion of auction purchasers as 'strangers' into *pattis* with traditional solidarities based on longstanding communal ties.[15] However, not all parts of the district which were hard-pressed thus by revenue assessment and proprietary right transfers responded to the mutiny in the same manner or to the same degree. This shows that in order to understand why an insurrection actually breaks out in a particular locality rather than in another it is imperative to look beyond the immediate context of economic loss or gain.

The rebellion of Shah Mal started as a local affair. It is stated that the people of Baoli and Barout villages were the only members of the Jat caste in that neighbourhood to rise actively against the British. Yet in its intensity rebellion had assumed an importance which was acknowledged thus by the commissioner: 'The rebellion in the part of the district is kept up by Shah Mull of Byrout, his principal abettors being Bagta and Sajja . . . with them joined 60 villagers, who took no more part than individually swelling the ranks of the ringleaders'.[16] A large number of these rural leaders were *lumbardars*. For example Jeerum, Badan and Gulab, lumbardars respectively of Jowhree, Journawa and Jafarbad, were prominent commanders in Shah Mal's rebel force. The lumbardars of Barout, such as Shon Singh and Bud Singh, also cast their lot with the rebels. Out

[14] Board's Letter, 12 October 1822, BR, NWP, Proc 22, ibid.

[15] For two such instances see D.B. Moorison's Letter, 20 August & 17 September 1850, BR, NWP, Proc 59–60, UPSA; and Suit of Laik Ram vs. Govt., No. 34/1859, MCR, UPRA.

[16] Sapte to Williams, 2 December 1858: 'List of the Leaders and Instigators of the rebellion in Meerut Division Unfit for Amnesty', F101/1859, RD, MCR, UPRA.

of the sixty persons named, no less than twenty were lumbardars
who had made common cause with Shah Mal. There were also the
co-sharer of the patti, i.e. *hissadar* Askaran, and Harjus, hissadar of
Doghauta, who sided with him and 'attacked the tehsildar of Sir-
dauh and village of Daha'. Hargopal of Baraut and Mehir Chand of
Sirsalee belonged to the same category. But there were also men of
lesser social standing, such as Caloo and Dilsookli, sons of Shyam
Singh, a humble 'Jat inhabitant of Dhokowlee', who took command
of the insurgent forces. Again, Rajee of Kandhoura, and Hurdhyal a
Gujor of Jewahanpur, were followers of Shah Mal but do not seem
to have been lumbardars or hissadars.[17]

Thus Shah Mal had support among the village headmen and small
zamindars in the area. The term 'lumbardars' referred to a village
headman with whom an engagement for revenue had been made. In
fact many village *muqaddams* functioned as such in an altered context. They were elected by other co-sharers and allowed to collect a
percentage of the revenue. Through them the state approached the
cultivators, offered loans and received representations. However
they too were subjected, like all other petty proprietors, to the
severities of the fiscal demand and the process of survey and settlement. Asiya Siddiqui has pointed out how these groups were torn
between the contradictory prospects of economic advancement and
the loss of their *sir* lands. Many of them were poor or at best marginally above the level of the rest of the cultivators. On the other hand
they could in opportune moments use their connections with the
state to enrich themselves.[18] In the days of the rebellion these
groups, vexed by the state's revenue demand and interference and
propelled by their ambition, rallied around Shah Mal.

Upon the outbreak of the mutiny in Meerut on 10 May 1857 the
English authority was soon 'entirely suspended from Barout', when
'a number of cultivators left their fields and took to plundering and
many old proprietors took the opportunity of acquiring possession
of their lands'. At this time, on 12 or 13 May, the first act of open
defiance by Shah Mal was 'an attack and plunder of a large party of
Brinjara [Bunjara] Merchants'. He followed this up by an attack on
the tehsil of Barout and its destruction. After this he was appointed

---

[17] **Sapte's** report: 'Persons eminent for disloyalty and proposing reward for
apprehension . . . Meerut, May 1858', MCR, F79, 1858, UPRA.
[18] Asiya Siddiqui, *Agrarian Change in a North Indian State* (Oxford, 1978),
pp. 91–3, *passim.*

to a *subahdarship* by order from Delhi. He consolidated his position during May and June, Jat villages like Baoli joining him with their cultivating populations.[19] He gained further strength when the prisoners of Meerut gaol joined his forces. His rise to power was described thus by an official:

> Shah Mull, a Jhat [*sic*] . . . by collecting some bad characters, and getting aid from the rebels at Delhi, had gradually gained strength and boldness to attack and plunder the tehselee of Barouth, then to destroy the bridge of boats over Jamuna, at Baghput; then, with the assistance of a force of mutineers from Delhi, again to destroy the Baghput bridge which had been reconstructed by Mr. J. Campbell and was defended by the contingent of the Jheend Rajah . . . and finally, after all these successes, to seduce the inhabitants of eighty-four villages, principally Jats, known as the *Chowrassee des* from their allegiance to Government and *from nothing become the rebel of some importance*, collecting and sending supplies to the mutineers at Delhi, and entirely stopping the direct communication between headquarters' camp and Meerut and when he was attacked had threatened to raise the whole country to the west and northwest.

Another official wrote of him as 'a Jat of the Mavway tribe, Governor of the purgannah of Barout with the title of Rajah' whose control 'of this and three and four purgunnahs on the left bank of Jumna . . . enabled the people and garrison of Delhi to live during the siege'.[20]

These reports underlined the importance of a local leader who, unlike Walidad Khan, was not distinguished by lineage, but proved to be no less of an obstacle to the counter-insurgency operations. His first act of rebellion was the 'plunder and pillage' of the tehsil of Barout and the bazaar of Baghpat, visible symbols of authority and wealth. In this he was by no means atypical. But, more than many others, he developed a supra-local perception of power and forged an alliance beyond his own area. On his own he sent emissaries to Delhi to make contact with the rebels there. Allah Dyah, son of Nubee Baksh, a Baluchi of Baluchpara, was appointed an officer by Shah Mal and sent to Delhi 'to get help and to bring men to fight' against the English. Wazir Khan, the *thanadar* of Baghpat, also sent

[19] Sapte to Lowe, 6 December 1858, MCR, F19/1859, UPRA; R.H.W. Dunlop, *Service & Adventure with the Khakee Ressalah or, Meerut Volunteer Horse, during the Mutinies of 1857–58* (London, 1858), pp. 45–6; *DG:* Meerut, p. 201.

[20] Williams' Report, Meerut, 7 August 1857, *PP*, pp. 884–5 (emphasis added); Wilson to Edmonstone, 24 December 1857, *NE*, p. 20.

an *arzee* to the emperor for the same purpose. Mehtab Khan, son of Noor Khan at Baghpat, was yet another contact. These men had 'friends at Delhi and presented him before the King and it was consequently through these men that Shah Mall was pointed out as a man likely to benefit the rebel cause'.[21] He disrupted the lines of communication between the English forces, mobilized the villages within his own territory, and otherwise made himself essential to the Delhi rebels for whom his area came to serve as a strategic rear and supply base. In return his authority was recognized and legitimized by the emperor. The danger of such supra-local linkages between a local insurgent and the seat of rebellion in Delhi was not lost on Dunlop, who wrote in some alarm: 'Unless some vigorous measures are taken to assist our friends and punish our foes, we shall be totally deserted by the mass of people, those still faithful to us are becoming disgusted at our apparent apathy, and the mutiny and rebellion of today may become a revolution'.[22]

However, not all the villages in that area were in favour of Shah Mal. Before the counter-insurgency operations began in mid-July, Williams reported that 'many of the Jats had declared they would not assist him [Shah Mal], on the contrary would help in capturing him'.[23] Dunlop mentioned a Rajput village, Deolah, and another called Burka, both 'friendly to the English', as having been under a threat of attack from Shah Mal.[24] In fact Newal Singh, a Rajput of Deolah, acted as the principal guide and informant to Dunlop's volunteer force as it moved against Shah Mal on 15 July 1857. Both Deolah and Hussaodah paid their *kists* to the government. Shah Mal had taken exception to this and intended 'to attack and plunder the village' with a force of 3,000 insurgents. How close he was to executing this plan was found out by the English when on 17 July they captured the village of Bussowadah (Bussoud), inhabited by Mussalman Juggars, and discovered 8,000 maunds of grain, wheat and *dal* in a 'large store house collected for the Delhi rebels'. Shah Mal had taken shelter in this village the night before and escaped just in time. Government troops put all men to the sword and destroyed all arms, while 'two ghazees from Delhi continued fighting desperately

[21] Source as in fns. 16 & 17 above.
[22] Dunlop to Hewitt, 28 June 1857, *PP*, p. 894. Also Sapte's list and report as in fns. 16 & 17.
[23] Williams' Report, 7 August 1857, *PP*, para. 2, p. 884.
[24] Dunlop, *Khakee Ressalah*, pp. 87, 99 & 93.

in a mosque'. But Shah Mal's authority was so pervasive that the Deolah people refused to touch any of the captured provisions 'for fear of Shah Mal's vengeance'.[25] The case of Francis Cohen provides yet another instance of selective violence against the allies of the English. Cohen, a tehsildar under Begum Sumru, was 'a Christian and acted a Christian's part' in giving shelter to some fugitives from Delhi. For this he was punished by the Gujars and the followers of Shah Mal who 'plundered him of 7 and 8000 rupees worth of property' and took him prisoner, 'releasing him on a ransom of 600 rupees'.[26]

Shah Mal had transformed the bungalow of an officer of the irrigation department around the Jumna canal into 'a hall of justice for himself' and thus appropriated the office of the *sarkar* for the exercise of his own authority. He also set up a parallel network of intelligence to which Dunlop was obliged to pay a tribute when he wrote: 'The excellence of the intelligence received by the rebels on all occasions proves them to have had many friends amongst those not committed to rebellion'.[27] As we have noticed, Shah Mal managed to slip away from a surprise attack on Busoudh. After his death 'on his person was found a letter from Salek Ram and Lal Muin' who held undivided shares in the village of Painga. They had apparently warned him of the impending operation against the insurgents and given details about the strength of the army on the basis of information 'picked up . . . in Meerut'. These persons were caught and hanged as spies. 'These treacherous rebels and spies hanging about the Magistrate', wrote the commissioner, 'found out the intended attack on Shah Mull and strength of detachment and communicated the intelligence to him. The consequence was that the small detachment of 129 men had to fight thousands for hours and nothing but most determined courage saved the party from destruction. The spies were condemned and executed'.[28] It was with 'agents' like these that Shah Mal built up an organization at the nerve centre of the district authority. They moved in the night from village to village ro rally the people against the English, as Dunlop

[25] Dunlop to Meerut Commissioner, 26 July 1857, *PP*, p. 886; Williams to Meerut Commissioner, 31 July 1854, *PP*, p. 887.

[26] Petition from Francis Cohen, 18 october 1858, F48/1858, BR, MCR, UPRA.

[27] Dunlop, *Khakee Ressalah*, p. 119.

[28] Sapte's report, 19 February 1858. Confiscation of Estates, class III, entry no. 125, F105/1859, MCR, UPRA.

was to recall later.[29] In practice, they functioned as an arm of the rebel authority, helping it to distinguish friends from enemies and defend itself from attacks by the latter.

In the period of the pacification campaign, the government considered it 'fair to make a distinction between those who joined the rebels at Delhi and Rohilkhand and those who joined with any upstart
who took the occasion of authority weakened by a military revolt
and a contest of supremacy raging in the neighbourhood to strive
for independence'. And by placing Shah Mal and his followers in
the latter category,[30] the officials helped to emphasize the political
character of his revolt. References to 'the authority weakened by the
military revolt', to 'a contest for supremacy' and 'striving for independence' were all indices of that politics as seen from the stand-
point of the rebel's enemies. Among the latter, Dunlop, a shrewd
observer, had noticed 'various symptoms' showing 'how rapidly the
neglect of this part of the district had led to the belief that the British
rule had terminated for ever'. And as the battle for Delhi continued
and the fate of the court, which had provided support for Shah Mal,
hung in balance, 'the people of the district', said Dunlop, were 'in a
fever of excitement to know *whether "their raj"* or ours was to
triumph'.[31]

The distinction made in these reports between the two contending authorities, 'their raj or ours', speaks of an awareness that went
beyond the calculus of economic gain and loss and related to a concept of power. However, there are some other aspects of this struggle on which these official statements do not throw much light.
How did Shah Mal emerge as a leader over these individual villages?
In the contest for supremacy that was raging in the countryside,
how was his supremacy established? These are questions which no
historian on peasant insurrections can ignore. Indeed, two historians, Eric Stokes and Ranajit Guha, have tried to answer them in
their works.

In their respective discussions of Shah Mal both underline the elements of solidarity and their limits in the insurrection. Stokes locates the basis of solidarity in 'factional alignments'. These alignments took the form of local groupings involving both territorial

[29] Dunlop, *Khakee Ressalah*, p. 95.
[30] Lowe to Muir, 30 November 1858. List of the Confiscated Estates of Zillah
Meerut. F105/1859, MCR, UPRA.
[31] Dunlop, *Khakee Ressalah*, pp. 97, 127.

and kinship units, such as *tappas* and *khaps*, many of which were bitterly hostile to each other. Thus Barout was the centre of the Salaklain Jats who, under the leadership of Shah Mal and Suraj Mal, were actually in the process of renewing their old feuds against the neighbouring Ghatwal Jats. It was such clan and territorial linkages as well as the tradition of old feuds which, according to Stokes, contributed to Shah Mal's success in rallying a number of villages.[32] Guha argues that 'the role of territoriality as a positive factor behind rebel mobilization' was clearly demonstrated in the massive jacqueries triggered off by the mutiny. To him the notion of territoriality includes both geographical and social space. In citing numerous cases he puts the emphasis on local dimensions of the targets of rebel attack. This localized character of the rebellion also drew its sustenance partially from the 'revolt of particular ethnic masses'. The very nature of the distribution of castes and clans in an area helped to spread as well as limit an insurgent movement to a particular zone or particular castes. He cites the case of Shah Mal as a typical Gujar rebellion which 'convulsed the north-western district of Uttar Pradesh'. Its specific Gujar character was underlined by 'their attack on the Jat villages, who behaved notably in support of law and order'.[33]

There is much truth in both these arguments. In fact there was intense fighting between Jats and Gujars in this area during the mutiny and this rivalry determined, to an extent, loyalty and enmity towards the government. The Gujar village at Seekree, about sixteen miles from Meerut cantonment, took an active part in the disturbances and began to encroach on the land of other villages. The combined forces of three Gujar villages, Seekree, Nugla and Deosa, defeated a force of Jats 'who commenced collecting at the important village and bazaar of Begumbad for the purpose of defending themselves'. The incident took place on 8 July before the arrival of the government forces to save the 'loyalist' Jats. The victory of the Gujars was possible because 'they were better armed, less divided among themselves, more habituated in the acts of violence'.[34]

Here is a clear case of clan alignment and rivalry. But Shah Mal's mobilization cut across these alignments. Although he was himself a

[32] Stokes, pp. 17–18.

[33] Ranajit Guha, *Elementary Aspects of Peasant Insurgency in Colonial India* (Delhi, 1983), pp. 305–32, 313–14.

[34] Dunlop to Meerut Commissioner, 11 July 1857, *PP*, p. 883.

Jat—and his successors and next in command were his own relatives—the Gujars rallied around him. His army included villagers of various castes. In fact Dunlop, the leader of the counterinsurgency force, found it difficult to decide whether a village in this area was hostile or friendly, irrespective of the caste or clan of its residents. Thus two hostile villages, Chouparah and Jafarbad, both deserted on the approach of his troops, were inhabited respectively by Taga Brahmins and Muslim Jaggars. Bussoudah, where Shah Mal had his stock of grain, belonged to the Jaggars. 'A goojur village', Bichpooree, 'had taken an active part in all Shah Mall's misdoings'. Dunlop mentioned a *sipahi* who deserted his *ressalah* for Shah Mal's army because he was a Mussalman.[35] Again, the people of the Gujar village, Ahehra, were prominent in an attack on Cohen and actively assisted Shah Mal in all his operations, including the plunder of Barout and Baghput and the destruction of a vital bridge.[36] Suraj Mal sought help in the Jat village of Sirsalle, while the rebels from Mullurpore, who were willing to join Shah Mal, were said to have been led by 'one old white-bearded sikh'.[37]

A clue to the logic of these wide-ranging solidarities may be sought in the notion of 'Chowrasee Des'—a term which occurs again and again in Shah Mal's messages. Williams talked of an attempt made by the rebel leader 'to seduce the inhabitants of eighty-four villages, principally *jats*, known as Chowrasee Des, from allegiance to government'. The villagers from Burka advised Dunlop to fly 'as fast as possible . . . as the whole of Chowrasee Des was being raised by Shah Mall'. On the night before the latter's fateful confrontation with the volunteer forces, his emissaries were reported to have 'traversed every village of Chowrasee Des, calling all who could bear arms to assist them and declaring that Shah Mall would meet the pale-faced invaders of his territory on the morrow and annihilate the entire party or die in the attempt'. And after his death Sajjaram tried to rally the Jats of 'Chowrasee Des', while it was to all of 'the Chowrasee Des' that Dunlop addressed his proclamation calling on them to surrender.[38] Thus the messages of in-

---

[35] Dunlop to Meerut Commissioner, 26 July 1857, *PP*, paras 6–8, p. 886; Dunlop, *Khakee Ressalah*, pp. 95–9.

[36] Sapte, 8 July 1858, F8/1858, RD, MCR, UPRA.

[37] Dunlop, *Khakee Ressalah*, p. 91.

[38] Ibid., pp. 95, 99–100, 108; Dunlop to Meerut Commissioner, 26 July 1857, *PP*, p. 887.

surgency and counter-insurgency were both transmitted on a common wavelength.

Chowrasee Des offers us a rare glimpse into rebel perception. 'Chowrasee' or 'eighty-four' refers to a tract of country containing that number of villages in the occupation of a particular tribe.[39] It is a notion associated with clan settlements and the spread of kinship linkages over an area among Jats as well as the other castes in Uttar Pradesh. The very fact of the growth of hamlets from original villages and their establishment by junior members of particular clans at the time of their expansion in an area might have led to this notion. Each of the principal clans of the Jats in Meerut—the Gathwalas, the Baliyans and the Salaklain—had its claim to an area comprising eighty-four villages. That area would first be demarcated by the khaps. The khap itself was a unit comprising villages, most of which were linked with each other by people claiming common descent from the original settlers. Such descent groups formed their own thokes based on lineages and tried to restrict the transfer of proprietary rights among themselves. When these thokes organized themselves into a council for common action, it took the shape of the khap. The khap was named after the dominant caste and clan, but did not exclude other clans within the village when a common decision was taken. A khap could be divided into smaller units like *ganwands*. But its jurisdiction was said to extend over eighty-four villages or the Chowrasee, although the actual number could in fact be smaller. For example the Baliyan khap had its jurisdiction over no more than fifty-four villages, twenty-four having been depopulated and 'conquered' by the Pathans. Yet the area was still called the 'Chowrasee' of the Baliyan khap. It was thus that clan settlement corresponded to territorial space.

Equally important was the persistence of the notion of Chowrasee Des in collective memory. Thus, in Pandit Kaha Rambhat's eighteenth-century chronicle of the Jats of this area, political action against outsiders and resistance to the oppression of the state since the time of the Delhi Sultanate are often traced to decisions taken at

[39] The argument in this and the next para is based on H. Elliot, *Memoirs on the History, Folklore & Distribution of Races of the North West Provinces of India*, vol. II, ed. J. Beames (London, 1869), pp. 46–7; ibid., *Meerut Settlement*, p. 191; Gillan, p. 10; W. Crooke, *The Tribes & Castes of the North Western Provinces and Oudh*, vol. II (Delhi, 1974), *passim*; M.C. Pradhan, *The Political System of the Jats of Northern India* (Bombay, 1966), appx. 2–4.

khap council meetings. Baraut, in this chronicle, was mentioned again and again as a place where the panchayat met to decide upon measures which would be obeyed by the various clans and villages. Baoli and Sirsauli were the other villages in which such councils resolved on actions against the sultans and the Mughal rulers. Whatever the reliability of this chronicle, the fact remains that by the late eighteenth century the Jats of this area were thinking in terms of political units like khaps and describing their memory of common actions in the past in terms of those units. The names of the villages which were prominent in the chronicle were also important centres of rebellion. In the 1830s Elliot noted the existence of the Chowrasee 'in almost their pristine integrity' among the Jat and the Rajput communities. He recognized 'the ceremony of the binding of the turbans' as an important source of prestige and respectability for the headmen of the khaps by the members of the Des. Later, decades after the mutiny, other administrators too were to acknowledge the persistence of the notion of designating particular areas called Des by the Jats. Thus Shah Mal's appeal for the defence of Chowrasee Des against the intruders relied both on lineage and tradition to make itself understandable to the people of his locality. For they were aware of the tradition of common action against the state even in pre-colonial days. It was therefore possible for the rebel leader to summon to his aid the collective memory of a teritorial space over which he could claim to wield an authority hallowed by tradition. And by the same token the English force could be identified as tresspassers ('pale-faced invaders') violating the sanctity of Chowrasee Des, the country of his ancestors and his clan.

What emerges from our discussion is that there were various levels in the mobilization for rebellion. At a primary level a notion of community organized along ethnic settlements and an aversion to the encroachment of an alien power into this territorial unit determined the domain of rebel authority. However, that space was not a mere geographical notion. It was embedded in a collective consciousness, sustained by clan memory and history, to which the rebel appealed. However, in this type of mobilization it was by no means certain that each village belonging to the khap would join the rebellion. As has been noticed above, Shah Mal, after his escape from Busodh, collected his forces by 'raising village after village', and sixty villages were said to have 'individually' joined his forces (although many of them withdrew as soon as the victory of the En-

glish was imminent after the fall of Delhi). However, the other
thokes of Shah Mal's own village remained aloof. Dunlop, during
his counter-insurgency operations, noted how some of the villages
were hostile and others were vacillating or friendly.[40] Thus he found
Deolah and Hussaodah docile enough to pay up the instalments of
revenue due to them, while Bulaynee prevaricated, and the Gujar
village of Bichpoorie, which 'had taken an active part in all Shah
Mall's misdoings', was considered so hostile as to deserve destruction. And, again, the village Burka was friendly, while the neighbouring village Mánee Ghat, 'where Shah Mall and some of his principal dacoits were assembled', was certainly not so. Any single factor such as faction, feuds, clan or caste would therefore not explain
the variations in rebel mobilization. An understanding of the latter
must also take into account the perception of conflicts and alliances
by the participants themselves in terms of their own codes and the
transformations of symbolic relations within that code.

On this was grafted the authority of Delhi. Jat clans have earlier
been known to seek adjustment with the power in Delhi. In our case
both Shah Mal and the rebel force at Delhi needed each other. Each
was aware of the other's strength and importance. And this recognition was overlaid with an intense hatred of alien rule. The Meerut
commissioner noticed how even after Shah Mal's death some of his
followers continued to show 'the bitterest animosity against us',
how 'in order to show their hatred' they dug and ploughed up the
'made road as a Feringhee institution', while, according to Stokes,
the Jats of Lagoswar and the Chauhan Rajputs of Khair, despite
their traditional hostility towards each other, combined in 'their
hatred to British rule'.[41] This hatred was a rubric that was ever present in the rebellion of Shah Mal, and was more clearly focused in
the events following his death.

The elimination of Shah Mal was important for the reduction of
Delhi. The government 'had promised a reward of 1,000 rupees for
the apprehension or head of Shah Mall'.[42] In July the counter-
insurgency operations against him ran into a massive resistance
from 'a large crowd of armed men seven thousand in number', and
to an official who witnessed it all it appeared as if 'the whole coun-

[40] Dunlop to Meerut Commissioner, 26 July 1857, *PP*, p. 886.
[41] Williams' comments on the Amnesty List, F101/1859, MCR, UPRA: Stokes,
pp. 192–4.
[42] Williams' Letter, 7 August 1857, *PP*, p. 885.

try was rising; native drums, signal to the villagers to assemble were
beating in all directions and crowds were seen to be moving up . . .'
Dunlop, who led these operations, was forced to fly from 'Black
Douglas Shah Mall' and remarked ruefully that 'flight from villagers, in whatever numbers, was rather a shock to dignity', for the
'sundry flowers of the rhetoric in which the Hindoostani language
is rich . . . were gracefully accorded to me by Shah Mall's men'. He
narrowly escaped from the charge by Bhagta, the rebel's nephew,
and was chased upto Barout. There, in an orchard south of Barout,
the Khakee Ressalah—as the volunteer force was named—and the
followers of Shah Mal fought a pitched battle in which the rebel
leader was killed.[43] The private who killed the rebel gave a vivid description.

> I saw, in the distance, two horsemen armed with spears flying from us
> as fast as their horses could take them. I put spurs to my horse and
> overtook them after a chase of two minutes. The horseman nearer to
> me whom I never for a moment imagined to be Shah Mall dropped his
> sword at that time, but still retained his spear, the folds of his turban
> were also trailing on the ground.

The soldier twice shot him in the back. 'But recovering himself at a
moment when I never fancied he could have risen, he took me at a
disadvantageous turn and wounded me in two places'. The second
wound might have proved to be fatal, 'had I not suddenly held the
spear which he was driving with all his force at me and just at this
moment Azeem Beg, Sowar came up, thrust him with his spear on
which he fell swearing and abusing the sowar'.[44] His body was
hacked to pieces and the head severed by the order of Parker who
recognized him.

Now the head of Shah Mal, the rebel leader, became a symbol.
To the English this was a great victory and that victory needed to
be demonstrated. The force marched through the area with two
symbols of power and authority. As Dunlop wrote:

> We carried on a small silken Union Jack as the banner of the Volun-
> teers and on this occasion an ensign also, in the shape of Shah Mall's
> gory head struck on a long spear. The last was necessary, to prove to

[43] For details, see Dunlop, *Khakee Ressalah*, pp. 99–106. Dunlop's letter, as in
fn. 40. William's report, cited in *DG: Meerut*, pp. 178–9.

[44] Tonnochy to Tyrwhitt, 20 July 1857, *PP*, p. 888.

the country people who knew the sternly resolute features of old ruf-
fian well, that their leader was really dead.[45]

To the rebel, Shah Mal's head was a symbol of defiance, an object of honour. There were 'sundry reports of a meditated attack
by Rajputs and others to recover Shah Mall's head'. Dunlop's
army was under constant threat from insurgents led by Suraj Mal
and Bhagta, who were raising the countryside. 'We were followed
down to the ford by a large body of Mawee Jats who hoped they
might find an opportunity of taking the head of Shah Mall from
us', wrote Dunlop. The rebel died but the rebellion continued.
Shah Mal's successors refused to surrender and sided with the rebels in Muzaffarnagar, Rohilkhand and Awadh.

### III. *Devi Singh*

Devi Singh, a village rebel of Tappa Raya in Mathura, had in his
biographer his principal enemy, Mark Thornhill, magistrate of
Mathura, who wrote the biography for future generations 'as illustrative of native habits and of the condition of the country at that
time'. But the political implication of rural rebellion was not
altogether lost on even such a biographer. 'Dayby Sing's career was
brief and in its incidents, rather ludicrous', wrote Thornhill; 'it
might have been otherwise. With as small beginnings Indian dynas-
ties have been founded. He was the master of fourteen villages.
Runjeet Sing commenced his conquests as lord of no more than
twenty-five'.[46]

Devi Singh's brief and 'ludicrous career' is important for us
because in his rebellion there was no outside intervention or mediation. It was entirely the affair of a peasant community of a small
area. Raya, which was included in pargana Mat until 1860 and there-
after in pargana Mahaban, was a busy market town at the centre of a
group of villages. It followed the usual pattern of Jat settlement in
this area. Raya itself had no arable land. But it was considered 'as
the recognised centre of as many as twenty-one Jat villages which
were founded from it'. The very name of the town was derived from
that of its founder, Rae Sen, the ancestor of the Jats of Godha clan.

[45] Dunlop, *Khakee Ressalah*, pp. 110, 112. Dunlop to Meerut Commissioner, 26
July 1857, *PP*, p. 887.
[46] Mark Thornhill, *The Personal Adventures and Experiences of a Magistrate
during the Rise, Progress and Suppression of Indian Mutiny* (London, 1884), p. 109.

It was the Jats of this clan who were the dominant cultivators of this area.[47]

The most visible symbol of authority in tappa Raya was an old fort built by Jamsher Beg and renovated by Thakur Daya Ram of Hathras in the early nineteenth century. The latter's control over this area ended with his subjugation by the English in 1817. Still, his family continued to be the dominant magnates in this area and the loyalty of Thakur Govind Singh, his son, in 1857 helped the house to recover much of its old position.[48] During the mutiny Tappa Raya had a police station and tehsil. But more important than that, it was dominated by the Baniyas. Janaki Prasad, Jamuna Prasad, Matilal and Kishan Das were leading mahajans who lived in this town. It was their masonry houses that were 'the most conspicuous buildings in that place', and a 'large orchard of mango and Jaman trees, twenty-two bighas in extent, that adorned the tappa was planted by Kisan Das'. Gokul Dass Seth, who headed a list of prominent mahajans made on the eve of the mutiny, lived in Raya, as did Nanda Ram, head of the rising Baniya family in the region.[49]

The region around Raya was not as fertile as that of Barout. The soil varied in quality and irrigation was carried on from wells rather than from canals.[50] The Jats were the largest group in a population devoted exclusively to agriculture. In Mahaban pargana, which included tappa Raya and its villages, the Jats cultivated in the 1870s 22 per cent of sir lands and 35 per cent of the area as occupant ryots and tenants-at-will. From the malik Jats to the tenant Jats they cultivated 58 per cent of the entire area between themselves. Each clan had settled in a compact area: the Rayat had their holdings in Sankh, the Dusar in Sonai and the Godhe in Raya.

The very history of village settlement and the nature of holding had strengthened the community and clan feelings. 'It would seem',

[47] F.S. Growse, *Mathura, A District Memoir* (third edition, 1883), pp. 401–2. All the three editions of this work have been used in this essay and references will be made hereafter by the author's name followed by a numeral in parenthesis to indicate the edition used: e.g. Growse (3), p. 86. R.S. Whiteway, *Report on the Settlement of the Muttra District* (Allahabad, 1879), p. 33.

[48] *Statistical, Descriptive and Historical Account of the North Western Provinces of India*, vol. VIII, *Muttra*, pt. I (Allahabad, 1884), p. 132. Hereafter *Statistical, etc.*

[49] Growse (3), p. 402. Also D.L. Drake-Brockman, ed., *DG: Mathura*, pp. 323–4. List of Principal Mahajans and Sahukars in the District of Mathura, BR, Mathura, ACR, vol. 146, UPRA.

[50] Drake-Brockman, pp. 278–9; Growse (2), p. 86; Whiteway, p. 32.

wrote a settlement officer,[51] 'that all the Jat share-holders... are really or theoretically descendants of one man, the original founder of the estate. As his descendants increased and the cultivation around the old site grew, so new colonies of shareholders planted themselves in hamlets near their fields separating off their cultivation but still retaining their share in the ancestral Khera'. Nowhere was 'this tendency of the Jat caste to find new offshoots from the parent village as the community grows while at the same time the interest in the parent site remains undiminished' better illustrated than in Raya and Sonai.

Raya had twenty-four estates, covering nearly 12,000 acres. There was a group of older settlements comprising fourteen villages called Chaudah Taraf. The others were its offshoots. The history of the adjoining tappa, Sonai, with its town, Ayra Khera, had similar features. It was the recognized centre of eighteen villages. Nain Sin had established the *khera*, and it was his sons and grandsons who founded the surrounding villages after their name and became the owners of new settlements. But the bazar of Ayra Khera remained the joint property of the clan and their joint permission was necessary for the establishment of any new shop. It was obligatory too that all members of the clan should gather at the Phul Dal festival in the month of Chait. All of the arable land was occupied by the members of Godha subdivision of the Jats.[52]

Thus in this area community or clan-feeling sustained itself by a close correspondence between landholding and clan-settlement. It also had tradition, memory and customs to feed on. The khera, 'often an uninhabited site', but 'still remembered as the one that threw out separate villages as colony',[53] was the most visible symbol of a common origin, and attachment to it as the joint property of clan leaders the expression of a primordial solidarity. Each area had its dominant clan, which again had a local village or town to look back upon as the place which their common ancestor was said to have founded. Thus, tradition combined with the concentration of proprietorship in the hands of a particular clan to generate a consciousness that would express itself in any collective action such as an insurrection.

[51] Whiteway, p. 39.
[52] Growse (3), pp. 399–401.
[53] *Statistical, etc.* p. 136.

The land tenure was a bhaiyachara in perfection. By the 1830s the estates had been minutely subdivided into the various pattis and it was the pattidars who mattered most to the settlement officers. The pattidars were differentiated in terms of ownership. Some could own more than 500 bighas of land whereas others did not have more than sixty.[54] In the twenty years before the mutiny, however, the relations between pattidars and *biswadars* had come under strain. Stokes has argued that the revenue demand of the state as well as the administrative arrangements connected with the settlement operations were major factors which caused this strain. The settlement operations, for instance, were aimed at determining the precise ownership of each sharer, although, as J.G. Deedes, the officer on the spot in tappa Raya and Sonya pleaded with his superiors, 'an undivided patti or an undivided property in land', however 'foreign to all European ideas of property', was 'well understood by the people themselves', and therefore 'to make an individual family quarrel and divide their patrimony' could 'not tend much to the advantage of the society'. But the Board insisted on the recording of rights as joint proprietorship under 'the name of the managing and ostensible member of the family' and decided to change the village measurement to a new standard because such a measurement, they thought, would be 'correct and therefore more satisfactory to all'.[55]

The inflexibility of the settlements operations was compounded by the heavy revenue demand. In his report on the settlement in tappa Raya Deedes referred to 'the over-assessment and the resultant mortgages by which the government demand was provided for'. As the revenue demand was in many cases levied 'with little reference to the capabilities of the estate', its obvious result was 'in driving away the proprietary cultivator of the soil and eventually the loss of government is much greater than would have been incurred by granting relief in time, to say nothing of individual misery which has been caused by the numerous and repeated transfers'.[56]

[54] Deedes' letters, 1 December 1831, 4 February 1832. BR, NWP, 8 March 1833, Proc 43, UPSA.

[55] Macsween to the Board, 9 August 1832, BR, NWP, 8 March 1833, Proc 44, UPSA; Deedes to Macsween, 26 November 1832, BR NWP, 8 March 1833, Proc 47, UPSA. On measurements in Raya and Sonya, see Macsween's letter, 31 December 1832 & Deedes' letter, 5 December 1832, BR, NWP, 8 February 1833, Proc 65–70, UPSA.

[56] Settlement of Tappa Raya, Deedes' letter, 4 February 1832, ibid.

Moreover Deedes had noted the signs of a depression in the area during the 1830s. The loans from the indigo factories had dried up since the failure of farms. There was a sharp decline in the price of cotton—from Rs 50 per maund to as little as Rs 20. As Deedes observed, 'the village bohra ceased to make advances and the whole pargannah seems in distress'.[57] One of the effects of the depression was a substantial decrease in the number of wells in this area which was utterly dependent on well irrigation—a decrease related directly in the Agra division (and in Mathura district in particular) to a receding water-level caused by a drought as well as to the 'want of means . . . found in the co-parcener of a bhaiyachara village and in the non-proprietary tenant'.[58] Indeed by the 1840s the tracts of Sonya and Raya had been so reduced 'partly from drought and partly from overassessment' that Tyler, a local official, found a decrease in revenue demand essential in the former and a revision urgently needed in the latter. Yet in Raya the same official kept demands unchanged in eleven *mahals* and even increased it in two of them. Only six mahals out of nineteen got a minor revision, amounting to a mere 2 per cent decrease.[59] Arriving upon the scene on the eve of the mutiny, Thornhill was impressed by the consensus that was there 'among the natives . . . both respectable and lower orders' to the effect 'that the settlement of this district [was] severe'.[60]

In these circumstances the customary resistance of the bhaiyachara community to the alienation of its members' proprietary rights in favour of outsiders eroded slowly, over the years, before the onslaught of a few moneylender families. Nanda Ram, a petty trader who made a fortune from the sale of grains in the famine of 1838, was one of the first to penetrate into this region by mahajani transactions. He acquired a vast property extending over Mat as well as several of tappa Raya's villages—such as Acharu, Chura Hansi, Nagal, Gogu, Dhaku and Thana Amar Sing. Again, this pargana witnessed the rise of members of the Brahmin family of Jagdispore who had started their career as mere pedlars but made their fortune—they were moneylenders by profession—as they

[57] Deedes' letter, 1 December 1831, ibid.
[58] 'Note on the Decrease in the Number of Wells in the Agra Division', *Selections*, no. xxiv.
[59] Whiteway, p. 160.
[60] Thornhill to Unwin, 16 January 1855, Mathura—Revenue. ACR, Proc 14, vol. 145, UPRA.

built up 'a considerable estate out of lands which for most parts they held in mortgage'. Then there was the Brahmin Pachauri family of Gokharauli, members of which were sole proprietors of many of the villages in pargana Mahaban, while in each of the remaining villages of the pargana they owned at least one share, however small. This family had all the necessary political connections. They were traditionally tehsildars and one of their members, Kalyan Singh, was the *resaladar* major in the 17th regiment during 1857. Not on a par in social prestige with them, the Baniya called Jugal Kisore possessed one of the indigo factories in the town. It was to such moneybags that the proprietary rights in so many of the bhaiyachara villages of tappa Raya passed during the first half of the nineteenth century. Dhaku was established by the Dhokala Jats. The Jats were the chief cultivating caste. But Jamuna Prasad bought the rights of proprietorship in the villages from the descendants of the original settlers. Nagal was established by the Ram Singh Jats. Its Jat part was purchased by the baniyas. Tirwa and Saras were similarly lost to the Bohras. Acharu's share was held both by Nand Kishore and by Jamuna Prasad, the Baniyas of Raya. It is significant that these villages participated in their attack on Raya town during the mutiny.[61]

The process of mortgage and transfer was promoted to no small extent by administrative measures in the mid nineteenth century. Formerly in these bhaiyachara villages regular deeds against mortgages were not drawn up, an entry in a Bhai Khata being considered sufficient. When the money was paid up, the entry was also cancelled in the presence of witnesses. And there was no limit to redemption: 'land which has been mortgaged for upwards of 100 years being redeemed just as land which has only been in the possession of the mortgagee for one year'.[62] However, on the eve of the mutiny, legislation was brought to end this custom and a regulation introduced for the registration of the transfers and mortgages prior to the registration of a decree so that it could be accepted as a valid document in the court. As predicted by Wingfield, the act helped immensely to strengthen the position of moneylenders, who, thanks to their wealth and 'acquaintance with Civil Courts', made the most of it in order to undermine the bhaiyachara community by mort-

[61] Growse (1), part II (1874), pp. 86–7. These details are collated from the village lists in ibid., pp. 89–104.
[62] Whiteway, p. 43.

gages and transfers.[63] No wonder then that during the mutiny the moneylenders became the object of popular wrath in this area and confirmed, despite Stokes's arguments to the contrary, that the hatred of the Banias was caused by 'the loss of rights to urban moneylender and trader under the pressure of the British land revenue system'.[64]

Thornhill, magistrate of Mathura district at the time, was struck by the suddenness with which the rural jacqueries began: 'The news of the insurrection and the proclamation of the king of Delhi had now become known among the native population, the country immediately became disturbed . . . The news of the mutiny had spread with great rapidity and the whole country had risen almost instantaneously'. And he went on to say, 'A month before the country had been in profound tranquility; the sudden change to the anarchy without any apparent cause was very extra-ordinary and is a matter of the attentive consideration of the government'.[65]

To him the intensity and swiftness of the rebellion and the breakdown of authority in the countryside was a thing beyond comprehension. Nevertheless he attempted to describe a pattern. Thus: 'Kuar Dildar Ali Khan, a large Zamindar in Pargannah Mat was murdered by his villagers; on the 23rd May Omrow Bahadoor a relative of his who had estates in the Purgannah Noh Jheel had been besieged in his house; . . . several other murders were committed and other outrages, the particulars of which I do not remember'. And, the narrative continued, 'the whole district was in anarchy. The police and revenue establishments were everywhere ejected or if permitted to remain, allowed to remain on mere sufferance; the buniahs were plundered, new proprietors were ejected and murdered and the King of Delhi proclaimed . . .'.[66] Apparently, in the perception of the local guardian of law and order, there was nothing in the unfolding scene of a mighty rural upsurge except a generalized lawlessness which obliterated for him the individuality of the rebels and the specificity of the rebellion.

For us, however, these specificities are important as a guide to the social tensions in the area. Dildar Khan, for instance, had his estates

[63] Wingfield to Taylor, 2 January 1854, BR, Mathura, ACR, vol. 144, UPRA.
[64] Stokes, ch. VII *passim.*
[65] Thornhill to Harvey, 10 August 1858, *NE*, paras 5 and 22.
[66] Ibid., paras 10 and 19.

in Bhadanwara.[67] It seems that he was trying to consolidate his position by ejecting a large number of proprietors and thus came into conflict with the Jats. Harvey described him as 'an opulent but overbearing and unpopular Zamindar' who had 'met his end at the hand of his own dependants and neighbours'. This incidentally was the first jacquerie in Mathura district, and its seat was the pargana to which Raya belonged.

Thornhill and his forces remained at Raya for some days 'tranquilising the country'. All round him there was evidence of a collapse of British authority: 'in a circle of a few miles about five or six zamindars had declared themselves independent, assumed the title of Rajah and proclaimed the King of Delhi . . . *the impression that the English rule had ceased was universal*'.[68] The cessation of the existing authority was part of a general belief in rural areas. Dunlop had noticed the same in Meerut. Thornhill was to recollect later on how this belief was linked in popular imagination with the hope for an alternative authority in the form of a restoration of the Mughal emperor: 'Their talk was all about the ceremonial of the palace, and how it would be revived . . . As I listened, I realised as I had never done before, the deep impression that the splendour of the ancient court had made on the popular imagination, how dear to them were its traditions and how faithfully, all unknown to us they had preserved them'.[69] Thus the overthrow of colonial authority helped to rekindle an old tradition that got its verbal expression in proclamations in the name of the Mughal emperor. The idea of replacing the alien Raj by one that was the people's own—be it located in Delhi or nearer home at the seat of a rural insurrection—was very much in the air. It was in this context of political turmoil and high-pitched popular imagination that the revolt at tappa Raya broke out sometime between the end of May and early June.

The uprising, it has been stated, began with an attack on the township by the leading zamindars and the residents of the Chowdah Taraf, i.e. the core villages surrounding Raya. The zamindars of Acharu Laru named Dhani Ram and Sesh Ram (Sriram), Hulasi, Sawae and Akbar of Saras, and Chain Sukh, Jat lumbardar of Tirwa,

[67] Growse (1), part II, p. 72; M. Thornhill to G.F. Harvey, 10 August 1858; *NE*, para. 22.

[68] *NE*, para. 22. Emphasis added.

[69] Thornhill, *Personal Adventures*, p. 7.

were the persons prominent in the raid.[70] The role of the Chowdah Taraf on this occasion was particularly significant. 'The fourteen villages had in times gone by, formed a single estate', wrote Thornhill. He added

> During the half century of our rule they had been sold and resold, and the proprietors reduced to the condition of mere cultivators. But they still held the tradition of their former supremacy and looked forward to the time when they might recover it. On the breaking out of the mutiny that time seemed to them to have arrived, and they hastened to avail themselves of it. In each village they rose and turned on the new owners; of these most fled, the rest fought. In these fights Dayby Sing came to the front. ... Eventually, Dayby Singh's fellow caste-men obtained the victory, re-established themselves in their ancient position, and this done, Dayby Sing elected himself as their Rajah.[71]

It was thus that a peasant king was made, deriving his authority from an age-old tradition of the Jats. That tradition asserted itself in the colour of the yellow dress Devi Singh put on as the insignia of his new status, 'yellow among the Hindoos being the sign of royalty', and even in the language used by fellow-villagers in addressing him (as Thornhill was amused to remark) 'with the usual string of adulatory epithets which Eastern etiquette demands', such as 'the lord of beneficence, the source of wealth ... the supporter of the poor ... the great Rajah Dayby Singh, monarch of the fourteen villages, the victorious in war'. But, although the sanction behind the raja of Raya was a tradition much older than the idioms and institutions of politics introduced by the Raj he had subverted, he had to rely on some of those institutions for the exercise of his authority.

> On entering the town, Dayby Sing proceeded to the school-room, a building lately erected by our Government. In this he established his headquarters ... He then constituted a government of his own, which he formed on the English model. He appointed a Board of Revenue, a Supreme Court of Judicature, a Commissioner, a Magistrate and a Superintendent of Police. For this last office he did not consider any of his own people properly qualified; so he sent a message to the late incumbent begging him to return and promising him an increase of salary.

In modelling his own government thus on the very structure of authority he aimed at destroying, Devi Singh demonstrated very

---

[70] Growse (2), Village Lists.

[71] This and all other direct quotations in the rest of this section are taken from Thornhill, *Personal Adventures*, pp. 100–9, unless otherwise mentioned.

clearly indeed the historic limitations of the insurgent consciousness of his time. The rebel had not yet found his way to his own world.[72]

Within such limitations the new regime appears to have settled down to a fairly well-defined, if simple, administrative routine. According to Thornhill, Devi Singh would come to the town at dawn every day, take his seat at his headquarters in the schoolhouse, receive petitions, hear complaints and dictate despatches. 'This done, he devoted the rest of his day to plundering the Bunniahs which he did very deliberately, all the town assisting'. Settling accounts with the moneylenders was perhaps the most distinctive feature of this insurrection. Indeed this turned out to be the primary expression of the new regime's coercive powers—its powers to judge and to punish. Every morning a Baniya would be brought to trial before the raja, cross-examined, entreated to declare his hoardings, and surrender bonds and mortgage deeds. He would be let off if his response was found satisfactory. Otherwise he would be 'put to the torture', but apparently without any excessive severity, for Thornhill testifies to having 'found no case where any Bunniah had been seriously hurt'.

It was not corporal punishment but pillage that was used by Devi Singh to reduce the moneylenders of Raya. Their shops as well as houses were subjected to this particular form of violence. 'Every shop was completely plundered and not only plundered but wrecked. The doors were torn out, the verandahs pulled down, the floors dug up, and also great holes dug in walls. Whatever was worth carrying off had gone to the villages, the rest lay in the street. The roadway was covered with torn account-books, broken bottles, fragments of jars and boxes, besides the debris of the floors and verandahs'. The dwelling-houses fared even worse. 'In the search for hidden treasures the smaller ones had been nearly pulled to pieces; all of them were more or less reduced to ruins'. Such disciplinary proceedings would usually terminate in the release of an offending Baniya, for 'like a cobra deprived of its poison bag, without his documents he was considered harmless'.

It was with pillage that the insurrection had started, when according to a *barqandaz* of the local thana, 'carts laden with salt and gram' were plundered by a crowd of 1,000 men in tappa Raya.[73]

[72] Cf. Guha, pp. 75–6.

[73] Deposition of Dindar Khan, Barqandaz of Thana Raya, *FSUP*, v, pp. 695–6.

And pillage, that 'quintessential aspect of insurgency',[74] continued to articulate the violence of the people in its most radical form under Devi Singh's authority. More than any other it was indeed this collective action that effectively mobilized the masses around his power base. For the highly popular character of the attacks on the moneylenders is clearly attested by Thornhill: 'When Dayby Singh advanced to call them to account he had with him the sympathies of the entire population', and the raja plundered their shops and houses 'very deliberately, all the town assisting'.

But Devi Singh did not reckon with the strength of the empire. To him the colonial state was a local affair and 'having driven out the police he thought he had overthrown our government'. This want of maturity, perhaps historically inevitable, was soon to cost him his life and his little kingdom. For the audacity of the armed peasantry, roused *en masse* to settle accounts with the Baniyas—the element of local society still loyal to the Raj in 1857—and Devi Singh's expressed intention to drive Thornhill, the district magistrate, out of his refuge in an opulent banker's house in Mathura city, prompted the latter to make an example of Raya. On the arrival of the Kotah contingent from Agra to free him from a state of virtual seige, he led it into an attack on the rebel village on 15 June, where he seized Devi Singh and Sri Ram and hanged them. That marked the end of the short-lived counter-Raj in tappa Raya and the beginning of the restoration of colonial authority in the area by early November.[75]

'Dayby Sing's career was brief, and in its incidents rather ludicrous', wrote Thornhill in concluding his reminiscences of the village raja. This condescension followed to no mean extent from his discovery of the utter ordinariness of his adversary. He was 'a very ordinary-looking man' who, when captured by the counter-insurgency forces, was hardly distinguishable from the other peasants; the seat of his power was 'an ordinary village, large and very ugly, a mere collection of mud huts closely huddled together'; the only document of state that fell into the hands of his captors was a letter from a fellow-villager that 'reported only the purchase of a few pennyworths of pepper and about an equal amount of sugar and vegetables'. But it is precisely in such ordinariness, scorned by the administrator turned historian, that the student of Indian history

[74] Guha, p. 156.
[75] *DG: Mathura*, p. 217. *Statistical, etc.*, p. 169.

must learn to identify and acknowledge the hallmark of a popular rebel leadership—a leadership which, even when it stands at the head of the masses in a struggle, bears on it all the marks of its emergence out of the ranks of the masses themselves.

## IV. *Gonoo*

Like the high farming areas of the Doab, the tribal areas of Chotanagpore too were affected by the rebellion of 1857. But here the sepoy element was marginal. The tribal people and their chiefs provided the main thrust of revolt against the government. However, once the insurrection gathered momentum the chiefs fell behind and an initiative began to grow from below. Gonoo, a Kol, was an ordinary cultivator in Singhbhum. The events of 1857 made him a rebel leader. The lowliest in terms of social status among our rebel characters, he is the least known to us. The material I have on him is scarce and fragmentary.

Singhbhum was divided by the river Samjai. The southern side of the river happened to be directly under British rule whereas the northern side was a part of the feudatory estate of the raja of Porahat and divided among various members of his family. However, the latter exercised only a loose authority over the ordinary inhabitants. The Larka Kol were organized into the militia of the feudatory chiefs and claimed a share of the booty from plunder and conquest as their remuneration. The raja on his part was satisfied with the nominal acceptance of his sovereignty by them and extracted no rent from them as cultivators.[76]

For the Kols the functional unit of their society was their village and clan. In the Kolhan estate the villages happened to be communities of corporate owners, and zamindari and the other intermediate tenures were but a superimposition.[77] The Kols' right to their land was as immutable as their relation with their clan. 'According to their theory', wrote Dalton, 'dispossession for generations can no

[76] L.S.S. O'Malley, *Bengal District Gazetteers: Singhbhum, Saraikella and Kharsawan* (Calcutta, 1910), p. 10. S.R. Tickell, 'Memoirs on Hodesam Improperly called Kolehan', *Journal of Asiatic Society of Bengal*, vol. IX, part II, 1840, pp. 689–700. E.T. Dalton, 'The Kols of Chotanagpore', *Transactions of the Ethnological Society of London*, vol. VI (London, 1867), pp. 10–12.

[77] T.S. Macpherson, *Final Report on the Operations for the Preparaticn of a Record of Rights in Pargana Porahat, Dist. Singhbhum* (Calcutta, 1908), p. 83.

more annul their rights in land than it can extinguish ties of their blood'.[78]

The Kols had two institutions—(1) *Manki* and *Moonda*, and (2) *Killi*. A moonda was the chief of his village, but he was merely *primus inter pares* and did not hold any special tenure. A group of such villages, usually seven to twelve in number, formed a *peer* or a *Ho* unit. The leader of this group was called 'manki'. A manki was probably 'a lineal descendent of the leading settler in the chief village in the group'. He might also have functioned as a military chief to organize the armed people for the raja and maintain a link with him on behalf of the villages. However, his rights were not very different from those of ordinary subjects, and according to a knowledgeable officer, 'in the interior of the Kolhan, there had been, before the advent of the British, no acknowledged head or any king'.[79] Most of these villages conformed to the killis or clans who chose a particular area and settled there.

After the Kol insurrection of 1831 the colonial government took away fifteen peers from the Porahat king, and, along with eleven other peers, brought the southern Kolhan under its rule, leaving the northern part under the rajas. In this estate the government formalized the position of the mankis and the moondas, who were entrusted with the duty of revenue collection and the general superintendence over law and order in lieu of a commission. They became a functionary of the government and bound themselves by an oath taken to that effect before the agent to the Governor-General. The oath ran as follows: that they would not receive or obey 'any order' verbal or written, of any rajah or any zamindar or any of their subordinates'. This amounted to a transfer of their allegiance to a new authority. Hereafter in the selection of a manki his local influence would be considered, but the final right of selection lay with the government—which could exclude anybody thought to be unfit.[80]

In these peers the government fixed a tax on each cultivator at the rate of eight annas for every plough. Between 1844 and 1850 it made

[78] Dalton, 'The Kols', p. 21.

[79] Macpherson, pp. 14, 108–9; O'Malley, pp. 173–4; J.A. Craven, *Final Report on the Settlement of the Kolhan Government Estate, District Singhbhum* (Calcutta, 1898), p. 29.

[80] P.C. Raychaudhuri, ed., *Singhbhum Old Records* (Patna, 1958), pp. 54–5. Also see K.K. Basu, 'Early Administration of the Kol Peers in Singhbhum and Bamanghati', *Journal of the Bihar and Orissa Research Society* (Sept.–Dec. 1956).

several attempts to increase the assessment paid by the killis and to estimate the lands actually cultivated. Such official interventions 'had the effect of making the Koles restless'. So the mankis made a compromise by agreeing to pay one rupee instead of eight annas and the government promised to make no enquiry and levy no new tax for a period of twelve years. This fiscal adjustment relieved the headmen of the task of sending annual reports on the acreage of cultivation and enabled them to impose assessments on their ryot according to their own judgement. But the compromise was not unattended with the usual threats. A recalcitrant moonda refusing to pay the higher rate would not obtain *pattahs* and villages refusing to comply would be assessed strictly. It was also considered 'prudent' that military presence in the area should be strengthened 'against every possible contingency'. By this combination of compromise and threat the revenue was already doubled before 1857. Between 1837 and 1852 the amount had risen gradually from Rs 5,108 to Rs 8,523, but the figure for 1854 was Rs 17,000.[81]

There is no doubt that this assessment was light in comparison to that of other regions, and led the English officials to believe that the revolt of 1857 in Chotanagpore was merely an expression of the innate fighting nature of the Larka Kols. What they failed to acknowledge was that the very presence of the colonial power and its attempt to tinker with the traditional institutions had created a new situation. The writen oaths, annual visits by the commissioner, insistence on the regular payment of tax, the attempts to increase the rate of assessment and to change the mode of assessment had led to the development of a structure much stronger and more formal than that of the older segmentary authority. The traditional mankis and moondas had become revenue collectors as well as police functionaries on behalf of the government. As a result around 1857 the mankis were a divided group: a large number of them tried to uphold their older loyalties whereas quite a few looked up to their new masters. In fact, it is reported that in 1857 only those Kols who 'had in former times been retained by the rajah of Porahat' joined the rebellion.[82] Again, the sanction of the mankis' power lay within the community. By giving them some police powers the colonial state entrusted them with the task of punishing such newly defined 'crimes' as witch-hunting, which were in fact a part of traditional

[81] Raychaudhuri, pp. 40–5, 48–9.
[82] O'Malley, p. 40.

practice in Singhbhum.[83] Altogether, it was the attempt made by the colonial regime to intervene in the traditional institutions of the Kol and thereby to disrupt older communal ties which prepared the ground for the conflicts of 1857 in this area.

The rebellion began in Chotanagpore with the mutiny of the Ramgarh batallions. But the mutineers were opposed by the Kols who looked upon the plundered treasury as their own and resented its appropriation by the sepoys.[84] Meanwhile, the traditional rivalry between the chiefs of Porahat and Khursawan surfaced at this juncture, and Arjun Singh, maharaja of Porahat, who was to play so confusing a part in the struggle just begun, 'appeared on the scene. . . vacillating. . . at one moment acting the part of a loyal feudatory and doing good work for government and the next in rebellion, leagued with the sepoys he had just been opposing'.[85] While he vacillated, pressure built up from below for action. Juggo Dewan and his supporters were preparing for a showdown. A proclamation appears to have been issued in the king's name but without his concurrence. The arrow of war, that traditional method of transmission of war-like messages, began to circulate, defying the warnings issued by the English to the mankis against its use.[86] On 20 November the king was attacked and fled. Juggo Dewan, thought to have been responsible for the attack, was summarily executed by the authorities in the centre of the bazaar at that place 'and his body was left exposed until dark'. By that time 'the character of the Mutiny . . . had entirely changed', as an official observed, and 'the Sepoy element had disappeared'.[87] The mutiny of the Ramgarh battalions was transformed into a rebellion of the Kols.

[83] Ricketts had noted how the mankis and moondas were reluctant to report the cases of witch-hunting because, to the community, it was no crime. H. Ricketts, *Report on the District of Singhbhum, 1854*, Selections from the Records of the Bengal Government, no. 16, para 107.

[84] E.T. Dalton, *Descriptive Ethnology of Bengal* (Calcutta, 1872; reprint Delhi, 1978), p. 183.

[85] F.B. Bradley-Birt, *Chotanagpore, A Little Known Province of the Empire* (London, 1903), p. 220.

[86] Dalton to Lushington, 30 Sept. 1859, JP, 27 October 1859, Proc 167, WBSA, para. 14. Deposition of Dubroo, son of Sikur, resident of Mouzah Kossee, Purgunnah Colehan, JP, WBSA. Birch's letter, 23 November 1857, *PP*, 625–8. W. Crooke, 'Secret messages and symbols used in India', *Journal of the Bihar and Orissa Research Society*, vol. v, part iv, Dec. 1919.

[87] Bradley-Birt, p. 225.

Out of this process of transformation Gonoo emerged as a leader.
His own perception of that process was recorded thus in his testimony at his trial:

> The whole country was in revolt. . . All the moondahs and mankis
> went to the Rajah; I was with them. The Rajah asked us what we were
> going to do. We replied that the Sahibs have run away and you are
> now our ruler, we will hold to you. Afterwards, the Rajah called us
> and said see I have been hunted from Chuckradherpore and Porahat
> and am now obliged to live in jungles. What will you do? Will you
> fight for me? We said we would fight and swore to do so. Then he
> assembled all the *Bhuiyas* and *Dhorrowas* and gave their pay and arms
> and an army was collected and we went to Ajoodiah with the intention
> of fighting with Chuckdher Singh of Seraikellah [the traditional rival of
> the Raja of Porahat].[88]

Apparently the initiative came from below. The people, headed by
their chiefs, appealed to the raja to perform his traditional role as a
leader of the whole people at a time when the belief had gained
ground that the authority of the English had vanished and all the
older ties between king, headmen and people had been revived. The
raja on his part asked the subjects for their support and, on obtaining that, ordered armed action to begin. The will of the people thus
merged with royal consent, inaugurating the rebellion as a project of
the entire community.

Dalton described Gonoo as 'the most active adherent of the ex-
rajah of Porahat amongst Singhbum or Larka Kols and the principal
agent in spreading disaffection amongst them and the leader of the
men of that tribe'. One witness testified that 'during the disturbances of 1857 he was the leader of all the Hoes from Kolehan who
joined the rajah', and another that 'his name was in everybody's
mouth'. And according to the manki of Barpeer, the Kols who
opposed the English army at Seringsaraghaut 'acted under Gonoo's
orders'.[89]

It is as a leader of the Barpeer Kols that Gonoo first made his
name. He was an inhabitant of Jyunteegarh in Barpeer. This area
had a tradition of rebellion, and was, according to Dalton, 'one of
the most disaffected Peers during the disturbances'.[90] Here, by all
accounts, Gonoo mobilized the community: 'the people all ack-

[88] Gonoo's Testimony, JP, May 1864, Proc 30–31, WBSA.

[89] Dalton's letter, 15 March 1864, and Evidence of Rainse and Konka, ibid.

[90] Dalton to Lushington, 6 September 1859. JP, 29 September 1859, para 4, Proc
55, WBSA.

nowledged him as a leader'.[91] As he was to recall later: '. . . the rajah sent emissaries to Buntrea and Barpeer to collect men . . . I had come to the Bar Peer and heard from the Kols that they had defeated the sahibs . . . Then all the Mankees and Moondahs determined to fight again . . . and we assembled at Seringsara Ghat'.[92]

However, it was at Koordiha that Gonoo established his authority as one of a triumvirate (the others being Raghu Deo and Sham Kurran) who had, for all practical purposes, taken over control from Arjun Singh when the latter found refuge there after the fall of Porahat. Here the raja was virtually a prisoner in the custody of the rebel army dominated by the Barpeer Kols. He 'had no intention of opposing the Sahibs . . . but the others used to abuse him for this and say that they will fight'. His feeble-mindedness made him suspected as well as despised by the rebels. He was 'always attended by the *nugdees* (armed guards) placed to look after him', and was 'subjected to great indignities by the people and no one showed him any respect or minded what he said'.[93]

As one of the supreme command of the rebel forces whose authority had replaced the raja's, Gonoo was involved in disciplining traitors and informers. The official policy of making mankis into local agents of the colonial administration had its allurements; a number of them worked as spies and informers to provide the regime with intelligence against the insurgents. Raghu Deo and Gonoo were anxious to wipe them off. Buddo Mahato was killed on an order from them because 'he was suspected of being a *Meriah* [a spy and go between]'.[94]

Gonoo is also known to have used the threat of collective violence in order to enforce co-operation from vacillating elements within the tribal community. The testimony of the manki of Chynepore peer, which remained loyal to the government, offers an interesting example in this respect.

> I am the mankee of Chynepore Peer . . . He came to my village after burning Chynepore with a force of coles. There was then in the village, a lot of *suggars* laden with the provision for Chuckerdherpore. The bullock-drivers had fled when they heard of the burning of

[91] Evidence of Bhogwan, JP, May 1864, Proc 30–31, WBSA.
[92] Gonoo's Testimony, ibid.
[93] Depositions of Anadhee and Muddo, JP, 27 October 1859, WBSA.
[94] Depositions of Dhunno, Sreedhar Mahato, and Madho, JP, ibid. Examination of Singa, JP, 11 August 1859, Proc 62–63, WBSA.

Chynepore . . . he ordered me to collect cattle to yoke in *suggars*. He threatened to burn the villages if cattles and coolies were not provided. So to save the village I gave them both . . . A very large body of insurgents were with Goono on this occasion. They filled the village and were in every house demanding food and drink. Goono was their leader. They all said so, I had not seen Goono before but they said this is Goono our leader, Don't you know him and what he will do to you if you disobey.[95]

'Gonoo our leader'. To be designated thus, Gonoo had to come a long way from his humble beginnings. His father Mata was the moonda of village Chonpattea of Barpeer. Gonoo was a pupil of Chybasa school, 'but when he left the school', said an acquaintance who knew him from his childhood, 'he became poor and took to evil ways, thieving and the like'. And yet another man of his tribe spoke of his murky background: 'He bore a bad character. His father died in jail for rebellion. His brother was hanged'.[96]

It was not unusual for a 'bad character' to emerge as a leader in the course of a peasant revolt. In the Santal *hool* Domon Dakait had been transformed into Domon Darogah, and as recently as in the 1970s the dacoit Rameshwar Ahir had become Sadhu Rameshwar, the legendary peasant leader of Bhojpur.[97] The same process which had transformed the sepoy rebellion into an uprising of the masses in Chotanagpore was also what transformed a poor Kol who had taken to 'evil ways'. The *talpatras*, seized by Birch in Kordiha, with their references to the emperor of Delhi, to Nana Sahib and Koer Singh, registered a dim awareness of this process among the tribal population of Singhbhum and a vague expectation of help from those quarters.[98] It was the displacement of authority both at the supra-local level of the colonial regime and at the local level of the Porahat raj that helped to generate among the rebels the sense of an alternative authority and invest a law-breaker from a family of law-breakers with a new legitimacy for his role as a leader. However, even that legitimacy had to justify itself in the name of that very au-

[95] Deposition of Chumro, JP, May 1864, WBSA.

[96] Evidence of Konka and Martum, ibid.

[97] For a discussion of Domon Darogah's career, see Guha, pp. 95–7. For Rameshwar Ahir, see K. Mukherjee and R. Jadav, *Bhojpur: Naxalism in the Plains of Bihar* (Delhi, 1980), pp. 73–8.

[98] For these *talpatras* see Appendix A: Abstract translation of the letter writings on the *tal*-leaves found in the village of Koordiha by L.T. Birch, JP, 27 October 1859, WBSA.

thority which the rebellion was busy undermining. In the days of the insurrection Gonoo was said to have constituted himself as 'chief of Singhbhum', and, 'styled as a mankee', he 'rode about on a horse'. But he claimed to derive the authority that went with such title and carriage from no other source than the raja himself. 'He came to my house', said a witness at his trial, 'with a writing on talpat which he said was an order from the Rajah and he asked us if we [would] obey it and collect men'. And he told someone else that 'he had been appointed sardar in Singhbhum by the Rajah and the Rajah had invested him with a turban and given a horse'. When Gonoo described himself to his captors as 'not a leader', but as 'a mere follower of the Rajah', he was not trying to evade responsibility for his actions, but expressing in his own words the authentic limitations of his political consciousness as a typical Kol rebel of his time.

### V. *Maulvi Ahmadullah Shah*

Unlike Devi Singh or Gonoo, Maulvi Ahmadullah Shah is well known to the historian. He was one of a number of maulvis who figured prominently in the rebellion of 1857. Among these there were celebrities like Maulvi Liaqat Ali of Allahabad and Fazl Huq Khairabadi of Delhi and Awadh, as well as lesser known ulema and maulvis whose names occur in the lists of proclaimed offenders drawn up by the British administrators for their respective jurisdictions in Aligarh or Bulandshahr or in the towns and *qasbahs* of Rohilkhand. Indeed their role was so suspect that the authorities made up a list indicating the behaviour of *maafi* landholders in each district of the North-Western Provinces during the mutiny. In view of this it may be quite in order here to discuss the career of the Maulvi of Fyzabad as an aid to our understanding of the popular movements of that time.

The Maulvi was a member of a grandee family of Carnatic. Educated in Hyderabad, he became an itinerant preacher when he was very young. It is said that he travelled widely and visited Arabia, Iran and even England. His spiritual preceptor was Mehrab Shah, a *pir* of Gwalior. He passed through several places in Rajputana and northern India preaching jehad against the English. In November 1856 he was in Lucknow and attracted large crowds to meetings where, according to a local newspaper, he called for jehad against the government. He was soon forced out of the city by the kotwal, who prohibited the public from seeing him and restrained his movements. A contemporary account describes him as a Sufi from Agra, who had a thousand disciples and rode in a palanquin, with a drum beaten in front and a line of his followers bringing up the rear. His disciples swallowed burning charcoals before the crowds, for those who did so would, according to the Maulvi, bring forth fire tomorrow and go to heaven after death. Among the people he was called 'Danka Shah' or 'Naqara Shah', the Maulvi with the drum. And 'the city was full of uneasy news'.[99]

From Lucknow the Maulvi came to Fyzabad where he settled in the serai of the town with his entourage and began to draw large crowds. The authorities suspected 'that there was an evident intention on the part of the Faqir to raise a riot and dissension among the people'. An officer sent to contact him 'found the road, the entrance and interior of the Suraee very much crowded'. Asked to disarm himself, 'the Faqir said he could not and would not give up his arms as he had received them from his Peer'. On the request to leave the town he replied that he would go away at his leisure. On 17 February the officer, with a group of soldiers, arrested the Maulvi after a clash in which the latter was wounded and three of his disciples were killed.[100]

The activities of the Maulvi had been taking place in an atmosphere of tension and apprehension. The talk of a war of jehad against the English was very much in the air since the deposition of Wajid Ali Shah. Then on 8 June 1857 the irregular cavalry and native infantry rose, and the Maulvi, who was not without his supporters even in jail, was freed and elected a leader by the mutineers.[101] He led the rebel forces, the 22nd Native Infantry, from Fyzabad to Lucknow. On 20 June the decisive battle at Chinhat took place and Sir Henry Lawrence was defeated. The Maulvi 'fought stubbornly' and was wounded in the foot.[102] It is to be noted that it was mainly the sepoys and the lower class who were involved in this crucial battle. A contemporary witness described their activities thus after Lucknow was taken:

[99] Iqbal Husain, 'Lucknow between the Annexation and the Mutiny' (Mimeo, Department of History, Aligarh); Amritlal Nagar, *Ghadar Ke Phul* (Delhi, 1981), pp. 193–4, 234–5.

[100] *FSUP*, I, pp. 381–2.

[101] Ibid., p. 386. G. Hutchinson, *Narrative of the Mutinies in Oudh* (London, 1859), p. 33.

[102] *FSUP*, II, p. 54.

At first, the *shuhdas* and other rifraffs of the town reached there early in the morning and plundered whatever they could lay their hands on. Suddenly, one of the shuhdas of Roomi Darwaza reviling his own men (shuhdas) said, 'Do not indulge in plundering. Draw the cannons and place them, in position at Machhi Bhawan [the old fort of Lucknow]. Gird up your loins and fight. This will give us a good name. People will say "how bravely a debased class of people stood against such a great enemy" '. Everyone agreed and got ready to fight.[103]

In taking the initiative the lower orders sensed a pride which was denied to them in ordinary times. Insurrection, they felt, was a moment when they could behave like the great and could challenge the great. They encircled the Bhawan and shelled it, forcing the English to evacuate it at night. On 2 July the shuhdas entered the palace, where they were joined by 'other rifraffs . . . from the different quarters of the city', and pillage went on until the evening. The popular excitement was described as below by an upper-class observer:

Encouraged by their unexpected success the debased *shuhdas* commited greater reprisals. They secured two guns and stood against the Machhi Bhawan front. They set up a *morcha* at Munshi Iltifat Hussain's Bunglow in Bhim Ka Takia and another under the tamarind tree opposite the hospital and began firing. Although all that fight was merely puerile still the *shuhdas* exceeded their limits indulging in taunts and jokes. Then they recruited a *Paltan* of their own with the permission of the Government. They went round to the doors of the wealthy, and gave threats and exacted money, which they lavishly spent on spicy and tasteful food. They took Halwa, Puri and sweets from the shops without making any payments. They reviled all sorts of people. They took gunpowder and other explosives from makers of fire-works (*atash-baz*) and paid them inadequately. There was a heap of hay in the garden of the school *Kothi* to which they set fire and thus produced huge bonfires which lit the city. They brought Mir Baqar Ali who lived at Pakka Pul and cut him into pieces at the gate of the Bara Imambara with the sword. Nobody can say why they committed that sacrilege for he was a Saiyid. They moved about with naked swords in their hands.[104]

This description catches some of the atmosphere of the rebellion. According to its author, an Ashraf, the lowly 'exceeded their limits', and consequently their servility gave way to self-assertion. They formed their own armed contingents and indulged in language and

103 Ibid., p. 55.
104 Ibid., p. 58.

behaviour that violated the norms of address and etiquette due from
the lower orders to their superiors. In the mood of the shuhdas
there was an element of festivity as well as defiance. The latter was
expressed in such actions as making up a platoon of their own, threatening the wealthy and exacting money from them, roaming about
with 'naked' swords and killing a Saiyid. The bonfire and fireworks
as well as their enjoyment of food, 'spicy and tasteful', had an element of celebration, celebration at the tasting of a power undreamt
of by the poor classes in ordinary times of order and peace.

It was from this 'festival of the oppressed' of Lucknow that the
Maulvi drew his support,—'his considerable following of pig-
headed persons', as an Ashraf contemptuously called it.[105] But his
authority was soon challenged by Birjis Qadir's newly formed rebel
court which was virtually led by Begam Hazrat Mahal and Mammoo Khan. To the latter the Maulvi's popularity seemed to be a
threat to the royal court. 'So popular a commander was the Moulvie
with the Mutineers both on account of his bravery and his holy
character', said Wazir Khan, 'that the Begum after a time began to
dread his paramount influence as dangerous to her authority.
Accordingly she organized a party to diminish the Moulvie's power
and the measures she took to that end did not stop short of open
attack. He then left the capital and took up his abode in a garden
house in the suburbs'.[106] His concern for the civilian population
also upset the court and was used by it to undermine his authority.
'He had it proclaimed that the citizens might put to death all persons attempting to plunder them, and taking up his abode in the
beautiful building known as the Observatory, adopted all the airs
and ceremonials of the royalty'. That played into the hands of the
party in the palace, which 'incited the troops to resent the proclamation, which was particularly directed at them; and the Moulavie was
robbed and ignominiously driven from the Observatory'.[107]

It is also known that Ahmed Ali, the darogah of Hussainabad,
was sent to arrest the Maulvi, and five hours of continuous fighting
took place, after which the Maulvi retreated. Again, when after the
fall of Delhi Fazl Huq Khairabadi came to Lucknow and joined
Mammoo Khan, his assistance was sought to curb the influence of
Ahmadullah Shah. He even accompanied the force sent out by the

[105] Nagar, p. 237.
[106] *FSUP*, II, p. 147.
[107] Ibid., p. 139.

court to confiscate the Maulvi's estate.[108] After this his influence declined somewhat. But after the fall of Kanpur and Havelock's success he gradually regained his power over the troops. He personally
led the attack on Bailey Guard where the English were besieged. By
then 'he had somehow gained a high reputation for courage, of
which the authorities of the Palace were utterly destitute'.[109]

In fact the Maulvi's authority, apart from the factor of personal
courage and 'his penetration of character', i.e. his ability to choose
his followers, had two other elements, one of which was that 'the
Mahomedans had great faith in him as an inspired prophet', a faith
which 'became generally diffused among all classes of every religion
in Oude by the apparent confirmation of his predictions as to the
downfall of the British rule afforded by the temporary success of
the rebellion in the province'.[110] Kavanagh, an English officer, also
wrote about 'the religious credulity of his troops' who 'believed in
his invulnerability, even after a bullet . . . smashed his thumb'. He
had apparently 'impressed his followers with the belief that his
Whip and Handkerchief possessed magical qualities'. With his claim
to 'being an Incarnation of the Deity' and his 'predictions of complete success; of the ultimate extension of the rule of the army to the
sea; and of "beating his drum in London" '—all done in the manner
of a prophetic leader—the Maulvi succeeded in spreading his appeal
gradually to all classes of people and isolating the party at the
court.[111]

Such faith in the invincibility and predictions of an inspired
prophet was rooted in a religio-political type of popular consciousness. A real human being was transformed by this consciousness
into a superhuman and supernatural entity. Hence, even after his
wound, the Maulvi could be regarded as immune from English
weapons. He was himself conditioned by this consciousness since
he thought of himself as directly inspired by Allah. He refused to
look upon his destiny as a function of his own will; to him it was
more a product of a divine inspiration, a will independent of himself. The reasons for political action were expressed in a religious

[108] For these details see S.A.A. Rizvi, ed., *Sangharsh Kalin Netaon Ki Jiwaniyan*
(Lucknow, 1957), pp. 69–70; Depositions of Abdul Alee and Abdul Hakim in Trial
Proceedings of Fazl Haq Khairabadi, no. 6, UPRA.
[109] *FSUP*, II, p. 142.
[110] Ibid., p. 147.
[111] Ibid., pp. 142, 144; *FSUP*, V, p. 541.

code. It was the consciousness of someone 'who has either not found himself or already lost himself again'. Only a prophet could talk of success against heavy odds, and only then could the rebels realize their true nature in 'a fantastic reality of heaven'.[112] This fantasy was the ideological basis on which the authority of the Maulvi rested to a large extent. It was one of the sources which sustained the heroic resistance of Lucknow against the English.

Another factor behind the authority of the Maulvi was a fear of betrayal by the court, a fear of aristocratic plots. He shared that fear with the troops, whose attitude towards the court was graphically described thus by Kamal-ud-Din-Haidar Husaini:

> Everyday the Tilangas . . . sat scattered at the shops of Khas Bazar, sang Bhajans in accompaniment with *daira* and *dhaphili*. They reviled everybody. They called Mirza Birjis Qadar from the palace, embraced him and said 'you are Kanhaiya. Don't become slothful like your father. *Be cautious of your turbaned men, otherwise you will get spoilt*'.[113]

'Be cautious of your turbaned men' was a warning, a disbelief in the magnates who were supposed to be leaders. In fact the Maulvi's appeal lay against them, against their cowardice and the possibility of betrayal. He was known to have organized the assassination of Sharf-ud-dowla, the Begam's minister, after the initial success of the British, 'on the allegation that he had favoured the British attack by previously introducing European soldiers in *doolies* within the works and through whose aid within, the assault from without succeeded'.[114] This want of faith in the nobility is worth emphasizing as a corrective of the notion of a presumed symbiosis between the magnates and their subjects, i.e. of the people unthinkingly following their rulers as natural leaders. The persistent fear of an aristocratic plot turns the evidence in the opposite direction. For such suspicion, whether based on fact or not, must have originated from an awareness that the court's commitment to the rebel cause was not total, that its interest was not identical with that of the common insurgent, and that the latter should beware of betrayal. Such sentiment was the outcome of a contradiction fundamental in a class-divided society, dimly perceived by the rebels despite their common

[112] K. Marx, 'Contribution to the Critique of Hegel's Philosophy of Law' in *Marx & Engels Collected Works*, vol. 3 (Moscow, 1975), p. 175.

[113] *FSUP*, ii, p. 166. Emphasis added.

[114] Ibid., p. 148.

fight against the English. By contrast, impelled both by their religious instincts and the experience of struggle, they had come to place their trust in the Maulvi, and at a critical juncture, with trouble brewing between the Awadh and Delhi sepoys over pay and with the enemy advancing, 'the army appointed the Moulvi their Chief' on 8 December 1857.[115]

Between November 1857 and February 1858 the sepoys made six attacks on General Outram's position in Alumbagh. The Maulvi himself led the fourth attack, which was nearly successful. Lucknow fell on 14 March but the Maulvi stayed 'with unaccountable pertinacity' at the temple of Hazrat Abbas in the heart of the city. On 21 March Lugard captured the last stronghold after stiff resistance, but the Maulvi retreated safely to Muhamdi and made it a focal point of yet another stand against the English forces.[116] Assuming command in the name of his pir, he sent out *hukumnamahs* to several taluqdars, calling on them to rally their forces and arrange for provisions for the coming fight.[117] In these he expressed his yearning for solidarity, both on material and moral grounds. He declared that half of the *jama* of the taluqdars would be exempted for five years if 'they fight and kill the English; if not they would be punished'. All were urged 'to co-operate whole-heartedly in winning this war and extirpating and killing the English and thus, by exhibiting bravery and manliness, to prove themselves worthy of the patronage of this Sarkar'.

However, the Maulvi's attempt to reinforce his authority by rallying the taluqdars proved to be of no avail. The base at Muhamdi had to be abandoned and he withdrew to Pawayan where, on 15 June 1858, he was killed in the course of an engagement between his troops and those of the local raja, Jagannath Singh. The latter, described as 'two-faced' by a British official (for he had flirted with the rebels from time to time, but had 'on the whole a leaning to the English Government'), produced the Maulvi's head ('cut off by order of Buldeo Singh', the raja's brother) to the magistrate of Shahjahanpore and collected the official reward of Rs 50,000 for bringing to an end the career of 'one of the most determined and influential of the rebel leaders'. There followed the usual public demonstration of the might of the colonial state:

[115] Ibid., p. 258.
[116] *FSUP*, v, p. 513.
[117] For these hukumnamahs, see *FSUP*, ii, pp. 365–79.

The head . . . identified by several persons, both at Powayan and at Shahjehanpoor, as being that of the Moulvee Ahmud Oollah Shah . . . has been exposed to the public gate (gaze) in the front of the cotwalee; and the body has been, publicly, burnt this morning, and the ashes thrown into the river.

That gory display was the tribute that the Raj had to pay to one of its most feared adversaries, and it complemented the sigh of relief with which the small-town administrator, who had 'bagged' that head, wrote to his superior officer: 'I am happy to think [that] . . . a rebel leader, who was proud of himself, a most troublesome enemy owing to the wonderful influence possessed by him over his followers, has now disappeared from the scene'.[118]

What was there in the Maulvi's ideas to account for 'the wonderful influence possessed by him over his followers'? For an answer we may turn to the pamphlet, *Fateh-i-Islam*, published anonymously at a time when, after the battle of Chinhat, Ahmadullah Shah's influence was at its highest.[119] It is not known whether he wrote it himself; but in its tone and tenor it was evocative directly of many of his ideas and policies, such as an insistence on jehad, allusions to Quranic laws, warning against indiscriminate plunder, a vituperative attack on alien rule, and commitment to total warfare against the English. As such it may be said to have been fairly representative of his thoughts and actions. Written as a proclamation, it served as a vehicle of the ethical and political ideas of the rebellion much in the same way as the Maulvi's own prophetic statements. It was certainly meant to be read out in public places in Awadh and Lucknow city. 'The proclamation', said a loyalist Indian of Awadh at that time, 'is a highly dangerous and inflammable document for its contents are explicitly believed by the common people who are consequently much exasperated against the English'.[120]

The idiom in which the proclamation was written was religious. It represented the loss of religion as the loss of life, property, home, and finally, honour. '*Religious* distress is at the same time the *expression* of real distress and also the *protest* against real distress'.[121]

---

[118] *FSUP*, v, pp. 536, 538, 539, 545.

[119] See note in *FSUP*, II, p. 150. The source of all extracts from *Fateh-i-Islam* is an English translation of the text as given in ibid., pp. 150–62.

[120] W. Edwards, *Personal Adventures during the Indian Rebellion in Rohilkhand, Futtehghar & Oude* (London, 1858), p. 176.

[121] Marx, p. 175.

So, the appeal to the feelings of the oppressed and the narration of oppression began with an appeal for the defence of religion under an alien rule. It described the pre-colonial period as an age of religious freedom: 'formerly the Mahommedan Kings protected (as they felt it incumbent on them to do) the lives and property of the Hindoos with their children in the same manner as [they] protected those of the Mahomedans', whereas under British rule, 'the accursed Christians were anxious to make both the Hindoos and the Mahomedans, Christians'.

The alleged plan for conversion to Christianity was given a political meaning: the indictment of the spiritual immorality of the Raj was made into an indictment of its record of secular administration. It was a regime based on tyranny and violence: 'O Brethren! at this present time, the execrable Christians . . . are killing innocent men, plundering their property, setting fire to their houses and shutting up their children in houses, some of which they burn down . . .' The current conflict was interpreted as an episode in a campaign of genocide authorized by the Queen of England. 'Before the quarrel regarding the cartridges took place', read the proclamation

> these accursed English had written to the Impure Victoria thus: 'If your Majesty will permit us to kill 15 Moulvees out of every hundred in India and the same number out of every hundred Pundits, as well as five hundred thousand of Hindoo and Mahomedan sepoys and Ryuts, we will in a short time make all the people of India "Christians" '. Then that ill-starred, polluted Bitch gave her consent to the spilling of this innocent blood.

Such direct condemnation of the Queen of England in the most abusive terms sets the *Fateh-i-Islam* apart from other contemporary statements of this genre. 'The good Queen Victoria' who was to figure in popular imagination during some of the peasant rebellions later on in the century was condemned here as 'an ill-starred polluted Bitch'—words which stand for a defiance of the whole chain of British colonial authority from the crown to the common soldier and administrator. If the Maulvi had a hand in drafting this proclamation, his knowledge of England and its institutions might partially explain why the whole structure of colonial authority was put in the dock. If not, the perception in the proclamation implies a total rejection of alien rule, with no distinction made between the Queen and her functionaries.

'To destroy the English' is the religious and political mission proclaimed by the tract, and all Indians—Hindus and Musalmans, men as well as women—are urged to join in it. However, in this struggle a distinction had to be carefully maintained between enemies and friends. It was 'lawful to plunder the property of the enemy'. But the sepoys had to be prohibited from plundering Indians, 'especially the people of the places' conquered by them. 'Punish immediately the plunderer and cause the plundered property to be restored to its owner'. To direct popular wrath against the enemy and not against the people was a judicious plan for recognizing and handling various types of contradictions which were often forgotten by the insurgents themselves.

Yet another set of distinctions emphasized in the text is that between leaders and followers. The struggle requires leadership: 'It is . . . incumbent on us to appoint a leader or Chief forthwith and to obey his commands for the purpose of destroying the English'. Once a leader is appointed, 'a report of the commencement of a religious war will be spread'. Who should be chosen as a leader? Here the recommendation is clearly sectarian as well as theological: 'any Mahomedan Chief endowed even with a few of the qualities of a leader and observing the tenets of the Mahomedan Law can, as a matter of necessity, be selected as Chief.' And, as far as possible, it was necessary not to interfere with the existing chiefs. Their authority was to be maintained and invoked. Only where no chief was found, the rebels would assert their choice.

The theology of leadership had as a foil to it the notion of a hierarchical order. This leader would 'select other Chiefs among [sic] the army', thus making up a chain of hierarchical command from God through King and to Chief and his subordinates to the people. In fact this insistence on leadership and the necessity of accepting the older, traditional chiefs might be a pointer to a certain kind of political concern. For in the course of the struggle, in many cases, various claimants came forth and many different sources of initiative were thrown open. No single chain of any universally acceptable authority had emerged yet. Hence there was an appeal to 'order'. However, that alternative authority was by no means egalitarian. It was to be sustained by a relation of command and obedience between the chief and the subjects, and sacralized by Quranic precepts and Shariat laws. And thus, one could say with Marx, 'the tradition of all the dead generations' was brought to bear 'like a nightmare on the brain of the living'.

Yet, in this very proclamation, in terms of actual action, popular initiative was not altogether forgotton. The experience of the insurrection urged the author to talk of the strength of mass violence against alien rule, and the logic of the upsurge left its imprint on the tradition of order regulated and sanctioned by a hierarchy. In that vision of insurrection everybody was a participant, everybody was his own commander.

> all the people whether men, women or children, including slave-girls, slaves and old women, ought to put these accursed English to death by firing guns, carbines and pistols, from the terraces, shooting arrows and pelting them with stones, bricks, earthen vessels, ladles, old shoes and all other things, which may come into their hands. They should stone to death the English in the same manner as the swallows stoned the Chief of the elephants. The sepoys, the nobles, the shopkeepers, the oilmen, etc. and all other people of the city, being of one accord, should make a simultaneous attack upon them, some of them should kill them by firing guns, pistols, and carbines and with swords, arrows, daggers, poignando, etc., some lift them on spears, some dexterously snatch their arms . . . some should cling to their necks, some to their waists, some should wrestle and through strategem break the enemy to pieces; some should strike them with cudgels, some slap them, some throw dust in their eyes, some should beat them with shoes, some attack them with their fists, some scratch them, some drag them along, some tear out their ears, some break their noses . . . Under such circumstances they will be unable to do anything though they may amount to lakhs of men.

The role of the leader thus dissolves in a vision of popular resistance against the English. Initiative, it is suggested, ought to be everybody's, and then would victory be assured. There was on the one hand an implicit faith in the chief, and a demand for absolute obedience to him. On the other hand there was the vision of a popular uprising in which the lowly would also fight. This dual character of the proclamation made it unique. It was the same duality that had informed the prophetic leadership of Maulvi Ahmadullah Shah.

## VI. *Conclusion*

This narrative has of necessity been fragmentary and episodic. Its range is wide and the characters drawn only in outline. Yet this episodic and fragmentary narrative points to the existence in 1857 of what Gramsci has called 'multiple elements of conscious leadership'[122] at the popular level. There could be any number of variations in these elements. The Maulvi could not be compared with Gonoo, and Shah Mal's political aspirations were not of the same kind as Devi Singh's. Except for the Maulvi, most of them were bound in their activity within a locality. Because of his relatively longer political experience and the scope of his ideological appeal, the Maulvi had a bigger horizon than the others and could operate on a broader political platform. Devi Singh, Shah Mal and Gonoo lived and fought under very different social and economic conditions. Those differences to an extent conditioned their activities and the nature of mobilization under their leadership. They did not know each other; yet pitted as they were against the same enemy at the same historical moment, they shared, thanks to the logic of insurrection, some common characteristics.

Their leadership was of short duration. They were products of the movement and their influence declined with its recession. Hence an official could say of Shah Mal that out of nothing he had become a leader of importance. Devi Singh had hardly any mark of distinction. Gonoo was a misfit. Of the antecedents of the Maulvi the government knew virtually nothing. The ephemeral appearance and short duration of these rebels' leadership have led academic historians like S.N. Sen to dismiss their intervention in the events of 1857 as 'minor incidents', and soldier-historians like Dunlop to mock them as 'mushroom dignities'.[123] But, as this narrative has amply demonstrated, the role of such leaders, far from being incidental, was indeed an integral part of popular insurgency. They asserted themselves through the act of insurgency and took the initiative hitherto denied to them by the dominant classes; and in doing so they put their stamp on the course of the rebellion, thereby breaking the long silence imposed on them politically and culturally by the ruling classes. The suddenness of their rise was an indication that colonial society had been 'unhinged' under the hammer blows of an insurrection.

It is the 'ordinariness' of these rebels which constituted their distinction. Devi Singh could hardly be distinguished from his followers. Shah Mal was a small zamindar among many and Gonoo was a

[122] A. Gramsci, 'The Modern Prince' in *Prison Note-Books* (New York, 1973), p. 196.

[123] S.N. Sen, *Eighteen Fifty-seven* (Delhi, 1957), p. 407; Dunlop, *Khakee Ressalah*, p. 46.

common Kol. Even the Maulvi was hardly a learned man and knew only 'little Arabic and Persian'. The consciousness with which they all fought had been 'formed through everyday experience'; it was an 'elementary historical acquisition'. It was the perception and day-to-day experience of the authority of the alien state in his immediate surroundings that determined the rebel's action. Only the Maulvi could be said to have risen, to an extent, above this immediate experience and particularity, because he had found a comprehensive logic for his actions in the political doctrines of a world religion. Yet all he could do was talk of a jehad and the restoration of the old order led by the chiefs. He had only that within his experience to put forward as an alternative to the all-embracing alien rule. All of our rebels were firmly committed to their cause. It was they who made the thrust of insurgency in 1857 so violent and uncompromising. Yet their partial and empirical understanding of the world necessarily limited the potentiality of that movement.

The recognition of the strength and weakness of these rebels would be a step forward in understanding their role beyond stereotyped categories and formulae. They were not mere adjuncts to a linear tradition that was to culminate in the appropriation of power by the élite in a post-colonial state. Nor were they mere toys manipulated by the latter in a historical project in which they played no part. Nor can they be merely described as faceless elements in an omnibus category called 'the people'. To seek after and restore the specific subjectivity of the rebels must be a major task of the new historiography. That would be a recognition of the truth that, under the given historical circumstances in which he lives, man makes himself.

# III Domination Analysis in the Pre-Capitalist Context

# Conditions for Knowledge of Working-Class Conditions: Employers, Government and the Jute Workers of Calcutta, 1890-1940 *

## DIPESH CHAKRABARTY

## I

At the heart of this essay are two rather general propositions: first, that the ruling-class documents often used for historical reconstructions of working-class conditions can be read both for what they say and for their 'silences'; and secondly, that an attempt to understand their silences cannot stop at the purely economic explanation—though the economic is undoubtedly important—but has to push itself into the realm of working-class culture. It will also be claimed here that in arguing thus we are arguing with Marx and not against him.

The discussion in the first volume of Marx's *Capital* raises the possibility of a relationship between the day-to-day running of capitalism and the production of a body of knowledge about working-class conditions. Marx in fact presents us with the elements of a possible theoretical approach to the problem. Even at the risk of appearing to digress a bit, it may be worthwhile to go over that theoretical ground once again, as the rest of this essay will examine one particular working-class history—that of the Calcutta jute mill workers between 1890 and 1940—in the light of Marx's discussion. Perhaps it should also be emphasized that what we are borrowing here from Marx is essentially an *argument*. Marx used the English case to illustrate his ideas but the specifics of English history are not a

* This essay owes a great deal to discussions with Imran Ali, Katherine Gibson, Ranajit Guha, Stephen Henningham, Anthony Low and Roger Stuart. I am, however, solely responsible for any errors of fact or judgement.

concern of this essay. We are not reading Marx as a historian of England and this is not an exercise in comparative history.

As is well known, Marx used the documents of the English state for the wealth of detail they usually offered on the living and working conditions of the English proletariat. But Marx also noted in the process that the English state's interest in closely monitoring the conditions of labour had an extremely useful role to play in the development of English capitalism. 'This industrial revolution which takes place spontaneously', wrote Marx, 'is artificially helped on by the extension of the Factory Acts to all industries in which women, young persons and children are employed'.[1] This the Acts achieved in two important ways. First, they sought to make 'the conditions of competition' between different factories uniform: Marx referred in his discussion of the Factory Acts to the 'cry of the capitalists for equality in the conditions of competition, i.e. for equal restraint on all exploitation of labour'. Secondly, by regulating 'the working day as regards its length, pauses, beginning and end'—that is, by making 'the saving of time a necessity'—they 'forced into existence' more developed and complex machinery and hence, by implication, a more efficient working class.[2]

For the Factory Acts to secure these aims, however, the state needed to ensure that the knowledge generated by the administration of the Acts was not influenced by the narrower considerations of any particular industrialist. Individual masters, it is true, were often in 'fanatical opposition' to the Acts. But the very fact that Marx derived many of his details of the 'cruelties' of early capitalism directly from factory inspectors' reports speaks of the 'political will' that the English state was capable of mustering, the will that allowed it to distance itself from particular capitalists and yet serve English capitalism in general.[3]

Marx's discussion clarifies some of the conditions for this success. The 'political will' of the English state did not fall from the skies. While Marx did see the Factory Acts as 'that first and meagre concession wrung from capital' by the government and the working people, he also noted that important sections of English industrialists were in fact themselves in favour of the Factory Acts, their humanistic

[1] Karl Marx, *Capital*, I (Moscow. n.d.), p. 474.
[2] Ibid., pp. 474, 476-9, 490.
[3] Ibid., pp. 480, 482-4.

impulses often spurred on by the forces of competition. Competition was the key to the demand for 'equal restraint on all exploitation of labour'. 'Messrs. Cooksley of Bristol, nail and chain, &c., manufacturers', Marx noted, '*spontaneously* introduced the regulations of the Factory Act into their business' (emphasis added). The Children's Employment Commission of the 1860s explained why: 'As the old irregular system prevails in neighbouring works, the Messrs. Cooksley are subject to the disadvantage of having their boys enticed to continue their labour elsewhere after 6 p.m.' Marx also gave the instance of one 'Mr. J. Simpson (paper box and bag maker, London)' who told the Commission that 'he would sign any petition for it [legislative interference]. . . .' Summarizing such cases, the Commission said:

> It would be unjust to the larger employers that their factories should be placed under regulation, while the hours of labour in the smaller places in their own branch of business were under no legislative restriction. . . . Further, a stimulus would be given to the multiplication of the smaller places of work, which are almost invariably the least favourable to the health, comfort, education, and general improvement of people.[4]

Even if competition in the economy is regarded as instrumental to the autonomy of the English state, one still has to explain however why the factories, in the first place, produced the necessary documents without the state having to do much policing. Marx's answer lies in his discussion of the industrial discipline that the capitalist system of manufacture involved. In the process of the 'disciplining' of the labour force, the interests of the individual capitalists and those of the state meshed, since, in England, the pressure towards discipline arose both from within and without the factory. If one effect of the factory legislation was to produce 'uniformity, regularity, order and economy' within 'each individual workshop',[5] these were also produced internally, according to Marx, by the capitalist division of labour: 'continuity, uniformity, regularity, order . . .' are also the words that Marx used to describe discipline.[6]

Discipline, in Marx's discussion, had two components. It entailed a 'technical subordination of the workman to the uniform motion of the instruments of labour'; hence the need for training, education,

[4] Ibid., pp. 488-91.
[5] Ibid., p. 503.
[6] Ibid., p. 345.

etc. Secondly, it made supervision—'the labour of overlooking'—an integral part of capitalist relations of production. The supervisor or foreman was the executor of the 'private legislation' of capital, the 'factory code in which capital formulates . . . his autocracy over his workpeople'. The supervisor thus embodied the authority of capital, and documents representing factory rules and legislation—e.g. attendance registers, finebooks, timesheets—became both symbols and instruments of his authority. Supervision, so crucial to the working of capitalist authority, was thus based on documents and produced documents in turn. In Marx's words:

> The place of the slave-driver's lash is taken by the overlooker's book of penalties. All punishments [in capitalist production relations] *naturally* resolve themselves into fines and deductions from wages (emphasis added).[7]

The every-day functioning of the capitalist factory, therefore, produced documents, hence knowledge, about working-class conditions. This was so because capitalist relations of production employed a system of supervision—another name for surveillance—that, in the language of Michel Foucault, 'insidiously objectified those on whom it is applied'.[8] It was thus in the nature of capitalist authority that it operated by forming 'a body of knowledge' about its subjects. In this it was different from, say, pre-capitalist domination which worked more by deploying 'the ostentatious signs of sovereignty' and could do without a knowledge of the dominated.[9]

In pursuing Marx's ideas on the relationship between industrial discipline and documentation of the conditions of workers, we thus end up with the notion of 'authority'. Marx was quite clear that the supervisor represented the disciplinary authority of capital over labour; but 'authority', in Marx's hands, was never a one-sided affair. Quite early in his discussion on capital, Marx wrote: '*A* . . . cannot be "your majesty" to *B*, unless at the same time majesty in *B*'s eyes assumes the bodily form of *A* ...'.[10] Or a few pages later:

> Such expressions of relations in general, called by Hegel reflex-categories, form a very curious class. For instance, one man is King only because

[7] Ibid., pp. 423-4.
[8] Michel Foucault, *Discipline and Punish. The Birth of the Prison* (Harmondsworth, 1979), p. 220.
[9] Ibid.
[10] Marx, op. cit., p. 51.

other men stand in the relation of subjects to him. They, on the contrary, imagine that they are subjects because he is a king.[11]

A particular form of authority or a system of power, then, implies a particular cultural formation. In Marx's exposition of 'capital' as a category, it is quite evident that the figure of the worker invoked was that of a person who could be produced only by a society where the bourgeois notion of equality (before the law or the market) was ingrained in culture. Marx saw labour as a 'moment' (that is, a constituent element) of capital, and capital 'is a *bourgeois production relation*, a production relation of bourgeois society'.[12] The labourer of Marx's assumption had internalized and enjoyed 'formal freedom', the freedom of the contract (which brought legal and market relations together), and he enjoyed this not just in abstraction but as 'the individual, real person'.[13] Until this was ensured and so long as pre-capitalist, particularistic ties made up and characterized the relations of production, capital, as Marx understood it, was 'not yet *capital as such*'.[14] This is why Marx thought that the logic of capital could be best deciphered only in a society where 'the notion of human equality has already acquired the fixity of a popular prejudice'[15] and hence chose the historical case of England as the one most illustrative of his argument.

Indeed, as we now know from historians of our times, the 'notion of equality before the law' was an essential ingredient of the culture with which the English working class entered and handled its

[11] Ibid., p. 57, n. 1
[12] Marx quoted in Roman Rosdolsky, *The Making of Marx's 'Capital'* (London, 1980), p. 184, footnote 3. Emphasis in the original. For Marx's conception of labour as a 'moment of capital', see his *Grundrisse: Foundations of the Critique of Political Economy* (Harmondsworth, 1974), pp. 293-301. *Capital*, I, p. 333, sees labour as a 'mode of existence of capital'. *Hegel's Logic* (tr. W. Wallace; London, 1975), pp. 79, 113, uses 'moment' to mean both 'stage' as well as a (constituent) 'factor'. Jindrich Zeleny, *The Logic of Marx* (Oxford, 1980), p. xi, defines 'moment' as 'one of the elements of a complex conceptual entity'.
[13] Marx, *Grundrisse*, p. 464.
[14] Ibid., pp. 296-7. Emphasis in the original.
[15] Marx, *Capital*, I, p. 60. Admittedly, Marx made this statement with reference to the problem of deciphering the 'secret of the expression of value'. But then one has to remember that for Marx capital is self-expanding value and labour a moment of capital. For these and related points also see I. I. Rubin, *Essays on Marx's Theory of Value* (Montreal, 1975).

experience of the Industrial Revolution.[16] It is this working class that is present—though only as an assumption—in Marx's discussion of the disciplinary authority of capital that the act of supervision embodies. If our exposition of Marx's ideas is correct then it would mean that such authority was rooted as much in the factory codes that capital legislated out of its own needs as in the culture of the working class over whom the authority was exercised. The point seems important even in another respect. By assuming a particular kind of culture on the part of the worker, Marx assigns the working class a place—an active presence, in fact—in the whole process of disciplining by supervision and record-keeping. And this he does, not just for moments of protest when the working class is obviously active and shows its will, but even when it does not protest and is seemingly a passive object of documentation and knowledge.

For a historian of the jute mill workers of Calcutta, the relevance of all this is immediate. Any projected history of the conditions of this working class is soon bedevilled by the problem of paucity of sources. True, some of this scarcity of documents can be explained by the characteristics of the Bengali intelligentsia who never produced social investigators like, for instance, Henry Mayhew.[17] Some of it may also be explained by the non-literate nature of the working class. A problem still remains. What puzzles is the relative poverty of information in the documents of the state—especially documents that needed the co-operation of capital, the factory inspectors' reports, for instance—which compare rather badly with the apparent richness of similar English documents that Marx put to such effective use in the first volume of *Capital*.

Marx's argument could then be used as a measure of how different capitalism in colonial Bengal was from the one described by him. There is yet another question that Marx's argument helps us raise. The Calcutta jute mill workers, being mostly migrant peasants from Bihar and UP, did not have a culture characterized by any ingrained notion of 'human equality' and were thus very unlike the workers of Marx's assumption. Their's was largely a pre-capitalist, inegalitarian culture marked by strong primordial loyalties of community,

[16] The classic statement is in E. P. Thompson, *The Making of the English Working Class* (Harmondsworth, 1968), p. 213.

[17] Cf. my article, 'Sasipada Banerjee: A Study in the Nature of the First Contact of the Bengali Bhadralok with the Working Classes of Bengal', *The Indian Historical Review*, Jan. 1976.

language, religion, caste and kinship.[18] Since, in Marx's argument, the question of documentation of conditions of work within a factory was linked to the problem of 'disciplinary authority', and that in turn was linked to the question of working-class culture, the cultural differences of the Calcutta working class raise a whole series of problems. Were relations of production within a Calcutta jute mill still characterized (in spite of differences in working-class culture) by the disciplinary authority that Marx described? The answer would appear to be in the negative. What then was the nature of 'supervision' in a Calcutta jute mill? Did it behave like a huge apparatus documenting the conditions of labour? Did it have a bearing on the problem that a historian of the working class faces today: paucity of 'sources'?

The following sections will pursue these questions. This essay aims at two objectives. It aspires to draw a picture, however incomplete, of the conditions of the jute mill workers of Calcutta in the period mentioned. At the same time, it also intends to account for the gaps in our knowledge and argues that the gaps are as revealing of working-class conditions as any direct reference to them. It is thus a history both of our knowledge and of our ignorance. And the explanation offered here is both political-economic and cultural.

II

Government interest in working-class conditions in India is of relatively recent origin. It was only after the end of the First World War that the conditions of the Indian working class became an object of knowledge for the Government of India. A Labour Bureau was set up in May 1920 'to collect all available information on labour conditions in India, and classify and tabulate it'.[19] One important factor contributing to this development was the establishment of the International Labour Office (ILO) immediately after the war. The Indian government had been an 'active participant' in the process of the ILO's formation and was pledged to its goals.[20] A second important factor was one internal to the Indian political scene. The conclusion

---

[18] See my 'Communal Riots and Labour: Bengal's Jute Mill-Hands in the 1890s', *Past and Present*, May 1981.

[19] *Report of the Royal Commission on Labour in India* (London, 1931; hereafter R.C.L.I), vol. V, pt. I, p. 327.

[20] Ibid., and West Bengal State Archives, Calcutta (hereafter W.B.S.A.), Com[merce] Dept. Com [merce] Br[anch], Apr. 1922, A5-9.

of the war and the subsequent period of nationalist agitation had seen trade unions mushroom all over the country on a scale previously unknown. This was accompanied by a countrywide outburst of labour unrest. With the Russian revolution still fresh in its memory, the Government of India's reaction to these developments was coloured by a fear of Bolshevism.[21] 'Labour is growing more conscious of its own wants and power', the government warned its provincial heads in 1919, '[and] it is showing signs of a capacity for organization'.[22] By its militancy, thus, labour was drawing upon itself the gaze of the government.

What distinguished this new outlook on labour from the traditional law-and-order view of the state was a desire to reform the conditions of labour and thus change the nature of the working class. In an impressive range of labour legislation considered (and partly enacted) in the twenties and afterwards, the Government of India sought to take a direct role in structuring the situation of the working classes. The amended Factories Act (1922), the Workmen's Compensation Act (1923), the Trade Unions Act (1926), the Trade Disputes Act (1928), the Maternity Benefits Bill (1929), the Payment of Wages Act (1933), etc., were all aimed at creating a working class different from the traditionally-held image of the industrial labour force in India. The worker was henceforth to receive a new 'legal' personality, more welfare, and even some official help to organize into trade unions (naturally, of a non-communist kind). Introducing a bill for the 'registration and protection of trade unions', the Government of India wrote to the local governments in September 1921 that 'in so far as the [trade union] movement makes for the organization of labour, and for the steady betterment of the conditions of labour . . . every facility should be offered for its development along healthy lines'.[23]

The government's concern for a 'steady betterment of the conditions of labour' was sustained and animated by a recently-acquired vision of a burgeoning industrial growth in India. The war had left the government in a 'developmentalist' mood[24] from which sprang the arguments regarding working-class conditions.

[21] See for example W.B.S.A., Home Political (hereafter Poll.) Confidential (hereafter Confdl.) 405(1-3)/1919.

[22] W.B.S.A., Com. Dept. Com. Br., Nov. 1919, A11-25.

[23] W.B.S.A., Com. Dept. Com. Br., Aug. 1922, A32-51.

[24] See Clive Dewey, 'The Government of India's "New Industrial Policy", 1900-1925: Formation and Failure' in K. N. Chaudhuri and C. J. Dewey (eds), *Economy and Society: Essays in Indian Economic and Social History* (Delhi, 1979), pp. 215-57.

> There are indications of a considerable expansion in the near future in the number and size of industrial establishments. Moreover machinery and power are being employed in factories to a much larger extent than . . . before. Mines are being worked at greater depths. . . . The transport industries are developing.

With these words the government pleaded in August 1921 the case for creating a system of rules for compensations to be awarded to workmen injured in accidents in the course of work.[25] The argument was elaborated during the discussion that followed. The Government of India explained that the 'growing complexity of industry . . . with the increasing use of machinery' required a more efficient labour force than had hitherto been available. It was therefore 'advisable that they [the workers] should be protected . . . from hardship arising from accidents', because this would not only increase 'the available supply of labour' but also produce 'a corresponding increase in the *efficiency* of the average workman. . . .'[26]

'Efficiency', in this logic, was a function of working-class conditions. The government noted in 1919 that while there was 'a keen and increasing demand for factory labour' in India, there was 'little apparent desire on the part of the labourers to increase their efficiency', and—more to the point—'little prospect of their being able to do so under present *conditions*' [emphasis added].[27] Improving efficiency meant improving these 'conditions', and they included not only 'education, housing and social welfare' but also such aspects as the 'comfort' and 'spare time' of the worker.

> The efficiency of workers is closely connected with their education, and their standard of comfort; the shortening of hours may not prove an unmixed good, if the workers are not put in a position to make a proper use of their spare time.[28]

The argument was broader than it might appear at first sight. For it was not only a question of giving the workers 'spare time', but of structuring that 'spare time' as well, of ensuring that the workers made 'proper use' of it.[29] It was thus that the government's eyes fell—for the first time in Indian history—on several aspects of the

[25] W.B.S.A., Com. Dept. Com. Br., July 1922, A34-72.
[26] W.B.S.A., Com. Dept. Com. Br., Jan. 1923, A65-107. Emphasis added.
[27] W.B.S.A., Com. Dept. Com. Br., Nov. 1919, A11-25.
[28] Ibid.
[29] See also W.B.S.A., Com. Dept. Com. Br., May 1927, A1-6.

worker's life that had so far been held to be beyond the ken of capital. Issues of indebtedness, the 'monetary reserve' of the worker, his wages, food, health, home life—all came under the scrutiny of the government.[30] 'Efficiency' produced its own code of ethics which opposed the image of the vigorous and healthy worker to that of the overworked and fatigued.

> They [the Government of India] believe that the longer interval [of rest] is desirable in order to enable the worker to maintain his *vigour*, and that its enforcement should ultimately prove beneficial to the employer. There are grounds for believing that the absence of sustained work, characteristic of many factory employees in this country, has been due . . . to the fact that the hours fixed did not in the past allow sufficient opportunity for the *rest* necessary to prevent fatigue.[31]

It was only in the context of this search for an 'efficient' working class that working-class conditions became an object of knowledge. How did the Government of India propose to produce and gather this knowledge? Provincial governments were equipped with new departments meant to perform this task. For instance, under pressure from the Government of India, the Bengal Government established in July 1920 an office of the Industrial Intelligence Officer, later named the Labour Intelligence Officer, whose duty it was to 'maintain a proper watch over the industrial situation', and 'in particular to investigate and report on labour conditions and the facts and causes of labour disturbances'.[32] The Government of India also realized that much of this knowledge would have to be generated within the factories and that the provincial staff of factory inspectors might be employed to collect and monitor the information. Since 'leisure', 'rest', 'fatigue', 'sparetime', etc., were some of the key concepts supporting the government's notion of 'efficiency', control over the labourer's working hours naturally emerged as a problem of the highest importance. It is in this context that attendance registers maintained by individual factories and the factory inspectors' reports came to be regarded as crucial documents from the Government of India's point of view. With this end in view, the Factories Act was amended in 1922 with a new section 35 now requiring the manager of

[30] See for instance W.B.S.A., Com. Dept. Com. Br., Feb. 1927, A1-8, and May 1929, B196-9.

[31] W.B.S.A., Com. Dept. Com. Br., Mar. 1924, A45-61. Emphasis added.

[32] W.B.S.A., Com. Dept. Com. Br., Apr. 1922, A5-9.

a factory 'to maintain . . . [an attendance] register of all persons employed and of their hours of work . . .'.[33]

## III

The conditions of jute mill labour in Bengal never fully received the documentation that the Government of India had arranged to give them. In other words, the desired knowledge was not produced. The inaccuracies in the attendance registers of the jute mills were witness to this failure, for, as the Chief Inspector of Factories admitted to the Royal Commission on Labour, 'the records given in such registers do not represent the true conditions . . . of . . . labour'.[34] The Labour Office of Bengal, too, suffered from a peculiar bureaucratic malaise, the history of which only shows that the Bengal Government never shared the Government of India's eagerness for knowledge of labour conditions. For one thing, as the Labour Commissioner of Bengal recalled in 1935, the office was set up with 'no immediate purpose of having a large investigating office, with cost of living indices and other standard concomitants of an organised labour office'.[35] Besides, so low was the priority of this office in the eyes of the Bengal Government that 'when the first Retrenchment Committee' reported in 1921, 'the Labour Office seemed bound to go'; but 'instead of abolishing it, the [Bengal] government changed its character'. To economize, the Labour Intelligence Officer was saddled with various responsibilities and his investigative functions suffered badly in consequence. He was placed 'in charge of the Commerce Department, and later of the Marine Department [as well]'. He was made responsible for the administration of all the labour laws that were to come in the twenties, as well as for other legislative measures only 'partly concerned with the welfare of labour, e.g., the Boilers Act and the Electricity Act'. The Labour Intelligence Officer thus became, in his own words, 'an ordinary secretariat officer' who had little time to investigate the conditions of labour.

> With the growing volume of office work and the addition of one duty after another, the Labour Intelligence Officer found it impossible to continue his personal investigations regarding every strike, and also to some extent,

[33] W.B.S.A., Com. Dept. Com. Br., Feb. 1926, A1-46.
[34] *R.C.L.I.*, vol. V, pt. 1, p. 92.
[35] W.B.S.A., Home Poll. Confdl. No. 392(1-3)/1935.

his visits to factories ...; although, as far as possible, he continued these visits up to 1929 when the enormous increase of work due to the advent of Whitley Commission tied him completely to his desk.[36]

The atrophy of the Labour Office was not a matter of simple bureaucratic mindlessness. What calls for an analysis is precisely the 'mind' of this bureaucracy. To this 'mind', any interest in labour conditions beyond that called for by the immediate needs of capital or of law and order, was suspect. 'For some peculiar reason', wrote a rather frustrated Labour Commissioner in 1935, 'in Bengal, interest in labour matters or desire for knowledge of labour developments is read as sympathy for the labour point of view.'[37]

The 'reason' for this suspicion is not difficult to analyse. The Government of India's 'desire for knowledge of labour developments' assumed that the investigating authority would be capable of maintaining a degree of independence from the point of view of particular capitalists. The government desired to stand above the 'unevenness' of such particular views. For example, in insisting on 'uniform rules' for fines or accident-compensations, the Government of India argued that the question of 'welfare of the working classes' could not 'any longer be left to the uneven generosity of employers'.[38] Such 'neutrality' of the state, however, threatened to rupture the almost 'natural' unity that had existed in Bengal for years between the provincial government and owners of capital (especially those represented by powerful organizations such as the Bengal Chamber of Commerce and the Indian Jute Mills Association).

This 'natural unity' received its fullest expression in the nineteenth century when the moral order of the day was unashamedly procapitalist and when the Government of Bengal plainly considered it its duty 'to do all it can to afford moral support to the [jute] millowners' in the face of labour unrest.[39] In those years even the meagre provisions of the first two Factories Acts of India were seen by senior officers of the Government of Bengal as 'needlessly harassing to the [mill] managers'.[40] A factory inspector who once insisted on age-

[36] Ibid.
[37] Ibid.
[38] W.B.S.A., Com. Dept. Com. Br., July 1922, A34-72.
[39] W.B.S.A., Judicial Dept. Police Br., Jan. 1896, A6-11.
[40] W.B.S.A., General (hereafter Genl.) Dept. Miscellaneous (hereafter Misc.) Br., July 1882, A73-81.

verification for all jute-mill child-workers in his jurisdiction was sharply pulled up by the Chief Secretary of the Government of Bengal. 'Inspectors', he was told, 'by making the [medical] examination of every child compulsory, would give to owners or managers of factories the maximum of trouble, and to the government the maximum of expenses without conferring any compensating benefit on the majority of the children employed'.[41]

It would not be very profitable to see this merely as an instance of ruling-class hypocrisy. The evidence yields more value when treated as an expression of the ruling-class outlook on conditions of labour. The Bengal officials were not just displaying their lack of respect for the factory laws; underlying their statements was also the conviction that the labour conditions themselves did not leave much to be desired. To most of the factory inspectors, therefore—contrary to the aims of the factory legislation—the conditions always seemed satisfactory. A typical example is the report of the working of the Factories Act in Bengal for the year 1893. The 'general conditions of the [mill] operatives' were found 'very satisfactory', the coolie-lines were 'well laid out', their work 'not arduous', the water supply 'good', the latrines 'well kept', the children 'thoroughly healthy' and their work 'in no way detrimental to them', and arrangements for the workers' medical care 'satisfactory'. Even the 'fact' that 'five or ten per cent' of the children were 'weak, feeble in growth and stunted for their age' could not be attributed, it was said, 'to the work they perform in the mills, as about the same proportion of undersized and weakly children may be observed among the outside population'.[42]

To such an official 'mind', labour conditions deserved investigation only when they posed law and order problems. A Government of Bengal file discussing a sudden outburst of working-class unrest in the jute mills in 1894-5 gave some attention to the question of housing for labour. But this attention was merely bestowed for reasons of control and no more. The Lieutenant Governor of Bengal welcomed the IJMA (Indian Jute Mills Association) to 'co-operate with the [Bengal] Government in improving both direct control [i.e. policing] over the mill-hands in case they should break into violence, and also indirect control which will make acts of violence less likely by *bettering* the *conditions* of the employees':

[41] Ibid.
[42] W.B.S.A., Genl. Dept. Misc. Br., Aug. 1893, A1-36.

His Honor therefore confidently invites the co-operation of the mill-owners to provide comfortable and well-ordered homes for mill-hands, and thus avoid such conditions as those at Samnagar and Titanagar, which offer temptations to the disorderly and make control difficult.

But the amount of improvement desired in the 'conditions' was severely limited. Too much 'bettering' of conditions might make the task of control harder. 'Rice is very cheap, and this makes them [the labourers] independent', was the diagnosis of a police officer in the same file, who quoted jute mill managers' views in support of his own: 'Experienced mill managers seem to think that . . . when the labour market becomes once more over-stocked, as they say it will be, mill hands will grow less independent, and matters will quiet down to their normal state.'⁴³ In taking a law and order view of labour conditions, then, the state just reproduced the point of view of capital.

Much of this nineteenth-century spirit can be read off twentieth-century documents as well, especially those coming from the years before the First World War. There was for instance the Civil Surgeon of Serampore who thought (in 1909) that 'the mills in Hooghly need no legislation for the well-being of the operatives'; or the factory inspector who felt (in 1910) that 'an Inspector' was 'legitimately entitled to place the telescope to his blind eye' if he came across 'a child of seven or eight years sewing or hemming a gunny bag in the vicinity of the mother', even though the law demanded 'the Manager . . . be prosecuted for employing a child under nine'; or there was the even more striking case of C. A. Walsh, the Chief Inspector of Factories, boldly declaring in 1912: 'I see no poverty in the quarters surrounding the great [jute] mills in Khardah, Titagarh, Shamnagore, Kankinare, Naihati, Budge-Budge or Fort Gloster. . . .'⁴⁴

The tone of official pronouncements changed somewhat after 1920, thanks to the efforts of the Government of India and of nationalist and radical politicians who espoused the cause of labour. 'The increasing solidarity of labour' entered the calculations of the Government of Bengal and the realization dawned that 'industrial disputes will in future form an integral part of the industrial life of this province'.⁴⁵ Yet this did not bring about any 'epistemological

⁴³ W.B.S.A., Judicial Dept. Police Br., Jan. 1896, A6-11.
⁴⁴ W.B.S.A., Genl. Dept. Misc. Br., Aug. 1910, A33-86; Aug. 1911, A18-63; and Medical Dept. Medical Br., Jan. 1914, B287-95.
⁴⁵ W.B.S.A., Com. Dept. Com. Br., Dec. 1923, A8.

shift' in the status of the 'conditions of labour' question. It never acquired any priority over the question of control. The Industrial Unrest Committee of 1921 recommended that the Bengal Government set up some means for investigating strikes but made it clear that the means proposed 'must be designed for the purpose of alleviating unrest . . . rather than for a detailed investigation of current labour conditions'.[46] It was the same 'disease' that had warped the career of the Labour Office in Bengal. The periodic reports the Labour Intelligence Officer sent up to the Government of India were, it was admitted, 'nearly always' the views of the local police—'merely thana officers' views', as Donald Gladding, a senior official of the Bengal Government, once described them. 'Neither superior police officers nor Magistrates go about seriously to find out the truth by questioning the workmen on the one hand and the employers on the other—and this', Gladding insisted, was 'polite and correct'.

The factory inspectors' reports bore ample testimony to this absence of a spirit of investigation. A good example is the treatment that the question of the 'health' of the workers received in these reports. This was an important question from the Government of India's point of view, carrying obvious implications for the dietary conditions, the standard of living, the wages situation and finally the efficiency of the worker.[47] None of these latter considerations, however, ever influenced the Bengal factory inspectors. For years, their reports carried a section called 'General Health of the Operatives' where the workers' health was always described as 'good' if there had been no epidemics. 'The general health of operatives has been good', said the Factories Act report in 1928, 'no outbreak of disease in epidemic form having been reported during the year'.[48] Why was health a question of epidemics, and not one of diet, nutrition or standard of living? The following quotation from the factory inspection report for 1921 suggests the answer:

> The Naihati Jute Mills at Naihati, Baranagar Jute Mills at Baranagar, [etc.] . . . reported a shortage of labour in the month of August last owing to

[46] W.B.S.A., Com. Dept. Com. Br., July, 1921, A43-5.

[47] For evidence of Government of India's interest in these questions see W.B.S.A., Com. Dept. Com. Br., Feb. 1927, A1-8; Nov. 1933, A1-27; June 1935, A35-48. For Government of Bengal's reluctance to carry out a wage-census, see W.B.S.A., Com. Dept. Com. Br., Nov. 1921, B200-1.

[48] W.B.S.A., Com. Dept. Com. Br., Sept. 1929, A12-15..

outbreaks of malaria and influenza. The shortage . . . was not serious and the general health of the operatives . . . has on the whole been satisfactory.[49]

Or, to put the argument in an even more precise form, as did the report for 1923:

The general health of operatives during the year . . . has been comparatively good, no shortage of labour on account of epidemic diseases or sickness having been reported by the mills.[50]

At heart, this was the employer's argument. In the jute mills, health-care for workers was essentially aimed at the prevention of epidemics. Information regarding diseases treated free by the doctors of twenty-three jute mills in 1928 was collected by the Government of Bengal for submission to the Royal Commission on Labour. It is interesting to observe that none of the diseases treated were of nutritional origin: cholera, small-pox, malaria, enteric fever, relapsing fever, kala-azar, dysentery, diarrhoea, pneumonia, tuberculosis of the lungs, and respiratory diseases 'other than infections'.[51] Clearly, most of them were infectious diseases or water- or food-borne diseases, capable of affecting a number of people at the same time, especially under conditions of over-crowding. In other words, potential epidemics. Epidemics were what caused large-scale absenteeism that affected production; besides, they respected no class-barriers. Speaking to the IJMA in 1918, Alexander Murray, then hairman of the Association, referred to a proposal put by mills 'in four different municipalities up the river . . . to spend anything up to Rs 100 per loom' in improving workers' housing, and remarked that he could 'imagine no more profitable investment from a mill labour point of view'. Supporting this view, he said:

In proof of this I might refer to the experiences during the influenza epidemic last year of the mills with which I am most closely associated. Our mill doctors' reports show that the hands living in the bazar suffered far more severely than those living in the mills' own coolie lines. At most of our mills the production for the week ending 20th July, which witnessed the epidemic at its worst, was anything from 15 to 30 per cent below normal. But in the case of one of our mills which houses nearly all its labour in its own lines, the drop was only 5 per cent. . .[52]

[49] W.B.S.A., Com. Dept. Com. Br., June 1921, A29-30.
[50] W.B.S.A., Com. Dept. Com. Br., Aug. 1924, A34-7.
[51] W.B.S.A., Com. Dept. Com. Br., Apr. 1930, A7-12.
[52] W.B.S.A., Com. Dept. Com. Br., July 1919, A1-2.

Clearly, to Murray, as to the jute industry, the measure of the severity of epidemics was the drop in production. Hence the health of the workers was mainly a question of epidemics.

One implication of such an outlook was that large areas of working-class life escaped official notice. Once again, the health question illustrates the problem. As a result of the recommendations of the Royal Commission on Labour, an investigation was carried out into the conditions of women workers in jute mills in 1931-2. The investigating doctor discovered several diseases that had never found their way into the records of the mill dispensaries. She noted that many of the working-class children 'have a tendency to rickets, shown by slight bending of the legs and bossing of the forehead'. This was 'probably due to deficiency of vitamin D in the food'. While many children looked 'fine' 'in the first year of life', a 'healthy appearance was less common' after that age. Venereal diseases were 'said to be wide-spread', yet there was 'no evidence on the subject'. In the lines of one mill, she came across a young girl 'obviously dying of a pernicious type of anaemia', but 'she was having no treatment'. 'In the lines of another mill', she found 'a woman suffering from a severe degree of ostcomalacia, unable to walk. This is a very great danger in childbirth and with careful treatment can be cured or greatly relieved.' She noticed 'several cases of children reduced to almost extremity'. Another time she saw 'a woman obliged to stop her work for blindness and suffering great pain in the eyes [which] . . . would have been susceptible to treatment'. But a certain kind of 'blindness', in these cases, was what characterized the employer's outlook. The investigating doctor remarked: 'None of these cases were known to the mill doctors, who always accompanied me when I visited the lines.'[53]

Thus, in claiming as their own a view of labour conditions that really belonged to the owners of capital, the documents of the Bengal Government reproduced something else as well: the 'optical errors' of that vision. Significant aspects of working-class conditions remained hidden from it. This was what in the end undermined the Government of India's project for 'knowledge' of these conditions. The Government of Bengal lacked the political will necessary to distance itself from the employers in the jute industry. This was open knowledge even to the Government of India who, however, never

[53] W.B.S.A., Com. Dept. Com. Br., July 1932, A2-6.

felt powerful enough to force anyone's hand. On 13 September 1928
Lord Irwin, the Viceroy, wrote to the Secretary of State:

> We had a discussion in Council thi- week on the contemplated enquiry
> into labour matters . . . no Local Government except Bengal had any
> objection to our announcing now that such an enquiry would be held;
> but the Bengal Government entered a strong protest . . . Bengal have on
> other occasions lately shown a disposition to act as a brake in questions of
> this kind; for example they stood alone in adopting an uncompromising
> attitude in respect of minimum wages, and they were nearly alone in
> pressing for the circulation of the Trade Disputes Bill when we asked if
> Local Governments would agree to our pushing on with it.

Irwin's conclusion was significant: 'The influence of the employers
—and particularly the European employers—is strong there [in
Bengal], and they were not likely to receive the news of an enquiry
with joy.'[54]

It would once again be wrong to see this 'influence' as a conspiracy
of state and capital against labour. Its expressions were too above-
board and direct for it to be treated as such. It is better seen as part of
the existing political culture. In deciding, for instance, if commercial
bodies like the IJMA should be approached directly with the recommendations of the Industrial Unrest Committee (1921), Sir J. H.
Kerr, a member of the Governor's Council, wavered:

> We must walk warily [he wrote] . . . Sir Alexander Murray warned me
> specially that the Jute Mills Association would have to be led, not driven,
> and I think we should be safer in leaving the matter in his hands.[55]

Kerr felt frightened even to start an office like a Labour Bureau with
some pretension towards investigation of labour conditions: 'the
term bureau frightens people', he wrote; 'I would not start anything
in the nature of a Bureau even on paper without consultation with
employers.'[56]

So keen was the Government of Bengal in its desire to avoid any
confrontation with the owners of the jute mills that factory inspectors
were actually encouraged to leave all 'controversial' matters out of
their reports. Further, capitalists themselves sometimes had a direct
role in weeding out statements unfavourable to their interests. The

[54] India Office Library, London (hereafter I.O.L.), Mss. Eur. C152/4, Irwin
Papers, letter to Birkenhead, 13 Sept. 1928.
[55] W.B.S.A., Com. Dept. Com. Br., July 1921, A43-5 K.W.
[56] Ibid.

report for 1923 had to be redrafted because of objections from industrialists like Alexander Murray. As the Labour Intelligence Officer explained:

> Normally the Chief Inspector of Factories sends in his report to Government without previous sanction, but last year owing to a number of controversial paragraphs being inserted, the report was first unofficially examined. The report had ultimately to be reprinted as strong objection was taken by Sir A. Murray and others to the remarks of the Chief Inspector. There is nothing objectionable in the report [now being] put up, but I have toned down some of the remarks . . .[57]

Even the attendance register that the 1922 Factories Act required the factories to maintain was modified in Bengal to suit the convenience of the jute mill managers. It was made into a less detailed document than it could have been and as a result, admitted the Chief Inspector of Factories in 1930, it became 'a type of register satisfying the view of the employers [in the jute industry] but futile and inadequate for ensuring establishment of the provisions of Chapter IV [relating to working hours] of the [Factories] Act . . .'[58]

Thus if working-class conditions in the jute mills never quite became an object of knowledge in the way envisaged by the Government of India, the 'failure' occurred at two levels. The industry never produced the necessary documents; and the government lacked the political will to carry out its own investigations.

## IV

The question of the lack of a 'political will' on the part of the Government of Bengal, its inability to force any issue on the IJMA or the jute industry, can be partly comprehended as a negative illustration of Marx's argument. I say 'partly' because some of the spirit of co-operation between the state and capital must have derived from the tight racial bonds that existed between European employers and the British bureaucracy in colonial Bengal.[59] But one also has to note that the industry (or any sections of employers) never exerted any pressure on the government to equalize 'the conditions of competition'

[57] W.B.S.A., Com. Dept. Com. Br., Aug. 1924, A34-7.
[58] *R.C.L.I.*, vol. V, pt. 1, p. 328.
[59] See A. K. Bagchi, *Private Investment in India 1900-1939* (Cambridge, 1972), Ch. 6.

between different mills. 'Conditions are different in different [mill] centres', said the IJMA to the Royal Commission on Labour. 'One mill provides housing accommodation for all their workers whereas another mill provides none whatever. One mill provides good water, another provides no water.'[60] An official of the Government of Bengal was to use much stronger words:

> Perhaps in no industry in the world, situated in such a circumscribed area, is the wage position more inchoate. The mill groups under different managing agents work under wage systems which have developed many local idiosyncrasies during the long and short years of their existence. Even in mills under the same managing agents there are differences which to persons not acquainted with the position would seem incredible. . . . In . . . groups of mills situated close to each other and under different managing agents, the wage-rates in individual mills are kept, or are supposed to be kept, strictly secret.[61]

Yet the jute industry was always content to let all this be; there never arose any significant demand for standardization of wage rates. At the instance of the Royal Commission, the IJMA decided in 1931 to set up a sub-committee to look into the latter problem. The committee admitted in its report the following year that 'nothing can be done in the direction of general standardization [of wages] for all the mills' as there were 'circumstances which preclude any immediate steps being taken'.[62] The report ended with extremely cautious re-commendations for slow and gradual standardization of rates for mills 'in the same districts', but very little came of this. A confidential report on 'Jute Mill Labour Conditions' written in October 1945 by J. Lee, the Senior Labour Officer of the IJMA, referred to the lack of standardization of wage rates as a continuing problem:

> Over the last year I have collected statistics of wage-rates paid in the mills and these have all been transferred into a rate paid as "pies per hour" . . . I prepared a list of all occupations, and then gave the maximum rate paid as well as the minimum. The differences in many occupations was very great, and in itself, was . . . a good case for wage-standardization.[63]

[60] *R.C.L.I.*, vol. V, pt. 2, p. 163.
[61] Ibid., vol. V, pt. 1, p. 141.
[62] *I.J.M.A. Report for 1932* (Calcutta, 1933), pp. 314-15.
[63] I.J.M.A., Labour Department, 'Confidential Circulars and Notes' file, 1945-6.

The case for standardization remained 'good' and valid into the 1950s.[64]

Why was it that the jute industry, notorious for the feelings of rivalry that mills often harboured against one another, was happy to carry on with an 'inchoate' wage position? Several answers suggest themselves. To consider outside competition first, the relationship between the Calcutta and the Dundee industries was never one of straight-forward competition—as it was between Bombay and Manchester. With Dundee branching off into finer products for survival and Calcutta providing a big employment market for Dundee technicians and managers, the pressures of that potential competition eased off a great deal after 1914-19. The kind of uproar that Dundee industrialists often caused in the 1890s over labour conditions in Calcutta,[65] became a matter of the past in the twentieth century. Also, the state of organization of the Calcutta jute mill workers was too weak for them to exert any effective pressure on the wage question. Thirdly, the 'individualism' of individual (or a group of) mills was something that the IJMA accepted as the price for its organizational unity, which the industry saw as crucial to its overall prosperity. And fourthly, one must take into account the concentration of economic power within the industry; this must have gone some way towards mitigating any spirit of competition between the mills.

There were, however, two other factors which were perhaps more important than those mentioned above. Paradoxical though it may sound, the per capita expenditure incurred by the mills on their respective labour forces might have varied in fact far less than the discussion on wage rate differences suggests. In other words, it is possible that the 'conditions of competition' between mills remained more or less at par and thus made state intervention superfluous. It will be interesting, in this respect, to depart from the practice of calculating bonuses by themselves and try instead to study these along with other expenditures on labour, e.g. housing, sanitation, water supply, health clinics, etc. Since the amount spent under these latter heads also varied from mill to mill according to differences in the volume of labour supply, employers who paid lower wages might

[64] See Raghuraj Singh, *Movement of Industrial Wages in India* (Bombay, 1955), pp. 223-5.

[65] See, for instance, *The Dundee Advertiser*, 28 Jan. 1893, and *I.J.M.A. Report for 1893* (Calcutta, 1894), pp. 22-4.

well have ended up by spending more on housing, etc., and vice versa. It then seems quite possible that the average amount spent per unit of labour worked out to be roughly the same for different mills, so that the disparities in the 'conditions of competition' did not matter very much.

The point cannot be statistically verified here, detailed information on wage rates and other matters being extremely hard to come by. But there is some evidence to suggest that the industry had developed certain informal means for equalizing 'labour conditions' between the mills (especially those close to one another) or at least for keeping the 'inequalities' well within 'tolerable' limits. For one thing, it was hard to keep the information about wages a secret however much the managing agents might desire such secrecy. 'The total earnings [for different occupations] are not necessarily kept secret', the Government of Bengal told the Royal Commission, and the piece-rates or bonus rates could easily be 'ascertained by spy-work in the bazar'.[66] Further, the worker's idea of a 'fair wage' often involved a principle of parity with those paid by mills in the neighbourhood. Localized strikes therefore often tended to bring local wage rates in line with one another.

Even more important perhaps was the fact that managers could effectively create an informal climate (and pressure) of opinion which also had a homogenizing influence on labour conditions. When an American firm, the American Manufacturing Company, started a jute mill in Calcutta in the early 1920s, it was said that 'the Directors in the States . . . sanctioned large amounts to be spent on sanitation and welfare of workers, as they were accustomed to such outlay in connection with their jute mills in the United States'. Yet the eventual amount spent turned out to be much less than that sanctioned, for the managers of the other jute mills had objected.

> In many cases they [the Directors] would have been willing to go much
> further than they had actually gone e.g. to give electric light in the
> workers' houses, as well as a plentiful installation outside in the lines, but
> had been told that this had never been done here. So at present electric
> light is limited to the durwans' houses.

It is significant that this mill ultimately settled for the 'district rate' of wages and followed 'the custom in jute mills in the district' in respect

[66] *R.C.L.I.*, vol. V, pt. 1, p. 141.

of accident compensation. It also 'modelled' its leave rules (or the laxity of them!) on those at the 'neighbouring jute mills'. And while the 'agents had been willing to put in as good a drainage system as possible', the actual 'type copied was that used by the other Calcutta Jute Mills'.[67]

A lack of standardization in wage rates therefore did not necessarily reflect a competitive situation among the mills regarding their labour conditions. Effective pressure from international competitors was also conspicuously absent. The Bengal Government's views on labour conditions were therefore governed solely by its relationship with capitalists in the jute industry, and in this relationship the latter always predominated. What the state therefore reproduced in its documents was the blinkered vision of capital.

V

But that leaves us with the more crucial question: why was the 'vision' of capital 'blinkered'? Why did the jute mills fail to produce the daily records that the Government of India had asked for? Or to put the question differently: why were the attendance registers kept in such a state that they did not 'reflect the true conditions of labour'? Once again, Marx's argument is useful. To understand the lack of documentation at the level of the factory we have to turn to the problem of 'discipline'. A discussion of 'discipline' has to begin by considering the nature of work and technology in a jute mill, for discipline is, in the first place, a question of training and skills, the 'technical subordination of the worker' to the motion and requirements of the machine. Discipline of course also involves supervision, but we shall take that up later.

Work inside a Calcutta jute mill involved mechanical processes broadly similar to those in a nineteenth-century cotton mill, except that jute was a rougher material than cotton and the humidification necessary for cotton was not needed for jute.[68] After the raw jute was sorted and batched as it came into the mill, it went through a process

[67] W.B.S.A., Com. Dept. Com. Br., Apr. 1923, B77.
[68] This description is based on the following sources: Centre for South Asian Studies, Cambridge (hereafter C.S.A.S.), Papers of Sir Edward Benthall (hereafter B.P.), Box XVIII, Note entitled 'Indian Jute Industry' (n.d. [1940s?]), and N. C. Saha, 'Inside a Jute Mill', *Jute and Gunny Review*, Feb.–Mar. 1950, pp. 139-43.

of softening and preparation for the eventual spinning and weaving of
jute. Softening included passing the jute 'through a softening machine
consisting of fluted rollers under heavy pressure when simultaneously
an emulsion of oil and water...[was] applied', the oil being necessary
'to facilitate the succeeding process of manufacture as jute fibre
contains no natural lubrication.' After softening came the preparation
stage which included three distinct operations: carding, drawing and
roving. The object of carding was 'to break down long stalks or strips
of fibre into a continuous broad ribbon of fine fibres' and to lay the
fibres parallel to one another. The carding process involved the use of
two machines—the breaker card and the finisher card. The former
'breaks and hackles the stalks of [the] fibre' to make it into a broad
ribbon 'termed sliver in the trade'. About twelve such slivers were
then fed manually into the 'finisher' card 'where the carding operation
is continued on finer scale'.[69] The carded slivers were still not uniform
or straight and were therefore subjected to processes called drawing
and doubling, where the aim was to obtain 'a greater length of
[uniform] fibre for the same unit of weight'. The operations of
drawing and doubling were 'combined into one machine called [the]
drawing frame'. Drawing thinned out the sliver, doubling counter-
acted it by combining 'two or more such drawn out slivers into one at
the delivery end of the machine'. The last of the preparatory processes
was roving, the object of which was to draw out the slivers even
further, according to the spinning requirements, while strengthening
them by giving them a partial twist. The twisted sliver was called
'rove'.

The next step was spinning, where yarns were made by spinning
frames which further drew out the rove, spun it, and finally wound it
on spinning bobbins. Warp yarns were twisted harder than weft
yarns. The winding department followed next and 'the yarn forming
the warp of the cloth . . . [was] wound round . . . bobbins into the form
of comparatively large rolls, thereby obtaining a greater continuity in
length'. The yarn for the weft in the cloth was wound into ' "cops"
fitting exactly into the shuttles employed in weaving'. Warp yarn,
saturated with a starchy material to prevent breakage in weaving, was
then 'drawn on to large beams' (the 'beaming' process) and placed at

[69] Ibid.: 'The principle of these [carding] machines is a rapidly revolving cylinder
armoured with pins whilst smaller pinned rollers revolving at a slower speed are placed
parallel to this cylinder and retard the fibre, thus promoting the combing action.'

the back of the loom for weaving. The final stages in the manufacture constituted the finishing process, where the woven cloth was passed through the heavy rollers of a calendering machine for ironing and eventually cut and sewn into bags. The bags again were 'made into bundles of 25 or 30' and packed by a hydraulic press.

The technology accompanying these processes had been 'perfected' in the nineteenth century. S. G. Barker, who investigated the technical side of the Calcutta jute mills in the 1930s, found the technology so stagnant that he likened the industry to a gramophone needle: 'It runs in a groove and plays a nice tune. If either needle or record gets worn, new ones are demanded.'[70] The 'groove' in Barker's description referred to the lack of diversification of products in the history of the industry and to the crude and rough nature of what was produced. This he saw as a fundamental factor behind technological stagnation: 'hessian, sacking or canvas has not called for any alteration in machinery'. In Barker's words:

> Jute being a cheap material producing fabrics for rough usage . . . the machinery and technique in India became standardised upon an elementary mechanical basis. Simplicity of operation without the necessity for textile science since changes were practically non-existent . . . soon led to the mass production of the limited range of Indian jute products becoming almost automatic. The conversion of Jute fibres into fabrics therefore became a mechanical engineering proposition, a position largely maintained to this day. The mechanical influence was greatly enhanced by conditions in India, since spare machine parts and renewals were difficult to get from home. Thus each mill or group was equipped with an efficient mechanics' workshop, which not only maintained the machinery in excellent order but even extended to the construction of duplicates of existing looms, etc. Again the simplicity of the machine principles facilitated this. . . . Machinery in the mills in general, therefore, has had a long working life, perhaps too long.[71]

The industry considered this technology so adequate for its purpose that it placed very little premium on the scientific and technological training of its workers and the superior technical staff. Barker was surprised to discover many large and crucial gaps in the technical knowledge of the Scottish managers and assistants—gaps which they

[70] S. G. Barker, *Report on the Scientific and Technical Development of the Jute Manufacturing Industry in Bengal with an Addenda on Jute, its Scientific Nature and Information Relevant Thereto* (Calcutta, 1935), p. 42.

[71] Ibid., pp. 41-2.

usually filled up with that rather undefined human quality called 'experience'. The softening process contained a number of 'unknowns' like 'temperature, moisture content and distribution in the [jute] pile' as well as the optimum pressure between the rollers, 'the actual value for which seemingly . . . [had] no criterion but *experience*'. He was also struck by 'the lack of finality in technical knowledge of the carding process'. The same went for drawing and doubling, where 'the ideal roller pressure' and 'the size of flutings for Jute . . . [had] been determined by *experience*'. For the process of roving, the list of things unknown was formidable. 'Roller covering and pressure, surface speeds, spindle speeds, the flyer mechanism, the distribution of fibre length in the rove, the degree of levelness along its length, fibre control and, in addition, the factors concerning twist and the form of bobbins' were all yet 'to be studied'. Barker's correspondence with some of the mill managers on technical problems dramatically revealed the low priority that the industry gave to technical education. Technical issues were often treated merely as matters of the 'experience', 'opinion' or personal judgement of the people concerned:

> From my experience [wrote one manager to Barker] I have found that certain makers' machines are suitable for one class of fibre, while others are suitable for a different class. . . . Pinning [on the rollers]. A number of people favour pinning with light pins whilst others prefer a coarser pinning with a corresponding heavier pin, again only a matter of opinion.
>
> Another point which allows a certain latitude to be taken is roller speeds and ratios, but to my mind this item is not nearly as important as pinning and setting.[72]

If the manager's knowledge of the machinery had such a glaring 'lack of finality' about it, one can imagine the want of understanding that separated the worker from the machine. This is not to say that the machine did not in any way affect the worker's life in the factory. The mechanical processes in a jute mill were continuous, with one process feeding another, and the work was heavier and noisier than in a typical cotton mill.[73] The continuous motion and speed of the machinery was something that the worker had to adjust to. 'Continuous and even flow' of the jute sliver was the responsibility of the

[72] The quotations in this paragraph are from ibid., pp. 26-7, 30-1, 33, 36. Emphases added.

[73] See B. Foley, *Report on Labour in Bengal* (Calcutta, 1906), note (dated 19 Sept. 1905) on Bengal Cotton Mill.

labourers working on the softening, carding, drawing and roving machines.[74] 'The work of feeding the breaker cards', for instance, was 'heavy' and needed 'constant attention'. The finisher card required the co-operation of three women at a speed matching that of the machine: 'one arranges the slivers side by side at the feed end, one takes delivery at the other and one carries'.[75] In the spinning department, the shifting of bobbins 'must be done quickly for with bulky material such as jute, the bobbins fill fast and require frequent changing, which necessitates stopping the machine'.[76] But as the payment of the managing agents and managers often depended on the output, such stoppages were seen as time lost and therefore had to be as brief as possible. Pace also characterized the work in piece-rated departments like weaving or sack-sewing where the worker's earnings depended on how much, and hence how rapidly, he could produce.

This 'subordination' to the machine that the worker suffered in the jute mill, however, was not very 'technical'. The worker did not come to terms with the machine on the basis of even an elementary understanding of its working principles. The story is poignantly told in the nature of accidents which occurred in the jute mills. Many of the fatal ones resulted from the workers attempting to clean the machinery while still in motion or from their (especially women's) loose-fitting clothes getting caught in the moving parts of the machinery.[77] Accidents of this kind revealed the emphasis that the mill managements placed on the continuous running of the machinery, the laxity of factory rules (about dress) and the little value attached to a worker's life, but also the worker's incomprehension of the running principles of the machinery. In fact, the worker's relationship to the machine, instead of being mediated through technical knowledge, was mediated through the north Indian peasant's conception of his tools, where the tools often took on magical and godly qualities. A religious outlook rather than 'science' determined this relationship, with the difference that in a jute mill, the labourer's tools were far more powerful and malignant than the peasant's implements and were

[74] See *Report of the Central Wage Board for Jute Industry* (Delhi, 1963), Appendix XVII.

[75] J. H. Kelman, *Labour in India* (London, 1923), p. 82.

[76] D. H. Buchanan, *The Development of Capitalistic Enterprise in India* (New York, 1934), p. 247.

[77] The factory inspection reports for different years have material supporting this observation.

even capable of claiming lives at the shortest notice. The vivid details of the following report from the 1930s bear witness to this religious consciousness:

> In some of the jute mills near Calcutta the mechanics often sacrifice goats at this time [autumn: the time of the *Diwali* festival]. A separate altar is erected by the mechanics of each of the four or five departments in the mill. Various tools and other emblems of their work are placed upon it, together with heaps of sweetmeats and decorations. Incense is burned during an entire day and . . . the buildings are effectively filled with smoke. Towards evening a male goat is thoroughly washed, decorated with proper colors and flowers and prepared for a parade and final sacrifice. The little procession, made up principally of the goat and a band, then marches through the grounds and up and down the aisles of the department to the altar. The animal is fed as many sweets as he will accept, and is then decapitated at one stroke by a long knife and sword. With proper ceremony the head is deposited in the river, in this case . . . the sacred Ganges, while the meat is retained for a feast in the evening. . . . The factory and the power-machine have been readily adopted and given due place in religious ceremony.[78]

It is of course not being claimed here that this religious outlook of the workers would have vanished if only they had been given a scientific knowledge of the machinery. The fact that modern Indian 'holy men' have always counted a good number of Ph.Ds in physics among their camp-followers should act as a sufficient deterrent against such a point of view. Besides, cultures have their own ways of surviving even the most 'hostile' of environments. But what is relevant here is that the Calcutta jute worker's subordination to the pace and requirements of the machinery was not affected through training and education. It was not, in that sense, a case of the '*technical* subordination' of Marx's description. The mills in fact were largely averse to the idea of giving their workers or their children any education at all. In 1929, the IJMA said to the Royal Commission

---

[78] Buchanan, op. cit., p. 409. The practice of worshipping machine-tools seems to have been widespread among factory workers in eastern India. The present writer remembers being present, as a child, at some of the these ceremonies at a small engineering factory in Calcutta. The Jamshedpur steel-industry workers had their annual day of 'Hathyar Puja' (tool-worship) when 'tools and implements attained the status of deity'. 'Bedecked with flowers, the giant cranes and travelling derricks clanked to their appointed tasks; caparisoned with blossoms, the locomotives snorted about on the sidings; streaming garlands, the wheelbarrows squeaked from coalpit to furnace.' Lillian Luker Ashby (with Roger Whatley), *My India* (London, 1938), pp. 287-8.

that it did not think that the provision of education was a 'duty' of the employers.[79] But their deeper attitudes were revealed in 1914-15 when the Government of Bengal, acting under pressure from Delhi, made some money available for the education of working-class children in the jute mill areas and was forced by the IJMA to confine such education only to those children who were not yet old enough to work in the jute mills. And the lessons, insisted the mill owners, had to be confined to the teaching of 'the three "R"s' and nothing beyond.[80]

The argument that the IJMA put forward to the government (and one that was accepted by the latter) contained an important 'reason' for their lack of interest in workers' education:

> The character of the education must not be such as to draw the children away from the profession which they would adopt if they were allowed to continue illiterate... it must not render them unfit for *cooly* work.[81]

Literacy, in other words, was irrelevant to work in the jute mills. This was so, for, according to the employers, the work was easily learnt and required no rigorous training. Indeed, the bulk of the labour force was made up of totally unskilled labourers (called coolies) employed without exception on manual work. The Census of 1921 found that of a total of 280,854 workers in the Calcutta jute mills no less than 156,633 (i.e. over 55 per cent) were engaged in work involving no machinery at all.[82] Even of the work that involved the use of machinery it was said in 1937 by jute mill owners themselves that 'up to spinning... most of the work is mechanical or routine and can be easily learnt, and labour for these departments is plentiful; winding, weaving and [machine] sewing required skilled labour'.[83] How 'easily learnt' was explained in 1906 by the Chairman of the IJMA who spelt out the different amounts of time that were needed to train in the different occupations in a jute mill:

[79] *R.C.L.I.*, vol. V, pt. 2, p. 160.

[80] W.B.S.A., Genl. Dept. Edn. Br., Mar. 1913, A69-85; Jan. 1914, A31-36; Apr. 1915, A172-75.

[81] W.B.S.A., Genl. Dept. Edn. Br., Apr. 1915, A172-75.

[82] *Census of India 1921* (Calcutta, 1923), vol. V, pt. 2, Table XXII, pts. IV and V. This Census report defined all work involving machinery as 'skilled work'.

[83] C.S.A.S., B.P., Box XII: Mimeographed note dated 27 Apr. 1937, captioned 'Jute Strike Situation' by J. R. Walker, M.L.A.—circulated for the information of the European Group, Bengal Legislature.

| | | |
|---|---|---|
| Coolie ['s] [work] | ... ... ... ... | [one] week |
| Women ['s] [work: mainly preparing and hand-sewing] | ... ... ... ... | [one] week |
| Shifter ['s] [work] | ... ... ... ... | [one] week |
| Spinner ['s] [work] | ... ... ... ... | Graduate from shifters; may be a year or more on shifting. |
| Weaver ['s] [work] | ... ... ... ... | A year to be first-class workman[84] |

This 'learning', again, was purely experiential. It was pointed out by several witnesses to the Royal Commission that there was no appren-ticeship system in the jute mills.[85] The IJMA said in its evidence that 'the bulk of the work in the mill is unskilled, and where training is necessary, as for instance in the spinning department, this is obtained in the course of actual employment, by ɪe efforts of the worker himself'.[86] On the preparing side, 'a few weeks at any of the machines . . . [was] long enough to make the worker proficient'. Weaving needed 'skilled' work 'but, generally speaking, weavers become proficient very quickly'. Even mechanics, joiners, blacksmiths had no system of formal training: '[they] . . . start as boys, and are paid a nominal wage until they become of use'.[87]

The informality of the jute mills' system of recruitment and training—two important features of industrial discipline—was the subject of comment in 1945 in a note on 'Apprenticeship to Jute Mill Weaving Departments' prepared by the newly-formed Labour Department of the IJMA. 'Notwithstanding that the Jute Industry has prospered and expanded upon the output of its many looms', the note said, 'there haꞩ never been established any common method of selecting recruits or of teaching young workers the business of weaving.' Worse still, such informal training as the workers could receive by watching or helping others was often a matter of breaking factory rules or legislation: '[the] knowledge of power loom weaving could only be gained by the efforts of the novice himself in time spent, *usually surreptitiously*, beside a friendly weaver already employed in a mill factory'. What permitted such a state of affairs to continue was the stagnation in technology which reflected, as we

[84] Foley, op. cit., Appendix.   [85] *R.C.L.I.*, vol. V, pt. 1, p. 262; pt. 2, pp. 129, 157.
[86] Ibid., vol. V, pt. 1, p. 280.                                   [87] Ibid., p. 298.

have seen, a lack of diversity in the products of the mills and their rather crude nature. This, again, was commented on in the note:

> Of recruits who had any specialised tuition in weaving there were none, and there are very few today. . . . No lasting improvement of quality or quantity of outturn could possibly result from this system, and it is probably true that the operative himself is no better equipped technically to turn out good fabric today than was his grandfather fifty years ago. Pride of craftsmanship has not been fostered, nor have any efforts been made to improve or widen the outlook of the operative who frequently never attains greater proficiency than is needed for operating a loom weaving [only] one type of fabric.[88]

This discussion helps explain why the owners in the jute industry took a rather selective view of working-class conditions. Given the easily-learnt nature of jute mill work, individual workers remained highly replaceable as long as the supply of labour was adequate. The task of structuring a labour force was therefore largely a supply proposition to the mills and not a question of skill formation, training or efficiency. An 'ample supply of [cheap] male labour', and not efficiency, was what was always seen as an important key to the prosperity of the mills.[89] It was in fact the concern with the supply of labour that often produced a certain atmosphere of laxity of rules within a jute mill. As the Factory Inspector explained in his report for 1893:

> A number of men, women and children can at most times of the day be seen in the grounds of the large [jute] mills, either asleep under the trees or shady parts of the building, taking their meals, bathing or smoking in a special shed . . . built for the purpose. The question might suggest itself to some . . . as to why so many are able to leave their work at all times of the day when in the Home Mills everyone is kept under lock and key. The answer is simple but a very striking one. There are 100 per cent more hands employed in every Jute Mill in Bengal than is required to work a similar sized mill in Dundee.[90]

The mills obviously found it cheaper to carry with them some excess labour (to meet contingencies like epidemics and absenteeism) than

[88] This and other quotations in this paragraph come from IJMA, Labour Department file on [confidential] Circulars and Notes of the Committee, 1945-46: Note on 'IJMA Apprenticeship Scheme'. Emphasis added.

[89] W.B.S.A., Com. Dept. Com. Br., Nov. 1919, A11-25: Alexander Murray's note on the jute industry.

[90] W.B.S.A., Genl. Dept. Misc. Br., Aug. 1893, A1-36.

to invest in a healthy, vigorous, efficient working class. As late as 1929, the Indian jute mill worker was half as efficient as a worker in Dundee. The IJMA explained that this was not because 'the work [in India] is unduly hard'. Nor was it caused by 'climatic conditions', but 'simply because this has been the custom so far as the Calcutta jute mills are concerned'.[91]

In the eyes of the employers, then, certain aspects of working-class conditions gained priority over others and received more attention. And the knowledge produced as a result of this attention bore the unmistakable stamp of the employers' concern about labour supply. The 'areas of origin' of the workers, for instance, became an object of investigation, especially at moments of inadequate labour supply. Hence the availability of such information. Foley's report of 1905, itself a document on labour supply, gave evidence of this. J. Nicoll of the IJMA told Foley that 'he [Nicoll] had experienced some difficulty [in procuring labour] in his three Jute Mills in 1902, and had *therefore* caused a census to be made that year, showing the districts from which the hands came', and it was this data that Foley reproduced in his report.[92] But Foley also noted that such information was not collected except in times of labour scarcity. The average jute mill manager, who was 'usually a kindly Scot from Dundee', was 'generally . . . unable to say from where his hands come, and if told the information would convey no meaning to him'.[93] Foley's impressions are confirmed by a 1921 report on 'The Conditions of Employment of Women Before and After Child-Birth in Bengal Industries' by Dr D. F. Curjel of the Indian Medical Service.[94] Of the twenty-five jute mills Curjel visited, none were able to offer any information about the number of children born to their female workers. Curjel was also struck by the managers' lack of interest in working-class conditions. The manager of the Soorah Jute Mill 'did not concern himself with conditions affecting lives of the workers'. Curjel found the manager of the Lawrence Jute Mill 'rather vague as to [the] class of labour employed', and he 'seemed to take little interest' in their conditions. The manager of the Union Jute Mill who 'had been in charge 6 months' told her that 'he had been too busy to think about the health of the workers'. This

[91] *R.C.L.I.*, vol. V, pt. 1, p. 304.
[92] Foley, op. cit., Appendix.
[93] Ibid., para 23.
[94] W.B.S.A. Com. Dept. Com. Br., Apr. 1923, B77.

lack of interest was once again reflective of capital's view of labour conditions: they mattered only if and when they affected labour supply. 'It is interesting to find', Curjel noted after talking to the manager of the Howrah Jute Mills, 'how little managers know of the origins of the labour employed in their mills. As long as the sirdars produced the required number of workers, it does not concern them from what district it is drawn.' Even more telling was the reception that Curjel had from the manager of the Ballighata Jute Mill. The manager 'would scarcely discuss' the subject of labour conditions with Curjel. He said 'he did not concern himself with the workers' lives'. 'He took no interest in modern labour questions [and] "thought it all useless".' Curjel notes why this was so: The manager who had been in this mill for many years, did not appear to be the very least interested in conditions affecting his workers, so long as he got the labour.'[95]

Thus it was that in the jute mills of Calcutta the employers' vision of labour conditions developed its particular blind spots: the worker's health became a question of epidemics and not one of nutrition; sanitation became a matter of interest but not the standard of living of the worker;[96] and while the areas of 'origin' of labourers became on occasion a subject of documentation and research, the individual worker remained largely undocumented almost throughout the period under consideration.[97] The political economy of the jute industry thus goes a long way towards explaining why the mill managers were not particularly careful about the proper maintenance of records relating to conditions of labour.

## VI

The selectiveness with which the industry treated the question of labour conditions meant that the factory documents covered a narrow

[95] Ibid.

[96] For examples of the jute mills' interest in sanitation see W.B.S.A., Local Self-Government Dept. Public Health Br., Oct. 1928, A7-42; Dec. 1931, A15-21; Dec. 1931, B24-26; June 1932, A70-81. For evidence relating to the extreme scarcity of information about the workers' indebtedness, see *R.C.L.I.*, vol. V, pt. 2, p. 172 and W.B.S.A., Com. Dept. Com. Br., Jan. 1933, B242-74.

[97] For example, up to 1924 the jute mills did not keep any records of the home addresses of individual workers. The Workmen's Compensation Act made such records necessary (see *R.C.L.I.*, vol. V, pt. 2, p. 21). Up to 1937 the mills did not keep any employment cards bearing the service histories of individual workers. These were to be introduced in 1937 at the instance of the Bengal Government but not properly till 1948. See *Report of the I.J.M.A. for 1937* (Calcutta, 1938).

range of issues, touching upon only a few aspects of the workers' lives. But apart from the narrowness of their scope, there was yet another problem that the authorities faced in handling these documents: their unreliability. This is why the attendance registers of the jute mills were described in 1930 as not reflecting 'the true conditions' of labour. Factory inspectors, courts of justice trying cases involving jute mill workers, the managers of the mills—all complained of this. 'You will admit', Alexander Murray of the IJMA was asked by Sir Victor Sassoon of the Royal Commission on Labour, 'that it must be very difficult for the management to be sure that the attendance books that come before them are accurate?' 'It is difficult', Murray admitted.[98] The extent of the 'difficulty' was underscored in the Factory Inspector's report for 1927 where he quoted a letter 'from a Subdivision Officer' as only 'an example of the value' of such documents. The letter read:

> In connection with a bad-livelihood case one ✳✳✳ said to be the clerk in charge of the attendance register of the ✳✳✳ Jute Mills, was summoned on behalf of the defence as witness. He gave sworn testimony that the undertrial prisoner ✳✳✳ had attended the mill from the 10th to 13th January 1927 and had drawn Rs 4-11 as wages. He stated that he had noted the attendance personally. It transpired, however, that the said ✳✳✳ was arrested by the Police on 30th December 1926 in connection with a dacoity case and since that day he was continuously in the Jail lock-up to the end of February 1927. The entries in the attendance register must be false entries. . . . The attendance register has been kept in a very slovenly manner and there are many unattested corrections and many entries are in pencil.[99]

Similar remarks were made by the Subdivisional Officer of Serampore who tried the 'Time Babu' of the Champdany Jute Mill in 1913 for employing a child on the basis of a cancelled medical certificate.

> I would point out [he said] that the provisional certificate shown to me does not bear any doctor's signature, and appears to be merely a blank form filled up by an unknown person. This suggests a lack of supervision, specially as I was told [that] this was the customary practice.[100]

The problem of the unreliability of documents then takes us back to a question already highlighted in our discussion of Marx's argument—the nature and quality of supervision inside the mills. The 'subordinate supervising staff' in the jute mills were of two classes. 'In the first class there would be the more or less educated

[98] *R.C.L.I.*, vol. V, pt. 2, p. 144.
[99] W.B.S.A., Com. Dept. Com. Br., Sept. 1928, A21-25.
[100] W.B.S.A., Finance Dept. Com. Br., Mar. 1915, A58-59.

babu who has never been a mill operative himself'. Initially appointed as an apprentice, the *babu* was soon promoted to supervisory work under a Scottish assistant. The duties of the *babu* would be to 'check attendances, to keep attendance registers', to prepare wage books and 'generally assist in the supervision and work of the department'.[101] Below the *babu* was the *sardar* who was both a supplier and supervisor of labour and whose social origins were often the same as those of the ordinary worker himself. The Government of Bengal pictured the *sardar* thus:

> The immediate employer of a worker is his sirdar. The sirdar gives him his job and it is by his will that the worker retains it. . . . The sirdars are the real masters of men. They employ them and dismiss them, and, in many cases, they house them and can unhouse them. They may own or control the shops which supply the men with food. The operative, too, pays his lump or recurring sum to the sirdar to retain his job. His life, indeed, at every turn is coloured by sirdarism.[102]

The IJMA described the sardars and the under-sardars as constituting 'the lower subordinate supervising staff of the mills'.[103]

The *sardar* assisted the *babu* in the latter's task of maintaining factory documents. The process was explained in the conversation that took place between Victor Sassoon and Alexander Murray during the proceedings of the Royal Commission on Labour:

| | |
|---|---|
| Sassoon [S]: | Is the only check as to attendance after the men are at their machines? |
| Murray [M]: | That is right. |
| S: | Token [designating shifts] are not taken at the gate and put on their machines? |
| M: | No. The check is taken after the workman is at the machine. |
| S: | The *baboo* walks round the machinery and puts down the number of people he happens to see working at the machines or probably the *sardar* tells him are present? |
| M: | He is supposed to check up each worker individually. |
| S: | But I take it the *sardar* tells him who is there and he takes the word of the *sardar* to a great extent? |
| M: | That may happen.[104] |

[101] *R.C.L.I.*, vol. V, pt. 1, p. 280-1.
[102] Ibid., p. 153.
[103] Ibid., pp. 280-1.
[104] Ibid., vol. V, pt. 2, pp. 144-5.

We have quoted earlier the Government of Bengal's description of the *sardar*. As that description will have made clear, *sardari* was primarily about supervisory workers making money at the expense of the ordinary worker through such means as moneylending, bribery, etc. More *sardars* 'dismissed labour and engaged fresh hands just at their pleasure', the IJMA complained to the Royal Commission, and 'each man who signed on had to pay for the job'.[105] In this the *sardar* often acted in league with the *babu*.

It is easy to see that the 'corruption' of the *sardar* and the *babu* would have necessarily imparted a perverse character to the mill documents relating to working-class conditions—wage books, attendance registers, fine books, shift tokens, medical certificates, etc. This at any rate was the burden of the official complaints. One example that the authorities often gave to support their contention was the way the medical certificates of child workers were treated in the mills. In point of law, these certificates were meant to protect the health of the working class by preventing the employment of under-age children. But the practice of each child recruit having to bribe the *sardars* and the *babus* made this impossible of attainment. As the Chief Inspector of Factories explained to the Royal Commission:

> The sirdar produces the children and, in many cases, allows them to be employed whether they are fit, certified or not, and he being illiterate cannot satisfy himself as to the correctness of the entries in the register. He must, however, keep the spindles going, if not directly to maintain continuity of production, to maintain his receipts on a child capitation basis.[106]

This apparently led to a fairly rapid turnover of children from individual mills, a process that contributed to the 'unreliability' of documents. Captain O'Connor, the Senior Certifying Surgeon of Factories, Barackpore district, wrote: 'The principal reason why children migrate from mill to mill is that they are focibly turned out by sirdars for pecuniary gain'. The result was that it became 'quite normal ... for a child to have a certificate in each of a number of mills in a district', and a child 'whose certificate is cancelled for not being produced' could 'easily be re-certified under another name'.[107] Colonel Nott, the Civil Surgeon of Howrah, reported a case in 1913

---

[105] Ibid., p. 142.
[106] Ibid., vol. V, pt. 1, p. 92.
[107] Ibid., pp. 333-4.

in which the same child applied to him on the same day for certificates in two different names, one Muslim and the other Hindu—Pir Mahomed and Banojowah. Enquiries revealed that he had done it at the *sardar*'s instruction.[108]

A similar phenomenon could be observed in the case of adult labour as well. 'When checking registers', wrote the Factory Inspector in 1930, 'a woman under examination may give two or three names with a certain amount of persistence'.[109] The manipulation of the attendance registers (and other documents) by *sardars* and *babus* invariably led to an inflation of the wage bill. 'You may have 10 per cent of the names on your books', the Royal Commission suggested to the manager of the Caledonian Jute Mill, 'who actually do not exist as far as working is concerned and that money goes somewhere?' 'Yes,' replied the manager, 'it is divided between the baboos and the sardars and the man who is doing the two men's jobs.'[110] Another manager admitted in his evidence that about 7.5 per cent of his labour force were probably such ghost workers.[111] The Chief Inspector of Factories however thought these figures to be underestimates. While 'theoretically' and 'according to the register', the multiple shift mills carried 22 or 25 per cent more labour than single-shift mills, the Inspector knew that in reality it was 'considerably less than 10 per cent'.[112]

A study of the process of 'supervision' within a jute mill—a problem that Marx saw as central to the question of documentation of the conditions of work—turns on the problem of the 'corruption' of the supervisory staff. Why was 'the labour of overlooking' in a Calcutta jute mill riddled with 'corruption'? How does one account for the widespread practice of falsifying documents?

## VII

One could obviously and easily develop a 'needs of capital' type argument in response to these questions. It could be argued, for instance, that the *sardar* existed only because he served the 'needs of

[108] W.B.S.A., Finance Dept. Com. Br., Mar. 1915, A58-9.
[109] W.B.S.A., Com. Dept. Com. Br., Aug. 1931, A33-6.
[110] *R.C.L.I.*, vol. V, pt. 2, pp. 142, 144-5.
[111] Ibid., p. 143.
[112] Ibid., p. 195.

capital' in the jute industry and that his so-called 'corrupt' practices—recruiting workers for bribes, housing them, lending them money at high interests—constituted a kind of service to capital in a labour market that the industry had done very little to structure.

There is a body of evidence that supports this view. The mills, it would appear, were prepared to tolerate the 'corrupt' practices of the *sardar* as he was considered indispensable. Even though the IJMA bitterly complained to the Royal Commission about *sardari* 'corruption', they nevertheless insisted that 'you [could] not do without sardars'.[113] The financial outlays made by the mills on wages to be paid to the labourers clearly allowed for a certain amount of leakage through *sardari* corruption. Admittedly, this was not true of the (relatively) high-wage, piece-paid department of weaving where 'a check [was] made by calculating the total production of each section of the department, so that the total amount actually earned by production must equal the amount to be paid out'.[114] In weaving, therefore, *sardari* extortion of ordinary workers took the form of bribery, moneylending, etc.[115] But in every other department the wage policy followed the simple aim of keeping the 'corrupt' practices of the *sardar* and the *babu* (e.g. inflating the wage bill by employing 'ghost workers') under control rather than attempting to abolish them altogether.

> In each department throughout the works . . . a complement is drawn up, showing the number of hands it requires to run satisfactorily; and against this number is shown the amount in wages that such departments are bound down to.[116]

There is also evidence suggesting the direct complicity, in some cases, of the Scottish overseers and managers of the mills in the 'corrupt' acts of the *sardar* and the *babu*. The Kankinarrah Labour Union (formed in 1922) 'once exposed a case of bribery when Rs 3000 had been paid for the position of a Head Sardar'. The President of the Union, K. C. Roy Chowdhury, noted in his diary that 'the money had been received by a friend of the manager of the [jute] mill

[113] Ibid., p. 150.
[114] Ibid., vol. V, pt. 1, p. 281.
[115] Ibid., vol. V, pt. 2, p. 120.
[116] Ibid., vol. V, pt. 1, p. 281.

concerned'.[117] His diary also had the following entry which is even more revealing:

> Sen, the Head Babu of the Union [Jute] Mill, informed me today that numerous false tickets [tokens] are distributed every day at their mill. This means that tokens are distributed in the names of people who have not actually done any work. The money is then divided between the sardars, the Head Babu and the European overseer sahib. Bima sardar reportedly even supplies the weekly groceries for the overseer sahibs free of any cost.[118]

How did all this suit the 'needs of capital'? Why were the owners of capital in the jute industry prepared to overlook, and at best contain, this 'corruption' rather than stamp out the practices? Obviously, the *sardar* in his role of labour-supplier was important to the industry's view of its own interests. The Chief Inspector of Factories explained this in 1913:

> All mills have to rely on the Sirdars and Time-Babus of their various departments for the supply of labour, [and therefore] the Manager has either to overlook irregularities practised by these men or to deal strictly with them and face a shortage [of labour] which results in a reduced weekly outturn in tonnage of gunnies, and seriously affects his position with the Managing Agents.[119]

But as we shall see, finding inexpensive ways of controlling labour was a problem of greater concern to the industry than that of labour supply. And this was the reason for the continued importance of the *sirdar*. To understand why this was so we have to look at the nature of the demand for labour that the industry created and the way it proceeded to meet that demand.

A plentiful supply of labour was considered necessary for the progress of the industry. Between the years 1895 and 1926, when the industry enjoyed an almost uninterrupted period of prosperity and expansion of output, the number of workers employed in the mills grew from 73,725 to 338,497. The supply of labour had to be adjusted to the IJMA-devised strategy of short-time working which frequently

[117] Papers of K. C. Roy Chowdhury (hereafter K.C.R.P.), Bengali diary no. 3, entries for 25 Aug. to 28 Nov. 1929. These papers, at present in my possession, were made available to me through the kind courtesy of Mr Basudha Chakrabarty and Mrs Nabaneeta Deb Sen.

[118] K.C.R.P., Bengali diary no. 3, entry for 6 Oct. 1929.

[119] W.B.S.A., Finance Dept. Com. Br., Mar. 1915, A58-59.

imposed weekly 'idle days' on the mills as a way of reducing output (to match temporary fluctuations in demand) and wage bills.[120] From 1913 onwards, the mills kept changing 'from four to five days a week or from five days to six days a week and so on at different intervals', sometimes changing 'twice or three times a year'.[121] But as the mills offered no incentives for long-term service, a temporary closure of a mill often meant a temporary loss of labour. The problem was an old one,[122] but assumed critical importance in the prosperous years of 1895-1926 when individual mills always wanted to conserve labour for days when they might be called upon to expand output.

The means devised to meet this end was the multiple shift system whereby the labour force was worked in three or four shifts during the day and into the night.[123] Between 1913 and 1926 more than 90 per cent of the jute mills worked on this system.[124] Its main advantage was not economy. An 'abundance of labour or surfeit of it . . . [was] a necessary concomitant of multiple-shift employment', as that was the only way it could be ensured, at least on paper, that the workers did not work beyond the legally allowed hours.[125] There was for instance an elaborate relief system for weavers which necessitated employing extra 'daily-weavers'.[126] It was generally agreed in 1929 that a multiple shift mill carried 25 to 30 per cent more labour (at least on its books) than a single shift mill.[127] But therein lay its advantage, a reduction in the risk of a bottle-neck developing in labour supply should the trade ever demand an increase in output.

By an accident of history, the industry's search for an ample

[120] Cf. *The Report of the I.J.M.A. for the Half-Year Ending 30 June 1886* (Calcutta, 1886), p. 14.

[121] *R.C.L.I.*, vol. V, pt. 2, pp. 168-9.

[122] *The Jute Mills of Bengal* (Dundee, 1880), p. 48, mentions the case of Seebpore Jute Manufacturing Co. Ltd. whose directors decided to continue working 'rather than temporarily close the mill and lose the workpeople', even when they were faced with a depressed 'bag market'.

[123] For a good description of the multiple shift system, see W.B.S.A., Com.|Dept. Com. Br., Jan. 1929, B261-8.

[124] See *R.C.L.I.*, vol. V, pt. 2, pp. 168-9, 195. Between 1926 and 1929 half of the mills transferred to the single shift system as a result of a deterioration in the trade position. After 1930, all the mills were working single shift. Ibid., vol. V, pt. 1, pp. 81-2.

[125] W.B.S.A., Com. Br., Com. Dept. May 1929, B196-99 and Jan. 1929, B261-68.

[126] *R.C.L.I.*, vol. V, pt. 2, p. 167.

[127] Ibid., vol. V, pt. 1, p. 15.

supply of labour took place at a time that saw enormous increases in the emigration of labour from Bihar and UP and other regions into Bengal. 'Twenty years ago', Foley wrote in 1905, 'all the hands [in jute mills] were Bengalis. These have been gradually replaced by Hindustanis from the United Provinces and Bihar . . . so that at present in most of the mills two-thirds of the hands are composed of up-countrymen.'[128] And once the flow started 'from up-country', it flowed—as the Royal Commission on Labour was told—'very strongly'.[129] The situation was considered so satisfactory by 1895 that an official enquiry committee formed to investigate the question of labour supply to the Bengal coal mines felt that 'there was no necessity' to conduct any 'exhaustive enquiry into the subject of labour supply for jute mills'. Nor did the mills particularly press for one.[130] Foley was 'somewhat astonished' in 1905 to find that large increases in demand for jute mill labour between 1895-6 and 1903-4 had been easily met despite there being 'no recruitment on any systematic method . . . at all', and without any 'material' rise in wages.[131] Even the problem of a seasonal shortage of labour—as during harvesting months, for example—that Foley and other early observers of the industry often commented on seems to have lost its importance in the later years. In their memorandum dealing with 'methods of recruitment' the IJMA said to the Royal Commission in 1929 that 'labour is in good supply all the year round'. When asked about the seasonal shortage of the 'olden days', the IJMA representatives remarked that even those conditions had changed after 1914: 'the fact remains that since 1914 labour has never been scarce'.[132]

Evidence of the industry's sense of satisfactior. regarding the supply of labour may also be seen in certain siginificant changes in the geographical location of the mills. In the early days, when the mill hands were local—that is, 'mostly Bengalis'—an 'isolated site' for a mill was 'recognized as an advantage, the hands . . . living in the neighbourhood'.[133] In those years 'it was considered by the mills a

128 Foley, op. cit., para. 28.
129 *R.C.L.I.*, vol. V, pt. 2, p. 237.
130 *Report of Labour Enquiry Committee of 1895* (Calcutta, 1896), pp. 49-51. See also A. K. Bagchi, op. cit., p. 135.
131 Foley, op. cit., paras 18, 21-4.
132 *R.C.L.I.*, vol. V, pt. 2, p. 162.
133 Foley, op. cit., para 26. The early mills like Fort Gloster, Gourepore, Budge Budge, Kamarhati, etc., all followed this policy: see *The Jute Mills of Bengal*, pp. 27, 35-6, 43, 45, 68, 81.

matter of life and death to prevent a rival company settling down in proximity to their labour supply'.[134] The first two years of the Victoria Jute Mill built in 1885 on the river bank opposite the Samnugger Jute Mill were marked by what Wallace called 'the celebrated land dispute' between the two mills.[135] 'We are a little short of hands this week', ran a typically complaining letter from the Samnugger Mill to its directors in 1887, '. . . and this may affect us. The Victoria [Mill] has taken up all our spare hands . . . [and] we do not have so many to fall back on and that injures us a bit.'[136] The Hastings Mill's rather 'unremunerative'[137] decision in 1894 to work day and night by electric light was 'said to have been suggested by a rumour that another . . . firm contemplated putting up a large Mill near Hastings, whereupon the proprietors of the latter thought they might as well find employment for all the hands in the neighbourhood . . . by running 22 hours, instead of from daylight to dark'.[138] As labour became 'chiefly immigrant' and came of its own in abundant numbers, the situation soon reversed itself. Mills were no longer located in isolation from one another. Instead, noted Foley, 'it is considered now [1905] . . . an advantage to have a site in a centre, such . . . as Kankinara, where immigrant labour congregates'.[139] This explains why the number of mills on the 24 Parganas side of the river Hooghly—where Kankinara, Jagaddal and other centres of immigrant labour were located in very close proximity to one another—eventually grew much faster than the numbers in other districts (see Table 1).

A significant aspect of this migration of labour from UP, Bihar and other places into Bengal was that it enabled the industry to replace Bengali workers by their 'cheaper', up-country substitutes and this at a time when the industry was looking for ways of reducing expenses. The IJMA's move in 1886 to reduce wage expenditure by short-time working was in fact preceded by 'most of the Mills . . . taking action to effect a reduction of wages', for 'the tone of the market . . . [was] still very unfavourable'.[140] Just how large these reductions were is suggested

---

[134] D. R. Wallace, *The Romance of Jute* (Calcutta, 1909), p. 38.          [135] Ibid.
[136] Archives of Thomas Duff and Company, Dundee (hereafter T.D.A.), letter from the Calcutta Agent dated 10 May 1887.          [137] Wallace, op. cit., p. 47.
[138] John Leng, 'The Indian Dundee' in his *Letters from India and Ceylon* (Dundee, 1896), p. 79.
[139] Foley, op. cit., para 26.
[140] T.D.A. Minute books of the Titaghur Jute Factory, letters from the Calcutta Agent dated 25 June 1884 and 20 May 1885.

## TABLE 1

| District | No. of jute mills in the year | | | |
|---|---|---|---|---|
| | *1880* | *1896* | *1911* | *1921* |
| Hooghly | 4 | 6 | 7 | 9 |
| Howrah | 5 | 6 | 9 | 12 |
| 24 Parganas | 6 | 15 | 31 | 38 |
| Calcutta | 3 | 3 | 3 | 5 |

*Sources:* For 1880, *The Jute Mills of Bengal* (Dundee, 1880); for 1896, John Leng, 'The Indian Dundee' in his *Letters from India and Ceylon* (Dundee, 1896); for 1911 and 1921, *Census of India 1921*, vol. V, pt. 1, p. 403.

by a letter that the Dundee directors of the Titaghur jute factory received from their Calcutta manager towards the end of 1885. The letter reported, to the directors' delight, 'that the wages at the works have now been reduced Rs 1000 per week below what used to be paid, which the Directors considered very satisfactory and creditable to the Manager'.[141] The prolongation of working hours with the introduction of electricity into the mills about 1895[142] also seems to have caused a decline in the Bengali component of the labour force.[143] Whatever the specific factors aiding these changes in the social composition of the jute mill working class, the result was that by the 1920s the labour force was of a predominantly migrant character (see Table 2).

It is important to emphasize that the industry did little to help these migrant workers to settle down in the city, and thus develop a permanently stable labour force. The reason for this inaction lay in the very mercantilist notion of profit that the jute mills employed in handling their affairs. To the Scottish (and later Marwari) entre-preneurs in the industry, profit was firmly linked to the idea of 'cheap products'. It was thought that their cheapness gave these products—sacking and hessian of a very crude quality—a com-petitive edge over any natural or synthetic substitutes. Hence the insistence within the industry on keeping their products crude and

[141] Ibid., Minutes for 21 Oct. 1885.
[142] Wallace, op. cit., pp. 49-50.
[143] See the *Report of the Indian Factory Labour Commission* (London, 1909), vol. 2, p. 271.

## TABLE 2

| Year | Areas of origin of jute-mill workers, 1921–41 (figures in percentages) | | | | | | |
| | Bengal | Bihar | Orissa | United Provinces | Madras | Central Provinces | Others |
| --- | --- | --- | --- | --- | --- | --- | --- |
| 1921 | 24.1 | 33.4 | 11.4 | 23.2 | 4.6 | N.A. | 3.2 |
| 1928 | 24.8 | 37.1 (inc. Orissa) | | 15.7 | 11.2 | 9.1 | 1.9 |
| 1929 | 17 | 60 (inc. Orissa) | | 5 | 14 | 4 | N.A. |
| 1941 | 11.6 | 43.1 | 3.4 | 36.4 | 1.6 | N.A. | 0.8 |

(Figures have been rounded off to the first decimal place.)

*Sources* : Ranajit Das Gupta, 'Factory Labour in Eastern India: Sources of Supply, 1855–1946—Some Preliminary Findings', *The Indian Economic and Social History Review*, vol. XIII, no. 3, p. 297, Table 6, except for the column for 1928 which is derived from W.B.S.A., Com. Dept. Com. Br., Apr. 1930, A7-12. The 1921 figures apply to the whole of the labour force and the 1928 figures relate to 25 jute mills. The 1929 figures are very approximate, and the 1941 figures were drawn from a sample survey of mill workers in the Jagaddal area and hence are not representative of the whole working class.

inexpensive[144]—a policy which resulted in a stagnant technology and an unskilled labour force. Besides, an inexpensive product had to be produced at a low cost, and the availability of cheap labour in eastern India was seen as a definite advantage in this regard. Thus developed the labour-intensive nature of the industry, where labour alone accounted for about 50 per cent of the cost of converting raw jute into the finished material (see Table 3).

The bulk of this 'labour cost' was constituted of wages. Given their concern for keeping down the prices of their products while using labour-intensive methods of production, the owners of the jute mills were reluctant to spend on labour anything beyond such minimum necessities as wages. And even the wages paid were single-worker wages; they were not enough to support a worker's family. According to an estimate of 1929 the 'average income' of a jute mill worker was Rs 5 per week, while it would cost him at least Rs 7 to maintain a family of himself, his wife and, say, three children.[145] The increase

[144] Space does not permit any substantiation of the statements made here about the industry, but the reader may be assured that they are based on a careful consideration of the available evidence.

[145] *R.C.L.I.*, vol. V, pt. 2, p. 132.

## TABLE 3

| Year | Labour cost as percentage of the cost of conversion (figures relate to different mills) | Remarks |
|------|------|------|
| 1880[a] | 45 | Figures for two mills |
| | 40 | |
| c. 1900[b] | 55 | Figure for a hypothetical Calcutta mill |
| 1927[c] | 50 | Figure for one mill |
| 1957[d] | 49.6 | Figure for four mills |
| | 55.4 | |
| | 50.7 | |
| | 49.5 | |

*Sources* : for (a), *The Jute Mills of Bengal* (Dundee, 1880), pp. 20, 47; for (b), Archives of the Modern History Department, Dundee University, Card Collection on Cox Brothers, card entitled 'Cost of Mill and Factory' (c. 1900); for (c), D. H. Buchanan, op. cit., p. 250; for (d), C.S.A.S., B.P., Box XIII, 'Paul' to Edward Benthall, 20 Sept. 1937, Enclosures.

over the years in investment in workers' housing was extremely tardy. An 1897 survey of about 73,000 of the Bengal jute mill workers showed only 13.5 per cent of them living in company-built coolie-lines. The rest had had to make their own arrangements.[146] Thirty years later in 1929 when the mill labour force had increased to 339,665, only 30 per cent of the jute mill labour were housed by the mills, according to the Bengal Chamber of Commerce and the IJMA.[147] Stability of labour was obviously not in itself a crucial concern to the industry—semi-skilled or unskilled workers being highly replaceable—so long as the supply of labour remained abundant.

One can also see this in the extremely underdeveloped nature of the factory rules that were in operation in the jute mills. The service rules, for instance, had been left largely uncodified. Graded wage systems (with provisions for regular increments), pensions, provident funds, sickness insurance, leave rules—all the usual inducements for long-term service and stability—were conspicuous by their absence. Leave as a rule was without pay and the amount of pay due to a worker during his or her sickness remained 'a matter for the manager's

[146] W.B.S.A., Judicial Dept. Police Br., Sept. 1897, A95-99.
[147] *R.C.L.I.*, vol. V, pt. 1, p. 282; pt. 2, p. 284.

discretion'.[148] Sickness insurance was considered 'impossible'[149] and so were provident funds and pensions. When the workers of the Fort William, the Howrah and the Ganges jute mills went out on strike in February 1937, the Secretary to the Government of Bengal concluded that they could not have had any 'serious grievances' as their leaders asked for 'such obviously impossible terms as provision of provident funds and pension'.[150]

For such an uncared-for and poverty-ridden working class, the *sardar* performed functions that ideally should have been performed by the employers, such as supplying work, credit and housing. R. N. Gilchrist, the Labour Intelligence Officer of Bengal, pictures the average migrant worker 'as he sets out from his village to find work' thus:

> The sirdar may oblige him with his fare and a little money to buy food on the way. . . . The sirdar may advance him a little more money, for a job may not be immediately available, and he may also direct him to live in certain quarters and to buy his rice at a certain shop. The day when there is a vacancy comes, and the sirdar may say: 'Your pay on the books of the mill is twelve rupees a month, but I have incurred some expense for you. Usually when I give a job, I require thirty rupees down and one rupee a month for two years. You have no money to give me as a lump sum, so you will pay me two rupees a month for as long as I secure you a job. If you do not, I cannot be certain your job will last.' The grateful youth . . . gratefully accepts. . . . As he grows older and wiser, he gradually finds out that the sirdar owns the house in which he shares a room with six others and for which they all pay rent, and that he also owns the shop where he buys his rice.[151]

This of course was part of the 'corruption' that the industry and the government complained of. The *sardari* practices undoubtedly constituted a kind of secondary exploitation of ordinary workers by their supervisory or superior colleagues.[152] But it could be legitimately

[148] Ibid., vol. V, pt. 2, p. 155.
[149] Ibid., vol. V, pt. 1, p. 283-5.
[150] W.B.S.A., Home Poll, Confdl. No. 60/1937.
[151] R. N. Gilchrist, *Indian Labour and the Land* (Calcutta, 1932), pp. 6-7.
[152] The words '*sardari* practices' are used here in a generalized sense to designate activities not only of the Head *sardars* but of the under-*sardars* and some other workers as well. In an industry devoid of any structuring of skills or promotions, exploitation of the fellow worker was one important means of material advancement. The more ambitious and the luckier worker often followed the *sardar*'s example of being a moneylender or a landlord to the less fortunate. *Sardari* is thus best treated both as a real institution and as a working-class ideal of success. See *R.C.L.I.*, vol. XI, pt. 2, pp. 358, 365.

argued that the employers allowed such 'corruption' to exist because it saved them the expense of investing in institutions otherwise typical of the capitalist control of labour. *Sardari* control was cheaper than housing, health care or an articulated body of rules guiding the conditions of work.

## VIII

A 'needs of capital' type of argument then tells us that the *sardar* existed along with his invariably 'corrupt' practices mainly because they were allowed so to exist. They suited the strategy of capital. This is fine and important but it does not go far enough for the purpose at hand. Most important, it does not answer the question that Marx helps us to raise: what was the relationship between the *sardar*'s authority and his 'corruption'? As we have seen, it was *sardari* 'corruption' that ultimately distorted the documents which the supervisors in a jute mill were required to produce and keep. The nature of supervisory authority in the Calcutta jute mills was thus significantly different from the one discussed in Marx's argument. For Marx, the supervisor's authority in capitalist relations of production manifested itself in the keeping of time sheets, fine books, attendance registers, wage rolls, etc. Such maintenance of documents implied a keeping of the wage contract between capital and labour. And the notion of the contract took us back to Marx's specific assumptions regarding working-class culture, assumptions that informed his category of 'capital'. Our jute mills, however, present a very different picture. The supervisory authority of the *sardar* (or of his accomplice *babu*) produced unreliable, falsified documents. One could in fact go further and argue that falsifying documents was integral to the operation of the power and authority that the *sardar* wielded over the ordinary coolie. What appeared to the state as 'corruption', 'abuse', breaking of the rules, etc., was precisely the form in which the *sardar*'s authority was manifested. Or to put it in another way, it was an authority that was incompatible with any bourgeois notions of legality, factory codes and service rules.

We would be mistaken, for example, to see the bribe that the ordinary coolie gave the *sardar* simply as an economic transaction. The bribe was also a sign, a representation, of the *sardar*'s authority and its acceptance by the worker, which is why an act of refusal to

pay the bribe was seen as a gesture of defiance and exposed the
worker to a degree of anger, vendetta and violence from the *sardar*
that was often out of proportion to the amount of money involved.
K. C. Roy Chowdhury's diaries mention the not untypical case of
one Abdul, a worker of the Hukumchand Jute Mill, who was stabbed
by the followers of a certain *sardar* called Sujat for having refused to
pay the latter his *dastoori*, or customary commission.[153] The nature of
the *sardar*'s authority and power is visible in the details of the following
letter that some twenty-eight workers of the Budge Budge Jute Mill
once wrote to a Bengali barrister in December 1906:

> We have to get permission for leaves from the Sahib. But we have to pay
> bribes to the babu and the sardar at the time of the leave; further, they take
> bribes from us every month and also when the Durga Puja season ap-
> proaches. If we refuse to pay them they get the sahib to fine or dismiss us
> on false charges of bad workmanship. Till recently we felt compelled to
> meet their unjust demands. But as prices ran very high last year at the time
> of the Durga Puja, we expressed our intention to pay them a little less than
> in earlier years. At this the Head Sardar Haricharan Khanra has been
> going around instigating the Assistant Babu Atul Chandra Chattopadhyay
> to collect even more *parbani* [gifts customarily due at times of religious
> festivals; *parban* = religious festival] than usual. The two of them have
> even advised the in-charge Panchanan Ghose, a nice gentleman otherwise,
> to force us to pay a much larger *parbani* this year. When [in protest] we
> stopped paying any *parbani* whatsoever, they got the sahib to fine us on
> cooked up charges. . . . But, in truth, we are not guilty.[154]

A large part of the *sardar*'s authority was then based on fear: 'we
felt *compelled* to meet their unjust demands'. So great was the fear of
the *sardar*'s vengeance that several of the workers interviewed by the
Royal Commission strenuously denied having paid any bribes for
their employment. But their denial lacked the force of conviction.
Sorju, an under-*sardar* of the Anglo-Indian Jute Mill, admitted that
there was bribery 'in every department' of the mill but claimed that
there was none in his own. Kalil, a weaver in the same mill, said that
he had heard 'that *sardars* take Rs 5 or Rs 10 but so far as I am
concerned I did not pay anything'.[155] Harilal, a spinner in the Titaghur

---

[153] K.C.R.P., Bengali diary no. 2, entry for 12 Apr. 1928.
[154] The letter is quoted in Sumit Sarkar, 'Swadeshi Yuger Sramik Andolon: Kayekti
Aprakashita Dalil', *Itihas*, vol. IV, No. 2, Bhadra-Agrahayan 1376 (1969), pp.
113-15.
[155] *R.C.L.I.*, vol. V, pt. 2, p. 26.

Jute Mill, insisted that he 'did not pay any *bakshish* for getting my job' while he thought it possible that 'other people might be paying *bakshish* to the *sardar*'.[156] A Madrasi female worker of the Howrah Jute Mill told her interviewers that she got her employment only after promising the *sardar* two rupees from her 'first wages'. On the statement being read out to her, however, she retracted it. 'It is probably true', remarked the interviewers.[157]

It is of course undeniable that much of this fear of the *sardar* derived from the employers allowing him to 'dismiss and engage fresh hands just at [his] pleasure' (to repeat the words of the IJMA). Babuniya, a Bihari female worker of the Titaghur Jute Mill, expressed her fear to the Royal Commission thus:

> When I was first entertained I had to pay Rs 4 *bakshish* to the *sardar* who appointed me. Each time I return back from the village I have to pay the same amount as *bakshish* to the *sardar*. I also pay him 2 as. every week. My husband paid Rs 6 when he was first appointed. He pays 4 annas a week to the *sardar*. If we refuse to pay the *sardars* we will not get work. Every worker pays a similar amount to the *sardar*.[158]

Another important element in the *sardar*'s domination was the use of naked physical force. For the ordinary worker, as we have noted, there was always 'the fear of being beaten'. The child workers, it was said, would not normally speak up against the *sardar* for this very reason.[159] Narsama Kurmi, a female worker of the Howrah Jute Mill, was 'obliged to leave' Howrah as 'she had trouble with a sirdar'. She returned only after 'she found [that] the sirdar who annoyed her [had] gone'.[160]

Like all domination, however, the *sardar*'s domination was not based on fear alone. There was always an undercurrent of tension between the *sardar* and the ordinary worker and pushed beyond a certain point, the worker could become openly hostile. To be effective therefore the *sardar*'s authority also needed legitimacy and acceptance. Fear had to be balanced by respect. In fact, according to R. N. Gilchrist, the typical jute-mill *sardar* was more respected than feared. 'The sirdar [is] a man of considerable importance', Gilchrist wrote. 'He is... respected, perhaps even feared.'[161]

[156] Ibid., p. 78.
[157] Ibid., vol. XI, pt. 2, p. 360.
[158] Ibid., vol. V, pt. 2, p. 77.
[159] Ibid., vol. V, pt. 1, p. 333.
[160] Ibid., vol. XI, pt. 2, p. 360
[161] R. N. Gilchrist, op. cit., p. 6.

What made the *sardar*'s authority effective? Our tentative answer would be 'culture', the culture to which both the *sardar* and the worker belonged. In essence this was a pre-capitalist culture with a strong emphasis on religion, community, kinship, language and other primordial loyalties. The evidence on this point is not direct but is extremely suggestive. It seems significant, for instance, that all the words used by the workers (and others) to describe *sardari* extortions—extortions summed up in the legalistic expression 'corruption' or 'abuses'—were words of pre-capitalist, pre-British origin: *dastoori, bakshish, batta, parbani, salami,* etc. *Dastoori,* the most widely used of these words, came from the word *dastoor* which meant 'custom' or 'tradition'. Even the word *sardar* in its meaning of 'labour supplier'—though literally it meant 'a headman'—was in vogue in the late eighteenth century and perhaps even earlier.[162] Besides, the *sardar*'s mode of operation had certain crucial pre-capitalist elements. He usually recruited on the basis of the often overlapping networks of community, village and kin. The Government of Bengal wrote:

> Sirdars in the jute mills, engineering works, and other concerns recruit in their own native villages and surrounding areas; hence there is a tendency for people from the same village or the immediate neighbourhood to congregate in the same industrial area in Bengal.[163]

Much of the basis of the *sardar*'s social control of the work force lay in community, kin or other primordial relationships and in the ideas and norms associated with them. For example, it was usual for important up-country *sardars* to build temples or mosques for the workers under them. On this depended a lot of the *sardar*'s prestige and authority. Mosques in jute-mill areas are even today named after important *sardars* and stand as monuments to their one-time enormous presence. 'Manbodh sardar ki musjid', 'Birbal sardar ki musjid', 'Ishaque sardar ki musjid' are, to give a few instances, the names

[162] See, for example, the use of this word by Krishnakanta Nandy in his account books of 1787-8 in S. C. Nandy, 'Krishnakanta Nandy's Book of Monthly Accounts of 1195 B.S. (1787-88)', *Bengal Past and Present*, Jan.-June 1980, p. 10. Bishop Heber's *Narrative of a Journey through the Upper Provinces of India from Calcutta to Bombay 1824-1825* (1828) had references to such labourers as 'Sirdar bearers and bearers': Heber quoted in Brajendrath Bandopadhyay's 'Introduction' to Bhabanicharan Bandopadhyay's *Kalikata Kamalalaya* (Calcutta, 1951), p. 21.

[163] *R.C.L.I.*, vol. V, pt. 1, p. 11.

of three working-class mosques that exist today in the Kankinara area.[164] *Sardari* was thus possibly an instance of a pre-colonial, pre-capitalist institution being adapted to the needs of industrialization in a colony.[165]

The *sardar* then embodied contradictory elements of authority. He owed his formal position of being a foreman to the managers and owners of capital and, in that sense, was a functionary in the capitalist production system of the jute mills. He was also different from the traditional village headman of north India in that '*sardar*-ships' could be bought and sold on the market. Yet he was not quite the industrial foreman of nineteenth-century Western Europe whose role 'became increasingly technical' as time passed.[166] *Sardars* were selected not for any technical ability but for 'the authority which they display[ed] over their fellowmen' even before becoming *sardars*.[167] *Tumko apná sardar ká hukum manna hoga* ('you will have to obey the order of your own *sardar*') was one sentence that the Scottish managers and assistants in the mills were expected to learn in order to use it in dealing with a refractory worker.[168] The sentence brings out the ambiguity of the *sardar*'s authority. His *hukum* (order) was obviously subordinate to yet another imperative ('You will have to'), that of the manager, the representative of capital. But the world *hukum*, once again an ancient word familiar to the north Indian peasant, would have had long and deep resonances within the worker's consciousness and culture.

The legally required factory documents on working-class conditions were thus largely irrelevant to the exercise of the *sardar*'s authority which was in the nature of pre-capitalist domination. He ensured obedience to his *hukum* through means that were either 'illegal' or fell outside the rule of law. His was not the 'disciplinary authority' that Marx outlined in his argument. When the Government

[164] This information comes both from my field investigations and from K.C.R.P., Bengali diary no. 3, entries for 25 Aug. to 28 Nov. 1929.

[165] *R.C.L.I.*, vol. 1, pp. 22-4, describes jobbery as the ubiquitous form of labour recruitment and control in Indian industrialization.

[166] Michelle Perrot, 'The Three Ages of Industrial Discipline in Nineteenth Century France' in John M. Merriman (ed.), *Consciousness and Class Experience in Nineteenth Century Europe* (New York, 1979), p. 159.

[167] *R.C.L.I.*, vol. V, pt. 1, pp. 280, 298. 'Capability, efficiency, services' were the other qualifications required.

[168] Mohiuddin Ahmed, *Essentials of Colloquial Hindustani for Jute Mills and Workshops* (Calcutta, 1932), p. 89.

of India grafted a disciplinary apparatus of documentation on the culture that supported (and sometimes resisted) the *sardar*'s domination, these documents found their own place and meaning within that culture: as additional vehicles of the *sardar*'s power and authority. The *sardar* now proved his power by bending rules and falsifying documents. Hence the phenomenon of 'false fines', 'cooked up charges', 'wrongful dismissals', etc. The very exercise of this authority therefore produced 'unreliable' documents.

## IX

In conclusion, we may repeat our principal argument. An attempt to write a history of the conditions of the jute mill workers of Calcutta on the basis of documents emanating from the state and the owners of capital invariably reveals certain gaps in our knowledge of these conditions. In this essay we have argued that in so far as that knowledge has a history, the gaps have a history too. In fact it was the same history that produced both the knowledge—enshrined in archival documents—and the gaps which the same documents also contain. An examination of that history (with the aid of an argument borrowed from Marx) led us to investigate the political economy of the industry and the nature of the 'industrial discipline' operative with the mills. The latter question took us into the problem of 'supervision' and working-class notions of 'authority', and hence into the realm of culture.

# IV Nationalism: Gandhi as Signifier

# Peasant Revolt and Indian Nationalism:
# The Peasant Movement in Awadh, 1919-22

## GYAN PANDEY

In January 1921 the peasants of Awadh burst onto the national stage in India. Huge peasant demonstrations at Fursatganj and Munshiganj bazars in Rae Bareli district led to police firing on 6 and 7 January. At other places in Rae Bareli, Faizabad and Sultan-pur districts, peasant violence—the looting of bazars (as at Fursat-ganj), attacks on landlords, and battles with the police—broke out around this time. For some weeks, indeed, many a landlord was too scared to appear anywhere on his estate. 'You have seen in three districts in southern Oudh [Awadh] the beginnings of something like revolution', Harcourt Butler, the Governor of UP (the United Provinces of Agra and Awadh, modern Uttar Pradesh), observed in March 1921.[1] The peasants' actions received wide publicity in the nationalist press, too, especially after Jawaharlal Nehru had been drawn into the Munshiganj events of 7 January.

Virtually for the first time since 1857 the Awadh peasant had forced himself on the attention of the elites in colonial India. The debate was quickly joined. The leaders of the major nationalist party, the Congress, who had been involved in some of the peasant meetings and demonstrations of the preceding months, now stepped forward to defend the peasants in the courts and to prevent further violence. Colonial administrators rushed to consider remedial legislation: 'It has for long been obvious', as one of them put it, 'that the Oudh Rent Act requires amendment.'[2] The Liber-als, moderate nationalists who were moving away from the

[1] Harcourt Butler Colln., Mss. Eur. F. 116 (India Office Library, London), vol. 80: Note of Butler's interview with taluqdars, 6 March 1921.

[2] Uttar Pradesh State Archives, Lucknow (hereafter UPSA), U.P. General Administra-tion Dept. (hereafter GAD), File 50/1921, Kw: Commissioner, Lucknow Division to Chief Sec., U.P., 14 Jan. 1921.

Congress as it adopted a more militant posture at this time, shared something of both the Congress and the Government positions. With local Congressmen, some of them had supported the initial organizational efforts and demands of the tenants. After January 1921, they were foremost in pressing for legislation to improve their conditions.

The underlying causes of the peasant protest that brought forth these reactions lay in a pattern of agrarian relations that had evolved over a long period. In 1856 Awadh was brought under direct British rule in order, it was said, to rescue the province from the effects of misrule and anarchy. The mutiny and civil rebellion of 1857-9, which brought some of the fiercest fighting and severest reprisals of the century, formed, from that point of view, an unfortunate interlude. After that the benefits of Pax Britannica flowed freely, towards some. Chief among the beneficiaries were the two hundred and eighty or so taluqdars who, for their part in the recent uprising, were now held up as the 'natural leaders' of the people. The taluqdars were mostly local rajas and heads of clans, officials and tax-farmers who had secured an independent position in the land before the British annexation, plus a handful of 'deserving chiefs' who were given estates confiscated from the most notorious of the rebels. On this motley crowd the new rulers formally conferred many of the rights of the landowning gentry of Britain. Three-fifths of the cultivated area of Awadh was settled with them in return for the regular payment of revenue and assistance in maintaining order in the countryside. And British policy was now directed towards ensuring the taluqdars the wealth, status and security necessary to fulfil this role. The extent of the British commitment to the taluqdars was indicated by Harcourt Butler when he wrote, in the 1890s, that for political purposes 'the Taluqdars are Oudh'.[3] By the Encumbered Estates Act of 1870 and subsequent measures, the colonial administrators even agreed to bale out any insolvent taluqdari estate by taking over its management for as long as twenty years—although this ran counter to all their principles of political economy.

Some effort was made to secure the intermediary rights of other traditionally privileged groups: village proprietors, coparcenary

[3] T.R. Metcalf, *Land, Landlords and the British Raj: Northern India in the Nineteenth Century* (Delhi, 1979), p. 198; see also Metcalf in R.E. Frykenberg, (ed.), *Land Control and Social Structure in Indian History* (Madison, 1969), p. 147.

communities controlling various plots of land and privileged tenants of several categories. This was necessitated in part by the prolonged resistance of many of these inferior right holders, such as the Barwar Rajputs of Amsin Pargana and the under-proprietors on the Raja of Pirpur's estate (both in Faizabad district).[4] Legally and in terms of actual power, these intermediary groups retained something of their earlier position in the taluqdari as well as the non-taluqdari areas of Awadh.[5] Yet Pax Britannica and the compromise sub-settlements of the 1860s tended to work against the interests of the lower classes.

Generally it was laid down that under-proprietors would pay the Government revenue plus a further 10 to 50 per cent. Thus they bore the entire burden of any enhancement of revenue while the taluqdars escaped any new obligations. In the years after the first round of settlements and sub-settlements had been completed, the smaller under-proprietors lost more and more of their remaining rights to the taluqdars and, to some extent, to money-lenders and other men from outside. Many groups of once privileged tenants also suffered losses in the general process of enhancement of rents. The Government contributed fully to these developments. On the Government-managed estates of Mehdona, Kapradih and Sehipur in Faizabad district, for instance, several arrests were made for the non-payment of rents in full by underproprietors; and

> where tenants held reduced rates only by favour of the taluqdar, without any legal claim based on a former proprietory title, the Government exerted itself vigorously to bring rents up to the level of those paid by ordinary cultivators.[6]

Among the tenants, then, Brahmans and Thakurs suffered a progressive decline in terms of favoured rental rates as well as the areas of land leased out to them. Yet the pressure on them was light by comparison with that on the Kurmis and Muraos, cultivating castes with a reputation for efficiency who formed a considerable part of the tenantry, numbering in all about a million in Awadh in the 1880s. In Rae Bareli, in the decade following the first regular settlement of the district, during which prices rose only gradually,

[4]Ibid., pp. 131-3.

[5]P.J. Musgrave, 'Landlords and Lords of the Land: Estate Management and Social Control in U.P., 1860-1920', *Modern Asian Studies*, 6:3 (July 1972).

[6]Metcalf in Frykenberg (ed.), *Land Control*, pp. 133-4; see also *Collection of Papers Relating to the Condition of the Tenantry and the Working of the Present Rent Law in Oudh*, 2 vols. (Allahabad, 1883).

the increase in their rents varied between what was described as 'nominal' and 30-80 per cent, and actually reached a 100 per cent in one or two cases.[7]

With the taluqdari settlement, the bulk of the population of Awadh (just under 11½ million in 1881, rising to over 12 million by 1921) had in any case lost all their rights, which were unrecorded earlier and now excluded from the record. The vast majority of cultivators emerged as tenants-at-will on small holdings, or as landless labourers. In Lucknow district at the beginning of the 1880s, only a half per cent of the agricultural population held more that 50 *bighas* of land (a *bigha* = 5/8 acre). Six per cent held from 20 to 50 *bighas*, 11½ per cent 10 to 20 *bighas*, 15 per cent 5 to 10 *bighas*, and 39½ per cent less than 5 *bighas*. This was at a time when officials, who could scarcely be accused of liberality in these matters, felt that a cultivator needed at least 5 *bighas* to live 'reasonably'. The remaining 27½ per cent of Lucknow's agricultural population were classified as landless day-labourers.[8]

The resistance of Kurmi and other tenants on various occasions[9] could do no more than slow down these developments in particular areas. Nor did legislation that aimed at providing a modicum of security for the unprotected tenants and some control on the level of rent enhancements, significantly arrest the general deterioration. The landlords had too many cards up their sleeves, most of them the gift of the British Raj itself, to be seriously affected by such paper threats. They collected more than the recorded rents, instituted a system of unofficial taxation whereby the tenant paid a large premium or *nazrana* to be admitted or re-admitted to a holding, and often ignored the law altogether.[10] C.W. McMinn noted in the 1870s that taluqdar power was still great, in some ways indeed 'more absolute' than before, but now (constricted to narrower channels) it had 'meaner developments'.[11] The taluqdars now concentrated their efforts on screwing up their incomes from their estates, without any concern for protecting old tenants and dependants or improving their lands. The peasants of Pratapgarh

[7]Ibid., vol. I, p. 135.

[8]Ibid., vol. II, p. 400.

[9]F.W. Porter, *Final Settlement Report of the Allahabad District* (Allahabad, 1878), pp. 47-8; S. Gopal, *Jawaharlal Nehru: A Biography, vol. I* (London, 1975), p. 46.

[10]See G. Pandey, *The Ascendancy of the Congress in Uttar Pradesh, 1926-34; A Study in Imperfect Mobilization* (Delhi, 1978), p. 21.

[11]Quoted in Metcalf, *Land, Landlords and the Raj*, p. 175.

described this situation in their own idiom in conversation with the Deputy Commissioner of the district in 1920. Referring to the *murda faroshi kanun* (literally, the 'law for sale of the corpse'), i.e. the law permitting immediate enhancement of rent on, or sale of, the land of a dead tenant, they said that a new kind of Mahabrahman (the lowest among the Brahmans on account of the fact that he lives on funeral gifts) had come into being. The one object of this creature was to pray for an epidemic—just as the grain dealer prays for a famine—so that he might reap a rich harvest of *murda faroshi* fees. This Mahabrahman was the landlord. 'Before the ashes are cold on the pyre this Mahabrahman has to be satisfied.'[12]

To add to the misfortunes of the lower classes, population pressure on the land and the cost of living steadily increased from the later nineteenth century. In these conditions a very large section of the Awadh peasantry, both smaller landowners and tenants, sank into debt. As time went on they relied more and more heavily on their valuable crops, especially rice and wheat, to pay off interest and other dues, and the acreage under these crops increased. For their own consumption the bulk of the rural population depended on the inferior grains—maize, barley, *jowar* and *bajra*. One result of the growing demand for these inferior grains and the decline in the area over which they were cultivated, was that their prices rose even more sharply than the prices of wheat and rice in the first decades of the twentieth century.[13] It was a somewhat paradoxical index of the social dislocation that lay behind the revolt of the Awadh peasantry after the First World War.

January 1921 was the culminating point of a movement that had advanced very rapidly indeed from its inception towards the end of 1919. Kisan Sabhas, or peasants' associations, were being organized locally in Pratapgarh from the early months of 1920. By the middle of that year they had found a remarkable leader and coordinator in Baba Ramchandra, a Maharashtrian of uncertain antecedents who had been an indentured labourer in Fiji and then a *sadhu* (religious mendicant) propagating the Hindu scriptures in Jaunpur, Sultanpur and Pratapgarh, before he turned to the task of

---

[12]U.P.S.A, U.P. Rev. (A) Dept. File 753 of 1920; 'Report on Agrarian Disturbances in Pratapgarh', by V.N. Mehta, Deputy Commnr., Pratapgarh (hereafter, Mehta's Report), p. 4.

[13]M.H. Siddiqi, *Agrarian Unrest in North India: The United Provinces, 1918-22* (New Delhi, 1978), ch. II.

organizing Kisan Sabhas. Led by Ramchandra, members of the Pratapgarh Kisan Sabha sought the support of urban nationalists. It was then that Jawaharlal Nehru 'discovered' the Indian peasantry and found the countryside 'afire with enthusiasm and full of a strange excitment';[14] and then that the Kisan Sabha workers of the Congress who had endeavoured to extend their links in the villages of UP since 1918, began to work in association with the organizers of these independent local Sabhas, especially in Awadh.

Before the involvement of the nationalists from the cities, the Awadh Kisan Sabha movement had already gained considerable strength. There were reported to be 585 panchayats (village arbitration boards established by the peasants) working in Pratapgarh district alone. In the month or two during which Rure, the village in Pratapgarh where the first Kisan Sabha was established, was a centre of the movement, 100,000 peasants were said to have registered themselves with the association. These early efforts at organization had received indirect encouragement from the sympathetic attitude of the Pratapgarh Deputy Commissioner, V.N. Mehta, who asked Ramchandra and other peasant leaders to forward the peasants' complaints to him for examination and instituted inquiries regarding some of the more tangible allegations.[15] Now, with the growth of urban nationalist support, the movement advanced more swiftly still until it had engulfed large parts of Pratapgarh, Rae Bareli, Sultanpur and Faizabad districts, and established important footholds elsewhere. Its strength may be judged from the numbers of peasants who were said to have turned out for very different kinds of demonstrations: 40-50,000 to press for the release of Ramchandra from Pratapgarh jail in September 1920, 80-100,000 for the first Awadh Kisan Congress held in Ayodhya (Faizabad district) in December 1920.[16] Such estimates of the numbers involved in mass gatherings are of course notoriously unreliable. But even if we scale them down to one half or a third, as colonial officials did at the time, they indicate the rise of a movement of massive proportions.

[14]J. Nehru, *An Autobiography* (London, 1936; 1947 rpt), pp. 57, 51.

[15]Baba Ramchandra Colln. II (Nehru Memorial Museum & ' Library, New Delhi'; hereafter NMML), Acc. No. 610: RC XI, 'Autobiographical Notebook', p. 13; Ramchandra Colln. I (NMML) Acc. No. 163: 'Note' of 8 Aug. 194[?] and incomplete letter of 1939, pp. 5-6. For Mehta's role, see also Mehta's Report, p. 3.

[16]Siddiqi, op. cit., pp. 146-7.

Matters came to a head in January 1921, and soon after, the Awadh peasant movement, by now bereft of support from its erstwhile urban allies, was repressed by a determined attack on the part of the Government. It was not crushed, however, and a few months later it arose again in northern Awadh in the modified form of an Eka (unity) movement. We write of this as a continuation of the earlier, Kisan Sabha, phase of the struggle because the same kinds of forces were involved in its creation, and there was the same kind of ambiguous relationship between the Congress and the peasant rebels.[17] The Eka associations were aided in their initial stages by some Congressmen and Khilafatists of Malihabad, Lucknow district. But they quickly outstripped their beginnings, spread out widely and became very militant. The movement was strongest in certain districts of northern Awadh where the evils of grain rents and disguised rents abounded. The peasant associations now raised the cry for commutation to cash rents and resistance to demands for anything more than the recorded rent. They called at the same time for non-cooperation with the colonial regime. Before long, colonialist observers were complaining about the fact that the Indian Penal Code and the Criminal Procedure Code had 'no provision for a whole countryside arrayed against law and order'.[18] Yet the Congress leadership spared little time for the protagonists of Eka, and in due course this new phase of the movement was suppressed by a large force of armed police and military men.

There could have been no other outcome, given the positions adopted by the various contending forces in UP in early 1921. In the following pages we examine these positions at some length, for what they tell us about different assessments of the nature of political struggle in colonial India and the role of the peasantry in that struggle. The urban nationalist leaders and British officials have left behind more or less detailed discourses on the Awadh peasant movement of these years, alternative perspectives which reveal, we believe, their basic concerns and the extent of their

[17] As the officer specially deputed by the U.P. Govt. to inquire into the Eka movement, Lt Col J.C. Faunthorpe, put it, 'The Eka movement, which commenced towards the end of 1921, is a revival of the *Kisan Sabha* movement.' *United Provinces Gazette,* 13 May 1922, pt VIII (hereafter Faunthorpe's Report), p. 273.

[18] Clipping from *Englishman* (Calcutta), 28 Feb. 1922 in GOI, Home Dept., Pol. Branch, File 862 of 1922 (NAI, New Delhi).

understanding of the contradictions and possibilities existing in the situation. There are of course subtle, and sometimes not so subtle, variations between the language, say, of Gandhi and of Nehru, or the comments of the Liberals and those of the young non-cooperating Congressmen of 1920-22. Again there is a world of difference, on the Government side, between the response of someone like the Pratapgarh Deputy Commissioner, V. N. Mehta, and that of H. R. C. Hailey, his Commissioner and immediate boss in Faizabad Division, or Harcourt Butler, Lieutenant Governor and then (after 1920) Governor of UP: the first undertook an intensive tour of his district, interviewed 1700 witnesses and collected a mass of material on the basis of which he drew up a 111 page 'Report on Agrarian Disturbances in Pratapgarh' in 1920; the second described the report as 'partisan', 'one-sided', painting peasant grievances in 'lurid' colours; the third dismissed it simply as 'long and crude'.[19]

An appreciation of these variations is important for a proper reconstruction of the history of the period. Yet, in general terms, an official and a Congress stand on the Awadh peasant movement in these years, can be discerned. So can a general landlord position, though the landlords of Awadh were so much the puppets of their colonial masters by this time that they have left no significant deposition of their own. As for the peasants who set off this debate, no one took the trouble of recording their discourse. A small collection of papers, notes and diaries written by Baba Ramchandra mainly in the late 1930s and 1940s has been discovered, and this is in some ways very valuable. But we have no peasant testament outlining the impulses that moved them or defending the actions they took in 1919-22, not even an elaborate statement from Ramchandra. The peasants' view of the struggle will probably never be recovered; and whatever we say about it at this stage must be very tentative. Yet it seems important to try and piece together some part of it, from the isolated statements of peasants found in the documents and from the only other evidence we have—the message contained in their actions. Without this the historical record remains woefully incomplete. And the exercise is relevant for another reason too.

Historians of India have long debated the question of how mass

[19]U.P. Rev. (A) Dept. File 753 of 1920: Hailey to Keane, 26 Nov. 1920 and Butler's 'Note' of 17 Dec. 1920.

mobilization occurred in the course of the struggle for liberation from colonial rule. In the earlier writings, nationalist as well as colonialist commentators tended to treat the 'masses' (in this agrarian society, predominantly peasants) as essentially inert. When peasant insurrection occurred and swelled the tide of anti-imperialist agitation in the latter part of British rule in India, it was for the colonialists a sign of manipulation by 'outside agitators', for the nationalists evidence of mobilization by popular urban leaders. Colonialist (and neo-colonialist) historiography has not moved very far from this early position, although the theory of deliberate instigation of disturbance among ignorant and unconcerned people has been rendered somewhat superfluous by the discovery of 'factions', their members ever ready, in their hundreds if not thousands or indeed tens of thousands, to rise behind 'faction-leaders' in the latter's quest for the prestige and profits of office.[20] Liberal nationalist and Marxist historians, on the other hand, have gone on to make significant new statements regarding the politics of mass protest in India.

First, research indicated that many of the most important peasant insurrections in the country were largely autonomous, and that the intervention of 'outside' leaders was a marginal and, often, a late phenomenon. But while it was recognized that peasants had at times exercised an independence of initiative, their actions were seen as having been non-political or at best 'pre-political'. More recently some scholars have granted that these actions were in fact (at times) political, in the sense that they threw up a challenge to the established structure of authority and sought to create alternative centres of power. Yet the previous view persists: indeed, it remains dominant in the universities and among others interested in the recent history of the subcontinent, finding expression for instance, in the common equation of the Congress movement with the 'political' movement and of workers' and peasants' struggles with a 'social' one. And where some acknowledgement has been made of the political content of the latter, a new argument seems to have arisen. It is now suggested, in what might be called the last stand of traditional nationalist historiography, that these sectional struggles, of peasants and workers and other labouring and exploited classes, were out of step with the primary need of the 'nation' at that stage in its

[20]See D. Hardiman, 'The Indian 'Faction': A Political Theory Examined', in this volume.

history—the need to advance the anti-imperialist movement.[21].

The validity of some of these propositions cannot be fully tested until a good deal more research has been undertaken into modern Indian history, especially in the domain of mass movements and popular consciousness. Yet enough is known already about particular struggles, like that of the peasants in Awadh from 1919-22, to raise doubts about certain long-standing assumptions regarding what has come to be described as the relationship between popular struggles and the Indian national movement. It is the limited purpose of this essay to examine these assumptions in the light of what we know, from secondary as well as primary sources, about the Awadh peasant movement. I shall first analyse the very different contemporary responses to the political events of 1919-22 in Awadh, and then go on to consider whether historians commenting on peasant revolt and Indian nationalism have not too readily accepted the viewpoint of the better-educated and more vocal participants in the anti-colonial struggle in nineteenth-and twentieth-century India.

## The Congress Response

In February 1921, when he visited UP, Gandhi issued the following *Instructions* to the peasants of the province:

Attainment of swaraj or redress of grievances is imposible unless the following rules are strictly observed.

1. We may not hurt anybody. We may not use our sticks against anybody. We may not use abusive language or exercise any other undue pressure.

2. We may not loot shops.

3. We should influence our opponents by kindness, not by using physical force nor stopping their water supply nor the services of the barber and the washerman.

---

[21] See Bipan Chandra, *Nationalism and Colonialism in Modern India* (New Delhi, 1979) for the view that Gandhi and the post-World War 1 Congress 'aroused [the masses] to political activity', and for the above distinction between 'political' and 'social' struggle, pp. 127, 165, 183 and *passim*. There is a faint echo of this 'political'-'social' distinction also in Sumit Sarkar, *The Swadeshi Movement in Bengal, 1903-1908* (New Delhi, 1973), p. 515; and it is commonly voiced at academic seminars in India and elsewhere. The view that a peasant struggle was ill-timed, or diversionary, is expressed most clearly in Siddiqi, op. cit., pp. 217, 219. It is also reflected in Bipan Chandra, op. cit., p. 347.

4.   We may not withhold taxes from Government or rent from the landlord.

5.   Should there be any grievances against zemindars they should be reported to Pandit Motilal Nehru and his advice followed.

6.   It should be borne in mind that we want to turn zemindars into friends.

7.   We are not at the present moment offering civil disobedience; we should, therefore, carry out all Government orders.

8.   We may not stop railway trains nor forcibly enter them without tickets.

9.   In the event of any of our leaders being arrested, we may not prevent his arrest nor create any distrubance. We shall not lose our cause by the Government arresting our leaders; we shall certainly lose it if we become mad and do violence.

10.   We must abolish intoxicating drinks, drugs and other evil habits.

11.   We must treat all women as mothers and sisters and respect and protect them.

12.   We must promote unity between Hindus and Muslims.

13.   As amongst Hindus we may not regard anyone as inferior or untouchable. There should be the spirit of equality and brotherhood among all. We should regard all the inhabitants of India as brothers and sisters.

14.   We may not indulge in gambling.

15.   We may not steal.

16.   We may not tell an untruth on any account whatsoever. We should be truthful in all our dealings.

17.   We should introduce the spinning-wheel in every home and all—male and female—should devote their spare time to spinning. Boys and girls should also be taught and encouraged to spin for four hours daily.

18.   We should avoid the use of all foreign cloth and wear cloth woven by the weavers from yarn spun by ourselves.

19.   We should not resort to law courts but should have all disputes settled by private arbitration.

The most important thing to remember is to curb anger, never to do violence and even to suffer violence done to us.[22]

These *Instructions*, directed especially towards the peasants of Awadh who had so recently been responsible for acts of violence, may be taken as the final Congress comment on the peasant movement in Awadh. They were issued, we may be sure, after

[22]*Collected Works of Mahatma Gandhi*, vol. XIX (Ahmedabad, 1966), pp. 419-20

much soul-searching on the part of Gandhi, and a long period of trial-and-error on the part of the Congress leadership as a whole. In the ranks of the Congress and other organized nationalist parties, there were still some who favoured a continuation of the peasants' struggle. But in the thinking of the most important Congress leaders in the province and the country, January–February 1921 marked an important turning-point.

Numbers *1-3*, *9* and perhaps *8*, in addition to the concluding sentence of Gandhi's *Instructions,* reiterate the deep Gandhian concern for the maintenance of non-violence in all circumstances. It is notable, however, that the specific injunctions contained in them flow not simply from an abhorrence of physical violence in any form, but also from a precise knowledge of the actions taken by the Awadh peasants in the course of the development of the Kisan Sabha movement over the preceding months.

*Instructions 1* and *2* were clearly intended to counter the kind of peasant activism that had broken out in Rae Bareli at the beginning of January 1921 and in Faizabad, Sultanpur and elsewhere a few days later. Peasants had attacked and looted bazars as well as stores of grain in the villages. They had destroyed and burnt property: straw belonging to the landlords, crops on the landlords' fields , large quantities of clothes, jewels and so on. *Instruction 2* related to this. So probably did *Instruction 15,* for destruction is no different from theft in the eyes of the propertied and their counsel.

*Instruction 9* inveighed against the repeated attempts of peasants to liberate their leaders when they were arrested. Such attempts had led on more than one occasion in recent weeks to serious clashes with the police and to police firing. The most famous of these was the incident at Munshiganj bazar, a couple of miles from the centre of Rae Bareli town, on 7 January 1921. On that date thousands of peasants converged on the town from the early hours of the morning. The common object of those who turned out was to obtain the release of a popular leader. Most came because of rumours that Baba Ramchandra had been arrested and imprisoned in Rae Bareli jail. Some reported having heard that Gandhi had been detained there as well. The crowds probably also included some followers of Baba Janki Das, a local Kisan Sabha leader, who had been arrested in the district two days earlier and brought to the town but not, it was reported, before he could instruct his men to get people from Arkha (an early base of the

Kisan Sabha movement) to come and free him.[23] The numbers had soon swelled to an estimated 10,000, and the 'largest and most determined' section of the crowd was said to be at Munshiganj. The assembly was peaceful but refused to break up until their leaders had been released or rather, as it turned out, until a landlord and the police had fired several rounds at them, killing a number and wounding many more.

Just over three weeks later, on 29 January 1921, another man who called himself Ramchandra was arrested near Goshainganj railway station in Faizabad district. He had for some time before this been active in the area, urging peasants to refuse to pay their rents in protest against existing conditions, and advocating the justice of land being owned by its tiller. He had developed a large following—on account, it was said, of his radical preaching, *sadhu's* garb and, not least, his adopted name. When he was arrested crowds gathered at the station following a false report that the authorities intended to take him away by train They lay on the rails and prevented the train from moving, and were dispersed once again only after police firing and the arrest of eighteen of their number.[24] By this time, indeed, such confrontations between the police and the people had become fairly common, 'Even when minor agitators are tried for petty offences', the Deputy Commissioner of Bara Banki wrote in an affidavit submitted to the Court of the Judicial Commissioner of Awadh in the case instituted against Baba Ramchandra in February 1921, 'enormous gatherings assemble at the court house with the object of intimidating witnesses or to rescue the accused.'[25]

Gandhi no doubt wished to prevent the recurrence of the violent incidents that developed out of these situations. But in the process he attacked the very action that had first demonstrated the organized strength of the peasantry to the British administration and, more importantly, to the peasants themselves. Towards the end of August 1920, the Pratapgarh district authorities had arrested Baba Ramchandra on what appears to have been a fabricated charge of 'theft'. Arrested with him were Thakur Jhinguri Singh, who was

[23]U.P, G.A.D, 50/1921, Kws: J.A. St. John Farnon to Dy. Commnr., Rai Bareli, 19 Jan. 1921, and A.G. Shireff's 'Note' of 29 Jan. 1921.

[24]Siddiqi, op. cit., pp. 168-9.

[25]Motilal Nehru Papers, Group C (Legal) (NMML), File No. 44, 'King-Emperor v. Ram Chandra. Charge Under Sec. 124A 1PC, Court of the Judicial Commnr. of Oudh', affidavit submitted by C.W. Grant, Dy. Commnr., Bara Banki, 10 Feb. 1921.

one of the men responsible for the establishment of Kisan Sabhas in the district even before Ramchandra took a hand, and about thirty other peasants. Their plea for bail was refused. Three days later, when the arrested men were due to appear in court in Pratapgarh, 4-5,000 peasants marched to the town to see them—whereupon the hearing was either postponed or held secretly in jail. Upon this the crowd marched to the jail and held a peaceful demonstration outside: it dispersed only after officials had made a number of promises, the nature of which is not clear. Ten days later, a larger crowd (estimated variously at 10,000 to 40-50,000) congregated at Pratapgarh, drawn there by the rumour that Gandhi had come to get Ramchandra released. Gandhi was absent, but the peasants refused to budge until they had extracted a promise from the officials to release Ramchandra the next morning, then spent the night on the banks of the river Sai and re-assembled outside the jail at dawn As the crowd began to swell even more, the authorities lost their nerve; Ramchandra was released, spirited out of the jail under cover to prevent a stampede, and taken to a spot some distance away where from a tree-top he gave an audience to his followers. In their fear, officials had also assured the crowd that the grievances of the peasants would be investigated; and, if nothing came of this immediately, a few days later the case against Ramchandra, Jhinguri Singh and their co-accused was withdrawn.[26] It was a noble victory, but not one that Gandhi's injunctions would allow the Awadh peasants to repeat.

The origins of *Instruction 8* are equally hard to locate in the principle of non-violence alone. On the occasion of two mass rallies of the peasants, the Awadh Kisan Congress at Ayodhya on 20-21 December 1920 and a later conference at Unchahar in Rae Bareli on 15 January 1921, thousands of peasants practised 'non-cooperation' by travelling ticketless on the trains, and, when evicted, offered 'passive reistance' by lying on the rails until officials gave in and permitted them to travel free of charge. In January 1921, too, as we have noticed above, the peasants practised satyagraha by lying on the rails at Goshainganj (Faizabad) on the day of the arrest of the pretended Ramchandra. Years later,

[26]Siddiqi, op. cit., pp. 130-3. Ramchandra reports that the case against him and his comrades was got up by the Ramganj Estate. See his incomplete, undated letter in Ramchandra Colln., Acc. No. 163, Subject File No. 1—'Papers Relating to the Peasant Movement in Awadh, 1921'.

Jawaharlal Nehru recalled with pride these spontaneous acts of the Awadh peasants. The Non-co-operation Movement had begun, he wrote, and

> the *kisans* took to travelling in railway trains in large numbers without tickets, especially when they had to attend their periodical big mass meetings which sometimes consisted of sixty or seventy thousand persons. It was difficult to move them, and, unheard of thing, they openly defied the railway authorities, telling them that the old days were gone. At whose instigation they took to the free mass travelling I do not know. We had not suggested it to them. We suddenly heard that they were doing it.[27]

In February 1921, however, Gandhi advised, nay instructed, the *kisans* to refrain from such actions; and Nehru went along with him.

Numbers 8 and 9 of Gandhi's *Instructions* indicate that, in Gandhi's view as in that of the colonial regime, the peasants bore the responsibility for the preservation of non-violence—and for its break-down in any situation of clash with the authorities. *Instruction 3* shows that this was his view also of any confrontation between the peasant and the landlord. The instruction referred to physical force, but what was unique in it was the injunction against social boycott. It was precisely through this traditional practice that the Kisan Sabhas of Awadh had first signalled their arrival in the post-war political arena and through it too that they had considerably extended their influence. Towards the end of 1919, certain taluqdars of Pratapgarh who were guilty of severe exactions or other oppressive acts, found themselves up against such 'strikes' by the villagers. *Nau dhobi band kar diye gae,* i.e. the services of the barber, the washerman and other performers of menial but essential tasks, were withheld. More than a year later, in December 1920 and January 1921, this form of protest was still widespread in Pratapgarh and Sultanpur districts.[28] Now, after the outbreak of violence at various places, Gandhi sought to restore 'peace' by asking for the voluntary surrender of this time-honoured and effective weapon. No corresponding sacrifice was demanded of the landlords.

Indeed, the concern for the interests of the landlords went further. 'We may not withold taxes from the Government or rent

[27]Nehru, op. cit., p. 59.
[28]*Collected Works of Mahatma Gandhi,* vol. XX, p. 544; Siddiqi, op. cit., p. 111.

from the landlord' (*Instruction 4*). This was in line with *Instruction 7*: 'We are not at the present moment offering civil disobedience [this 'further step' was adopted by the Congress only in November 1921]; we should, therefore, carry out all Government orders.' But it was actuated by an altogether different argument as well: 'It should be borne in mind that we want to turn zemindars into friends' (*Instruction 6*). 'We should influence our opponents by kindness' (*Instruction 3*). 'Should there be any grievances against zemindars they should be reported to Pandit Motilal Nehru and his advice followed' (*Instruction 5*).

The use of the first person plural pronoun in Gandhi's *Instructions* was a delicate touch, typical of the man. But the delicacy of *Instruction 5*—'Should there be any grievances'—is of a different order. The long-suffering peasant masses of Awadh exploded in anger in 1920-21 in a situation of severe hardship. We have referred above to the well-nigh unchallengeable position guaranteed to the taluqdars by the British administration and—what was perhaps seen as part of that guarantee—the extremely insecure legal position given to the vast majority of tenants in Awadh. We have pointed also to the more or less general trend of immiserization of the peasantry under the weight of a stagnant economy coupled with population growth, rising prices and increasing demands for rent, interest and other dues. The First World War and its immediate aftermath brought new and crushing burdens: rocketing prices, uncertain harvests, War Loans, recruitment and sudden demobilization, and finally a quite disastrous season of epidemic disease. Added to these was renewed pressure from the landlords for enhanced rents, and much increased *nazrana* and other cesses, backed by the force of legal and illegal evictions of *bedakhli*. It was against *bedakhli* and *nazrana* that the peasants of Awadh protested most bitterly in 1920-21. And officials admitted the legitimacy of their protest, and therefore hastily moved to amend the Rent Act. 'There is no doubt', wrote the Commissioner of Lucknow Division having awakened to a new awareness of his surroundings in January 1921,

> that in the worst managed taluqdars' estates in this district [Rae Bareli] and others the tenants have been treated with such want of consideration and in some cases with such oppression by the landlords that one is compelled to sympathise with them.[29]

[29] U.P.,G.A.D. 50/1921, Kws: Commnr., Luknow to Chief Sec., U.P., 14 Jan. 1921.

It was not as if Gandhi knew less than this official about the extent of distress among the peasants. Among the more prominent leaders of the national movement, it was he who first vowed to identify himself with the poorest in the land (in language, in dress, in the food he ate) and to work for their uplift, precisely because of his awareness of their misery. But in Awadh at the beginning of the 1920s, he sought to play down the significance of the clash of interests between landlord and peasant, for· tactical reasons as much, it appears, as out of any concern for non-violence. 'Should there be any grievances': in other words, if there were any examples of oppressive acts or punishment or cruelty which a peasant could not possibly tolerate any longer, he should—not protest, organize a social boycott of the oppressor, or perform satyagraha by sitting and fasting outside his house, but—refer the matter to Pandit Motilal Nehru, and follow his advice. Otherwise, outside the sphere of these extreme, absolutely intolerable grievances, 'You should bear a little if the zemindar torments you. We do not want to fight with the zemindars. Zemindars are also slaves and we do not want to trouble them.'[30]

Presiding at the Rae Bareli District Political Conference a few months later, Jawaharlal Nehru seconded Gandhi. The meeting appealed to tenants and zamindars to live in harmony, and 'although the recent Rent Act [the Awadh Rent Amendment Act which had in the meantime been rushed through the provincial legisature] had made their position worse, still they should patiently bear all their troubles, pay their rents and keep the welfare of the country in view'. Before then, the Congress message had gone out in still plainer terms: peasants in Faizabad Division were asked to give up organizing 'meetings', as well as 'disturbances', and to leave it to Gandhi to win Swaraj.[31]

It needs to be emphasized that Gandhi and other Congress leaders were concerned here not primarily with urging the peasants to foreswear violence and continue their struggle by non-violent means. They were urging that the struggle be abandoned altogether—in the interests of 'unity' in what they and later commentators have called the 'greater' struggle against the British.

[30]Gandhi to a peasant audience in Faizabad on 10 Feb. 1921, quoted in Siddiqi, op. cit., p. 180.

[31]Gopal, op. cit., pp. 61, 65. See also Siddiqi, op. cit., p. 179 for Jawaharlal's earlier expression of disapproval at the peasants' actions.

This idea of a united front with the landlords of Awadh in the anti-imperialist campaign bears pondering for a moment, for the landlords' dependence on the British (the 'slavery' that Gandhi spoke of) is obvious enough. Very few of the taluqdars performed any useful function in the rural economy, the man who was Settlement Commissioner of Rae Bareli in the 1890s recalled later: most of them were 'mere rent collectors'.[32] The British relied on these rent collectors. They were 'a very solid body', 'by no means a negligible quantity' and 'the only friends we have', the Lieutenant Governor of UP observed in 1920. Or again, as he noted in a memorandum justifying a demand for five reserved seats for the taluqdars in the new legislative council to be set up in the province under the reforms of 1919, 'they live on their estates. They are prominent in all good works. They take the lead in all movements for the improvement of the province and make generous subscriptions.'[33]

The mutuality of interests found here is noteworthy, for the taluqdars relied even more heavily on the British. Wherever the Kisan Sabha spread in 1920–21 their authority crumbled at a stroke: very few did 'anything else than shut themselves up in their houses or leave for the nearest town and complain of the supineness of the authorities'.[34] Then, like the village dog who sneaks out barking when danger has passed, the taluqdars returned to battle in February–March 1921, adamant in their refusal to agree to a liberal amendment of the Awadh Rent Act and insistent on the sanctity of the *sanads* (or patents) granted to them by the British after 1857. They were good landlords, one taluqdar asserted in a discussion regarding the proposed legislative amendments; therefore, 'the tenant . . . should only be the tiller of the soil, and he should not be given any rights'.[35]

[32]Butler Colln., vol. 75: S.H. Fremantle's comment on R. Burns's talk on 'Recent Rent & Revenue Policy in the United Provinces' in *Journal of the Royal Society of Arts* (20 May 1932), p. 674.

[33]Butler Colln., vol. 21: letters to H.E. Richards, 2 June 1920, and Vincent, 10 Nov. 1920; vol. 75: Memo prepared for the Southborough Committee, 1 Dec. 1918. Butler 'screwed' Rs 20 lakhs out of the Maharaja of Balrampur for the War Loan, and got him a knighthood in return. He had in fact intended to extract 50 lakhs, but because of a misunderstanding the subordinate official whom Butler sent to Balrampur asked only for 20 lakhs (Butler Colln., vol. 20: Butler to Hewett, 19 July 1918).

[34]U.P., G.A.D. 50/3/1921: Hailey to Lambert, 1 Feb. 1921; cf. also Butler Colln., vol. 80, Butler's notes on his meeting with taluqdars on 6 March 1921.

[35]Ibid; note on meeting with taluqdars, 12 Feb. 1921. For the emphasis on *sanads*, see esp. Raja Sir Rampal Singh's 'Taluqdars and the Amendment of the Oudh Rent Law' (Lucknow, n.d.), in ibid.

Nehru himself admirably summed up the position of the taluq-dars in his *Autobiography*:

> The taluqdars and big zamindars . . . had been the spoilt children of the British Government, but that Government had succeeded, by the special education and training it provided or failed to provide for them, in reducing them, as a class, to a state of complete intellectual impotence. They did nothing at all for their tenantry, such as landlords in other countries have to some little extent often done, and became complete parasites on the land and people. Their chief activity lay in endeavouring to placate the local officials, without whose favour they could not exist for long, and demanding ceaselessly a protection of their special interests and privileges.[36]

But that was a later reflection. In 1921 Nehru and Gandhi looked aghast at the actions taken by the Awadh peasants against these creatures of imperialism. The symbolic significance of the Mun-shiganj events of 7 January 1921 when the landlord and the Deputy Commissioner lined up with the armed police against unarmed peasants and their local Congress allies, was missed. Or at least it was overlooked; for even at the time Nehru described the landlord as 'half an official' and wrote bitterly of 'the twins' (the British Deputy Commissioner and the Sikh landlord) who stood shoulder to shoulder at Munshiganj.[37] Yet, the Congress leaders looked to their landlord 'brothers' for support in the great struggle that was then raging against the British.

### The Colonial View

A British intelligence official who travelled around a 'disturbed' area in December 1920 and January 1921 made what was in some ways a shrewder analysis of the political situation in the UP countryside, in spite of his need to justify the colonial power—which he did at every step. His assessment was based on a month's tour through the part of Allahabad district that bordered on Pratapgarh (Partabgarh in his report) and Jaunpur. Conditions differed here in significant respects from those that obtained in Awadh. Yet a strong Kisan Sabha movement arose in the same years, and there are so many features of similarity that this report on Allahabad, reproduced in full as an Appendix to this paper, may

[36]Nehru, op. cit., p. 58.
[37]*Selected Works of Jawaharlal Nehru*, vol. 1 (New Delhi, 1972), pp. 213, 224.

be taken as representative of the official discourse on the peasant movement in Awadh at this time.

Intended as a general report (and a secret one at that), this Intelligence Department document is far less selective than Gandhi's *Instructions*. Its ostensible purpose was to establish the identity of the opposing forces in the countryside and the reasons for peasant discontent. The report is therefore to the point about the causes of the Kisan Sabha movement.

> Everywhere . . . the great outcry is against bedakhli (ejectment), in spite of the large amount of marusi [*maurusi*, i.e. land held on a stable. occupancy tenure] land held by cultivators in these parts. (See p.193 below.)

The situation was far more serious in the neighbouring districts of Awadh where the great bulk of the tenants' land was *ghair-maurusi* (non-occupancy). But even in Allahabad,

> the idea prevails that the zamindars are avoiding the pinch of rising prices by taking it out of their tenants, both in the form of nazranas and by raising rents. When enhanced rents are not paid, the tenants are evicted, or in some cases the land is given for ploughing to others, without even the formality of an ejectment decree. (p. 193 below.)

The official's comments on the structure of colonial administration are equally frank. No one in the villages knew anything about the much-vaunted Montagu-Chelmsford reforms and the right of franchise conferred upon some people, he tells us, until Congress spread the word that votes should not be cast. But for the non-cooperators, the elections would have been 'even more of a farce' than they actually turned out to be. It would have meant, he adds in a significant observation, that 'the subordinate officials and well wishers of the government wishful to make the Reform Scheme a success would have brought voters to the polling stations as they did recruits to the colours and subscriptions to the War Loan.' (p. 195 below.) Elsewhere he pinpoints the contemporary social and political position of the landlords. 'The average zamindar is only concerned with collecting his rents and pays very little attention to improving the means of production, communication and irrigation on his estates.' 'The position taken by the zamindars is that they and their forefathers have been well wishers of the government, and it is up to that government now to help them out of their difficulties'. 'Their only wish is for things to go on the same as ever'. (p. 194 below.)

The major weakness in this report is the absence of any direct reference to the role of the colonial Government. The author plainly fails to make sufficient allowance for the fact that he is 'a European official', his assertion to the contrary notwithstanding. The point he wishes to stress most of all is that the Kisan Sabha agitation is 'not in any way anti-British nor even anti-Government'. The movement, he suggests, is basically directed against the landlords—and who can deny that the latter have in a large measure brought it upon themselves? He argues, further, in an interesting variation of the 'manipulation' theme, that the peasants are really quite ignorant of the larger issues at stake; they did not even know who Gandhi was, and actually said 'We are for Gandhiji and the Sarkar'. (p. 197 below.) We shall have more to say about this in a moment.

First, it may be noted that the intelligence official's clean chit to the Government and the Court of Wards, and his contention that the peasants were in no way anti-Government or anti-British, is contradicted by testimony that he himself inadvertently provides:

> The idea is a fixed one [in the minds of the villagers] that a poor man has no chance against a rich man in a contest in the courts, and who will say that there is not some truth in this under the system of civil and criminal justice as it has come to be practised in India. (p. 193 below.)

He admits, besides, that the peasants blame the Government for all their sufferings during the War and believe that they 'supplied the men and money' but got nothing in return. Finally, there is in the latter part of the report still more conclusive evidence against the intelligence man's claim that the Government was 'above it all'. Here it is stated that when it was announced to crowds of peasants that Gandhi had ordered that no votes be given, 'everyone' obeyed. 'For the present . . . Gandhi's word is supreme'. 'What he orders must be done'. (pp. 196-7 below.) That fact stood as an open challenge to the authority of the British. One should add that in a situation where the peasants were not even certain of who Gandhi was (as the intelligence report indicates), it is unlikely that they would always come to know what he had 'ordered'. Rather they must often have decided, by assumption, what his orders were. The point is of some importance for, as we shall see in the next section of this essay, in parts of Awadh Gandhi's name came to be used by peasant rebels, without any specific instructions from Gandhi, to deal out justice to the landlords and the police—the subordinate officials as well as the well-wishers of the regime.

The intelligence official's remarks regarding the supremacy of Gandhi, however, tell us a good deal more about the nature of the peasant movement in Awadh in 1919-22. They indicate the important role played by rumour in the rise of such movements. It is a common assertion that peasants, scattered and isolated by the conditions of their existence, are incapable of mobilizing themselves for political action. They need an 'outside leader', we are told—a Peasant King or a modern substitute, come to deliver the people from their thrall. Yet a Just, and usually distant Ruler has often been known to provide the necessary inspiration for peasant revolt. The belief in an 'outside leader' can also be seen as the obverse of a belief in the break-down of the locally recognized structure of authority; and rumour fulfils the function of spreading such a notion as efficiently as the leader from the town. Here lies the real significance of the myth of the Great Man: 'someone' has challenged the powers that be, 'someone' has come to deliver. Hence:

> The currency which Mr Gandhi's name has acquired even in the remotest villages is astonishing. No one seems to know quite who or what he is, but it is an accepted fact that what he orders must be done. He is a Mahatma or sadhu, a Pandit, a Brahman who lives at Allahabad, even a Deota. One man said he was a merchant who sells cloth at three annas a yard. Someone had probably told him about Gandhi's shop [the new Swadeshi store set up in the city of Allahabad]. The most intelligent say he is a man who is working for the good of the country, but the real power of his name is perhaps to be traced back to the idea that it was he who got *bedakhli* stopped in Partabgarh. It is a curious instance of the power of a name. (p. 196 below.)

A brisk trade in rumours arose in many parts of India during the First World War. Embellished, re-interpreted, modified and magnified as they were passed on from person to person, these rumours contributed significantly to the flood of mass risings in this period. There was a widespread belief that the British Empire was on the verge of collapse; the recruitment campaign grew ever more furious and fearful because its armies were decimated, there was a need to scrounge pennies from the people (the War Loans) because its coffers were empty. The advocacy of Home Rule took on a new meaning. The German King was sending troops to help the opponents of the Raj, it was said. The world was turning upside down. The day of the downtrodden had come. So stories concerning the coming of the Germans caused 'excitement' not only in the villages of Allahabad (p. 197 below.); they accompanied a whole variety of other mass uprisings in these years—agitation among the Oraons of Ranchi and Chota Nagpur (and in the distant tea-gardens of Assam) in 1915-16, violent revolt among the Santhals of Mayurbhanj (Orissa) in 1917 and the large-scale rioting in Shahabad (Bihar) on the occasion of the Baqr-Id in the latter year, for instance.[38]

The 'power of a name' was evident again in Awadh in the first years of the 1920s. Both 'Baba Ramchandra' and 'Gandhi' came to acquire an extraordinary appeal. This is highlighted by the huge demonstrations for the release of Ramchandra on different occasions, and the success of the 'pretender' Ramchandra at Goshainganj (Faizabad), noticed above. It is testified to also by the 'multiple personality' that Ramchandra appeared to develop during this period: he was reported to be 'in Bahraich on the 5th [January 1921] by Nelson, to be in Barabanki at the same time by Grant and in Fyzabad [Faizabad] by Peters'.[39]

Rumours about the presence of Gandhi added to the tumult on several occasions and, as we have already noted, brought thousands of peasants thronging to Pratapgarh jail in September 1920 and to Rae Bareli on 7 January 1921 when the firing at Munshiganj occurred. Less than a week later, the Commissioner of Faizabad reported that 'large numbers' of peasants were heading towards Rae Bareli (in which district a big meeting of peasant delegates was scheduled to be held, at Unchahar, on 15 January), having been told by their Kisan Sabhas that 'it was Gandhi's order that they are to go'.[40] But with these indications of the response to 'Gandhi' and 'Ramchandra', we have passed into the domain of the peasants' perspective on the political events of 1919-22.

---

[38] See IOL, London, L/P & J/6/1448 of 1916; L/P & J/6/1488 of 1917; L/P & J/6/1507 of 1918; GOI, Home Progs., Conf., 1919, vol. 52.

[39] U.P., GAD 50/1921, Kws: Hailey to Chief Sec., 15 Jan. 1921. Nelson, Grant and Peters were the Dy. Commnrs. of the three districts named.

[40] Ibid., Hailey to Chief Sec., 13 Jan. 1921.

## The Peasants' Perspective

'We are for Gandhiji and the Sarkar'(p. 197 below).The peasants of UP, like peasant rebels elsewhere,[41] appear to have retained faith in the justice and benevolence of a distant ruler, the 'Sarkar', even as they revolted against his despotic agents. From this point of view, even the statement in the intelligence report on Allahabad district that the reverence for Gandhi was partly due to the belief that he had influence with the Government may be said to have had a grain of truth in it.

It is perhaps significant that in the Awadh of the early 1920s, those who spoke of Gandhi displacing the King at Delhi or in London tended to be men from the towns.[42] The peasants' own 'kings' were recruited locally. 'Gandhi Raj' would bring reduced rents, and

> Baba Ram Chandra Ke rajwa
> Parja maja urawe na
> (In the raj of Baba Ramchandra
> The people will make merry).[43]

The peasants' Gandhi was not a remote, western-educated lawyer-politician: he was a Mahatma, a Pandit, a Brahman, even a merchant 'who lives at Allahabad'. (p. 196 below.) Baba Ramchandra was more emphatically still a local man—a *sadhu* of renown in the districts of Jaunpur, Sultanpur and Pratapgarh, even before he gained a position of importance in the Kisan Sabha movement.

M.H. Siddiqi, citing the folk-rhyme regarding Ramchandra quoted above, rightly observes that the notion of *raja* (king) and *praja* (subjects) was 'so deeply ingrained in the psyche' of the peasant that he spoke even of popular peasant leaders in these terms.[44] The evidence from Awadh is indeed striking in this respect. Shah Muhammad Naim Ata, the descendant of a pious Muslim revered by Hindus and Muslims alike in the village of Salon (Rae Bareli district), became 'King of Salon' when he joined

---

[41]Cf. Gopal, op. cit., pp. 49-50n; I.J. Catanach, 'Agrarian Disturbances in Nineteenth Century India', *Indian Economic & Social History Review*, 3:1 (1966); Daniel Field, *Rebels in the Name of the Tsar* (Boston, 1976), *passim*.

[42]U.P., GAD 50/2/1921, D.O. No. 1620 from Office of Publicity Commnr., Naini Tal, 25 June 1921, quoting article in the *Leader* entitled 'Perversion of Peasants'; Siddiqi, op. cit., pp. 173n, & 178n.

[43]Ibid, pp. 200, & 112n.

[44]Ibid., pp. 122-3n.

the rebels in 1920. Jhinguri Singh, founder of what was probably the first Kisan Sabha of the movement in Rure (Pratapgarh district), was acclaimed 'Raja of Rure' and said to have 'swallowed all laws'. The pretender Ramchandra established his 'kingdom' in the region of Goshainganj (Faizabad district), held court and meted out justice before his arrest in January 1921. Thakurdin Singh, a servant of the Raja of Parhat, had done the same in some of the latter's villages in Pratapgrah district a couple of months earlier. In February 1922, again, it was reported that the leaders of the Eka movement had begun to assume the title of Raja and were moving about the countryside with 'large bodyguards of archers and spearmen'.[45]

The pithy rhyme from the Patti tahsil of Pratapgarh district thus captures a central feature of the traditional peasant view of the political world. There are rulers and ruled. And rulers are usually just: they must be, for their subjects to remain contented and for the normal functioning of the prescribed order of things. As we shall see, it was a view that at least some sections of the Awadh peasantry were to discard as their struggle matured between 1919 and 1922.

In the early stages of the Kisan Sabha movement, however, traditionalism was pronounced. One of the earliest forms of peasant protest to come to notice in Awadh during this period was the age-old practice of social boycott—*nau dhobi band*. The customary sanction of village caste panchayats was used to enforce the boycott among the peasants.[46] Caste solidarity and the authority of the caste panchayat appears also to have been of significance in the setting up of the Kisan Sabhas. The villages where the first Sabhas were established, such as Rure, Arkha and Rasulpur, had in their populations a large proportion of Kurmis and Muraos, 'superior' cultivating castes with a tradition of solidarity and independence, and it was among these castes that the Kisan Sabhas found their initial base.[47]

In southern and eastern Awadh as a whole the Kurmis were

[45]U.P., GAD 50/1921: telegram from Commnr., Lucknow to Chief Sec., U.P., 12 Jan. 1921; Mehta's Report, p. 3; S.K. Mitral and Kapil Kumar, 'Baba Ram Chandra and Peasant Upsurge in Oudh, 1920-21', *Social Scientist*, No. 71 (June 1978); extracts from the *Englishman* and the *Leader* as in *notes* 18 and 42 above. Cf. Pushkin's *The Captain's Daughter* for a picture of Pugachev, the Pretender.

[46] Siddiqi, op. cit., p. 111.

[47]Ibid., p. 117; W.F. Crawley, 'Kisan Sabhas & Agrarian Revolt in the United Provinces, 1920-21', *Modern Asian Studies*, 5:2 (1971), p. 101.

thought to be the 'mainstay' of the movement all the way from the
last months of 1919 to the early part of 1921.[48] At more than one
place in his notes and diaries, Baba Ramchandra reports how
Thakur Jhinguri Singh and Thakur Sahdev Singh, the men who
were responsible for drawing him into the Kisan Sabha movement,
were aided in their earlier efforts to promote the movement by a
number of 'honest, dedicated, self-sacrificing' Kurmis named
Kashi, Bhagwandin, Prayag and Ayodhya. Jhinguri Singh, Sahdev
Singh and their families initially had to bear the entire cost of
looking after the thousands of peasants who in the early months of
1920 flocked to Rure to report their grievances. Then Bhagwandin, Kashi, Prayag and Ayodhya got together and proceeded to
mobilize support from their caste-fellows. This they did so successfully that several thousand rupees were raised in a short while,
and the movement gained a more secure footing.[49] Similarly, on
the occasion of the great Awadh Kisan Congress held at Ayodhya
in December 1920, the Rasulpur (Rae Bareli district) Kisan Sabha
leader, Mata Badal Koeri, raised Rs 6000 from the Koeris who had
come to attend the Congress.[50]

By the winter of 1920–21, the Kisan Sabha had gained considerable support among tenants and labourers of a wide range of castes,
including Muslims. Caste consciousness may now have posed other
problems for the organizers of the movement: hence, perhaps, the
need for Ramchandra's directive that after meetings, local Ahirs
should look after and feed Ahirs who had come from distant
places, and Kurmis, Koeris, Muslims, Brahmans and others should
do likewise.[51]

The peasant movement in Awadh was, in addition, marked by a
pervasive religious symbolism. At the early peasant meetings
Ramchandra and others commonly recited excerpts from Tulsidas's *Ramcharitmanas*,[52] the favourite religious epic of the Hindus in

[48]Ramchandra Colln. II, RC XIII; U.P. Rev. (A) Dept. File 753 of 1920: Hailey's 'Note'
on Mehta's Report, dated 17 Dec. 1920; U.P., GAD 50/1921, Kws: Commnr., Faizabad to
Chief Sec., U.P., 14 Jan. 1921.

[49]Ramchandra Colln. I, Subject File No. 1: 'Papers Relating to Peasant Movement in
Avadh 1921', incomplete letter of 1939 and 'Avadh, U.P., ke kisanon par mere niji vichar'
(14 July 1934). Translation from the Ramchandra papers is mine, except where otherwise
stated.

[50]Ramchandra Colln. II, RC XI: 'Autobiographical Notebook', p. 35.

[51]Ibid., p. 12.

[52]Nehru, op cit., p. 53; D.N. Panigrahi, 'Peasant Leadership', in B.N. Pandey (ed.),
*Leadership in South Asia* (New Delhi, 1977); p. 85. Old Congress workers of Sandila in Hardoi
district recalled how Madari Pasi also 'recited *kathas* and held peasant meetings'.

northern India and especially beloved of people in this region: their own language, Awadhi, was after all the language of Tulsidas's composition, and places like Ayodhya (a few miles from Faizabad), the seat of Ram's kingdom, very much part of their world. The phrase 'Sita Ram' early became the chief rallying call of the movement—used by peasants of all communities, Muslims as well as Hindus, to bring out supporters for meetings and (at a later stage) for resistance to Government and landlord agents attempting to overawe members of the Kisan Sabhas, confiscate moveable property or take other action against the peasants.

Baba Ramchandra has a good deal to say about the words 'Sita Ram' in the course of his fairly sketchy writings on the movement. He recalls, in a note written in 1934, that when he first came to Awadh, the greeting *salaam* (usually addressed by one in an inferior station to one in a superior) was widely used. He promoted the use of the alternative, 'Sita Ram', which did away with such discrimination on grounds of status, and thus earned the displeasure of 'many of the praiseworthy [*sic.*] and respectable folk of the upper castes'. Gradually, however, he writes, 'Sita Ram', 'Jai Ram', 'Jai Shankar', caught on in place of *salaam*. And as the movement developed, and his own popularity increased, it was enough for Ramchandra to raise the slogan 'Sita Ram': the cry was promptly taken up in one village after another, and thus in a remarkably short space of time thousands would assemble to see him and hear his discourse.[53]

Elsewhere, Ramchandra writes with still greater pride of the phenomenal power of the peasants' new slogan. On one occasion, early in the history of the Kisan Sabha movement, a confrontation took place at village Bhanti (in Pratapgarh district) between the police and the agents of the Ramganj and Amargarh estates, on the one hand, and Thakur Jhinguri Singh and his co-workers on the other. 'On that side were the wielders of *lathis* and spears', Ramchandra records dramatically. 'On this side was the slogan "Sita Ram". . . As soon as the cry of "Sita Ram" was raised, thousands of peasants poured out in waves from the surrounding villages.' It needed no more to make the police and other authorities change their tune: with the landlords' men, they left as quietly as possible.[54]

[53]Ramchandra Colln. I, Subject File 1: 'Avadh ke kisan par mere niji vichar' (14 July 1934); Nehru, op. cit., p. 52; interviews with the late Babu Mangla Prasad, one of the Allahabad Congressmen who had been drawn into the Pratapgarh peasant movement in 1920.        [54]Ramchandra Colln. II: 'Autobiographical Notebook', p. 26.

In retrospect, indeed, Ramchandra attributes miraculous powers to the phrase 'Sita Ram'. He describes an incident in which a servant of the Amargarh estate forcibly cut a peasant's sugarcane crop for the purpose of feeding the Amargarh estate's elephants. As he returned with his loot loaded on an elephant, he was stopped by a Kisan Sabha worker named Prayag. 'The driver urged the elephant to advance upon him. But Prayag stood his ground, crying "Sita Ram". The elephant refused to advance.' Ramchandra goes on to report that in the part of Awadh where he was first based, the mango trees in the villages for several miles around bore fruit only once every three years. 'Because of the slogan "Sita Ram" they began to bear fruit every year.' He concludes: 'In the most difficult of situations, the peasants turned to the slogan "Sita Ram". And the slogan fulfilled their many different desires. As a result the organization [of the Kisan Sabhas] grew ever stronger.'[55] In other 'notes' written at around the same time, i.e. in 1939 or 1940, Ramchandra rues the fact that the peasants of Awadh were forgetting the two simple words that had brought them such great victories as the extraction, from the British, of the Awadh Rent (Amendment) Act of 1921 and the passing, by a Congress ministry, of the far more thorough U.P. Tenancy Bill of 1939.[56]

These reflections of a man who was by then inclining more and more to a left-wing position point to the religious type of consciousness[57] that the peasants brought to their struggle. That it was not just a 'half-crazy' *sadhu* who attached a special significance to the words 'Sita Ram' is attested to by other contemporary observations. The 'most serious feature' of the situation in January 1921, according to the Deputy Commissioner of Faizabad, was

> the immense danger which arises from an organization which at very short notice is able to collect enormous crowds. The existence of a definitely arranged rallying cry is another danger.

The last part of this statement was later elaborated thus:

[55] Ibid., p. 26-7.
[56] Ramchandra Colln. II, RC XIII; Ramchandra Colln. I, Subject File No. 1: 'Note' of 27 Dec. 1939. The 1939 Tenancy Bill received the Governor's approval and became law only in 1940 after the resignation of the Congress ministries.
[57] Ranajit Guha has drawn my attention to this concept which occurs in some of the early writings of Karl Marx.

One of the most powerful weapons at their [the peasants'] command is the war cry—Sita Ram Ki jai. They all say that when this is sounded, most turn out and to a very large extent this is done. It has become the cry of discontent.[58]

The hold of religious symbols on the mind of the peasant is perhaps also indicated by a story relating to the selection of Rure as the place where the first Kisan Sabha should be established. V. N. Mehta, after his enquiries into the movement, suggested that Rure was chosen partly because legend had it that Ram and Lakshman, the heroes of the *Ramayana,* had once rested there. Tulsidas wrote: '*raj samaj virajat Rure*' [the company of Princes honour Rure with their presence], and the people of Rure claimed that this was a reference to none other than their own village.[59] What better traditional sanction than this for the launching from here of a just and righteous political movement?

The idea of a just, or moral, struggle appears to have been fundamental to the peasants' acceptance of the necessity of revolt. Exploitation as such was not unjust. It was inevitable that some ruled and some conducted prayers and some owned the land and some laboured, and all lived off the fruits of that labour. But it was important that everyone in the society made a living out of the resources that were available. It was when the subsistence needs of the peasants of Burma and Indo-China were threatened in the colonial era that the fiercest peasant revolts broke out there.[60] It was similarly when the landlord decided to levy new and oppressive imposts in a period of considerable hardship for substantial sections of the peasantry that resistance was taken up in Awadh as morally right and necessary.

In Allahabad district, the intelligence officer noticed that there was a difference in the peasants' response on the estates of resident proprietors on the one hand and absentee owners on the other, and among the latter especially those of 'new men'—city *banias* and *mahajans* and the like.

There is nowhere any genuine objection to performing *hari* and *begari* [forced labour] according to immemorial custom for zamindars who

[58]U.P., GAD 50/3/1921: H.R.C. Hailey to Butler, 24 Jan. 1921; and 'Note' by Hailey, regarding views of himself, Peters and Scott O'Connor (enclosed with Hailey's letter to Lambert, 1 Feb. 1921). See also Nehru, op. cit., p. 53.

[59]Mehta's Report, cited in Siddiqi, op. cit., p. 115n.

[60]James C. Scott, *The Moral Economy of the Peasant* (California, 1976), *passim.*

are seen and known, but there is a tendency to kick against working for and supplying nazrana, hathyana, motorana [all relatively new 'taxes'] etc. etc. for distant and unknown landowners at the bidding of foul mouthed karindas and sepoys.[61] (pp. 192-3 below.)

The feeling against 'new men' may have contributed to the peasant revolt in some of the Awadh districts too. The animosity displayed towards one or two Sikh taluqdars in Rae Bareli, it was suggested in January 1921, was because they were regarded as interlopers. On the estate of Sardar Amar Singh, the peasants were reported to have accepted the leadership of a Rajput occupancy tenant who had been dispossessed following the Mutiny.[62] In an attack on the estate of the small Kurmi taluqdar of Sehgaon-Pacchimgaon, also in Rae Bareli district, the peasants followed the Kurmi descendants of co-sharers likewise dispossessed after the Mutiny.[63] The adoption, as King of Salon, of Shah Naim Ata—descendant in a line of revered benefactors of the village—may also have been the result of a similar kind of sentiment.

There is evidence too of an acceptance of the long-established, 'fair' rights of the landlord—in Awadh as in Allahabad. A contemporary statement on the Awadh Kisan Sabha agitation made the point that the peasants' complaints regarding *begar, rasad* and so on were minor compared with their sense of outrage over *bedakhli* and *nazrana:* 'The former had been a custom for generations. The latter were of comparatively recent growth.'[64] In Pratapgarh, Mehta reported on the basis of his inquiries in October 1920, town-based politicians like Mata Badal Pandey had adopted the position that nothing more than the rent should be paid to the landlord; but 'the tenants have not yet fallen into line with them'.[65]

The 'Kisan pledge' to be taken on the formation of each new Kisan Sabha, which was drawn up in May or June 1920, still looked to the landlord (Thakur) for justice and protection from his oppressive agents (*ziladars,* peons and so on). It read as follows:

[61]*Nazrana* was the premium demanded from a tenant to allow him onto, or let him stay on the land. *Hathyana* and *motorana* were imposts levied on the peasants when a new elephant or a motor-car was bought by the landlord.

[62]U.P., GAD 50/1921, Kws: Commnr., Lucknow to Chief Sec., U.P., 14 Jan. 1921.

[63]H.R. Nevill, *Rae Bareli: District Gazetteers of the United Provinces of Agra and Oudh,* vol. 39, (Lucknow 1923), p.95; Siddiqi, op. cit., pp. 160-1.

[64]Faunthorpe's Report, p. 273.

[65]Mehta's Report, p. 57.

1.  We Kisans shall speak the truth—not the untruth—and tell our story of woe correctly.

2.  We shall not brook beating or abuses from anyone; we shall not lay our hands on anyone but if a ziladar or peon raises theirs on us we, five or ten of us, will stay his hand. If anyone abused us we shall jointly ask him to restrain himself. If he would not listen we would take him to our Thakur.

3.  We shall pay our rent at the proper time—and insist upon a receipt. We shall jointly go to the house of the Thakur and pay the rent there.

4.  We shall not pay illegal cesses like *gorawan* [*ghodawan*], *motorawan*, *hathiawan*. We shall not work as labourer without payment. If any peon catches hold of a Kisan (for forced labour) the rest of the villagers will not take their meals without setting him free. We shall sell *upli* (cow dung cakes), *patai* (sugarcane leaves for thatching) and *bhusa* (straw) at slightly cheaper than the bazaar rate but we shall not supply these articles without payment.

5.  We shall not quarrel and if we do we shall settle it by a panchayat. Every village or two to three villages combined will form a panchayat and dispose of matters there.

6.  If any Kisan is in trouble we shall help him. We shall consider other Kisans' joys and sorrows our own.

7.  We shall not be afraid of constables. If they oppress [us] we shall stop him [them]. We shall submit to no one's oppression.

8.  We shall trust in God and with patience and zeal we shall try to put an end to our grievance[s].[66]

Later a spokesman for the peasants explained, with reference to clause 4 above, that the amounts of *bhusa, upli,* etc. traditionally given, would still be provided free of charge; it was only anything demanded in addition that would have to be paid for as specified. And in October 1920, shortly after his liberation from Pratapgarh jail on account of the mass demonstrations of his followers, Ramchandra promulgated the rates of the customary dues, like *hari* and *bhusa, karbi* and *bhent,* that peasants were to pay.[67] It is in the light of the peasant's notion of a moral world, rather than in the simple terms of 'moderate' and 'radical' borrowed from elite discourse,

[66]This translation is found in ibid, pp. 109-10. The pledge appears over the name of Gauri Shankar Misra, vice-president, U.P. Kisan Sabha, but its language and Ramchandra's reconstruction of it in his writings (see undated, incomplete letter in Ramchandra Colln. I, File No. 1), suggest that Ramchandra and other local people had a major hand in drawing it up.

[67]Mehta's Report, p. 110.

that this position might best be understood. It is in this light too
that we might comprehend the 'not altogether simple' demands[68]
of the 3000 peasants led by Baba Janki Das and others, who
besieged the house of Thakur Tribhuvan Bahadur Singh of Chan-
danian (Rae Bareli) on 5 January 1921 to obtain an end to ejectment
and 'the turning out of a prostitute in the Taluqdar's keeping'.

The religious-ethical aspect of the peasants' demands was evident also in the oath taken by villagers in northern Awadh to
signify the support of their villages for the Eka movement in the
latter part of 1921 and the early months of 1922. An elaborate
religious ritual accompanied the oath-taking. A hole dug in the
ground and filled with water represented the sacred river Ganga.
Over this, and in the presence of all the villagers—summoned,
officials averred, by means of abuse, threats and social boycott—a
pandit recited a prayer. A collection of four annas or more per
head was made, and part of this was used to pay the pandit for his
services. Finally, an oath was administered and a panchayat
formed in order to settle disputes in the village. By the various
injunctions of the oath, the peasants bound themselves to:

1. Refuse to leave their fields if illegally ejected.
2. Pay only the recorded rent.
3. Pay rent regularly at the agreed times.
4. Refuse to pay rents without being given receipts.
5. Refuse to perform *begar* for zamindars without payment.
6. Refuse to pay *hari* and *bhusa*.
7. Refuse to pay for the use of irrigation tanks.
8. Refuse to pay for grazing cattle on jungle and pasture lands.
9. Give no help to criminals in the village.
10. Oppose oppression by the zamindars.
11. Take all disputes to their own panchayat and abide by its
    decision.[69]

There are several points of similarity between the Eka oath and
the earlier Kisan Sabha pledge. In both a traditional peasant
morality finds expression. There was a proper share that the
superior classes might claim: this was to be met promptly. Crime
was to be opposed (Eka oath), truthfulness and trust in God
maintained (Kisan Sabha pledge). Yet both emphasized, at the
same time, the peasants' need for unity and self-help, especially
reliance on their own panchayats for the purpose of settling all
internal disputes.

[68]Siddiqi, op cit., p. 154.     [69]Ibid.. pp. 201-2.

It seems evident that there was already, in the earlier stages of the peasant movement, a growing tension between the traditional structure of agrarian society and the peasants' insistence on implementing traditional practice. Thus rents would be paid, but only if receipts were provided. Customary cesses would be met, but not any demand for larger quantities than usual, nor any new and illegal imposts. More generally, the peasants would resist oppression by the police and the landlord's agents, although they might still turn to the landlord for arbitration.[70] By the time of the Eka movement, this tension had been resolved to some extent by the adoption of a more militant stand against the traditional system as a whole. A commitment was still made to pay rents as agreed between landlord and tenant, but this was no longer the case even with customary cesses such as *hari* and *bhusa*. The peasants would no longer perform *begar* without remuneration, or pay for the use of irrigation tanks or pasture lands; for water, like air, was a gift of God, and the jungles and other uncultivated lands had for long (before the arrival of the British legal system and record of rights) been used in common. Finally, the peasants now declared their determination to resist any attempt to evict them illegally from their fields, and indeed to oppose all oppressive acts of the landlords. The surviving elements of deference, found in the expression of hope of justice from the landlord in the Kisan Sabha pledge, had disappeared.

This change of tone reflects another feature of the powerful peasant movement under discussion, its ability to overcome some of its own traditionalist limitations. Seeing how their landlords had acted, the Awadh peasants were learning to defend their interests. Many of the old links between the landlords and their tenants, labourers and other servants, had been eroded by the imposition of British order, the registration of rights, rigorous collection of rent, revenue and interest, the enforcement of all this in the courts of law, and most recently the exceptional pressure brought to bear on the peasantry during the First World War. Now, with the emergence of the Kisan Sabhas (working at times in association with Congress and Liberal volunteers) and the later Eka associations, the peasants' subservience broke down further.

[70]At another level the use of the traditional greeting 'Sita Ram' reflected the same tension—since it was promoted in part to do away with the peasant's consciousness of hierarchy and attitude of deference, and was opposed (as we have observed) by members of the more privileged classes.

Soon they launched into a more open attack on the old order. The movement had entered upon a significant new phase.

For the beginnings of this phase we have to look back to the events of December 1920 and January 1921. The great Kisan Congress at Ayodhya on 20 and 21 December 1920, attended by some 80-100,000 peasants, appears to have marked the turning point. After the Congress, the peasants first lay on the rails until they were permitted to travel home on the trains without purchasing tickets; then, back in their villages, took to protracted discussion of the events and decisions of the meeting 'in the local panchaits [panchayats] which have since been formed in almost every village'.[71] For the first time, an official commented, these villagers 'had begun to realise the power of an united peasantry—to realise that they themselves had the remedy of the most flagrant of their wrongs, the illegal exactions of the landlords, in their own hands'.[72]

By January 1921, another official reported after an investigation in Faizabad division, while most tenants professed 'a certain amount of attachment to the estates to which they belong', they appeared 'firmly determined to obey their [Kisan Sabha] leaders'. He went on to comment on the mass meeting scheduled to be held at Unchahar in Rae Bareli district on 15 January 1921, at which it was said Ramchandra would decide whether future rents were to be paid or not: 'The organization of the tenants' sabhas is now so far complete that it is probable that these orders will carry great weight, if [they are] not implicitly obeyed.'[73] As in Allahabad, a new authority had arisen. 'Gandhi's word is supreme.' Baba Ramchandra will be 'implicitly obeyed'.

As it happened, the peasants did not wait for the word of Gandhi, or of Ramchandra who was by this time working in close association with the leaders of the Non-cooperation Movement. It is evident that the presence of Gandhi and the Congress, and rumours regarding Gandhi's achievements in Champaran, were an important source of inspiration to the Awadh peasant in these years. The support of local Congressmen, Khilafatists and Liberals, and the intervention of men like Jawaharlal Nehru was also of consequence, helping to further inject the Kisan Sabhas with

[71]U.P. GAD 50/1921, Kws: St. John Farnon, Dy. Commnr., Rae Bareli, 19 Jan. 1921.
[72]Loc. cit.
[73]Ibid., Commnr., Faizabad to Chief Sec., U.P., 14 Jan. 1921.

nationalist symbols and slogans and of course giving them wider publicity. Yet, one must not exaggerate the role of the urban politician in the growth of the movement. Any suggestion that it was the Congress (or the Liberals) who politicized the peasantry and thus drew the Awadh peasant into the wider campaign against the British Raj, is belied by timing of the peasants' revolt and the violence of their actions.

It is clear that masses of peasants returned from the Ayodhya Congress with their own unexpected interpretation of the stated purpose of the gathering: 'to end landlord atrocities'. Ramchandra had appeared at the Congress bound in ropes, a dramatic gesture alluding to the bondage of the Awadh peasantry. Before the end of the conference he agreed to throw off his ropes since 'owing to the gathering, ejectment had already been done away with'.[74] The peasant audience took this act literally. Ejectment symbolized the oppressive authority of the landlords, and over the next three months this authority was attacked time and time again. The period saw widespread rioting in Rae Bareli, Faizabad and Sultanpur districts, and the extension of protest into other areas over matters that had not until then been brought into contention.

From the Faizabad division, officials reported a 'general refusal' to till the landlord's *sir* in Pratapgarh, Sultanpur and parts of Faizabad district.[75] The Raja of Pratapgarh, a leading taluqdar, received confirmation of the changed character of the struggle in January 1921 when he found tenants refusing his 'liberal' offer of fourteen-year leases which they had a short while earlier readily accepted. Around the same time, protests were beginning to be heard against demands for *rasad* and *begar* in Bara Banki, a district that had remained largely unaffected by the Kisan Sabha movement until then.[76]

In January 1921 there were also several instances of attacks on landlord property. These were concentrated in Rae Bareli district and the Akbarpur and Tanda tehsils of Faizabad district, but occurred elsewhere too. In Rae Bareli large bands appeared in several estates, destroying the taluqdars' crops and looting and destroying their storage places. 'From 5 January for some days the

[74]Siddiqi, op cit., pp. 148-9.

[75]*Sir:* land held by the landowner under title of personal cultivation.

[76]U.P. GAD 50/1921 Kws: letters of Commnrs., Faizabad and Lucknow Division to Chief Sec., U.P., 14 Jan. 1921.

district was practically in a state of anarchy.' In Pratapgarh there was an assault on the *ziladar* of Raja Bahadur Pratap Bahadur Singh. In Faizabad the terminal weeks of 1920 and the early days of 1921 brought isolated attacks on the servants of taluqdars, and the looting and burning of their straw. Then, following a meeting on 12 January 1921, which led to an attack on and the looting of the zamindars of Dankara, widespread rioting broke out in the district. Bands of 500-1000 men, women and children marched from place to place for the next two days, settling scores with their enemies.[77]

By this time, as we have already observed, many of the lower castes and landless labourers were involved in the agitation. At Fursatganj and Munshiganj bazars in Rae Bareli district, where police firing occurred on 6 and 7 January 1921 respectively, the multi-caste composition of the crowds was especially noted. Among these crowds were numbers of Pasis and members of other 'crir inal' tribes who constituted a substantial section of the labouring population of the district. The prominence of the latter was attested to again by the official view that they were responsible for the 'indiscriminate' looting of village bazars and the concentration of rioting in the south-eastern tehsils of Rae Bareli.

In Faizabad, it was reported, Brahmans and Thakurs were not 'generally' in the movement, but 'all the lower castes are affected'. The rioters were said to consist chiefly of Ahirs, Bhars, Lunias and the untouchable Pasis and Chamars, i.e. the castes that provided the majority of the small tenants and agricultural labourers. Deo Narain, one of the two major Kisan Sabha leaders active in the district (the other was Kedar Nath), appears to have concentrated his propaganda efforts among the *halwas* (labourers) of the Brahman and Thakur zamindars and tenants, organizing them into numerous Kisan Sabhas. Consequently Pasis, Chamars, Lunias and other labouring castes were to the fore in the riots in Akbarpur and Tanda tehsils: they plundered the houses of high-caste villagers and their women too came out to attack the high-caste women.[78]

[77]Siddiqi, op cit., p. 165.

[78]U.P., GAD 50/1921 Kws: St. John Farnon to Dy. Commnr., Rae Bareli, 19 Jan. 1921; U.P. GAD 50/3/21: telegram from Commnr. of Faizabad to U.P.A.O., Lucknow, 16 Jan. 1921: and L. Porter to Governor, 19 Jan. 1921, report of interview with Raja Tawaqul Husain of Pirpur; also Siddiqi, op. cit., p. 166 and Panigrahi, op. cit., p. 95. C.A. Bayly has noticed the same sort of development in the neighbouring Allahabad district: by December 1920, he writes, the 'enraged lower peasantry had been joined by landless labourers,

The interests of the landless labourers and the smaller, unprotected tenants of Awadh converged to a large extent. And after December 1920, the actions of the peasants highlighted the concerns of these sections of the rural poor. Their attacks were extended to the bazars and other points where wealth was concentrated. The chief targets were the *banias* (merchants) who had exploited the difficult times to make large profits, but *sunars* (goldsmiths), weavers and others who were thought to have profited from the situation were also attacked in some places. Stores of grain belonging to the taluqdars were looted and destroyed. The houses of upper caste and prosperous villagers were attacked, and quantities of clothes, jewels and so on burnt and destroyed.[79]

At this more advanced stage of the struggle, the peasants also identified more clearly the forces that were ranged against them.[80] In Faizabad the targets of the peasants' violence spread out from the taluqdars and their direct agents to patwaris,[81] small zamindars, large cultivators and the high castes in general. They now covered all those who were on the side of the 'enemy'. This explains the attacks on upper-caste tenants, for as the Commissioner of Faizabad observed, many of these in Faizabad (and in Sultanpur) belonged to 'the same clans as the landlords' and 'opposed the formation of Sabhas in their villages'. Indeed, at this stage the higher castes in Faizabad turned more openly against the movement, welcomed the police, and on the latter's arrival 'plucked up spirit' to defend their property.[82]

suddenly caught by the rise in prices and the sharp turn of the labour market against them after the good months following the influenza epidemic of 1918. Offences against the liquor laws and attacks on the police by Pasis became frequent and in north Allahabad and Patti [Pratapgarh district] disorderly 'swarajya' crowds composed of unemployed Pasi and Chamar labourers became increasingly active during the next six months.' Bayly, 'The Development of Political Organization in the Allahabad Locality'. (Oxford D. Phil. thesis, 1970, pp. 369-71, 382.)

[79]U.P. GAD 50/3/1921; Siddiqi, op cit., pp. 151-3, 165.

[80]Siddiqi seems to accept the contemporary officials' view that the peasants were 'indiscriminate' in their attacks, and describes the local Sabhas as becoming 'totally anarchic' 'at the level of action' (ibid., p. 154). Yet the weight of the evidence points to a quite different conclusion, in spite of the instance Siddiqi singles out of an attack on weavers by 'some ten men'. (Ibid., pp. 150, 153.)

[81]In Awadh the patwari was looked upon as a servant of the landlord though he also performed several duties for the Government. Metcalf, *Land, Landlords and the Raj*, pp. 302-3.

[82]U.P., GAD 50/3/21: Commnr. of Faizabad to Chief Sec., U.P., 24 Jan. 1921; & U.P., GAD 50/1921 Kws: Commnr. of Faizabad's telegram and letter of 16 & 17 Jan. 1921; also Panigrahi, op. cit., p. 97.

It was in the very nature of these developments that the peasant rebels should soon come into direct confrontation with the law-enforcing authorities, who were unquestionably on the side of their enemies. An official diagnosis suggested in February 1921 that

> the kisans have come to appreciate the strength of numbers and having successfully defied the landlords are quite ready to defy Government authority. They have to a large extent lost all fear of the police.

It also reported a growing feeling of antagonism towards Europeans and the abuse of policemen for deserting their countrymen and serving an alien race. An important part of the local Kisan Sabha propaganda at this stage declared the taluqdars to be 'evil creations' of the Government; or, alternatively, described the Government as being 'in league with taluqdars, as guilty of murders and crimes, and above all as being condemned by Gandhi'.[83] All this had little to do with the Congress leaders. It was rather a product of the experience gained by the peasants in the course of their struggle. Given the structure of the colonial administration, the necessity of opposing European officials and the police arose from the very fact of opposing the landlords. This is evident from an examination of the circumstances surrounding even a few of the clashes between the peasants and the police in the Awadh countryside.

In the village of Sehgaon-Pacchimgaon, the peasants were aroused by news of the demonstrations and battles at Fursatganj and elsewhere in Rae Bareli district. In this situation they accepted the leadership of the dispossessed Kurmi co-sharers earlier mentioned and responded to their appeals to unite against the landlord. After the third week of January 1921 tension increased in the village. The villagers set loose the zamindar's cattle to graze on his sugarcane fields. Then, on a bazar day, they gathered and threatened to attack the landowner. The police intervened—to be attacked by the peasants. 'One constable was killed by a *lathi* blow, which smashed the back of his skull. The others retired two or three hundred yards using their guns.' It was some time before the so-called 'ringleaders' could be arrested and the crowd dispersed.

Not long after this event another major clash occurred near the railway station of Goshainganj in Faizabad district. Here the

[83]U.P. GAD 50/3/21: Hailey's 'Note' enclosed with Hailey's letter to Lambert, 1 Feb. 1921.

pretender Ramchandra, who will by now be familiar to the reader, was active for several days in the last part of January 1921, advocating the non-payment of rent and apparently also the doctrine of 'land to the tiller'. Propagandists like him, officials observed, made 'the strongest appeal to the low castes and landless castes who are always little removed from starvation and are told that a millenium in the shape of swaraj is coming through the intervention of Mahatma Gandhi'. The Goshainganj Ramchandra actually did better. Such was his following for a short while that he was able to return land to peasants who had been ejected and order the explusion of others 'not true to the cause'. On 29 January 1921, then, it required a force of some seventy mounted policemen to arrest this one man. That afternoon crowds gathered thinking that he was to be taken away by a train at that time, and lay on the tracks to prevent the train from moving. When a large police force came forward to remove them, the peasants responded by attacking them with bricks lying near the station. The police had to fire thirty-three rounds before the crowds dispersed.

Later, in March 1921, the familiar sequence of mobilization against a landlord (in this case a widowed landlady) and then against the police when they intervened, occurred at Karhaiya Bazar in Rae Bareli district. In this area Brijpal Singh, a demobilized soldier from Pratapgarh, Jhanku Singh, another ex-soldier, Surajpal Singh and Gangadin Brahman, delivered numerous 'objectionable speeches' in the first three weeks of that month. A meeting, scheduled to be held at Karhaiya Bazar on 20 March, the weekly market day, was prohibited by the authorities, and orders issued for the arrest of the 'agitators'. But on that day, the peasants battled with the police, trading brickbat for buckshot, and rescued Brijpal Singh and Jhanku Singh when the police tried to arrest them. Indeed, the police were forced to retreat into the taluqdarin's house and here they were besieged by 'a yelling mob of several thousand people'. The arrival and direct orders of the white Sahib, the English Deputy Commissioner, failed to move the peasants. They continued their vigil all night and maintained a barricade the next morning to prevent 'motors' from entering or leaving the courtyard of the house. Another round of police firing was necessary before the peasants withdrew and their leaders were arrested. Jhanku Singh who was shot during the firing, later succumbed to his injuries, and at least two other peasants are known to have been killed.[84]

The transformation that had taken place in the Awadh peasants' struggle was recognized by the Magistrate at Pratapgarh who reported that what had started as a 'genuine tenants' agitation' soon assumed an 'openly political form' [*sic*].[85] In Faizabad, an official summary informs us, the result of the lectures delivered every three or four days all over the district by Deo Narain Pande, Kedar Nath Sunar and Tribhuvan Dutt was that

> meetings are held nightly *in every village* and a regular system of non-co-operation is being preached. Cultivators are told not to go to the courts, or to the tahsil or to the police, and to pay no rent. [emphasis added.]

At one of these nightly meetings, at which two police constables were beaten and slightly hurt, a number of papers were confiscated from the speaker: in the main, these were petitions to Gandhi describing various grievances regarding the peasants' fields, but they also consisted of two lists of men to be appointed to the posts of Deputy Commissioner, 'Kaptan Sahib' (i.e. Superintendent of Police), Daroga, etc.[86] In Karhaiya, as in Goshainganj (Faizabad), there is evidence of the rebels having established something in the nature of a parallel government. Brijpal Singh and Jhanku Singh in the former, and 'Ramchandra' in the latter, held frequent panchayats and tried criminal cases. Some villages in Rae Bareli even elected their own Deputy Commissioners, who then tried local cases.[87] In Tajuddinpur village in the district of Sultanpur, at about the same time, 'for a few weeks *swaraj* was proclaimed and a parallel government set up'.[88] It was a measure of the distance that the Kisan Sabha movement had traversed between the end of 1919 and the early months of 1921.

At this point the peasant movement in Awadh was more or less abandoned by the Congress leadership, and an emboldened admin-

[84]The last three paragraphs are based on Siddiqi, op. cit., pp. 160-1, 162-3, 168-70 and U.P., GAD 50/2/1921: Judgement of Khan Bahadur Md. Abdus Sami, Magistrate First Class, Rae Bareli, 25 April 1921, in Criminal Case 69, King-Emperor v. Brijpal Singh & others.

[85]*Report on the Administration of the United Provinces of Agra and Oudh, 1921-22* (Allahabad, 1922), pp. 31-2.

[86]U.P., GAD 50/3/21: L. Porter to Governor, 19 Jan. 1921: report of interview with Raja Tawaqul Husain of Pirpur, and Hailey to Butler, 24 Jan. 1921.

[87]Faunthorpe's Report, p. 273.     [88]Gopal, op. cit., p. 55.

istation advanced to crush it—through the arrest of all of the most important peasant leaders, Ramchandra, Deo Narain and Kedar Nath among them, the widely publicized,[89] but ultimately trivial, amendment of the Awadh Rent Act, a sustained campaign of propaganda on behalf of the Government and a massive display of armed force.[90] Yet the movement was far from finished. Towards the end of November 1921 it burst forth again in the form of the Eka campaign.

The revival of the movement in this novel form may have owed something to an All-India Congress Committee resolution in November 1921 sanctioning 'full civil disobedience' including the non-payment of taxes. It was also encouraged initially by the efforts of certain Congressmen and Khilafatists based at Malihabad in Lucknow district, from whom it was suggested the movement got its new name—'Eka' or 'Aika' for unity. However, the Eka associations spread swiftly and it was not long before 'they got out of the control of the Congress people who were quite annoyed about it'.[91]

In Hardoi district, where the Eka movement first took root, tenants began to organize locally towards the end of 1921 to resist landlord attempts to collect more than the recorded rent. In Bahraich in early January 1922, there were two occasions on which tenants beat up *thekadars* (long-term lease-holders who collected rents on behalf of the taluqdars) and carried away the grain extracted from them as rent. Later that month bands of tenants were reported to be moving from village to village in the district demanding the immediate abolition of grain rents, through which the taluqdars and *thekadars* reaped virtually all the benefits of high prices. In Kheri district, the arrest of a Congress volunteer was the occasion for a demonstration by a considerable gathering,

[89]On 13 Jan. 1921, the U.P. Government telegraphed to various newspapers and to the Associated Press a press communique along the following lines: 'With reference to the suggestion that an enquiry must be held into the relations between the landlords and tenants in Oudh the Government is in possession of full information and has already decided to take up the question with a view to early legislation.' Further, 'Sir Harcourt Butler [the Governor] hopes as an old friend of both the landlords and the tenants of Oudh that they will avoid all action likely to cause a breach of the peace and will trust the Government to do justice.' (U.P., GAD 50/1921 Kws.) The Government also telegraphed all Dy. Commnrs. to 'have intention to legislate published in every Tahsil' (UP GAD 50/3/21).

[90]P.D. Reeves, 'The Politics of Order: "Anti-Non-Cooperation" in the United Provinces, 1921', *Journal of Asian Studies*, 25:2 (1966); Butler Colln., vol. 21, Butler to H.E. Richards, 4 Feb. 1921.

[91]Faunthorpe's Report, p. 274.

which besieged the police station and released the man. In the village of Kothi in Bara Banki district, again, the peasants' wrath was aroused; here a zamindar's peon was killed in March 1922 when he tried to collect rents.[92]

These and other such incidents reflect the force of the peasant movement as it swept through Hardoi, Bahraich, Kheri, Bara Banki, Sitapur and Lucknow districts. By the end of January 1922 the movement was very strong indeed in the Sandila tehsil of Hardoi district, and the landlords of the area more than a little perturbed. In February 1922 one police circle in Hardoi reported twenty-one Eka meetings in three days, with assemblies of 150 to 2000 people. In the same month Kishan Lal Nehru visited Atrauli (Hardoi district) in order to try and reassert a Congress hold on the movement. But he found that Madari, an untouchable Pasi by birth who had become the acknowledged leader of the Eka movement, was 'in full command'. Indeed at this stage, as the movement spread to thirty more villages, Madari completely severed his connections with Malihabad and shifted the Eka headquarters to Sandila in Hardoi district.[93]

Yet this symbolic and significant break from the Congress did not make the Eka movement any less 'political', even if we take the narrow view of equating the political with the avowedly nationalist. On the contrary. The official report on the Eka movement, produced by Lieutenant-Colonel J.C. Faunthorpe, I.C.S., in April 1922, sought to draw a distinction on this ground between the Kisan Sabha and the Eka phase of the agitation. In the former, Faunthorpe wrote, 'the animosity of the peasants was directed entirely against the taluqdars and not against Government officials. In the Eka movement this is not so much the case.' The official biographer of Jawaharlal Nehru writes that 'though the Congress had little to do with the Eka Movement . . . the Eka associations soon began to pass political resolutions'. According to the police at the time, too, there was little to distinguish Noncooperation from Eka in the preachings of men like Baba Garib Das, a Pasi turned *sadhu* who was active in Bara Banki in March 1922.[94] Perhaps the most striking evidence of all is Madari's attempt to extend the appeal of the movement at the very time

[92]Loc. cit; Siddiqi, op. cit., pp. 196-204.
[93]Ibid., p. 200 & n.; Faunthorpe's Report, p. 274.
[94]Ibid., 273; Gopal, op. cit. p. 57; Siddiqi, op. cit., p. 204n.

when he shifted its headquarters from Malihabad to Sandila. In order to do this, it was reported, he 'adjusted local differences' and urged zamindars to join the Ekas. In the weeks that followed, large numbers of petty zamindars did so.[95]

The provincial authorities in UP were in no doubt about the political implications of the Eka movement. From the end of 1921 they used their 'most autocratic powers' to break the Eka and the Congress organizations.[96] In Awadh this intervention again led to open clashes between the police and the peasants. When the police tried to arrest Madari in February 1922—having made 'arrangements on a somewhat elaborate scale'[97] for the purpose—several thousand peasants gathered to frustrate their effort. Indeed Madari was not to be apprehended until June that year, in spite of the handsome Rs 1000 reward that the authorities offered for his arrest. In March 1922 the peasants of Hardoi provided further evidence of their political feelings, when a large crowd of Pasis attacked a police party that was making inquiries about Eka meetings in village Udaipur in the Shahabad police circle. In the police firing that followed, two of the attackers were killed.[98] Ultimately the forces at the disposal of the Government proved to be too great for the proponents of Eka to match on their own. Confronted by large bodies of armed and mounted police and a squadron of Indian cavalry, the Eka movement went under.

## Conclusion

When peasant violence erupted in January 1921 to set off the debate on the social and political condition of Awadh, the British were quick to sum up its causes. 'It has for long been obvious that the Oudh Rent Act requires amendment.' 'In the worst managed taluqdars' estate . . . the tenants have been treated with such want of consideration and in some cases with such oppression by the

[95] Faunthorpe's Report, p. 281. Siddiqi argues that the participation of the small zamindars was 'not entirely political'. He quotes the instance of one landowner whose involvement was attributed by officials to a desire to advance his personal interests, but then goes on to tell us that most of the zamindars who supported the movement did so either because they were Khilafatists or because of 'the crushing weight of the revenue demand which made them join the ranks of the tenants' (op. cit., pp. 206-7). It is not easy to conceive of many choices more political than that.

[96] Reeves, op cit., p. 273.

[97] Faunthorpe's Report, p. 274.

[98] Loc. cit. See also Siddiqi, op. cit., p. 204 & n.

landlords that one is compelled to sympathize with them.' The administrators themselves, fair-minded officials, representatives of a great empire, were above it all. Venerable justices of the peace, their influence would count, their neutrality could scarcely be called into question. The assessment turned out to be inaccurate. The days were gone when the Raj could pose as an impartial referee, standing on high and whistling 'foul play'. Local struggles tended more and more to get caught up in the general wave of anti-imperialism sweeping through India Even as the officials in Awadh were making their pious pronouncements on the reasons for the 'disturbances', the peasants had begun to attack the symbols and servants of the British Raj.

The colonialists could never comprehend this development. Then and later their explanation of it was to be in terms of the ignorance of the Indian masses and the manipulation of them by self-interested politicians. Yet they needed no prodding to realize its potential consequences. They wavered for a brief moment in mid-January 1921, even asking the bigger and more 'responsible' nationalist and peasant leaders to mediate and bring their moderating influence to bear on the peasants.[99] Then they moved with determination—and 'sympathy' was less in evidence than armed and mounted police and contingents of Indian troops.

Other participants in the debate could not match such clarity of vision or firmness in action. It was a period of learning, of trial-and-error, and uncertainty all round—among the peasants as among their urban well-wishers. Gandhi and Nehru recognized and indeed stressed that the Awadh peasant movement was anterior to and independent of the Non-cooperation Movement, though there is evidence too of the interaction between the two and the strength one lent to the other. Hesitantly, yet surely, the Congress leaders were drawn into the conflict between the peasants and their oppressors. In the end, however, they came around to the view that if the peasants' struggle was allowed to continue, it might hinder the development of the national movement against the British. The interests of that 'larger' struggle, the need for 'national unity', necessitated the shelving of such sectional struggles for the time being. The argument appears to have a good deal of force in it and some recent historians have been tempted to

[99]U.P., GAD 50/1921, Kws: telegram from Commnr., Lucknow to Collector, Rae Bareli, 14 Jan. 1921.

accept it *in toto*. The grounds on which they do so, however, require closer examination.

A united front of the whole Indian people—landlords and peasants, millowners and manual labourers, feudal princes and the tribal poor—in the anti-colonial campaign was scarcely feasible: no major struggle for change anywhere has ever achieved such unity. If, then, the statement is diluted to one urging the 'widest possible unity' on the basis of the only demand held in common by most Indians, the demand for Swaraj, we are still in the position of begging the question. What did the demand for Swaraj in fact signify? Is the idea of liberation from colonial rule to be equated with the narrow vision of the eviction of the white man from India? It is doubtful if a single one of the more important Congress leaders had a notion of Swaraj that was restricted to the simple physical eviction of the British from Indian soil. Had this been the sum total of the nationalist demand, the British would in all probability have been willing to submit to it long before they did. The concept of Swaraj had inherent in it the idea of greater individual freedom, equality and justice, and the hope of accelerated national and consequently individual development. Whether articulated by a Gandhi, as in his *Hind Swaraj,* or a Nehru, as in Jawaharlal's 'socialist' phase, or by the humblest nationalist sympathizer, the idea of Swaraj had built into it the dream of 'a new heaven, a new earth'—increased participation by all in the making of the decisions that affected them, reduced burdens (of rents and other taxes and imposts), an end to oppression.[100] The question then was how best to organize to bring this about.

The appeal to the need for *national unity* in the pursuance of this goal is plainly rhetorical. It needs to be re-phrased in terms of an appeal for *a particular kind of alliance,* seen as being necessary for the furtherance of the anti-imperialist struggle. It should be evident that the nature of the Swaraj that eventuated from this struggle would depend very much on the nature of the alliance (the 'unity') that was forged. From this point of view, the Congress' insistence in 1921-2 on a united front of landlords as well as peasants and others, was a statement in favour of the *status quo* and against any radical change in the social set-up when the British finally handed over the reins of power. The advice to peasants to give up organizing

[100]See Saadat Hasan Manto's story 'Naya Qanoon' for an interesting portrayal of such expectations.

'meetings' and 'disturbances' and to leave politics to the professionals, was a statement against mass participatory democracy and
in favour of the idea of 'trusteeship'—the landlords and princes
acting as trustees in the economic sphere, Gandhi and company in
the political. In the two and a half decades following 1922, sections
of the Congress did abandon this stance, under the impetus particularly of the workers' and peasants' struggles that arose in various
parts of the country during the years of the Depression and after.
But the main body of Congressmen stood by the position worked
out by Gandhi and other leaders in 1921-2.

The sort of alliance that the Congress leadership settled on at
that juncture was of crucial significance in determining the future
course of the anti-imperialist struggle in India. Yet it is too easy to
present a scenario of a dynamic urban-based party conducting the
struggle, and at certain points making a choice between a variety
of passive onlookers who might be expected to sympathize with
their objectives. Referring to the debate between pro-slavery
(conservative) and abolitionist (liberal) writers on American slavery, Genovese has pointed out that both viewpoints treat the
Blacks 'almost wholly as objects, never as creative participants in a
social process, never as half of a two-part subject'.[101] So, in the case
of colonial India, the peasants have generally been treated as
beneficiaries (economically) of an increasingly benevolent system
or victims of an oppressive one, 'manipulated' (politically) by
self-seeking politicians or 'mobilized' by large-hearted, selfless
ones. Both viewpoints miss out an essential feature—the whole
area of independent thought and conjecture and speculation (as
well as action) on the part of the peasant.

From the stand-point of many an Awadh peasant in the 1920s,
we would suggest, there was a Gandhi different from the one we
know and a promise of Swaraj also different from the one that we
do not so much *know* as *assume*; just as from his predecessor's point
of view there had been, in the nineteenth century, a 'benevolent'
but inaccessible white queen, quite different from the 'benevolent'
Queen addressed and perhaps seen by the western-educated Moderate members of the Indian National Congress. This man, with
his own peculiar expectations of Gandhi and Swaraj, jumped into
the fray in Awadh in the years 1919-22. Beginning with petititions,

[101] Eugene D. Genovese, 'American Slaves and their History' in A. Weinstein and F.O.
Gatell (eds.), *American Negro Slavery* (New York, 1973), p. 186.

and demonstrations against the landlords's agents, he went on to show his faith in locally-organized panchayats in preference to the British courts, to non-cooperation with the railway authorities and further, in places, to a campaign for the non-payment of taxes and attacks on the landlords and the police. At the very moment of Gandhi's imaginative Non-cooperation Movement, he and thousands of his comrades arose to present a parallel and powerful challenge to the entire structure of colonial authority in UP. They threw up thereby the real and immediate possibility of an anti-imperialist movement very different from any until then contemplated by the urban nationalist leadership. And to press their point they marched scores of miles first, in June 1920, from Pratapgarh to Allahabad, and then, in the succeeding months, to several Kisan Conferences to meet their Congress leaders and learn from them how they should proceed.

It was not, thus, an abstract question of whom the Congress might choose as ally, and then educate and train for political action. The peasants of Awadh had already taken the lead in reaching out for an alliance. As Ramchandra put it:

> It was felt that if we could link our Kisan movement with some established organization, or gain the support of well-to-do [privileged?] groups and lawyers, then this movement would become the future of India.[102]

As it happened, the Congress leadership declined this offer—on account of its concern for the maintenance of non-violence, its uncertainty as to the possible repercussions of encouraging a broad-based peasant movement, or a dim but growing awareness of its own class interests.

Recent statements on the peasant movement in Awadh have asserted that 'the Congress and the Liberals had helped the Kisans to stand on their feet'[103] and to 'defy not just the landlords but even the Government'.[104] How far and in what way this was true has already been indicated. For the sake of the completeness of the historical record, it needs also to be said that the same people helped, by their refusal of continued support, to bring the peasant movement to its knees. It has been argued, in addition, that while the Liberals appreciated the class interests of the peasants better

---

[102]Ramchandra Colln. I, Subject File No. 1: incomplete letter of 1939.
[103]Siddiqi, op. cit., p. 217.     [104]Gopal, op. cit., p. 55.

than the Congress—witness their support for the amendment of
the Awadh Rent Act—'the Congress, as a more advanced political
force that wanted to end British rule in India, devoted its energies
and attention towards preserving unity between different
classes'.[105]

Here the historian faithfully reproduces the Congress leaders'
assessment of the peasant movement in Awadh as fundamentally
misguided. On the basis of the evidence so far available, this is not
a position that is easy to uphold. Indeed it may more reasonably be
argued that, as their struggle matured, the peasants of Awadh
sensed more accurately than the urban leaders did, the structure of
the alliance that held up the colonial power in UP and the range of
forces that might combine to fight it. The very 'moderation' of
Madari Pasis' effort to enrol the support of the smaller zamindars
stands testimony to that. In this situation, a pronouncement of the
error, or ill-timing, of the peasant movement can come only out of
an uncritical acceptance of the Congress leaders' point of view. It
does not flow from an analysis of the actual conditions of anti-
colonial struggle in the 1920s.

Madari, Sohrab, Isharbadi: three names, and the caste affiliation
of the first-named (a Pasi), is all we know about these Eka leaders
who, with others as yet unnamed, for several months in 1921 and
1922, guided a powerful peasant movement against the colonial
regime and its local collaborators.[106] It is a telling comment on the
importance that historians and others have so far attached to the
history of the subaltern.[107] Some scholars have indeed expressed
their prejudice quite plainly. 'To organize was difficult enough, to

[105]Siddiqi, op. cit., p. 217.

[106]The long lists of 'freedom-fighters', *Svatantrata Sangram ke Sainik,* drawn up district by
district, by the U.P. Government in connection with the celebration of the Silver Jubilee of
Indian independence, does not contain entries for any of these leaders. Madari Pasi and the
village he is supposed to have come from are mentioned in the introductory note to the
volume on Hardoi district. In a brief visit to the district I sought to use this lead in order to
try and find out more about Madari, only to discover that Madari never came from a village
of that name, that a village with that name does not exist in the concerned tahsil, and that
old Congressmen (mentioned in the list of 'freedom fighters') spoke of Madari as they
would of a 'bad character' or at best an inconsequential one: so heavily does the élitist
heritage sit upon us. I did not have the time to pursue my inquiries after Madari and other
Eka leaders on that occasion, but feel sure that further effort will yield useful information.

[107]We use this term (as we use 'elite') as a convenient short-hand to distinguish the lower,
labouring and exploited classes from the upper, relatively privileged groups in different
parts of the society.

organize in the face of repression was not possible for Madari.'
Thus Majid Siddiqi, in the only published monograph on the
peasant movement in Awadh.[108] This comment on the configuration of forces then existing in the country betrays the élitist
viewpoint of its author, for the picture appears very different from
the peasants' perspective.

By the winter of 1921-2, the peasant movement in Awadh had
overcome many, though by no means all, of its own traditionalist
limitations. Yet, its localism and its isolation remained. To get
over these it needed an ally among other anti-imperialist forces in
the country. But the chief candidate for this role, the party of the
growing urban and rural petty bourgeoisie, had turned its back on
the peasant movement long before that time. What a commenta-
tor wrote on another popular struggle, in another time and
another land, is perhaps more appropriate in the context:

> The petty bourgeoisie encouraged insurrection by big words, and
> great boasting as to what it was going to do. [But] wherever an armed
> conflict had brought matters to serious crisis, there the shopkeepers
> stood aghast at the dangerous situation created for them; aghast at the
> people who had taken their boasting appeals to arms in earnest; aghast
> at the power thus thrust into their own hands; aghast, above all, at the
> consequences for themselves, for their social positions, for their for-
> tunes, of [at?] the policy in which they were forced to engage them-
> selves . . . Thus placed between opposing dangers which surrounded
> them on every side, the petty bourgeoisie knew not to turn its power
> to any other account than to let everything take its chance, whereby,
> of course, there was lost what little chance of success there might have
> been, and thus to ruin the insurrection altogether.[109]

---

[108]Siddiqi, op. cit., p. 202n. Kapil Kumar has recently completed a doctoral dissertation
on the peasant movement in Avadh, for the University of Meerut. When published, this
should tell us a good deal more about the Eka movement.

[109]F. Engels, *Germany: Revolution and Counter-Revolution* (London. 1969), p. 105.

# APPENDIX
## Kishan Sabha in Allahabad

(Source: Government of India, Home Department, Political Branch, Deposit, February 1921, No. 13. Extracted from CID Memo No. 1052, dated Allahabad 7 January 1921, signed P. Biggane, Asst. to D.I.G., C.I.D. UP, SB).

The following note is the outcome of personal observations and enquiries after a month's tour in the trans-Ganges tract of the Allahabad district, where the Kishan Sabha agitation has been most acute.

There is a very noticeable stirring of the pathetic contentment of the masses, but the discontent lacks definite aims. After due allowance is made for the fact that the enquirer was a European official there can still be no doubt that up to the present at any rate the disaffection is directed against the landlords and is not in any way anti-British nor even anti-Government. Naturally the strength of the movement varies with the locality, it being strongest in places along the pucca roads where agitators were on the motor cars near the Partabgarh border and in big market villages where extremist meetings have been held. Get away even a mile or two from these special localities and there is very little active interest. Of course people have heard of meetings being held and Kisan Sabhas being formed at other places, but at present there is very little inclination to follow suit without direct instigation from outside. The distinction is generally freely admitted between the condition of land tenure in Oudh and in the Allahabad district, but still there is a great longing for the Permanent settlement (or Duncani Bandobast) as it exists in Jaunpur. The difference is very noticeable between the state of affairs in villages where the landlords are small men residing on the spot and on the estates of long absentee landowners, particularly on those of city *banias* and *mahajans,* who have no interest in the tenants except what they can get out of them in the way of rent. It is freely recognised that the trouble there is that the landowners have to employ *Sujawals, karindas* and sepoys and it is these middlemen who are the cause of the oppression of the tenantry. There is nowhere any genuine objection to performing *hari* and *begari* according to immemorial custom for zamindars who are seen and known, but there is a tendency to kick against working for and supplying nazrana, hathyana, motorana, etc. etc. for distant and unknown landowners at the bidding of foul mouthed karindas and sepoys. Everywhere however except in Court of Wards Estates where the tenants have no complaints of any sort the great outcry is against bedakhli, in spite of the large amount of marusi land held by cultivators in these parts. To what extent the outcry is justified can be better decided by some one more acquainted with the working of the revenue courts than the writer, but the word is in every person's mouth. The idea prevails that the zamindars are avoiding the pinch of rising prices by taking it out of their tenants, both in the form of nazranas and by raising rents. When enhanced rents are not paid, the tenants are evicted, or in some cases the land is given for ploughing to others, without even the formality of an ejectment decree. It is all very well to argue that such proceedings are impossible under the law, and that the tenant has his redress in the courts. Whatever the facts may be the idea is firmly rested in the average cultivator's mind that this sort of thing is going on; and it is also a fact that there is very little faith left in the efficacy of the law courts as a means of obtaining redress. The idea is a fixed one that a poor man has no chance against a rich man in a contest in the courts, and who will say that there is not some truth in this under the system of civil and criminal justice as it has come to be practised in India? It is no use arguing with the cultivator that as a result of the prevailing high prices of food stuffs, he gets far and away more for his produce than he did, and that it is only fair that a ratio of the profits should go to the zamindar and to Government. His reply is that owing to the drought this year there has been little or nothing produced, and in any case cloth is so dear that he cannot afford to clothe himself and his children. This contention is unanswerable and the extent of the genuine distress is very great. It is naturally difficult for the Indian peasant who cannot see much beyond his nose either in space or time, to understand how the war has caused a world shortage of commodities and how the value of the currency has fallen. After all people in other countries with a greater claim to intelligence and education are as unreasonable on the subject of the high prices, and have a tendency to blame their Government of whatever form it may be. The Indian peasants' chief idea about the war is that they supplied the men and the money and [Government] issued them bits of paper instead. It will be noticed that these notions distinctly smack of Bolshevism, and it would be interesting to know whether they are in some way the indirect result of Bolshevik propaganda, or have arisen from the same causes as have produced them in other countries. The Bolshevik idea is also rapidly spreading from the extremist areas mentioned above, that it is the cultivators who plough, sow, irrigate and reap and are thus entitled to the whole of the produce of the land. There is no need of, and no right to be such things as zamindars. Here again the contention of the cultivators is very hard to refute, as there is no denying the fact that the Indian landlord is singularly backward in the performance of his duties. The old class of small proprietor who acted the godfather to his tenants and helped them on the occasions of their domestic ceremonies is being rapidly bought out, and even he did practically nothing to improve the economic lot of the cultivators. The average zamindar is only concerned with collecting his rents and pays very little attention to improving the means of production, communication and irrigation on his estates. No doubt the system of sub-division of estates militates against such improvements being effected as a general rule, but the fact remains that the population cannot go on increasing and the standard of living be raised unless there is more intensive cultivation and increase in yield per acre. The general attitude of the zamindars is even less reassuring than that of the cultivators. Their only wish is for things to go on the same as ever. In only very few places in this district up to the present are they meeting with any organized opposition from the tenants and they are content to get on by the force of custom and prestige and to hope that things will not get worse. In the few places, as in some villages near the Partabgarh border where the tenants have combined to oppose and boycott them, and where they can get no redress owing to the solidarity of their opponents they are biding their time and relying on Government to put things right. There is no attempt to combine or form a political party. The position taken up by the zamindars is that they and their forefathers have been well wishers of the British Government, and it is up to that government now to help them out of their difficulties. The curious part about the situation is that the vast majority of the cultivators also still look to Government as their only salvation. They can make no suggestions as to the remedy for their present distress; that is the function of Government. They have their grievances and their miseries and it is up to

Government to put things right. There is no other power under Heaven that can save them. *Upar Parmeshwar niche Sarkar.* They have generally heard the word swaraj but are quite incapable of explaining it. (In this perhaps they are not peculiar.) If they are told that it is the sarkar's own hukm that the government is to be handed over to Indians as quickly as possible they are filled with genuine consternation and quote instances of mismanagement under Indian officials. They all contend that such a thing is impracticable without unity among Indians themselves, and they are unanimous in the opinion that such unity is impossible. They allow that if even the cultivators of one village can combine they are then in a position to oppose the zamindar, but they generally refuse to admit that such union is permanently possible. Such a thing as any concerted action between Hindus and Muhammadans—in the opinion of the Muhammadan minority at any rate—is quite beyond the bounds of possibility. For the present then the cultivators like the zamindars are looking to Government to put their troubles right, and it is unfortunately undoubtedly true that they have completely failed to grasp the idea that they are themselves in a position to influence the decisions and policy of Government through the reformed councils and by that means to get the law altered if they choose to suit their ends. Up to within a few days of the General Election on the 30th November, hardly a soul in the villages had heard anything at all about councils or votes, and the whole system of representative government, in spite of District Board Elections, seems absolutely incomprehensible to the vast majority. In many places it was only when the non-cooperation agents spread about the injunction that votes were to be given to no one, that any one had heard of such a thing as a vote. Even then no one had any idea what it meant. It is no exaggeration to say that if there had been no non-cooperation agitation at all the elections in the rural parts of this district at any rate would have been even more of a farce than they actually were. It would have probably meant that the zamindars, subordinate officials and well wishers of the government wishful to make the Reform Scheme a success would have brought voters to the polling stations as they did recruits to the colours and subscriptions to the War Loan. The cultivators would have recorded their votes because it was a sarkari hukm and not with any conception at all of what they were doing. Even the election campaign conducted by Pandit Radha

Kant Malaviya through the Kisan Sabha proper seems to have educated only a negligible number of persons in the Handia tahsil. The elections occurred at a time when the cultivators were fighting the drought in order to produce some rabi crop. Every hour spent away from the irrigation well meant a certain loss of produce. Naturally the hard headed cultivator was glad of an excuse not to attend a function in which he took not the slightest interest. Two or three days before the election the candidates began a little propaganda in the form of distribution of leaflets, specimen voting papers, etc. These apparently made no impression. The method of attack adopted by the Moderate candidates seems to have been in the main to approach the zamindars and get them to round up some of their tenants at the polling stations. Those who went to the polling stations on the election day did so with a vague idea that they were going to attend some sort of sabha which was some affair of the zamindars. It was thus not difficult for the non-cooperation agents to persuade them that the whole thing was a ruse of the zamindars to get their signatures (or thumb impressions) on a paper which would lead in the end to bedakhli. The Indian villager is chary of giving his signature without knowing exactly what he is signing, and with good cause. Thus when it was announced to the hesitating assemblies that it was the order of Mr Gandhi that no votes should be given, every one heaved a sigh of relief and went home. The currency which Mr Gandhi's name has acquired even in the remotest villages is astonishing. No one seems to know quite who or what he is, but it is an accepted fact that what he orders must be done. He is a Mahatma or sadhu, a Pandit, a Brahman who lives at Allahabad, even a Deota. One man said he was a merchant who sells cloth at three annas a yard. Some one had probably told him about Gandhi's shop (the new Swadeshi store in Hewett Road). The most intelligent say he is a man who is working for the good of the country, but the real power of his name is perhaps to be traced back to the idea that it was he who got *bedakhli* stopped in Partabgarh. It is a curious instance of the power of a name. As mentioned above the Duncani bandobast is still a bye word in this part, and the writer was solemnly asked by more than one man whether he knew the Duncans and whether any of the family was now in India. Were a Duncan Sahib to come to settle the Allahabad district now, his name would probably supersede that of Gandhiji in a week. One cannot help being struck by the

chance that offers among a people of this nature to a real patriot,
should one arise from among the people themselves, not from
among the landowning or professional classes, to take the place of
the notoriety hunters and Bolshevik agents who now pose as
leaders of the people. For the present, however, the fact must be
faced that Gandhi's word is supreme, and even the local hero
Malaviji has been displaced, being accused of misspending funds
entrusted to him. When votes were obtained by Radha Kant
Malaviya by his agents, it was generally only because they told the
voters: 'Gandhi Babu says you are not to vote at all, or, if you do,
to vote for Malaviji.' The curious thing is that as a general rule
Gandhi is not thought of as being antagonistic to Government, but
only to the zamindars. The sarkar is still conceived of as something
above and aloof from such consideration.

The Reformed Councils are just a ruse of the zamindars. We are
for Gandhiji and the Sarkar. The reverence for Gandhi is undoubtedly partly due to the belief that he has great influence with the
Government. If therefore the result of the new councils is legislation in favour of the zamindars the effect is likely to be disastrous.
Undoubtedly what is required to allay the present unrest is some
amendment of the Land Tenure Laws in such a way as to appeal to
the imagination of the tenants. And the sooner some thing of the
sort is done the better. At present, as stated above, the cultivators
are much too busy irrigating their fields to be easily led away on
any other tack. Should, however, the rabi fail as the kharif has
done a delicate situation would be created. Generous remissions of
land revenue would be the first requisite. But even if they were
granted, assuming that Mr Gandhi's name continued in the ascendant till April, the mischief makers would be in a position to use it to
create an ugly situation, in the panicky condition in which the
people would then be. If on the other hand there are winter rains
and the Land Tenure act is tackled in a liberal manner as the first
business of the new council, Mr Gandhi's name will probably fade
from people's memories as quickly as did that of the Germans after
the first excitement at the outbreak of the Great War.

# Gandhi as Mahatma:
# Gorakhpur District, Eastern UP,
# 1921–2[1]

## SHAHID AMIN

'Many miracles, were previous to this affair [the riot at Chauri Chaura], sedulously circulated by the designing crowd, and firmly believed by the ignorant crowd, of the Non-co-operation world of this district'.

—M. B. Dixit, Committing Magistrate,
Chauri Chaura Trials.

## I

Gandhi visited the district of Gorakhpur in eastern UP on 8 February 1921, addressed a monster meeting variously estimated at between 1 lakh and 2.5 lakhs and returned the same evening to Banaras. He was accorded a tumultuous welcome in the district, but unlike in Champaran and Kheda he did not stay in Gorakhpur for any length

[1] Research for this paper was funded by grants from the British Academy and Trinity College, Oxford. I am extremely grateful to Dr Ramachandra Tiwari for letting me consult the back numbers of *Swadesh* in his possession. Without his hospitality and kindness the data used in this paper could not have been gathered. Earlier versions of this essay were discussed at St Stephen's College, Delhi, the Indian Institute of Management, Calcutta, and the Conference on the Subaltern in South Asian History and Society, held at the Australian National University, Canberra, in November 1982. I am grateful to David Arnold, Gautam Bhadra, Dipesh Chakrabarty, Partha Chatterjee, Bernard Cohn, Veena Das, Anjan Ghosh, Ranajit Guha, David Hardiman, Christopher Hill, S. N. Mukherjee, Gyan Pandey, Sumit Sarkar, Abhijit Sen, Savyasaachi and Harish Trivedi for their criticisms and suggestions. My debt to Roland Barthes, 'Introduction to the Structural Analysis of Narratives', in Stephen Heath (ed.), *Image-Music-Test* (Glasgow, 1979), Peter Burke, *Popular Culture in Early Modern Europe* (London, 1979), Ch. 5 and Ranajit Guha, *Elementary Aspects of Peasant Insurgency in Colonial India* (Delhi, 1983), Ch. 6 is too transparent to require detailed acknowledgement.

of time to lead or influence a political movement of the peasantry. Gandhi, the person, was in this particular locality for less than a day, but the 'Mahatma' as an 'idea' was thought out and reworked in popular imagination in subsequent months. Even in the eyes of some local Congressmen this 'deification'—'unofficial canonization' as the *Pioneer* put it—assumed dangerously distended proportions by April-May 1921.

In following the career of the Mahatma in one limited area over a short period, this essay seeks to place the relationship between Gandhi and the peasants in a perspective somewhat different from the view usually taken of this grand subject. We are not concerned with analysing the attributes of his charisma but with how this registered in peasant consciousness. We are also constrained by our primary documentation from looking at the image of Gandhi in Gorakhpur historically—at the ideas and beliefs about the Mahatma that percolated into the region before his visit and the transformations, if any, that image underwent as a result of his visit. Most of the rumours about the Mahatma's *pratap* (power/glory) were reported in the local press between February and May 1921. And as our sample of fifty fairly elaborate 'stories' spans this rather brief period, we cannot fully indicate what happens to the 'deified' image after the rioting at Chauri Chaura in early 1922 and the subsequent withdrawal of the Non-Co-operation movement. The aim of the present exercise is then the limited one of taking a close look at peasant perceptions of Gandhi by focusing on the trail of stories that marked his passage through the district. The location of the Mahatma image within existing patterns of popular beliefs and the way it informed direct action, often at variance with the standard interpretations of the Congress creed, are the two main issues discussed in this essay.

In a number of contemporary nationalist writings peasant perceptions of and beliefs about Gandhi figure as incidents of homage and offering. Touching instances of devotion and childlike manifestations of affection are highlighted in the narratives of his tour in northern India during the winter of 1920–2.[2] And if this spectacle of popular regard gets out of hand, it is read as a sign of the mule-like obstinacy (*hathagraha*) of simple, guileless *kisans*. The sight and sound of

[2] See Mahadev Desai, *Day-to-day with Gandhi* (Secretary's Diary), iii (Varanasi, 1965), pp. 143ff. and 262–6. For a condensed version of the same ideas, see D. G. Tendulkar, *Mahatma: Life of Mohandas Karamchand Gandhi*, ii (Bombay, 1952), p. 78.

uncouth peasants invading the train carrying Gandhi, rending the sky with cries of '*jai*' and demanding *darshan* at an unearthly hour, could be annoying and unnerving. But all was not yet lost because local Congress leaders could be counted on to restrain the militant exuberance of lathi-wielding, torch-bearing enthusiasts.[3] A passage titled 'Boundless Love' from the tour diary of his secretary is representative of how peasant attitudes towards Gandhi have been written about in nationalist narratives:

> It is impossible to put in language the exuberance of love which Gandhiji and Shaukat Ali experienced in Bihar. Our train on the B.N.W. Railway line stopped at all stations and there was not a single station which was not crowded with hundreds of people at that time. Even women, who never stir out of their homes, did not fail to present themselves so that they could see and hear him. A huge concourse of students would everywhere smother Gandhiji with their enthusiasm. If at some place a sister would take off her coral necklace and tell him, 'I give this specially for you to wear', at some other, *sanyasis* would come and leave their rosaries on his lap. If beautiful sheets of handspun and hand-woven cloth, many yards long, would be presented at one place, at some other place would turn up a loving villager from the woods, boastful of his trophy, saying, 'Maharaj (an address of reverence) this is my feat of strength. The tiger was a terror to our people; I am giving the skin to you'. At some places, guns normally used as fog-signals were fired in his honour. At some others, we came across railway officers who would not give the green flag, when our train came within their jurisdiction, in order to have and let others have Gandhiji's *darshan*. Not minding the fact that our 'Special' was certain to pass by them in terrific speed, people were seen at some places, standing along the railway lines in distant hope of having just a glimpse of Gandhiji or at least of making their loud shouts of 'Gandhi-Shaukat Ali-ki-jai' reach his ear. We have met with even policemen who had the courage to approach Gandhiji to salute him or touch his hand, and CID's [*sic*] also who would plaintively say, 'We have taken to this dirty work for the sake of the sinning flesh, but please do accept these five rupees'.[4]

Seeking darshan was obviously a fairly visible sign of popular reverence, and no wonder it occupies a prominent place in descriptions of Gandhi's tours. D. G. Tendulkar writes of the Mahatma's 'tour of mass conversions to the new creed' in 1921 as follows:

> Remarkable scenes were witnessed. In a Bihar village when Gandhi and his party were stranded in the train, an old woman came seeking out Gandhi. 'Sire, I am now one hundred and four', she said, 'and my sight has grown dim. I have visited the various holy places. In my own home I have dedicated two temples. Just as we had Rama and Krishna as *avatars*,

[3] See below, p. 21.

[4] Desai, pp. 142–3.

so also Mahatma Gandhi has appeared as an *avatar*, I hear. Until I have seen him death will not appear'. This simple faith moved India's millions who greeted him everywhere with the cry, 'Mahatma Gandhi-ki-jai'. Prostitutes of Barisal, the Marwari merchants of Calcutta, Oriya coolies, railway strikers, Santals eager to present khadi *chaddars*, all claimed his attention.

From Aligarh to Dibrugarh and then as far as Tinnevelly he went from village to village, from town to town, sometimes speaking in temples and mosques. Wherever he went he had to endure the tyranny of love.[5]

Examples of such darshan-seeking scenes could be multiplied, and we shall come back to them in our account of Gandhi's passage through Gorakhpur. It is worth stressing here that the Gandhi-darshan motif in nationalist discourse reveals a specific attitude towards the subalterns—the *sadharan janta* or ordinary people as they are referred to in the nationalist Hindi press. To behold the Mahatma in person and become his devotees were the only roles assigned to them, while it was for the urban intelligentsia and full-time party activists to convert this groundswell of popular feeling into an organized movement. Thus it would appear that even in the relationship between peasant devotees and *their* Mahatma there was room for political mediation by the economically better off and socially more powerful followers.[6]

The idea of the artifacts of the 'mythopoeic imagination of childlike peasants' being mediated by political intermediaries occurs in anti-nationalist discourse as well. Referring to stories about the power of Gandhi current in Gorakhpur and other districts of eastern UP in the spring of 1921, the *Pioneer* wrote in an editorial:

Mr Gandhi is beginning to reap the penalty of having allowed himself to be unofficially canonized (as we should say in the West) by his adoring countrymen. We say 'reap the penalty', because it is inconceivable that a man of his transparent candour and scrupulous regard for truth should hear without chagrin the myths which are being associated with him as a worker of miracles. *The very simple people in the east and south of the United Provinces afford a fertile soil in which a belief in the powers of the 'Mahatmaji', who is after all little more than a name of power to them, may grow.* In the 'Swadesh', a paper published in Gorakhpur, four miracles were quoted last month as being popularly attributable to Mr Gandhi. Smoke was seen coming from wells and, when water was drunk, it had the fragrance of keora (pandanus ödaratissimus) an aloe-like plant which is used in the manufacture of perfume; a copy of the Holy Quran was found in a room which had not been opened for a year; an Ahir who refused alms to a Sadhu begging in Mahatma Gandhi's name, had his gur

---

[5] Tendulkar, p. 78.                          [6] Cf. p. 19 below.

and two buffaloes destroyed by fire, and a sceptical Brahmin, who defied Mr Gandhi's authority, went mad and was only cured three days afterwards by the invocation of the saintly name! *All these events admit of an obvious explanation, but they are symptoms of an unhealthy nervous excitement such as often passed through the peasant classes of Europe in the Middle Ages, and to which the Indian villager is particularly prone.* Other rumours current in Ghazipur are that a man suffered the loss of his wife, sons and brothers because he had offended Gandhi, that the 'Mahatma' was seen in Calcutta and Multan on the same day, and that he restored two fallen trees. *In all these instances we see the mythopoeic imagination of the childlike peasant at work, and perhaps nobody is much the worse, but a case reported from Mirzapur would require sooner or later the attention of the police.* The story is told that a young ahirin who had been listening during the day to speeches took a grain of corn in her hands when playing with her companions in the evening, blew on it with an invocation of the name of Gandhi and, lo! the one grain became four. Crowds came to see her in the course of a few days and she quadrupled barley and gram and even common objects like pice. But it is reported that strange coins could not be multiplied. *While this is obviously a mere trick of mouth concealment, the agitator is proclaiming it as a miracle*, and all the neurotic girls of the countryside will be emulating the achievement.[7]

A fuller analysis of some of these stories is presented in another section of this essay. What is important to notice at this point is that while the *Pioneer* locates the *origin* of these stories in a popular imagination fired by 'nervous excitement', their *circulation* is attributed to 'agitators'. There is no room here for the 'deified' Mahatma inspiring popular attitudes and actions independent of élite manipulation and control.

Jacques Pouchepadass' sensitive study of Gandhi in Champaran can be read at one level as an elaboration of this theme.[8] In an extended discussion of Gandhi's presence in this district in 1917, the 'obstinate quest for his *darshan*' is picked out as the initial point of departure. Pouchepadass notes that Gandhi was 'invariably met by throngs of raiyats at railway stations' and elsewhere, and this, combined with the influx of peasants from a large number of villages to Bettiah and Motihari to give evidence against the planters, enlarged the area of agitation in the district. 'The name of god was frequently used to denominate Gandhi' and the 'obstinate quest for his *darshan* gives further evidence about the deification of the Mahatma' in the

---

[7] *Pioneer*, 23 April 1921, p. 1. Italics mine.

[8] Jacques Pouchepadass, 'Local leaders and the intelligentsia in the Champaran satyagraha (1917): a study in peasant mobilization', *Contributions to Indian Sociology* (NS) 8: 1974, esp. pp. 82–5.

district. The peasants' faith in Gandhi's power was indexed by 'fantastic rumours':

> Those rumours . . . reported that Gandhi had been sent into Champaran by the Viceroy, or even the King, to redress all the grievances of the raiyats, and that his mandate overruled all the local officials and the courts. He was said to be about to abolish all the unpopular obligations which the planters imposed on their raiyats, so that there was no need to obey the word of any planter any more. A rumour was also in the air that the administration of Champaran was going to be made over to the Indians themselves, and that the British would be cleared out of the district within a few months.[9]

Not all of these however were the product of popular imagination. Pouchepadass is of the opinion that 'many of these rumours were very consciously spread by the local leaders, who took advantage of Gandhi's charismatic appeal to give additional impetus to the agitation . . . . But what matters is that the peasants believed them because Gandhi's name was associated with them'.[10] This faith also broke the normal ties of deference in the countryside—the *hakims* and the *nilhe sahebs* held no terror for the peasants testifying before the Champaran Enquiry Committee. The implication of all this for direct political action by the peasants is unfortunately left unexplored. In fact a case is made out for the transference of Gandhi's charisma to the authorized local interpreters of his will. Pouchepadass warns against over-rating Gandhi's 'personal ascendancy over the humbler classes':

> When he is present, of course, only his own word counts. But once he is gone, the local leaders are apt to retain part of his prestige, and become the authorized interpreters of his will. It is a fact that from 1918 onwards, after Gandhi had left and the planters' influence had begun to fade away, the hold of the rural oligarchy grew more powerful than ever.[11]

[9] Ibid., pp. 82–3. It is interesting to note that most of these rumours can be classified under the motif 'redressal of wrongs done to the peasantry', a development of the popular idea that Gandhi had come to Champaran precisely for such a task. In war-time all rumours are concerned with war. Though not each and every one of the thirty rumours collected by J. Prasad after the great Bihar earthquake was about seismic upheaval, all of them were nevertheless concerned with disaster. See J. Prasad, 'The Psychology of Rumour: a study relating to the great Indian earthquake of 1934', *British Journal of Psychology*, 35:1 (July, 1935), p. 10 and *passim*.

[10] Ibid., p. 84; cf. Pandey: 'The belief in an "outside leader" can also be seen as an obverse of a belief in the break-down of the locally recognized structure of authority; and rumour fulfils the function of spreading such a notion as efficiently as the leader from the town'. See Gyan Pandey, 'Peasant Revolt and Indian Nationalism: the peasant movement in Awadh, 1919–22', in R. Guha (ed.), *Subaltern Studies I* (Delhi, 1982), p. 164.

[11] Pouchepadass, p. 85.

However, evidence from north Bihar and eastern UP suggests that no authorized version of the Mahatma could have been handed down to the peasants, either by 'local leaders' or by members of the District Congress Committees. The spate of *haat*-looting incidents in Muzaffarpur, Darbhanga, Rae Bareli and Fyzabad in early 1921 in the name of Gandhi was clear proof of a distinctly independent interpretation of his message.[12] Blaming agent provocateurs for misleading 'the poor ignorant peasants'[13] into committing these acts would, therefore, be to turn a blind eye to the polysemic nature of the Mahatma myths and rumours, as well as to miss out the stamp these carried of a many-sided response of the masses to current events and their cultural, moral and political concerns.

In existing literature the peasants of eastern UP and Bihar are often portrayed as more superstitious than those of some other regions such as western UP and Punjab. We have seen that according to the editor of the *Pioneer*, 'the very simple people of the east and south of the United Provinces afford[ed] a fertile soil in which a belief in the powers of the "Mahatmaji" . . . [might] grow'. In a recent piece of sociological writing the metaphor of 'fertile soil' seems to have been taken literally. In eastern UP, writes P. C. Joshi, summing up his experience of field work in the area, the 'very fertility of soil had minimized the role of human effort', as a result of which 'religion and magic permeated every sphere and occasion of life'.[14] Whether rice growing areas dependent on monsoon rains are more superstitious than canal-fed wheat growing tracts is a question which need not detain us here. Instead I propose, very briefly, to sketch those features of the political history of Gorakhpur in the late nineteenth and early twentieth centuries which throw some light on the specific response of the area to Gandhi's visit in February 1921.

## II

The spread of Gaurakshini Sabhas (Cow Protection Leagues) in the 1890s and the subsequent growth of the Nagri movement, Hindi journalism and Hindu social reform in the 1910s appear to have been

[12] See *Bihar and Orissa Legislative Assembly Debates*, 28 Feb. 1921, i, p. 279; Stephen Henningham, *Peasant Movements in Colonial India. North Bihar, 1917–42* (Canberra, 1982), pp. 98–9; Kapil Kumar, 'Peasants' Movement in Oudh, 1918–1922' (Ph.D. thesis, Meerut University, 1979), pp. 154–7.

[13] J. Nehru, *An Autobiography* (Delhi, n.d.), p. 61.

[14] P. C. Joshi, 'Fieldwork Experience: Relived and Reconsidered. The Agrarian Society of Uttar Pradesh', *Journal of Peasant Studies*, 8:4 (July 1981), p. 470.

the important landmarks in the political history of Gorakhpur in the period up to 1919–20.[15] These saw the involvement of a wide range of the district's population. Former *pargana* chiefs—rajas and ranis, members of the dominant landed lineages, schoolmasters, postmasters and *naib-tahsildars*, middle-caste Ahir and Kurmi tenants—all 'rallied round the Cow' (although the last two did so with ideas quite different from the rest).[16] The developments in the first twenty years of the present century relied on *rausa* and trader support but drew in the intelligentsia, religious preachers and sections of the rural population as well. Gorakhpur neither witnessed widespread agitation against the Rowlatt Acts, as had happened in the Punjab, nor did a Kisan Sabha movement of the Awadh type develop in this region.

The Gaurakshini Sabhas of Gorakhpur in their attempt at selective social reform anticipated the 'Sewa Samitis' and 'Hitkarini Sabhas'— Social Service Leagues—of the early twentieth century. A mammoth meeting of the Gorakhpur sabha held at Lar on 18 March 1893 laid down rules for different castes regarding the maximum number of *baratis* (members of the bridegroom's party) to be entertained at a wedding and the amount of money to be spent on the *tilak* ceremony—all in an effort to cut down 'foolish expenditure on marriages'. Observance of proper high-caste rituals was also stressed. Thus it was made obligatory for 'all *dwija* castes (i.e. Brahmins, Kshatriyas and Vaishyas) . . . to recite the *gayatri mantra* at the three divisions of the day', and he who failed in this was to 'be expelled from the brotherhood'.[17] Contributions 'for the protection of the Gao Mata' (Mother Cow) were also made compulsory for every Hindu household on pain of exclusion from caste. Rule 4 of the Lar sabha stated that 'each household [should] every day contribute from its food supply one *chutki* [handful], equivalent to one *paisa*, per member', and that 'the eating of food without setting apart the *chutki* [should] be an offence equal to that of eating a cow's flesh'. Women

[15] On the cow-protection movement in eastern UP and Bihar see John R. McLane, *Indian Nationalism and the Early Congress* (Princeton, 1977), Pt iv; Sandria B. Freitag, 'Sacred Symbol as Mobilizing Ideology: The North Indian Search for a "Hindu" Community', *Comparative Studies in Society and History*, 22 (1980), pp. 597–625; Gyan Pandey, 'Rallying Round the Cow: Sectarian Strife in the Bhojpur region, c. 1888–1917', in R. Guha (ed.), *Subaltern Studies II* (Delhi, 1983).

[16] Pandey, 'Rallying Round the Cow'.

[17] 'Note on the Cow-protection Agitation in the Gorakhpur District', c. 1893, L/P&J/6/365, India Office Records. This document is also discussed in Freitag and Pandey.

were to be 'instructed as to the contribution of *chutki* in proper fashion with due regard to *pardah*'.[18]

Again, the power of panchayats was brought to bear upon 'remorselessly [to] boycott' those who sold cows or bullocks to Muslims or butchers. It seems that these panchayats were of two kinds. In the 'Cow Courts' of Azamgarh 'whose proceedings . . . were a somewhat flattering imitation of the proceedings in the Magistrate's Courts' it was generally the zamindars who acted as judges.[19] In certain other cases, as in that of a 'respectable Hindu farmer' of Sagri pargana of that district in June 1893, a less formal and more militant boycott was undertaken by the peasants themselves. To quote Gyan Pandey:

> Villagers gathered at . . . [the house of Lakshman Paure], pulled down tiles from the roof, smashed his earthern vessels, stopped the irrigation of his sugarcane field, prohibited Kahars from carrying sweets which were needed for his daughter's entry into her bridegroom's house and slapped Lakshman, adding the threat that the house would be looted and he himself killed if he did not get the bullock back.[20]

The 'Gandhi Panchayats' of the early 1920s organized by local volunteers meted out punishment similar to what Lakshman Paure of the village of Pande Kunda had received in 1893. However, in the spring of 1921 when all was charged with magic, any mental or physical affliction (*kasht*) suffered by persons found guilty of violating panchayat decisions adopted in Gorakhpur villages in the Mahatma's name was often perceived as evidence of Gandhi's extraordinary powers, indeed as something providential and supernatural rather than as a form of chastisement devised by a human agency.[21]

Hindi was officially adopted as the language of the courts of law in UP in 1900. Soon after, the *Nagri pracharini* (Hindi propagation) movement began to pick up momentum in Gorakhpur as well. In 1913 the local branch of the sabha agitated successfully for judicial forms to be printed in Hindi, and in September 1914 *Gyan Shakti*, a literary journal devoted to 'Hindi and Hindu *dharma prachar*', was published by a pro-government Sanskrit scholar with financial support

---

[18] Rules 4 and 16. For analogous alms and subscriptions in the name of Gandhi, see pp. 46–7 below.

[19] Offg. Commr. Banaras to Chief Sec., NWP & Oudh, 29 Sept. 1893, cited in McLane, p. 311.

[20] Pandey, 'Rallying Round the Cow'.

[21] For a detailed discussion, see section VI below.

from the rajas of Padrauna, Tamkuhi and Majhauli, as well as some
from the prominent rausa of Gorakhpur.[22] In the following year
Gauri Shankar Misra, who was later to be an important figure in the
UP Kisan Sabha, brought out a new monthly—*Prabhakar*—from
Gorakhpur. Its object was to 'serve the cause (*sewa*) of Hindi, Hindu
and Hindustan'. However, the journal ceased publication within a
year;[23] only *Gyan Skakti* remained, and even this closed down
between August 1916 and June 1917. The full impact of Hindi
journalism was not felt in Gorakhpur until 1919. In April and August
of that year two important papers—the weekly *Swadesh* and the
monthly *Kavi*—made their appearance.[24] These, especially Dasrath
Dwivedi's *Swadesh*, were to exercize an important influence in
spreading the message of Gandhi over the region.

In the 1910s movements and organizations of Hindi, Hindu culture
and social reform—'nagri sabhas', 'pathshalas' (vernacular schools),
'gaushalas' (asylums for cattle), 'sewa samitis' (social service leagues)
and 'sudharak sabhas' (reform associations) of various sorts provided
the support and cover for nationalist activity in Gorakhpur. Each
type of these socio-political movements served nationalism in its own
way; but there was a considerable amount of overlapping in their
functions and interests. In August 1919 a branch of the Bhartiya Sewa
Samiti which had M. M. Malaviya for its head was established in
Deoria.[25] A number of 'sudharak' and 'gram hitkarini sabhas' (village
betterment societies) and subsidiary branches of the sewa samitis
were established in the smaller towns and bigger villages of the region
during 1919–20. The inspiration usually came from the local notables
and pleaders at the tahsil and pargana headquarters, though sometimes
appeals in the *Swadesh* for the setting up of community organizations
also bore fruit. At these sabhas, heads of Hindu religious trusts
(*mahants*) and celibates (*brahmcharis*) from nearby *ashrams* or
itinerant preachers (*pracharaks*) from neighbouring districts and from
Banaras discoursed on the Hindu way of life and its rituals. *Yagya*

[22] Arjun Tiwari, 'Poorvi Uttar Pradesh mein Hindi Patrakarita ka Udbhav aur
vikas' (Ph.D. thesis, Gorakhpur University, 1978), pp. 37, 49–50; *Statement of
Newspapers and Periodicals Published in U.P. during 1920 and 1921*, entry under
*Gyan Shakti*.

[23] Tiwari, pp. 107–8.

[24] *Statement of Newspapers and Periodicals . . . U.P.*, 1920, 1921.

[25] See Note on 'The Sewa Samiti Movement in the United Provinces', by
P. Biggane of the CID, dated 18 Dec. 1919, GAD File 604 of 1920, UP, State Archives,
Lucknow.

(sacrifice) was performed; a Sanskrit pathshala and a gaushala endowed with financial support from traders, arrangements made for the orderly running of Ramlilas and *melas*, and panchayats set up for the arbitration of disputes.[26]

Thus, the fourth annual convention of the Sanskrit Pathshala, 'supported by the zamindars and peasants' of *tappa* Belhar in Basti district, was the occasion for launching a 'Belhar tappa Hindu Sabha' for which more than 300 Hindus from some twenty-five neighbouring villages had gathered at *mauza* Kotiya on 23 October 1920. The proceedings started with the chanting of Vedic sacrificial mantras, and after deliberating on the progress of Sanskrit education in the locality, Pragyachakshu Dhan Raj Shastri discoursed on *samskar*, especially *upanayan samskar*. A Brahmchari from Ballia who for the past five months had been 'reciting continuously' from the Maha-bharata, the Bhagavad Gita, etc. followed with a powerful speech on cow protection. It was resolved that only those who were prepared properly to look after the welfare of Brahmani bulls (*sand*) should get them branded; those unable to do so should, as an alternative, contribute to the sabha for other religious deeds on a scale ranging from Rs 1.5 to 5 according to their means. The 'most important and topical resolution' passed at this sabha was 'that in every village of Belhar tappa, a . . . panchayat consisting of five persons [should] be established and a big panchayat . . . set up for the tappa as a whole'.[27]

The evolution of the Pipraich Sudharak Sabha at about the same time indicates how those who were active in the promotion of Hindu culture could also be promptly induced to espouse the cause of Non-Co-operation. Pipraich was the seat of an important market town owned by the pro-government Jawwad Ali Shah of Gorakhpur city. A railway town, it was an important centre of the grain and sugar trade which was mostly in the hands of Hindu traders.[28] A sudharak sabha was formed on 21 October 1920 at a meeting of 300 presided over by the local *raees*, Babu Munni Lal. The Sabha handled the arrangements for the Dussehra *mela* (fair) and the subsequent festivities of Bharat-milap (based on the story of the exiled Rama's

[26] Details of these activities are scattered through the 1920 volume of the *Swadesh*.

[27] Notice by Chandra Bali Visharad, B.A., in *Swadesh*, 14 Nov. 1920, p. 9. Unless stated otherwise, translations from the local Hindi journals are my own. *Tappa* is a grouping of villages, with the chief village as the seat of the dominant local landed lineage.

[28] See Statement of Bazar Collections at Pipraich, File I-A13-1917, Gkp. Collector's Rec. Room.

reunion with his brother, Bharat). After ten days of activity during the Dussehra fortnight, yet another meeting was held. Again presided over by the local raees, it was attended by 1,500 people including the *babus* of nearby Balua. However, on this occasion speakers from Gorakhpur town gave a different direction to the deliberations. The editor of *Swadesh* spoke on council boycott, and others on sewa dharma and commercial matters. A decision was taken unanimously to open a 'swatantra pathshala'—an independent school unaffiliated to the government—with the spinning of *khaddar* yarn specified as an important part of its curriculum.[29]

Traditional Hindu religious discourses addressed to large congregations lasting several days at a time were also put to a similar use on some occasions:

> In mauza Gointha, Post Office Dohrighat (Azamgarh) the discourse of Pt Ramanugraha Sharma, *dharmopdeshak*, went on for ten days. Many thousands turned up for these lectures. After the last lecture he organized a Vedic yagya and many indigents and Brahmins were feasted. He also established a Bharat Hitaishi Sabha to which both Hindus and Muslims have contributed 5 *panches* and 2 *sarpanches* each . . . . Many cases have been settled [out of regular courts].[30]

Caste sabhas could undergo interesting transformations as well. Thus on 12 December 1920 a Bhumihar Ramlila Mandal was established at Bhiti village in the Bansgaon tahsil of Gorakhpur; its 'object was to encourage unity and propagate satyagraha by revealing the [true] character of Sri Ramchandraji'.[31] Similarly, in a great many cases lower and middle-caste panchayats imposed novel dietary taboos as a part of the widespread movement of self-assertion which was also exemplified by acts such as the refusal of their women to work as housemaids or the withholding of *begar* (forced labour) both from the *sarkar* and the zamindar. A correspondent from Naugarh in Basti district wrote to the *Swadesh:*

> The sweepers, washermen and barbers of this place met in panchayats of their various *biradaris* on 27 January 1921. They have decided that anyone who partakes of meat, fish and liquor would be punished by the biradari

[29] *Swadesh*, 31 Oct., 7 Nov., and 19 Dec. 1920. *Babus*: members of the dominant local lineage of a tappa.

[30] *Swadesh*, 11 Sept. 1919, p. 11. Ramanugraha Sharma, resident of Bhelia (Rasra), Ballia district had followed this procedure in Shahabad, Pipraich and Paina, near Barhaj in present day Deoria district. See *Swadesh*, 4 July 1920, p. 8, 1 Aug, pp. 10–11, 30 Oct. 1920, p. 7. *Panch*: member of a panchayat; *Sarpanch*: head of a panchayat.

[31] *Swadesh*, 19 Dec. 1920, p. 8.

(brotherhood) and would have to donate Rs 51 to the gaushala. The Dhobis and Barbers have also decided not to wash the clothes and cut the hair of any of their patrons who partakes of meat, fish and liquor.[32]

A widespread boycott of meat and liquor 'due to the efforts of a Bengali sadhu' was reported from Padrauna in Gorakhpur in early 1921, though caste panchayats played a role in this instance as well.[33]

It must be emphasized that the very act of self-purification on the part of the ritually impure amounted, in some instances, to a reversal of the signs of subordination. 'All low caste Hindus, except those who are Bhagats or vegetarians by vow, almost without exception eat meat', observed a local ethnographer of Gorakhpur in the late nineteenth century.[34] For them, especially the sweepers, washermen and untouchable agricultural labourers, to give up meat in 1920 was not simply an instance of 'Sanskritization'. Thus at a sabha held in October 1920 the Chamars of Bareilly (central UP) had decided to forsake meat as well as liquor and other intoxicants; but they were also very forthright in their refusal to do begar for the district officials on tour. As they said in a petition addressed to the Governor on that occasion: 'We are ready to perform any legitimate services required of us appertaining to our profession but inhuman treatment, meted out to a Chamar every day, by petty servants of the thana and tahsil is nothing short of a festering sore'.[35]

By early 1922 indications of a 'growing restlessness among the . . . [Chamars] . . . arising out of the general spirit of revolt' were reaching the police headquarters in the districts. The movement for 'self-reform' now revealed 'a tendency to forsake hereditary callings' as well.[36] The eight resolutions passed at a large meeting of the Chamars of Azamgarh in January 1922 followed the standard pattern of caste reform in their concern about the prevalence of child marriage and co-habitation out of wedlock, and in the interdictions they imposed on toddy, liquor and animal sacrifice. What is perhaps equally significant

[32] *Swadesh*, 6 Feb. 1921, p. 8.

[33] *Idem*.

[34] Note by Ram Gharib Chaube on 'Eating Meat', William Crooke Papers, MS 131, Museum of Mankind, London.

[35] Extracted in Harcourt Butler to Chief Sec., UP, 26 Oct. 1920, GAD File 694 of 1920; *Swadesh*, 10 Oct. 1920, p. 1. For a discussion of the assertive nature of middle-caste movements in early twentieth century eastern UP, see Pandey, 'Rallying Round the Cow'. See also David Hardiman's essay on the Devi movement in the present volume.

[36] UP Police Abstracts of Intelligence (PAI), 1 April 1922.

is that members of this caste of leather workers also pledged themselves not to trade in hides and skins and to discourage young boys from taking up their ancestral profession.[37] In western and central UP, Chamars were refusing to skin carcasses and perform begar for the landlords and were 'allowing their women less liberty of movement',[38] an euphemism for the withdrawal of female labour from the homes of the upper castes.

## III

Gorakhpur in 1920 was no stronghold of the Congress or the independent Kisan Sabhas. In fact the relative backwardness of the entire region comprising Gorakhpur, Basti and Azamgarh districts was lamented repeatedly by the editor of the Congress weekly, *Swadesh*, and the main reason for this was thought to be the absence of an effective and dedicated leadership.[39] Political meetings in Gorakhpur city and in important market towns like Deoria and Barhaj Bazar picked up from July–August 1920, as the campaign for council elections by the rajas, rausa and *vakla* was sought to be countered by challenging the bona fides of 'oppressive landlords' and 'self-seeking pleaders'. Open letters appeared in the columns of *Swadesh* highlighting the oppression suffered by peasants in the bigger zamindaris and challenging the presumption of the rajas to be the natural spokesmen of their *praja* (subjects). At a public meeting of the newly-formed Voters' Association in Deoria the representative of a landlord candidate was faced with the charge that his patron's command of English was inadequate for him to follow the proceedings of the legislative council.[40] But increasingly, the boycott of council elections and, after the Nagpur Congress (December 1920) the propagation of Non-Co-operation, was being written up and broadcast as a part of the spiritual biography of Mahatma Gandhi. In a powerful editorial, prominently displayed by *Swadesh* on the front page on 11 November and reprinted the next week, Dasrath Dwivedi appealed to the local electorate in bold typeface:

[37] Report of the Chamar conference held at Gopalpur village, thana Madhuban, district Azamgarh, *Swadesh*, 8 Jan. 1922, p. 6.

[38] PAI, 1 April 1922.

[39] See *Swadesh*, 18 April 1920, pp. 13–14, 23 May, p. 9, 15 Aug., p. 14.

[40] See *Swadesh*, 16 May, 6 June, 4 and 18 July 1920.

OH YOU VOTERS OF THE GORAKHPUR DIVISION! HAVE SOME SELF RESPECT. BEWARE OF THE OBSEQUIOUS STOOGES! BE SURE WHO IS YOUR GENUINE WELLWISHER! MAHATMA GANDHI, PT MOTILAL NEHRU, PT MALVIYAJI or those who are now running after you, begging for your votes? Think for yourself; what good have the latter done for you so far that you may now expect them to help remove your sorrows and sufferings from inside the Council. Now cast your eyes towards Mahatma Gandhi. This pure soul (*pavitra murti*) has sacrificed everything for you (*tan-man-dhan . . . arpan kar diya hai*). It is for your good that he has taken the vow of renunciation (*sanyas-vrat*), gone to jail and encountered many a difficulty and suffering. Despite being ill, he is at this moment wandering all over [the country] in the service of your cause. It is the *updesh* of this same Mahatma Gandhi that you should not vote. And you should not vote, because approximately thirty thousand of your unarmed Punjabi brethren were fired upon in Amritsar, people were made to crawl on their bellies, and despite the hue and cry for justice you were shoed away like dogs (*tumhen dutkar diya gaya tha*). And no heed was paid whatsoever. Look out. Beware. DO NOT VOTE FOR ANYBODY.[41]

In this text, which may be regarded as representative of the local nationalist discourse on council boycott,[42] the 'Punjab Wrongs' and the callous indifference of the British are no doubt mentioned as reasons for not voting; but it is hard to miss the person of a saintly Gandhi, resplendent in his suffering for the people and, in turn, requiring and even demanding their obedience to his injunctions. Perceived thus the boycott of elections and the rejection of loyalist candidates appear as a kind of religiously prescribed abstinence from the polling booth, analogous to the observance of proper Hindu rituals and self-purification which was being propagated by many of the nationalist religious preachers and taken up by certain low-caste panchayats as well. It was to such a region, which was not unaware of the peasant rioting in southern Awadh in January 1921 but had not yet developed any comparable peasant movement of its own, that Gandhi came on 8 February 1921.

The decision to invite Gandhi was taken at a public meeting held in Gorakhpur city on 17 October 1920. Maulvi Maqsood Ali Fyzabadi

[41] *Swadesh*, 11 Nov. 1920, p. 1.

[42] In all likelihood the Congress volunteers who were to tour the district for a fortnight, spreading 'Gandhiji's message of council boycott', would have taken the above editorial as their central text. It seems that voting was thin in Bansgaon tahsil and at Siswa Bazar, Bridgmanganj, Pipraich and Parwapar in Maharajganj and Padrauna tahsils. See *Swadesh*, 14 Nov. 1920, p. 12, 12 Dec. 1920, p. 12.

presided over it and Gauri Shankar Misra was the main speaker. The meeting resolved to support the cause of those arrested in connection with the Khilafat agitation, pronounced *asahyog* (Non-Co-operation) to the *uchit* (proper) and decided to send a telegraphic invitation to Gandhi and the Ali brothers to visit Gorakhpur at an early date.[43] Gandhi was also approached by the Gorakhpur delegates (prominent amongst whom was Baba Raghav Das, successor to the spiritual *gaddi* (seat) of Anant Mahaprabhu and founder of the Paramhans Ashram, Barhaj) at the Nagpur Congress and he told them that he would visit the district sometime in late January or early February.[44] To the creed of *asahyog* that Raghav Das and Dasrath Dwivedi brought with them from Nagpur was added mounting excitement at the prospect of its author's advent. Propagation of the politics of Non-Co-operation in the Gorakhpur countryside in early 1921 had elements of a celebratory exordium, a preparing of the district for the Big Event. The peregrinations of Raghav Das and his brahmachari followers around their ashram in Barhaj, the 'melodious Gandhi-*bhajans*' sung by Changur Tripathi to a peasant assembly at Kuin nearby[45] and the 'poetical effusions' in the first issue of a rejuvenated *Kavi* magazine—'written with the set purpose of arousing in the masses and classes alike a yearning for the quick descent of Krishna, the Messiah'[46]—are the few surviving fragments of this picture of enthusiasm and expectation in Gorakhpur at that time.

An index of this popular expectation was the increase in the number of rumours which assigned various imaginary dates to Gandhi's visit. By the first week of January the news of his arrival had 'spread like wild fire'. Dasrath Dwivedi, the editor of *Swadesh*, was bombarded with hundreds of letters asking for the exact dates. To allay anxiety on this score the journal printed a column on its front page on 9 January assuring its readers that the date of Gandhi's arrival would be announced in the *Aaj* (Banaras), *Pratap* (Kanpur), *Bhavishya* (Prayag), *Vartman* (Kanpur); the *Leader* and *Independent* would also publish the news, while the *Swadesh* press would ensure that notices, posters and letters carried the word to all six tahsils of the district.

[43] *Swadesh*, 24 Oct. 1920: p. 11.
[44] Amodnath Tripathi, 'Poorvi Uttar Pradesh ke Jan-jeevan mein Baba Raghav Das ka Yogdaan' (Ph.D. thesis, Allahabad University, 1981), pp. 62–7, 77; *Swadesh*, 2 Jan. 1921. [45] Tripathi, p. 78; *Swadesh*, 6 Feb. 1921, p. 9.
[46] *Statement of Newspapers and Periodicals, U.P.*, 1921, p. 33.

Meanwhile the District Congress Committee (DCC) geared itself
into action. It had been decided to get a national school inaugurated
by Gandhi, and the DCC was active on this front. Advance parties of
lecturers (*vyakhyandata*) announcing his arrival were to be dispatched
to the tahsil headquarters and to Barhalganj, Dhakwa and Gola in the
densely populated southern tahsil of Bansgaon; to Rudarpur and
Captainganj in the central tract of Hata; to the railway towns and
marts of Deoria, Salempur, Majhauli, Lar, Bhatpar and Barhaj Bazar
to the south-east, and to Padrauna in the north-east. Within the
sparsely populated northern tahsil of Maharajganj, Peppéganj and
Campierganj—seats of European zamindaris—and Siswa Bazar, the
important entrepôt of gur and rice, were to be the target points. At
meetings held at these places, the visiting lecturers were to preach the
doctrine of the Congress and ask for contributions to the National
School Fund. In their turn the local residents were to ensure that
people within a radius of ten miles attended these public discourses on
the philosophy and advent of Gandhi.[47] The massive attendance at
the Gorakhpur sabha on 8 February and the crowds that thronged
the five stations on the fifty mile railway strip between Bhatni and
Gorakhpur city suggest that the news had spread widely enough.

On 30 January the *Swadesh* announced that the probable date was
now 8 February and requested the people of Gorakhpur to seek the
Mahatma's darshan and bring their donations with them. It also
wrote about the need for more Congress workers to come forward
and help in supervising the arrangements.[48]

An editorial which appeared in the columns of that newspaper on 6
February announcing the impending arrival is a significant text and is
reproduced in Appendix I. Besides illustrating how the image of the
distinguished visitor was projected in Gorakhpur by local Congressmen, it is also representative of nationalist understanding of the
relationship between the subaltern masses, the élite leadership and
Gandhi himself. Dasrath Dwivedi, the young author of this text, had
been trained as a journalist on the staff of the *Pratap* in Kanpur and on
Ganesh Vidyarthi's advice had come back to his home district in 1919
to start his own *Swadesh*.[49] The editorial, 'The Great Fortune of

[47] *Swadesh*, 9 Jan. 1921, p. 11; see also Appx II below.
[48] *Swadesh*, 30 Jan. 1921.
[49] The circulation of the paper in early 1921 was 3,500, though according to official
estimates it dropped to 2,300 in the course of that year. See Tiwari, p. 558; *Statement
of Newspapers etc.*, *U.P.*, 1921, entry under *Swadesh*.

Gorakhpur', was written by one who was obviously an ardent nationalist disappointed at the political stupor prevailing in the region, and who felt as if his dream of Gandhi bringing about a transformation was soon to be fulfilled. Addressed basically to lawyers and students whom it urges to cast off sloth, it is also significant in its attitude towards the common people:

> Our plea is that the common people (*sadharan janta*) of Gorakhpur are only anxiously awaiting for the darshan of the Mahatma. The Mahatma will arrive, the public will have darshan and will be eternally grateful for it. There will be no end to the joy of the people when they are able to feast their eyes on the Mahatma.
>
> But what about those who are openly co-operating with the government ... don't they have some duty at this juncture ...? A voice from the heart says 'Of course! ... *They should kneel before Mahatma Gandhi and pray to the Almighty for courage to enable them to row their boats out of the present whirlpool and into safety . . . . For Mahatma Gandhi to appear* [*avteern:* from *avtar*] *before us in these difficult times is a tremendous boon, for us, our society and our country* . . . . Don't vacillate, arise now to serve the oppressed brothers of your district. Blow the *shankh* (conch-shell) of Swaraj . . . . This movement is an elixir (*amrit-bati*) for you. Mahatma Gandhi is offering it to you.[50]

How the common people and the élite should respond to Gandhi's visit is thus clearly laid out. The task of the janta is to congregate in large numbers, 'feast their eyes on the Mahatma', count themselves lucky, and after such brief taste of bliss return to their inert and oppressed existence. So far as they are concerned the Mahatma is to be in Gorakhpur for no other purpose than to offer them darshan. They are not expected to proclaim the cause of *swaraj* on their own. The clarion call (written metaphorically, as *shankhnaad*, after the blast of conch-shells used for Hindu sacred rituals) of swaraj in villages requires only the power of élite lungs: for that rallying blast the 'oppressed brothers' of Gorakhpur must rely on the initiative of the élite followers of the Mahatma. The implication is that the peasants' pilgrimage to Gorakhpur and the mufassil stations will be useless from a nationalist perspective unless 'leaders' step in to channel the goodwill generated in the villages as a result of Gandhi's darshan. That such a journey, made often in defiance of landlord opposition, could in itself be a political act and that Gandhi's message might be decoded by the common villager on his own, without prompting by outsiders, were possibilities not entertained by Dasrath Dwivedi at

---

[50] 'Gorakhpur ka Ahobhagya', *Swadesh*, 6 Feb. 1921. Emphasis mine.

this time. Yet a perusal of local news published by him in subsequent months shows that these were the lines along which popular response to the Mahatma's visit expressed itself.

Apart from this the imagery, feeling and metaphors used by Dwivedi to convince educated waverers about the greatness of Gandhi and convert them to his cause are of interest in themselves. At this level there is no significant difference between the religiosity informing the peasants and the attitude Dwivedi wants the intelligentsia to adopt towards Gandhi; the language of belief seems to be the same in both instances with merely some variations in tone and accent. The italicized portions of the extract quoted above testify to the religious, indeed devotional nature of Dwivedi's writings. The boat and boatman imagery occurs frequently in rural and urban devotional songs. As Susan Wadley notes in her study of popular religion in a village in western UP, 'many . . . devotional songs use the whirlpool analogy for a crisis situation, along with other nautical imagery (the ocean of existence, boat, boatman, ferry across, the far side, etc.)'.[51]

Gandhi's visit to Gorakhpur was well organized and the gatherings of people on that occasion were truly phenomenal. An advance party of Gorakhpur Congressmen had been sent to Bhatni junction at the south-eastern edge of the district, and the train by which he travelled made its way very slowly through, stopping at every railway station where people had assembled for darshan. As Shyam Dhar Misra who led the reception party reported in *Swadesh*:

> At Bhatni Gandhiji addressed *(updesh diya)* the local public and then the train started for Gorakhpur. There were not less than 15 to 20,000 people at Nunkhar, Deoria, Gauri Bazar, Chauri Chaura and Kusmhi [stations] . . . . At Deoria there were about 35–40,000 people. Mahatmaji was very pleased to witness the scene at Kusmhi, as despite the fact that the station is in the middle of a jungle there were not less than 10,000 people even here. Some, overcome with their love, were seen to be crying. At Deoria people wanted to give *bhent* [donations] to Gandhiji, but he asked them to give these at Gorakhpur. But at Chauri Chaura one Marwari gentleman managed to hand something over to him. Then there was no stopping. A sheet was spread and currency notes and coins started raining. It was a sight . . . . Outside the Gorakhpur station the Mahatma was stood on a high carriage and people had a good darshan of him for a couple of minutes.[52]

[51] Susan Wadley, 'Power in Hindu Ideology and Practice', in K. David (ed.), *The New Wind: Changing Identities in South Asia* (The Hague: Paris, 1977), p. 144, n. 17.
[52] *Swadesh*, 13 Feb. 1921, p. 3.

Among the peasants who had come all the way from their villages for Gandhi-darshan on this occasion, there were many who would again in a year's time—in February 1922—march past the Chauri Chaura railway station to the adjacent thana as participants in another fateful event. Indeed, at the trial of the peasant-rioters of Chauri Chaura, some of those who acted as witnesses for the prosecution found it necessary to try and offer an innocuous explanation of their presence among the crowd at the station on 8 February 1921. As Shankar Dayal Rae, a prosperous contractor of the locality, put it to the Sessions Judge in June 1922: 'I never before went to the station to meet any *rajnaitik* (political) leader—to Gorakhpur or Chaura— except that I went to pay my respects to Gandhiji when he passed through Chaura in the train.'[53] The devotion of the Gorakhpuri peasants to the Mahatma seems to have acquired a militant edge. According to Mahadev Desai's account of the return journey from Gorakhpur, darshan was now demanded almost as a right:

> The train started from Gorakhpur at 8.30 p.m. at night . . . . It was a train that halted at every station . . . . Hordes and hordes of people began to rush upon our compartment . . . . At every station peasants with long long lathis and torches in their hands would come to us and raise cries loud enough to split the very drums of our ears. Of course, all of us in the compartment were making as many appeals for quiet as we possibly could. But whoever would care to listen to us? . . .
>
> Many of these devotees do not even know how their 'Mahatma Gandhi' looks like. A few of them thrust themselves into our compartment, and began to bawl out, 'Who is Mahatma Gandhiji?' 'Who is Mahatma Gandhiji?' I got desperate and said 'I'. They were satisfied, bowed down to me and left the compartment! What a difference between my pre-sumptuousness and these people's untainted love! But it was no use getting enchanted with that guileless love . . . .
>
> Any sleep for Gandhiji in the midst of this uproar was out of question . . . . The people's *hathagraha* (mule-like obstinacy) was repeated at each and every station that came after Bhatni: At last even Gandhiji's endurance and tolerance was exhausted . . . . He began to entreat the people 'Please go away. Why do you harass us at this dark hour?' He was answered only by sky-rending shouts of victory to him! . . . That was the height of the people's love-mad insolence . . . .[54]

## IV

If this was the way in which the peasants reacted to Gandhi, how was his message understood by them? Were there any ambiguities in what

[53] Evidence of Shankar Dayal Rae, Chauri Chaura Trials (Sessions Judge), p. 508.
[54] Desai, pp. 263–6.

Gandhi said or was believed to have said? If so, what implications did these have for peasant beliefs about Gandhi as revealed in the 'stories' about his power?

The main thrust of Gandhi's speeches at the 'massive gatherings of peasants' in Fyzabad and Gorakhpur was to condemn the recent acts of peasant violence and rioting in southern Awadh. As Mahadev Desai recounts in his diaries of this period:

> Gandhiji had only one message to give them, viz. those big sticks [lathis] were not to be used for killing or injuring anybody. The same thing was preached at Fyzabad also. Gandhiji's utterances were devoted exclusively to the outbreaks of robbery, villainy and rioting that had taken place in the United Provinces.[55]

This was indeed so, but a close reading of his speech at Gorakhpur suggests that it had enough ambiguity in it to cause semantic slides. After a laudatory poem written by the Hindi poet 'Trishul' and read by Dasrath Dwivedi, Gandhi started his speech to a mammoth gathering of over 1.5 lakhs, which included a 'fairly large number of illiterates and rustics',[56] as follows:

> This gathering is not the occasion for a long speech. This gathering shows that there is a commonality of purpose amongst us. The poem that was recited just now did not mention Mohammad Ali . . . . Now brother Shaukat Ali, Mohammad Ali and I are saying the same thing . . . .

After stressing the need for Hindu-Muslim unity, he warmed up to a condemnation of peasant violence in Awadh:

> What happened in Fyzabad? What happened in Rae Bareli? We should know these things. By doing what we have done with our own hands we have committed a wrong, a great wrong. By raising the *lakri* [i.e. lathi] we have done a bad thing. By looting haats and shops we have committed a wrong. We can't get swaraj by using the lakri. We cannot get swaraj by pitting our own devilishness (*shaitaniyat*) against the satanic government. Our 30 crore lakris are no match against their aeroplanes and guns; even if they are, even then we shall not raise our lakris. The Quran says so. Brother Mohammad Ali tells me that [according to the Quran] as long as the raising of the stick is unnecessary we cannot do so . . . .
>
> Our kisan brothers have committed a mistake. They have caused great anguish to my brother Jawahar Lal. If further difficulties [of this sort] are put in our way then you shall see that that very day it would become impossible for Gandhi to live in Hindustan. I shall have to do penance—this

---

[55] Ibid., p. 267. For a detailed discussion of Gandhi's 'Instructions' to the peasants at Fyzabad, see Pandey, 'Peasant Revolt and Indian Nationalism'.

[56] *Gyan Shakti*, Feb. 1921, p. 407.

is a peaceful struggle. Only after I retire to the Himalayas can it become a violent struggle. Our fight should be like the one put up by our Sikh brethren in Taran Taran . . . . They did not seek revenge against their oppressors . . . . This is our way, this the *asahyog dharma*, this is real *Brahmacharya*. This is *kshatriya dharma*. And today this is the dharma of the Musalmans. To go against it is to commit a sin . . . .

Right now we should forget about 'social boycott'. The time has not yet arrived for such actions. Nobody should prevent any brother from going to the burial ground, nobody is to prevent anybody from the use of the services of barbers or to have *chilum* [i.e. ganja] and liquor. In fact we want to rid everybody of chilum and booze (*daru*).⁵⁷ If all of you give up [these things] today then we shall attain swaraj straightaway . . . .

[Congratulating Gorakhpur on its organization of this meeting Gandhi continued] The real result of your organizational abilities and your work would be seen when in Gorakhpur lawyers give up their practice, schools no longer remain sarkari [i.e. affiliated to the government], titles are given up, no drinkers, no whoremongers, no gamblers remain in your district. When every house has a *charkha* and all the *julahas* of Gorakhpur start weaving [hand-spun yarn] . . . . You should produce so much khaddar in Gorakhpur that you people don't have to go to Ahmedabad, to Bombay or Kanpur [for your cloth] . . . .

I would request you to be patient and listen to Maulana Mohammad Ali's speech and carry on donating money to the volunteers. Please refrain from being noisy. I want to tell you, if you follow my programme—I want to assure [you] if you do as I tell you, we shall get swaraj by the end of September. We could also get the Khilafat and the Punjab Wrongs undone by the sarkar. But this is the right [task] of only those who accept the things discussed at the Nagpur Congress. This is not the business of those who are not with us in our work . . . . From those who are not with us, but still come to our meetings, I expect that they will at least keep the peace—we can attain swaraj by end September if God grants us peace; if all of us Indians have the spirit of self-sacrifice and self-purification then 30 crore people can achieve just about anything.⁵⁸

The main constitutive elements—*baat* in the indigenous parlance—of Gandhi's message to the Gorakhpur kisans could be arranged as follows:

1. Hindu-Muslims unity or *ekta*.
2. What people should *not* do on their own: use lathis; loot bazaars and haats; enforce social boycott ('*naudhobi band*').

⁵⁷ The words used were 'Koi kisi bhai ko kabristan jane se na roke, koi kisi ko hajjam, chilum aur daru se na roke'. *Chilum* is an earthen bowl for smoking tobacco, but is understood in popular parlance to refer to *ganja* smoking. It seems that Gandhi is here using the word chilum to refer to ganja, but this can also be understood to be an injunction against smoking as such.

⁵⁸ Translated from the verbatim report published in *Swadesh*, 13 Feb. 1921, p. 6.

3. What the Mahatma wants his true followers to do: stop gambling, ganja-smoking, drinking and whoring.
4. Lawyers should give up their practice; government schools should be boycotted; official titles should be given up.
5. People should take up spinning and weavers should accept hand-spun yarn.
6. Imminence of swaraj: its realization conditional on innate strength of numbers when matched with peace, grace of God, self-sacrifice and self-purification.

This sequential summary of Gandhi's speech is an attempt to reconstruct the way in which his utterances might have been discussed in the villages of Gorakhpur. It is reasonable to assume that such discussions would proceed by breaking up his message into its major ideological constituents.[59] If the practice, which is current even today, of communicating printed news in the countryside is any guide, then in all likelihood the main points of that speech summarized from the version published in *Swadesh* was conveyed to the illiterate peasants in the local dialect.

It will be seen that baat no. 4 does not greatly concern the peasants. No. 1 is very general and figures only marginally in the Gandhi 'stories'. Baat no. 5 is, in part, far too specific as an instruction addressed exclusively to weavers, while the advice in favour of spinning might have sounded rather too general, lacking as it did an infrastructure to make it feasible at this stage. It is the conflation of baats no. 3 and no. 6, and its contexualization within the existing ideas about 'power' and magic, which lay at the root of some of the 'stories' relating to the Mahatma in Gorakhpur. It seems that the complimentarity of his negative advice with regard to popular militancy (baat no. 2) and the positive actions enjoined on the 'true followers' (baat no. 3)—the complimentarity, so to say, of the do's and don'ts in these particular messages, was (*pace* Mahadev Desai) largely lost on his rustic audience. On the other hand baats no. 3 and 6 came to be associated in the popular mind as a linked set of spiritual command-ments issued by a god-like personage. As such these were consistent with those legends about his 'divinity' which circulated at the time.

[59] For an example of one such breaking up of Gandhi's message to the peasants into main (*mukhya*) baats, see 'Kisanon ko Mahatma Gandhi ka amritmay sandesh', *Abhyudaya*, 18 Feb. 1931, p. 19. For an extended use of the term baat, and its use as an organizing principle in the narrative of Bhojpuri fables, see George A. Grierson, *Seven Grammars of the Dialects and Subdialects of the Bihari Language etc.*, Pt. II (Calcutta, 1884), pp. 102ff.

The enforcement of social boycott was not widespread yet; it was to pick up only from late 1921. Meanwhile, that is immediately in the wake of Gandhi's visit, people, acting on their own or through their panchayats and sabhas, were still involved in efforts at self-purification, extending and transforming his message on this theme. It is with the intervention of the supernatural in this process and the Mahatma's role in it that most of the Gorakhpur 'stories' are concerned. To these we now turn.

## V

The feeling of devotion towards Gandhi in Gorakhpur was commented on in glowing terms in the nationalist press. Dasrath Dwivedi wrote in an editorial about the 'fantastic flow of *bhakti*' (devotion) caused by the Mahatma's visit. Mahavir Prasad Poddar, a Gorakhpuri merchant resident in Calcutta and a popular retailer of Swadeshi-sugar of yesteryears,[60] elaborated on this theme thus in the columns of the *Swadesh*:

> It had not occurred to us in our wildest dreams that the same Gorakhpur which was politically dormant would suddenly wake up like this. A crowd of 2–2½ lakhs for the darshan of Gandhiji is no ordinary thing. It can probably be said that this is the biggest crowd that has ever gathered for the darshan of the Mahatma . . . . But let no one think that this vast multitude came like sheep, inspired by blind faith (*andhbhakti*) and went back empty handed. Those with eyes can see that the darshan of 'Gandhi Mahatam' (this is the phrase used in villages) have not been in vain. The janta came with devotion (*bhakti*) in their hearts and returned with feelings and ideas (*bhav*). The name of Guru-Gandhi has now spread in all four corners of the district . . . .
>
> But roses have thorns as well . . . . A zamindar of the city had it proclaimed in his *ilaqa* that anyone going for Gandhi's darshan would be fined Rs 25 and receive twenty-five shoe-beatings to boot . . . . The people of this area wrung their hands in despair . . . . A Ramlila procession goes in front of the house with so much fanfare and the children are locked up in the attic! . . . I know there are other creatures like the above-mentioned raees in this district.[61]

Here is a far better understanding of the impact of that visit than we have so far encountered in nationalist prose. The janta does not just have bhakti; seeing and hearing the Mahatma also inspires *bhav*, a word suggestive not merely of feelings and ideas but of urge to action as well.[62] The laudatory poem read as a welcome address to Gandhi had ended on the note:

[60] *Swadesh*, 20 April 1919, p. 4.          [61] *Swadesh*, 27 Feb. 1921.
[62] I am grateful to Veena Das for this suggestion.

*jaan dalega yahan aap ka aana ab to; log dekhenge ki badla hai
zamana ab to . . .*
*aap aye hain yahan jaan hi aae samjho, goya Gorakh ne dhuni phir
hai ramai samjho.*[63]

By February 1921 times had indeed changed, beyond the 'wildest
dreams' of Poddar: a new life was already infused into a 'politically
dormant' Gorakhpur—a regeneration brought about by, as it were,
the powerful *tapasya* of Gorakhnath, the eponymous founder of the
city. Gandhi's advent was perceived as a major event by the zamindars
who had sought forcibly to prevent their peasants from seeking his
darshan. It was for them an event which stood out of the flow of
quotidian existence and as such threatened to bring about displacements in the local power structures. The analogy of eager children
being denied the joy of participation in an important religious procession was apt, for it suggests in the landlords a cruel paternalism
designed to prevent any subversion of the relationships of dominance
and subordination which constituted the stuff of everyday life in the
countryside. The enthusiasm Gandhi generated, the expectations he
aroused and the attack he launched on British authority had all
combined to initiate the very first moments of a process which, given
other factors, could help the peasant to conceptualize the turning of
his world upside down. This was an incipient political consciousness
called upon, for the very first time, to reflect—albeit vaguely and
intermittently—on the possibility of an inversion of many of those
power relations deemed inviolable until then, such as British/Indian,
landlord/peasant, high-caste/low-caste, etc. This process of conceptualization was set in train that spring in Gorakhpur by a clash
between the ordinary and the extraordinary, between the habitual
and the contingent—a clash triggered off directly by the Mahatma's
visit.[64]

## VI

Stories about Gandhi's occult powers first appeared in the local press
in late January 1921. An issue of *Swadesh* which announced his
arrival in the district also carried a report under the heading: 'Gandhi
in dream: Englishmen run away naked'. A loco-driver—presumably

---

[63] *Swadesh*, 13 Feb. 1921, p. 5. Your coming here will enliven this place; people
will notice how times have changed; you coming virtually brought back life to this
place and Gorakhpur has bounced back to life and pride.

[64] The argument in this paragraph owes a lot to discussions with Bernard Cohn and
Ranajit Guha.

an Anglo-Indian—who had dozed off while reading a newspaper at Kasganj railway station in Etah district woke up from a nightmare at 11 p.m. and ran towards a cluster of bungalows occupied by the English and some Indian railway officers shouting: 'Man, run, man! Gandhi is marching at the head of several strong Indians decimating the English'. This caused a panic and all the local white population emerged from their bedrooms in a state of undress and ran towards the station. The key to the armoury at the station was asked for, but could not be found as the officer-in-charge was away. English women were locked up in boxes and almirahs, and some Englishmen were heard saying, 'Man! The cries of "jai jai" are still reaching our ears. We shall not go back to our bungalows'. In the morning Indians who heard of this incident in the city had a good laugh at this example of English self-confidence (*atmik-bal*).[65] This story, first published in the Banaras daily *Aaj* and then in *Swadesh*, is illustrative of the wider tendency of the times to berate British power and boost Indian prowess by contrast.[66] The British emerge in tales of this kind as a weak-kneed race, mortally afraid of the non-violent Mahatma.

Other stories to appear in the press just prior to and immediately after his arrival were about a lawyer of Deoria who was cursed by a follower of Gandhi for going back on his promise to give up legal practice and had his house polluted with shit; about a high-caste woman who suffered the same polluting fate after she had denied a young boy a blanket to protect him from the cold when he wanted to go to the station at night to seek darshan; about a Kahar who tried to test the Mahatma's power with a foolish wish and came out the worse for it; and about a Pandit who sought to defy Gandhi by insisting on eating fish only to find it crawling with worms. These stories have the same sequential and structural characteristics as many others reported

[65] 'Swapn mein Mahatma Gandhi: Angrez nange bhage', writer Banwari Lal Sewak, *Swadesh*, 30 Jan. 1921 (extracted from *Aaj*).

[66] Thus Mohammad Ali addressing the Gorakhpur meeting on 8 February after Gandhi, concluded his speech with the following exhortation: 'We should only be afraid of Allah, and no one else. No Deputy Commissioner was sent saddled with his office from the house of God. No midwife ever said that the child-to-be-born would become a Commissioner, or a Viceroy. Even the Collector and Commissioner of Gorakhpur, even Sir Harcourt Butler must have emerged from their mothers' wombs as innocent babes, like the rest of us. Therefore [don't be afraid], have faith in Allah, keep the peace, all thirty crores work the charkha—you shall get swaraj in six month's time'. Reported in *Swadesh*, 13 Feb. 1921, p. 8.

from Gorakhpur. Taken together and classified according to their motifs, they may be said to fall into four fairly distinct groups:[67]

A. Testing the power of the Mahatma.
B. Opposing the Mahatma.
C. Opposing the Gandhian creed in general and with respect to dietary, drinking and smoking taboos.
D. Boons granted and/or miracles performed in the form of recovery of things lost and regeneration of trees and wells.

A. *Testing the Power of the Mahatma*

1. Sikandar Sahu of *thana* Mansurganj, mauza Mahuawa (Dist. Basti) said on 15 February that he would believe in the Mahatmaji when the *karah* (boiling pan) full of cane-juice in his *karkhana* split into two. The karah split in two in the middle![68]

2. On 18 February a Kahar (domestic servant; palanquin bearer) from Basantpur said that he would be prepared to believe in Mahatmaji's authenticity (*sacha manoonga*) only when the thatched roof of his house was raised. The roof lifted ten cubits above the wall, and fell back to its original position only when he cried and folded his hands in surrender and submission.[69]

3. On 15 March a cultivator in mauza Sohraghat (Azamgarh) said that he would believe in the Mahatmaji's authenticity (*sacha jaane*) if sesamum sprouted on 1.5 *bighas* of his field. Next day all the wheat in that field became sesamum. 'I have seen this with my own eyes at the house of Pt Brijwasi Vakil', wrote a correspondent. 'The ears look like that of wheat, but on rubbing with hand, grains of sesamum come out of them'.[70]

4. Babu Bir Bahadur Sahi of mauza Reaon was getting his fields harvested on 15 March. In order to test the Mahatma's powers he wished for some sweets. Suddenly sweets fell on his body. Half of the sweets he distributed among the labourers and the rest he kept for himself.

[67] These stories, unless otherwise stated, are taken from *Swadesh*, 27 Feb., p. 11; 6 March, p. 9; 13 March, p. 5; 10 April, pp. 1, 11; 17 April, p. 4; 24 April: pp. 11–2; 1 May, p. 7 and 8 May 1921, p. 2. I am aware that these stories can well be classified differently, and that a particular story can be grouped under more than one category. However, I have found the above classification useful for the purposes of the present discussion.

[68] These stories have been translated from the Hindi versions reported in *Swadesh*.

[69] 'These news items (*samachar*) have been sent in by Sri Sant Raj Chaudhuri of Rajpur. He maintains that all of these incidents are true'. *Swadesh*, 27 Feb. 1921, p. 11.

[70] Reported by Shyamnand Lal.

5. On 13 April a *karahi* was being set up as an offering to the Mahatma. The wife of one thakur saheb said that she would offer karahi to the Mahatmaji only if there were some miracles performed. Suddenly a dhoti hanging on a peg caught fire and was reduced to ashes, although there was no smell of burning whatsoever. 'I have seen this with my own eyes'.[71]

6. A reader of *Swadesh* from Barhaj wrote: 'Two chamars while digging were having a discussion about the *murti* (idol, image) that had emerged in Bhore village (Saran). One of them . . . said . . . "only if a murti emerges at that site as well will I accept that the one at Bhore is calling out for Gandhi". By a coincidence, while digging, a murti of Mahadev came out. On hearing the news people rushed for darshan, and *puja-paath* was done and offerings made. People are of the opinion that the cash offered should be sent to the National School [fund]'.

7. A similar incident was reported to have happened at the well of Babu Shiv Pratap Singh of Gaura [adjacent to Barhaj]. But it was said that as soon as people rushed to get the murti out of the well, it disappeared.

8. A Brahman of mauza Rudrapur (Post Office Kamasi) had the habit of stealing grass. People tried their best to convince him that Mahatma Gandhi had forbidden such evil deeds. He replied, 'I shall believe in Gandhiji if when I go stealing grass at night someone catches me, or I fall ill, go mad, or start eating *gobar* (cow dung)'. Strange are the ways of God: all these things happened. While stealing grass he started shouting that someone was coming to catch him. He fainted. He ran a high fever. People got hold of him and took him to his house. Soon after he ran out and started eating gobar. When after three days his family members took the *manauti* [i.e. pledged to propitiate Gandhi if the patient recovered], he started feeling better. 'As a result of this people in the village and its neighbourhood have given up theft etc. completely'.[72]

9. Shri Balram Das of the Gorakhpur School reported, 'On February 26th I had gone to the Rudrapur village in Maharajganj

[71] Reported by Jaikumar Singh. For the practice of karahi-offering see p. 47 below.

[72] Reported in Sarju Singh. *Manauti*: from *minnat*: taking of a vow; a promise to offer something (normally cash) in return for the fulfilment of a wish or the granting of a boon.

tahsil to give a lecture. Everybody agreed to follow the ways of Mahatma Gandhi. But one character did not give up his [old] habit and went to cut grass. On his return he went mad. He broke and smashed things around him. When he offered Rs 5 in the name of Mahatmaji he quietened down (*shanti hui*)'.[73]

Even a cursory reading of these 'stories' suggests that two obvious processes are at work here. First, the rumours are indicative of a considerable discussion about Gandhi in the villages of Gorakhpur in spring 1921. The recurring phrase, 'I shall believe in Mahatmaji only in the event of such an extraordinary happening', should be read as an index of a dialogue between sceptics and firm believers. It makes sense only in the context of such a discussion.

Secondly, this crucial phrase also suggests that what people thought of the Mahatma were projections of the existing patterns of popular beliefs about the 'worship of the worthies' in rural north India.[74] As William Crooke has observed, the deification of such 'worthies' was based among other things, on the purity of the life they had led and on 'approved thaumaturgic powers'.[75] The first of these conditions Gandhi amply satisfied by all those signs of saintliness which a god-fearing rural populace was prone to recognize in his appearance as well as in his public conduct. As for thaumaturgy, the stories mentioned above attribute to him magical and miraculous powers which, in the eyes of villagers nurtured on the lore of Salim Chishti and Sheikh Burhan, put him on a par with other mortals on whom peasant imagination had conferred godliness.

Turning to the stories themselves we find that they are developments of the basic idea of the genuineness of the Mahatma as revealed through various tests. In its simple version a test is set in the context of the immediate activity or environment of the person concerned, or there is the fulfilment of an expressed wish. The conditions are met and the story or the rumour connected with it goes no further. Examples of this are to be found in Nos. 1, 3 and 4, and to a lesser degree in No. 5 as well. In some of the other instances a further development takes place: the person who sets the test submits to the Mahatma's power. Thus the Kahar of Basantpur in No. 2 gets the roof of his hut back in position only after he makes amends for questioning the saint's authority by tearful repentance.

[73] *Swadesh*, 1 May 1921, p. 7.
[74] W. Crooke, *The Popular Religion and Folklore of Northern India*, i (London, 1896), pp. 183–96. We are not concerned with the deification of those 'who have died in a miraculous way', discussed by Crooke under this category.   [75] Ibid., p. 191.

A clearer example of the power of rumours in spreading the name of Gandhi in villages and reorienting normal ritual actions towards nationalist goals is contained in story No. 6. Of the two Chamars, one evidently believed in the rumour from Saran district in Bihar. But the other made his acceptance conditional on an extraordinary occurrence taking place in the context of his immediate activity—digging. When as a result of coincidence[76] his spade brought out a murti from the ground, the Chamar (perhaps convinced of the power of the Mahatma) retired as the subject of the narrative. Now others, who also had heard this particular rumour (further proof of which had been unearthed in their own area), entered the scene and propitiated the image of Mahadev in the usual way by having darshan and making offerings of flowers and money. But it is significant that the money which would otherwise have gone towards the construction of a concrete platform at that site was earmarked as a contribution to the National School Fund, a project with which Gandhi was directly associated in Gorakhpur.[77]

The story about finding a murti in Barhaj (No. 7) follows the line of popular interpretation adopted for the previous anecdote. That this particular rumour might have been spread deliberately by someone, and that the idol had 'disappeared' by the time people rushed to the scene, is immaterial for the purposes of the present discussion. What is important is that a series of 'extraordinary occurrences' in the villages of Gorakhpur were being read in a familiar way, that is according to the conventions of reading the episodes in a sacred text but with their religiosity overdetermined by an incipient political consciousness.

There is an element which story No. 2 shares with No. 5—where the *thakurain* makes her offering to the Mahatma conditional on the occurrence of a miracle and where this happens in the form of a dhoti bursting into flames. In both stories it is fear which imposes faith on non-believers. This penal motif recurs frequently in many religious ballads in eastern India. The doubting woman and the sceptical Kahar are persuaded to join the devotees—and do so ritually in the karahi episode—in the same way as a forceful display of an offended

[76] Phrases like 'by a coincidence', or 'strangely enough', which would otherwise qualify these miracles, occur very seldom in these stories. Besides, these should be read more as reflecting the viewpoint of the person reporting these occurrences to the press rather than as indicating a sceptical attitude on the part of the people as a whole.

[77] The fund was launched by the DCC in late 1920 so that Gandhi on his visit could open a National School at Gorakhpur.

godling's wrathful power breaks the resistance of a non-conformist in a *vratkatha* or *panchali*.

This motif is made explicit in No. 8 and its variation, No. 9, by the challenge to the Mahatma's power and the manner in which the latter is seen to triumph. The Brahman thief of Rudrapur village is representative not just of the ordinary village sceptic but of high-caste opposition to the Gandhian creed. His resistance questions by implication the conformism of the rest of the village (see the modified version in No. 9). But he pays for this by being subjected to physical and mental suffering. Only when his family relents on his behalf, joins the Mahatma's devotees by taking a vow in the latter's name and makes an offering does the man's condition improve. It is hard to miss the similarity between this and many other stories of opposition to the Gandhian creed, and between their predictable outcomes. (See Nos. 12, 21 and 23 below). The ending—'as a result of this particular occurrence people in the village and its neighbourhood have given up theft/drinking/gambling, etc.'—announces in each instance the victory of the new moral authority which is made all the more resplendent by the fact of having been deified at the outset.

## B. *Opposing the Mahatma*

This theme of personal suffering (*kasht*) and pollution recur in many other stories expressly concerned with incidents of direct opposition to Gandhi. Thus:

10. Pt Damodar Pandey from mauza Gayaghat, PO Uska Bazar (Dist. Basti) reported that a man in mauza Dumariya near his village had called Gandhi names, as a result of which his eyelids had got stuck . . .

11. In Unchava village, one mile from Chara Ghat, four seer of ghee belonging to Abhilakh Ahir had gone bad. The reason for this was that he had made some sarcastic remarks (*vyang vachan*) about Gandhiji.

12. Mauni Baba Ramugraha Das of mauza Benuakuti (Benuatikur?) had slandered Mahatmaji on several occasions. As a result of this his body began to stink of its own (*khud-ba-khud*). After some exertion in the right direction (*kuch yatn karne par*) things improved somewhat. Mauniji then made arrangements for a *lakshaad ahuti* (sacrifice).

13. Sri Murlidhar Gupt from Majhauli reported, 'When Mahatma Gandhi was going back on the night of 8 February from

Gorakhpur to Banaras there was a huge gathering at Salempur station to have his darshan. There was a lad of a Barai (betel-leaf grower) in that gathering as well. It is said that he had asked a Mishrain (wife of a Misr, a high caste Brahman) for a wrapper to come to the station. She reprimanded him and refused to give him the blanket. The poor soul came shivering to the station, had darshan of the Mahatma and went back home. In the morning I heard a rumour in the village that she suffered the same fate as befell the household of Babu Bhagavan Prasad, vakil of Deoria [i.e. shit rained all over, see Nos. 17 & 18]. In the end, only when she kept a fast, not even touching water for a day and a night and did *aradhana* (ritual praying) of the Mahatma, did peace finally return to her.'

14. In qasba Hariharpur, tahsil Khalilabad (District Basti) a big raees was getting a *mandir* (temple) constructed after the wishes of his deceased father. Babu Gyan Pal Dev—the raees—had been against Gandhiji, and had threatened his praja with a fine of Rs 5 if anyone even talked of Gandhiji or became his follower. On 4 April at 11.30 p.m. a huge figure with four hands appeared on the scene and announced aloud before a large gathering, 'I am a follower of Siva. All of you should do puja to him. Babu sahab give up your wrong policies (*aniti ko chor do*). Speak the Truth. Follow the Dharma; forsake *adharma*.' After this it assumed a diminutive form and disappeared. 'This is a factual and eye-witness account'.

In the first four stories (Nos. 10–13), physical ailment and pollution are seen as supernatural punishments meted out to those who opposed Gandhi or (as in No. 13) any of his devotees in word or deed. In No. 14 the idea of physical punishment is replaced by a divine warning which, since it was delivered in front of a crowd which included presumably his social inferiors, hurt the prestige of the anti-Gandhian raees of Hariharpur.

The story (No. 12) of the holy man of Banuatikur (Mauni Baba) who seems to have broken his vow of silence to criticize Gandhi, puts the usual image of religious preachers and peasant audiences in a slightly different light. It is generally believed that the manipulation of popular religious idiom by renouncers—babas, *sanyasis* and the like—was conducive to the spread of the nationalist message in the countryside.[78] The peregrinations of *dharmopdeshak* Pandit Ramanugraha Sharma in eastern UP and western Bihar and the career of the *Ramayana*-reciting Baba Ramchandra in Awadh were clear examples of this process at work.[79] However, the rumour about the Mauni Baba's criticism of Gandhi and the afflictions it caused suggest that the word of the local sadhu was not always taken at its face value in the villages of Gorakhpur. His suffering was interpreted in Benuatikur and broadcast through rumour over a wide area as an obvious punishment for his anti-Gandhian stance. Apparently the holy man himself found this explanation convincing enough to repent and make amends in an appropriate manner. We do not know whether it was a local Congressman or the common people who first thought up this explanation. Even if the former did, the wide currency of this and similar stories structured around the theme of physical suffering caused by opposition to Gandhi and his creed indicates that in these we have a moment representative of a very general idea.

Nos. 13 and 14 provide additional insights into the widespread phenomenon of Gandhi-darshan. In the first of these the resolve of the true darshan-seeker enables him to withstand personal discomfiture while bringing suffering and pollution to an opponent of Mahatmaji. Here fasting and puja add up to an act of penance; in other instances, to 'worship' the Mahatma would appear to be a part of the customary female ritual of *vrat* and aradhana, which were not necessarily linked with the notion of penance or *prayschit*.[80] The text of the story is also suggestive of the power and spread of rumour: the alleged pollution of the Mishrain's household as a divine retribution provoked by her anti-Gandhian attitude is identical to the terms of a

[78] The following description in a pro-government newspaper is illustrative of the crude view which projects the peasants as objects of their manipulation: 'The special correspondent of an Indian contemporary [newspaper] throws considerable light on the methods of certain politico-religious preachers professing to be followers of Mr Gandhi who have been carrying on active propaganda in the Rae Bareli district. They settle in a village, . . . dress themselves in saffron-coloured clothes, and in the beginning of their career refuse to take food for many days. The village people think that their saviour has come. The disciple of the Mahatma next takes to preaching, and gathers round him a great following of persons . . .'. *Pioneer Mail*, 28 Jan. 1921.

[79] For Ramanugraha Sharma, see p. 12 above. For Baba Ramchandra and his use of the Ramayana and the religious cry 'Sita Ram' in mobilizing peasants in Awadh, see M. H. Siddiqi, *Agrarian Unrest in North India: the United Provinces, 1918–22* (Delhi, 1978); S. K. Mittal and Kapil Kumar, 'Baba Ramchandra and the Peasant Upsurge in Oudh', *Social Scientist*, 10:71 (June 1978); Gyan Pandey, 'Peasant Revolt and Indian Nationalism'.        [80] See p. 46 below.

similar report received from Deoria twenty miles away a couple of days ago. (See Nos. 18 and 19 below).

The Mishrain from Salempur only rebuked the Barai lad for seeking darshan; there were landlords like Rai Kishore Chand (raees of Sarheri estate in northern Gorakhpur) and Babu Gyan Pal Dev (of Hariharpur in Basti) who sought to restrain their praja (tenants) in a more forthright fashion.[81] The supernatural occurrence at a mandir in Khalilabad tahsil on 4 April, timed by our correspondent for 11.30 p.m. and attested as factual, once again shows how such phenomena lent themselves to very different interpretations. Both Jamuna Prasad Tripathi who contributed this story to *Swadesh* and Babu Gyan Pal Dev agreed that a *daitya* (ogre) had appeared on the scene, but while the former understood this as a divine rebuke for the landlord's anti-Gandhian actions the latter denied the charge in a rejoinder and claimed that the apparition was merely a signal for the promotion of the Siva cult. How the assembled peasants read this supernatural sign we do no know for certain, but it is unlikely that they would have failed to identify in it an element of divine rebuke to landlord oppression.

### C. *Opposing the Gandhian creed in general*

15. A gentleman from Gorakhpur city wrote that a *mukhtar* of Alinagar *mohalla* had asked the women of the house to ply charkha. They said that they were not short of anything, so why should they ply the charkha? By a coincidence a trunk in the house caught fire in a strange way. 'The whole city was talking about this incident'.

16. There was a criminal case in mauza Bistauli. When the police arrived, both the accused and the aggrieved started telling lies. Someone, invoking the name of Mahatmaji (*Mahatmaji ka pratap batla kar*), told them not to tell lies. As soon as the evidence was taken down, the culprit's daughter-in-law died.

17. 'Sri Tilakdhari Rai from Dhoki (Azamgarh) writes that it was decided on 18 February at a sabha in mauza Ghaziapur that no one was to let his cattle loose. Qadir chaukidar had also pledged (*pratigya*) not to let his cattle loose, but later he broke his pledge. People reminded him of his solemn promise. He replied, "I shall let my cattle astray, let's see what your

[81] One of the zamindars referred to on p. 25 was Rai Kishore Chand Raees, a resident of Gorakhpur town and member of the District Board.

panchayat and Gandhiji can do?" An hour later his leg started
to swell up and pain. Even now the swelling has not stopped'.

18. 'A special correspondent writes from Deoria that Babu
Bhagvan Prasad vakil is in a strange predicament; shit is to be
found all over his house. Suddenly a murti that was kept in a
trunk fell down from the roof of his house. Even when he left
the house, the same predicament prevailed. The illiterates of
the town are of the opinion that this is due to the fact that the
vakil sahab had got into an argument with a speaker who was
discoursing on Non-Co-operation'.

19. 'The wife of the famous vakil, Babu Bhagvan Prasad of Deoria
has been in a strange predicament for the past few days.
Wherever she sits, she sees a bit of *vishtha* (shit) kept at a
distance from her. Sometimes she sees shit kept in a leaf-
container (*dona*) for food. There is a murti in the house. When
she keeps it back after puja it either disappears or is to be found
on the roof, or falls down from there. If she serves *poori* (a
type of fried bread) to someone, four of these become two; if
she serves five then they are reduced to three.

But it is absolutely false that she has been cursed by a
disciple of Gandhiji. People say that the vakil sahab had gone
to the Calcutta [Congress] and had agreed there to give up his
practice, but went back on his word. Subsequently a disciple
(*shishya*) of Gandhiji cursed him. Now wherever the vakil
sahab goes he encounters shit, and even his food, when served,
is transformed into shit. All this is untrue. Vakil sahab is
healthy, he does not see these things; neither did he go to
Calcutta nor did he promise to give up his practice, and
nobody has cursed him. Whatever his wife sees in the house,
people say, is the work of a ghost (*bhoot-leela*)'.[82]

20. 'On 11 April some people were gambling in the village of
Parasia Ahir. I told them not to. People accepted my advice.
Only one person did not listen to me and started abusing
Gandhiji. The next day his goat was bitten by four of his own
dogs, as a result of which he is now very unhappy and has
accepted his *qusoor* (fault)'.[83]

[82] *Gyan Shakti*, Feb. 1921, p. 407.
[83] Reported by Kasinath Tiwari, *Swadesh*, 1 May 1921, p. 7. Some other stories in
which Gandhi is not directly mentioned have been gathered together in Appendix III
and serialized as Nos. 42–50.

*Opposing the Gandhian creed with respect to dietary, drinking and smoking taboos.*

21. 'Rao Chokri Prasad writes, "The sons of a Tamoli (betel-leaf grower and seller) in the Tamoli neighbourhood of Lalchak near Bhatni station killed a goat and ate it up. Some people tried to dissuade them but they paid no heed. Later, all of them started vomiting and got very worried. In the end when they vowed in the name of Mahatmaji never to eat meat again their condition improved" '.

22. A Pandit of Rampur village, thana Mansurganj (Basti) was repeatedly told by many to give up his habit of eating fish, but he did not listen to anybody. He said—'I shall eat fish, let's see what the Mahatmaji can do.' When he sat down to eat [the fish] it was crawling with worms!

23. Babu Bhagirath Singh of Paisia, thana Naikot, district Gorakhpur wrote—'On 21 February the *riyaya* (peasants) of Babu Chandrika Prasad Singh promised to give up liquor as a result of his persuasion. But one Kalwar (of the caste of distillers) did not keep his solemn promise. As soon as he started for the liquor shop, brick-bats started to rain in his path. When he spoke the name of Gandhiji from the core of his heart the brick-bats stopped flying.'

24. On 22 February a sadhu came to Godhbal village and began puffing at his ganja pipe. People tried to reason with him, but he started abusing Mahatmaji. In the morning his entire body was seen covered with shit.

25. Pandit Krishnanand Misr from Paharipur village, PO Rampur, District Azamgarh wrote: 'It was decided at a sabha in mauza Kamal Sagar that nobody was to partake of any kind of intoxicant. Later a couple of persons, hiding from general view, started rubbing *surti* (tobacco-leaf, chewing-tobacco) on their palms. Suddenly the leg of a calf fell near the house of a Chaturvedi sahab. As a result of this strange occurrence everybody has given up tobacco, *surti*, etc. [as well]'.

26. A man in a sabha in mauza Majhwa had vowed not to smoke, but he took to smoking once again. Suddenly he was hemmed in by worms and insects from all sides. Because of this incident people in villages far away from Majhwa have also given up intoxicants.

27. In mauza Davani a Tambolin who used to smoke tobacco

dreamt that she was smoking and the pipe had got stuck to her mouth. She got afraid and has vowed not to smoke tobacco again.

In a sense these stories are variations on Nos. 10–13. The movement of the narrative as a sequence of personal suffering and/or pollution followed by repentance which, in its turn, generates a social impact, remains as of before. However, in the present series the punishments are seen to be meted out to those defying popular decisions taken in accordance with generally accepted tenets of the Mahatma. Nearly all rumours about the ill effects of breaking dietary and other taboos are indicative of a local elaboration of what was believed to be Gandhian ethics. Even Nos. 16–20 and No. 42 (in Appx III), not concerned with such taboos, suggest that an imbrication of popular attitudes and Gandhian ideas of self-purification was under way in the villages of Gorakhpur.

The story (No. 15) from the Alinagar ward of Gorakhpur city is the only one concerned with the refusal to ply charkha, while No. 20 about gambling refers to an activity specifically denounced by Gandhi on his visit there. Nos. 15 and 16 deal with truthfulness and attempts to regulate by a formal pledge the anti-social practice of letting one's cattle loose on other people's fields. The two variations of the story about the Deoria vakil and his wife (Nos. 18 and 19) draw on the familiar themes of pollution through human excreta and the breach of a solemn promise—that of Babu Bhagvan Prasad to give up his legal practice in accordance with the Non-Co-operation creed. It may be worth our while to pause for a closer look at these two versions.

The special correspondent of the *Swadesh* sought to distance himself from the popular interpretation of this story—'it is the opinion of the illiterates of the town'—without providing an alternative explanation. This mild disclaimer notwithstanding, he in effect gave currency to what had been thought up by the 'illiterates' of Deoria. The editor of the pro-government *Gyan Shakti* (whose pamphlet against Gandhi and Non-Co-operation was the standard text used by the district's loyalists),[84] provided a fuller account of the rumour, rebutting each and every ideological element of this popular story. In his account, which accepted the pollution of the house as a fact, it was the wife rather than the lawyer-husband who was the object of

---

[84] See for example the eleven-page pamphlet, *Hoshiyar ho jao* ('Beware'), written by Shiv Kumar Shastri and printed by him at the Gyan Shakti press for the Aman Sabha, Gorakhpur.

retribution. Any suggestion of the woman suffering for her husband's misdemeanour was rejected by the demonstration of all the rumours as being untrue, including the one about the lady having been cursed by a disciple of Gandhiji. The lawyer who, according to this report, had not broken any promise (made to the Congress), remained healthy in mind and body. Having taken the politics out of this rumour, the editor of *Gyan Shakti* offers an alternative explanation of this episode. The strange occurrence was not itself in doubt, it was just the reading of the signs which was problematic. In the popular version the rumour appears as a moment in the march of nationalist politics in the district. In the columns of the loyalist *Gyan Shakti* it loses that particular function: the empirical refutation put forward by the editor results in the spirit of Mahatma Gandhi being replaced by the activity of apolitical spirits (*bhoot-leela*)!

However, it is the stories in the next series which are truly illustrative of the way Gandhi's message was being decoded and amplified in terms of the popularly accepted notions of pollution, with coincidence and temporal sequence being read as indicators of casuality. Gandhi did not press his Gorakhpur audiences to forsake fish and meat, yet Nos. 21–2 reproduced above and Nos. 43–6 in Appendix III suggest that a considerable amount of discussion, ending sometimes in a collective resolve (e.g. No. 46), was going on in the villages on the subject of vegetarianism. In these texts Gandhi's name is not explicitly associated with any *pratigya* (vow) to give up fish, meat, liquor or ganja. However, as in Nos. 21, 22 and 24, the image and 'power' of Gandhi are the essential turning points in the progress of the narrative: they imbue what precedes and follows with a particular set of meanings. The defiant phrase, 'I shall eat meat/fish, smoke ganja, drink toddy/liquor, let's see what Mahatmaji can do' is crucial to the construction and progress of these rumours. It suggests an interlocution between persons for and against abstinence and the use of Gandhi's name as a part of the argument. A calamity befalling a non-conformist, its social impact and his repentance are then connected in popular imagination with the unpracticability and undesirability of going against locally imposed decisions in these matters.

Again, the absence of the Mahatma from the texts supplied in Appendix III (see Nos. 43–6, 48) suggests that he has been so fully internalized in this kind of discourse as to require no mention. It would indeed be a narrowly empirical reading which would see in these rumours no trace whatsoever of the popularly accepted notions of dietary taboos associated with the Mahatma in Gorakhpur. A comparison of the stories in which he figures explicitly (e.g. Nos. 21, 22) with those from which he is missing would suggest much affinity in the ordering of the two sets of texts. The sequence: interdiction-violation-consequence in Nos. 43, 46 and 48 is the same as in No. 21. In No. 44, the first step, interdiction, is absent (for no one warns Shankar Kandu against eating fish), but the follow-up—worms emerging from fried fish and the village giving up consumption of fish and fowl—is suggestive of the notice being taken of such evils as might result from transgressions of this kind, and of the tailoring of popular behaviour in accordance with them.

Why this concern for dietary purity? We have no evidence to enable us fully to answer this question. However, some plausible explanations may perhaps be suggested. We have already seen that conforming to the drive for ritual purity in the 1910s, a movement in favour of giving up not only liquor but also meat and fish had picked up momentum in the towns and bazaars of Gorakhpur and Basti districts.[85] Religious preachers were not alone in their advocacy of vegetarianism. Even the low-caste panchayats of Dhobis, Bhangis and barbers were insisting on heavy fines as a penalty for breaking the newly-imposed dietary taboos within their respective communities. This particular emphasis on purity in the spring of 1921 may therefore be seen as an extension of the Gandhian idea of self-purification (through abstinence from ganja and liquor) to a context where the prohibition enlarged its scope to include meat and fish and could be regarded as indicative of religiosity and lower-caste self-assertion at the same time. It is worth recalling in this connection that caste panchayats in northern Basti had decreed in January 1921 that fines imposed at a standard rate of Rs 51 for each violation of this taboo would have to be donated to the gaushala (asylum for cows).[86]

An example of this extension from one banned item to another is provided by the widening of the scope of interdiction against ganja to smoking and even chewing tobacco. It has been noticed above that Gandhi's injunction against smoking chilum, by which he meant ganja, could be regarded as applicable to smoking in general.[87] Nos. 25–27 of our stories show how this process was worked out in popular imagination. In No. 25 the ban on intoxicants (*maadak vastuven*) by which is generally meant liquor, toddy and ganja is already extended to surti—chewing tobacco. In that story divine

[85] See pp. 12–13 above.              [86] *Idem*          [87] See n. 57 above.

retribution helps to reform not only the culprit, but also the entire village. In No. 26 the violation, and the punishment which follows, has an impact not only on the village concerned but far beyond it. The story from mauza Dewani (No. 27) about a tobacco-addict frightened out of her wits in a dream may perhaps be read as a measure of the way in which the interdiction against the use of tobacco in any form had already been internalized.

In some cases (Nos. 22, 23, 43, 44) transgressors of dietary rules suffer physical harm and pollution of various sorts. The notion of pollution is articulated in a multi-faceted way, and for good reasons. In popular Hinduism, as Lawrence Babb has argued recently . . .

. . . Pollution has certain physical embodiments. All body effluvia are polluting, especially faeces, urine, body saliva, menstrual flow and after-birth. Products of dead cattle, especially beef and leather, are highly polluting. Decaying things are polluting (a common rationale for consi-dering liquor to be mildly polluting: 'It's a rotten thing'). Corpses, or anything having to do with death, are sources of extremely powerful pollution.[88]

In our collection of stories the same polluting agents—worms (as an embodiment of the idea of decay) or human faeces—are often associated with rather different acts or items of food. Thus faeces is associated in No. 19 with a curse for breaking a solemn promise, in No. 24 it is the consequence for abusing Gandhi and not conforming to the local advice against smoking ganja, and in No. 45 it is seen as a proof of and punishment for animal slaughter. Worms as polluting agents are associated with fish (Nos. 22, 44), though the idea of a miracle—live worms emerging from fish that had been fried or roasted—is also present. However, in No. 26 worms figure as a kind of calamity, while the frying of fish in No. 48 leads to the burning of huts.

Punishments for wrongs done could be (as in No. 42 below) visited on persons other than the actual wrong-doer. Thus in No. 46 the spread of an epidemic is associated with violating the generally accepted taboo against eating fish in a village near Pipraich. The gratuitous suffering by a high-caste person for the sin committed by another—the defilement of a Chaturvedi's house because of an attempt at surti-eating by others (No. 25)—is a theme that is encountered in other contexts as well. Thus Kashi Nath Tiwari of mauza Asiya Ahir

[88] Lawrence A. Babb, *Divine Hierarchy: Popular Hinduism in Central India* (New York, 1975), p. 48.

wrote to the *Swadesh* in early April that in his village 'one person had mixed water in milk, as a result of which the *dahi* (yoghurt) of several notable persons was infested with worms'. One can hardly miss here the echoes of a Brahmanical tradition going back to antiquity.[89]

D.	*Boons granted and/or miracles performed in the form of*
	*manauti and the recovery of things lost*

28.	Pandit Jiwnandan Pathak from mauza Devkali, PO Bhagalpur wrote, 'As a result of manauti of Mahatmaji a vessel of a Musalman which had fallen into a well six months ago came up on its own'.

29.	In Naipura village (Azamgarh), the long-lost calf of Dalku Ahir returned to its peg as a result of the manauti of Mahatmaji. Dalku Ahir has contributed the one rupee of the manauti to the Swaraj Fund.

30.	A gentleman from Ballia district wrote, 'In mauza Rustampur a *thaili* (purse) of a gwala-sadhu containing Rs 90 had disappeared from his hut. When he took manauti of Mahatmaji, he found it back in his hut, and the money was intact'.

31.	A well-known zamindar of mauza Samogar (tahsil Deoria) had taken a *minnat* [manauti] of Bhagwatiji and offered a goat as a sacrifice. Many took the meat as *prasad*. After some time the son of the zamindar found his hands stuck to his chest and his wife went mad. It was only when the zamindar vowed to contribute the price of the sacrificial goat to the National School Fund and feast Brahmans that both the son and the daughter-in-law began to feel well.

*Boons granted and/or miracles performed in the form of regeneration of trees and wells*

32.	'In mohalla Humayunpur, Gorakhpur city, two dead trees which had fallen in the garden of Babu Yugul Kishore, vakil, have planted themselves back! Many believe that this is due to the grace of Mahatmaji. This, because the person who cut the trees said that if the pratap (spiritual power) of Mahatmaji was

[89]	*Swadesh*, 10 April 1921. The idea of the sins of the lower castes visiting the higher castes is represented in its classic form in the Ramayana story of a Brahman child's death caused by a Sudra's insistence on engaging in the purificatory rituals of *tapasya* in order to attain a high degree of spiritual merit. For a Sudra to do so was to commit a sin. So a Brahman had to pay for it.

*saccha* (genuine) the trees would stand up on their own! Thousands gather at this site everyday and *batashas* (a kind of sweetmeat), money and ornaments are offered by men and women alike. It is said that the proceeds will be donated to the Swarajya ashram and the Tilak Swaraj Fund'.[90]

33. 'A frail mango tree had been bent by a storm. As a matter of fact its roots were not strong enough to withstand the weight of its branches . . . Because of the storm some of the roots were uprooted, but a part remained embedded in the ground. The tree dried up in a few days. People began cutting its branches and taking them home for fuel. As the weight of its branches was now reduced, the tree straightened up either on its own, or with the aid of some person. People proclaimed that [the] fallen tree [had] planted itself back. A crowd soon gathered, assuming the proportions of a *mela* (fair). They are now offering flowers, batashas and money to the tree. It is said that the tree has stood up because of the pratap of Gandhiji. The educated are laughing at the mela, and this particular exemplification of Indian beliefs'.[91]

34. A respected person from Basti district reported to the *Swadesh* the following incidents: 'Two saplings have sprouted from the *khunta* (peg) of a Mahua tree in Chakdehi village, two miles from the Khalilabad station. This khunta had been fixed in the month of Kartik (October-November), and every day the bullocks of one Pandeji used to be tied to it. It is also rumoured that a Chamar had seen a sapling coming out of the peg on an earlier occasion, but his wife had plucked it out. Subsequently, the Chamar was rebuked by some people. He then prayed to the Mahatma: "Oh! Mahatmaji, if you are a true Mahatma, then let another sapling sprout". And so it happened. Now every day crowds of men and women are coming to the spot to see the peg'.

35. 'In Basti town there lives a widow of Sri Raghubar Kasaudhan. She had a son who died three years ago. Her late husband had planted two mango trees; one was cut down some time back and the other dried up a year ago. Fifteen days ago it began sprouting fresh leaves. The old woman maintains that she had taken a manauti of Mahatmaji: "This tree is the only *nishani*

[90] *Batsha*: A light sweet-meat, in appearance like ratafia cakes.
[91] *Gyan Shakti*, April 1921, p. 34.

(sign) of my late husband, let this tree live". A large crowd gathers at this site as well'.

36. 'Last Saturday smoke started coming out of four or five wells in Gorakhpur city. People exclaimed that the water had caught fire: The whole city rushed to the spot. Some people drew water from one well: it had the fragrance of keora (*pandanus odaratissimus*). It is believed that this is also due to the 'pratap' of the Mahatma! Some money etc. has also been offered to the well'.[92]

37. 'Some days ago a major fire broke out in a village near the Gorakhpur Civil Courts. The entire village was burnt down. There is a *nala* (open drain) nearby. People started digging a *chaunra* (*katcha* well) in the nala to get some wet clay and water, but water was not struck even after digging several cubits. It is said that in the end one person took the manauti of the Mahatma. After this such a huge jet of water gushed out that not only was the 16–17 cubit deep well filled up, but the two adjacent *garhas* (depressions) were also submerged. Since then thousands of men and women gather at the site. Flowers, batashas and money are offered, they bathe and wash their faces there and some even carry the water back to their homes'.[93]

38. 'There is a big depression (garha) to the south of Bulandpur village [on the outskirts of Gorakhpur]. This garha is not less than twenty-three feet deep. The water level in Gorakhpur is around twenty-one feet. In some cases water is struck even before this depth is reached. An eleven cubit rope is normally used in these parts [to raise water from wells]. The present well from which water gushed out was dug in this deep depression. When water was struck it filled the chaunra to the brim. Now a mela is taking place here. When a chaunra is dug in a deep depression such an occurrence is only natural. The water level in Gorakhpur is eleven cubits; if you so desire you may measure it. We have seen scores of such wells which, when dug in a depression have been filled with water to the brim. People are offering flowers, batashas and money at the [above mentioned] well. They say that even this is an example of the grace of Gandhiji. This well is now called "Gandhi Chaunra" . . . Does one require this kind of intelligence for the attainment of swaraj?'[94]

[92] *Swadesh*, 13 March 1921, p. 5.     [93] *Swadesh*, 10 April 1921, p. 11.
[94] *Gyan Shakti*, April 1921, p. 34.

39. 'The *bhakts* (devotees) have . . . offered Rs 23-8-12 in Mirzapur Bazaar where water had come out on its own. Sri Chedi Lal has arranged for this sum to be sent to the Gorakhpur Swaraj Fund'.

40. The water of a well in Bikramjit Bazaar, tappa Belwa (Basti) had a very foul smell. Two *mahajans* took a manauti of the Mahatmaji. By morning the water had become pure.

41. 'Plague was raging through Sonaura village. People were living in [outlying] huts. The water in a well at this place was so shallow on 27 April that even a small drinking vessel (*lota*) could not be fully submerged in it. Seeing this, one Misrji offered to distribute Rs 5 in the name of Gandhiji. Subsequently, water began to rise slowly. By the afternoon of 28 April the well had filled up to five cubits, the next day it was eleven cubits deep'.

Once again we have in these stories the suggestion that the Mahatma's image takes form within pre-existing patterns of popular belief, and ritual action corresponding to these. In Nos. 28–30, Gandhi is fitted into the widespread practice of taking a vow (manuati) addressed to a god, a local godling or a saint on condition of the removal of an affliction or the fulfilment of a wish. In No. 31 we have an interesting development of this idea. Here the sacrifice of a goat in accordance with a manauti to Bhagwatiji boomerangs—it brings physical and mental suffering to the high-caste household of the zamindar of Samogar. The penance required is not limited to the traditional feasting of Brahmans; it now includes the donation of an amount equivalent to the cost of the sacrificial goat to the National School Fund.

The rational, if politically insensitive, explanations offered by the anti-Congress *Gyan Shatki* with regard to the regeneration of trees and wells (see Nos. 33 and 38) indicate the material basis for belief in these miracles. On the other hand, a couple of stories (Nos. 49 and 50 in Appx III) not strictly connected with Gandhi point once again to the existing stereotype of 'strange occurrences' in which the Mahatma's name figures so very often. It is thus that the traditional offerings made at the appearance of an image (No. 6) or at the site of a miraculous tree (Nos. 32 and 33) or a well can so easily be transferred to a nationalist fund.

The stories connected with wells (Nos. 36–41) which underline their importance for irrigation and even more for supplies of drinking water, call for some additional comments. The two major themes here are, first, the taking of a manauti by a banker or a high-caste person (usually a landlord) for the purification of drinking water (Nos. 40 and 41), and secondly, the more common offering of flowers, batasha and money to wells where water has appeared miraculously. Both these are readily understandable once it is realized that it was generally the bigger zamindars and bankers who invested in the expensive construction of pukka (masonry) wells. This was a highly ritualized activity in Gorakhpur and was described thus by a local ethnographer towards the end of the nineteenth century:

> When a man intends to sink a well he enquires an auspicious moment from the Pandit to commence it. When that hour comes, he worships Gauri, Ganesh, Shesh Nag, earth, the *kudari* (spade), and the nine planets. After worshipping these deities the person himself begins to dig with the *kudari* five times, facing the direction the Pandit has prescribed. Then the labourers begin their work. When they have sunk, so far as to make water appear, an auspicious moment is obtained to put the *jamuat* or wooden support on whom [sic] the brick structure of the well rests in the well. At the auspicious moment the person to whom the well belongs smears the *jamuat* with red powder in five places and ties grass (*dub*) and thread (*raksha*) on it, and then it is lowered down in the well. On this occasion a fire sacrifice (*homa/hawan*) is performed and Brahmans are fed. When the well has been sunk, cow-dung, cow-milk, cow-urine, cow-ghee, Ganges water, leaves of tulsi plant and honey are put in it before its water is made use of. Then a fire sacrifice (*homa*) is performed and Brahmans are fed.[95]

In Gorakhpur, according to the same informant, a mango tree was usually 'married' to a well.[96] Accounts from neighbouring Basti district suggest that the construction of a pukka well was both a communal and a ritual act. Neighbouring zamindars sent men, women and children to collect wood for the firing and baking of bricks, and the *sattu*, gur and liquor received by them were regarded 'in the light rather of a marriage feast than of remuneration'.[97] The 'marriage' of the well to an image (*jalotsarg*) was preceded by the carpenter spreading a *chaddar* (sheet) on the wooden frame. Into this the members of the brotherhood would throw coins of various denomination ranging from one paisa to one rupee, depending on their means and liberality. It was a measure of the importance of ritual in the consecration of pukka wells in this region that the

[95] Note by Ram Gharib Chaube, *North Indian Notes and Queries*, 3:12 (March 1894), no. 437.

[96] *North Indian Notes and Queries*, 4:12 (March 1895), no. 437.

[97] *Statistical, Descriptive and Historial Account of the North Western Provinces*, vi (Allahabad, 1881), p. 595.

'regular cost' of constructing a well, eight feet wide and nineteen feet deep, was reckoned to have been Rs 43 in the 1860s, while nearly twice as much was spent on ceremonial expenses.[98] As the settlement officer reported from Rasulpur Ghaus, Basti, 'On account of the expense the ceremony is often delayed one or two years, during which time the family of the builder makes no use of the water'.[99]

With this kind of worshipful attitude towards the construction of masonry wells, the offerings of flowers and money to those spots where water had appeared miraculously in the spring of 1921 and the transference of these offerings to a nationalist fund appear as an elaboration of existing ideas in a novel context. The practice of Gandhi manauti, of his vrat and aradhana (fast and worship), and of women begging alms in his name and making offerings of cooked food (*karahi charana*), as noticed in some of the earlier stories, can all be adduced as further instances of this process at work.[100]

[98] The break-up was as follows:

|  | Rs | annas |
|---|---|---|
| Offering to family god | 1 | 0 |
| Given to Brahmins: 5 dhotees and 5 rupees | 9 | 0 |
| Given to head beldar, 1 dhoty and 1 rupee | 1 | 12 |
| Liquor for remaining beldars | 0 | 4 |
| Feast to Brahmins (5 to 20) | 11 | 0 |
| Given to Brahmins and workmen, 5 rupees and 5 dhotees | 9 | 0 |
| Marriage ceremony from 10 rupees to an unlimited amount | 50 | 0 |
|  | 82 | 0 |
| Total: | 125 | 0 |

See Report on Pegunnah Rassolpore Ghaus, Appx L, in *Gorakhpur-Bustee Settlement Report*, i (Allahabad, 1871), p. 48.

[99] *Idem*

[100] In a study of popular religion in a north Indian village it has been suggested that the relationship between the devotees (*bhakts*) and the power-wielding deified beings moves along the grid of *Bhakti/Sewa: Krpa/Vardan*. Faith (bhakti) leads to the mercy (krpa) of the gods, while the sewa (service) of the devotees results in the granting of boon (vardan). On the other hand, the mercy of the gods leads to faith, and the accompanying boon results in further service (sewa) through the ritual of vrat (fast, puja and bhakti). Powerful deities have the ability not only to remove immediate distress, but are distinguished by their power to provide long-term shelter (*sharan*) and even *moksha* (salvation). See Wadley.

While the idea of boons and removal of distress is present in the stories collected above, the notion of the Mahatma providing sharan to his devotees seems to be absent, probably because Gandhi has not been constructed yet as a full-fledged deity in his own right. Rather, we have the suggestion that Gandhi, because of the fluidity of his 'powers', can stand in place of existing powerful beings and appropriate ritual actions connected with their worship, without upsetting the existing hierarchy of the divine and the deified.

The editor of *Swadesh* reported in April 1921 that 'news [had] been received from several places of women begging in the name of Gandhiji as they did for Devi Bhawani and offering karahi [to him]'. Women were also going round the threshing-floors, where the rabi crop had just been gathered, and asking for donations of grain, again to make offerings of karahi to the Mahatma.[101] The contemporary significance of the karahi ritual is somewhat unclear, though it appears to have been associated with propitation and the bringing of luck.[102] What is significant, in any case, is that this was an extension of a practice related to the worship of Devi Bhawani and that begging at the threshing-floor put the peasants under a moral obligation to donate some grain in the name of the Mahatma at a time when a surplus was readily available at the very site where it was being processed. In fact a similar obligation was placed on peasants manufacturing gur at the *kolhuar* as well: to turn a beggar away from a place where so much raw sugar was being made was an undesirable act which would seldom go unpunished.[103] It is hardly surprising, then, that the refusal of an Ahir in Nanusakh village (Azamgarh) to offer some gur to a hungry sadhu who came begging to his kolhuar (on 1 March 1921) was rumoured to have resulted within half an hour in the gur and the two buffaloes of the Ahir being destroyed by fire.[104] The version of this story, as reported in the *Swadesh*, did not mention Gandhi, although the *Pioneer* suggested that the sadhu was asking for alms in the Mahatma's name. True or not, it is possible that the Lucknow journal was not alone in associating him with this particular episode.

[101] *Swadesh*, 10 April 1921.

[102] Prof. A. N. Pandeya (IIT, Delhi) informs me that the phrase '*karahi charana*' refers in his part of the district (Padrauna tahsil) to the practice of women offering cake-like cooked food, prepared at the site of the local godling (usually female) in the open under a tree. Devi Bhawani, according to Crooke, is a north Indian mother goddess.

[103] Grierson's account of the worship of Makkar or Makar Bir in Bihar by the workmen of the kolhuar is worth recalling in this context. 'Near the place where the cane is cut into slips the men make a round idol of the deity called *makar bir* . . . He is said to have been originally a Dom, who once came to a sugar manufactory in the olden time and asked for juice, which the people refused to give to him. Thereupon he jumped into the boiler and was boiled to death. His spirit became deified, and is now worshipped by the workmen . . .'. G. A. Grierson, *Bihar Peasant Life* (1885: reprint, Delhi, 1975), pp. 55–6. The theme of suicide leading to the wrongdoer accepting his fault and then propitating and worshipping the spirit of the deceased is a recurring one in Indian folklore. See Crooke, pp. 191–5.    [104] *Swadesh*, 13 March 1921, p. 5.

## VII

Taken together, these stories indicate how ideas about Gandhi's *pratap* and the appreciation of his message derived from popular Hindu beliefs and practices and the material culture of the peasantry. Does not the fact of the reporting of these rumours in the local nationalist weekly suggest that these were actively spread by interested parties? It is true that such rumours enter our sources at the point where a correspondent communicates them to the *Swadesh*. But that need not be taken to mean that these did not exist prior to and independent of their publication. Their generalized circulation in the villages of Gorakhpur is also attested by their being reported and denied in the local anti-nationalist monthly, *Gyan Shakti*.

There can be no doubt that the reporting of these rumours in the local paper, *Swadesh*, must have added to their circulation and even to their authenticity. Lefebvre in his study of rural panic in revolutionary France observes how journalists imbued rumours 'with a new strength by putting . . . them into print'.[105] However, it seems unlikely that printing could have changed the character of these rumours to any significant degree; it merely increased their effectiveness as oral and unauthored speech.[106] People in the Gorakhpur countryside believed in these not out of any unquestioning trust in the weekly newspaper but because they accorded with existing beliefs about marvels and miracles, about right and wrong.

In Indian villages even printed texts often revert to their oral characteristics in the very process of communication. It has been noted that newspapers, pamphlets, etc. are made intelligible to the illiterate population in the countryside by reading aloud, paraphrasing the text in the rustic dialect and commenting on it.[107] In 'advanced cultural communities', Vachek notes, written texts are taken 'as a sign of the first order (i.e. the sign of an outside world)', the deciphering of which requires 'no detour by way of spoken language'.[108] It seems that one of the reasons for the reading aloud of newspapers in

[105] Georges Lefebvre, *The Great Fear of 1789: Rural Panic in Revolutionary France* (London, 1973), p. 74.

[106] For the characterization of rumour as oral and unauthored speech, see Ranajit Guha, *Elementary Aspects of Peasant Insurgency in Colonial India* (Delhi, 1983), Ch. 6.

[107] 'Language Problem in the Rural Development of North India', in *Language in Social Groups: Essays by John J. Gumperz* (California, 1971), p. 19.

[108] Josef Vachek, 'Some Remarks on Writing and Phonetic Transcriptions', in Eric Hamp *et al.* (eds.), *Readings in Linguistics*, ii (Chicago, 1966), p. 155.

Indian villages is that even for a large part of the technically literate population printed texts can be deciphered only by a detour through the spoken language. In such readings, it seems reasonable to suggest, a story acquires its authentication from its motif and the name of its place of origin rather than from the authority of the correspondent. It then spreads by word of mouth, and derives its credibility from any association, real or imaginary, it might have with place-names familiar to the local population.[109]

How did the local Congress leadership react to the spread of these stories? Maulvi Subhanullah, the DCC President, while recounting some of these to the Sessions Judge in June 1922, admitted that 'no attempt was made by the Congress or Khilafat to prevent [the] public from believing in them'.[110] *Swadesh*, the newspaper which published these stories under the sanctimonious rubric *bhakton ki bhavnain*— 'beliefs of the devotees'—adopted a double-edged policy in this regard.[111] On the one hand it published a note every now and then debunking some of the more fanciful stories and also let its satirist, Mannan Dwivedi, poke fun at them. On the other hand when attacked by the *Pioneer*, it came up with a spirited defence of its policy of printing these stories.

In March 1921 some people used the services of public criers to announce that 'Mahatmaji had emerged from fire [unhurt] and that Swaraj had been established'. They went so far as to swear by the truth of such statements. The editor of *Swadesh* promptly denounced this as an irresponsible act which had no sanction from the Mahatma. However, the same issue of the journal contained two columns of Gandhi stories under the heading 'strange happenings'. Elsewhere in the same issue Mannan Dwivedi, writing under the pen-name Shriyut Muchandar Nath, satirized some of these as follows:

> It is true that a felled tree in the front of Babu Yugal Kishore's garden has planted itself back and even sprouted leaves due to the grace of Mahatmaji. [See No. 32 above]. Every day lakhs of people come to see this [miracle],

[109] Thus in Satyajit Ray's film, *Ashani Sanket*, the foreign place-name Singapore is made meaningful to the peasants in a Bengal village by the suggestion that it is somewhere near Midnapore!

[110] Evidence, Chauri Chaura Trials, p. 556.

[111] Dwivedi, when queried by the Court about these miracles, proffered little information, and in fact maintained that in his paper he had 'given a summary . . . of the teaching of Mahatma Gandhi that he [was] not a god'. An extract from *Navjivan* in which Gandhi disclaimed to be an avtar was printed by *Swadesh* on the front page of its issue of 4 September 1921. See Evidence, Chauri Chaura Trials, p. 569.

as a result of which crores of rupees are being collected. Therefore, due to the efforts of Babu Krishna Prasad, neither will postal rates go up nor will there be a deficit in the budget this year . . .

It was rumoured that a well in Gorakhpur was smelling of keora. [See No. 36]. Now it has been confirmed by the Khilafat Committee that Sri Shiv Mangal Gundhi had emptied his karahs full of keora into the well, as it is said that he is going to perform the last rites for his Sundar Shringar Karyalay [a perfumary in the city] and is shortly to take up the running of a [nationalist] press.[112]

It is doubtful how many outside the city of Gorakhpur would have understood Mannan Dwivedi's allusions or allowed satire to get the better of belief. Even the editor of *Swadesh*, when pressed, could write an impassioned defence of the peasant's acceptance of these stories:

We do not consider . . . *Swadesh* to be the property (*miras*) of its editor. Therefore, we consider it as part of our duty to report the thoughts and feelings current among the people (janta), whether right or wrong, in our paper . . . . It is possible that some people might doubt these strange happenings, but the janta does not consider them so [improbable]. And there is a reason for this. It is because Hinduism has placed faith and belief (*shraddha aur vishwas*) on a high footing. It is because of this that those who worship stone images have their prayers answered. It is because of this that people take a dip in the holy waters of Gangaji and think that their sins have been washed away. In every age and country, every now and then, such things have happened. Even in the time of the Buddha, Mohammad and Christ such miracles were supposed to have taken place. Then we see no reason why miracles (*chamatkar*) should not be associated with Mahatma Gandhi whose name is perhaps even better known in India than that of Ram and Sita. It has been said: '*Vishwaso* [sic] *phaldayakah*': faith yields fruit.

'*jaki rahi bhavana jaisi,*
*prabhu moorat dekhi tin taisi*'.[113]

The editor of *Swadesh*, who had himself sought to inculcate an attitude of devotion in the district towards the Mahatma,[114] had thus no hesitation in printing rumours about the latter's pratap. It was only when these appeared to instigate dangerous beliefs and actions, such as those concerning demands for the abolition of zamindari, reduction of rents or enforcement of just price at the bazaars, that the journal came out with prompt disclaimers.[115]

[112] *Swadesh*, 10 April 1921, p. 5.

[113] 'Bhakton ki Bhavnain', editorial note, *Swadesh*, 1 May 1921. Whatever faith one has, the image of god appears accordingly.

[114] Cf. pp. 17–18 above.

[115] See *Swadesh*, 18 Sept. 1921, p. 8; 6 March 1921, p. 12.

## VIII

Just as the Mahatma was associated in Gorakhpur with a variety of miraculous occurrences, so did his name lend itself as a label for all sorts of public meetings, pamphlets—and of course for that polysemic word Swaraj. Surveying the background to the Chauri Chaura riot, the judges of the Allahabad High Court found it 'remarkable . . . how this name of "Swaraj" was linked, in the minds of the peasantry of Gorakhpur, with the name of Mr Gandhi. Everywhere in the evidence and in statements made . . . by various accused persons', they found that 'it was "Gandhiji's Swaraj"', or the "Mahatmaji's Swaraj" for which they [i.e. the peasants] were looking'.[116] 'Announcements in Urdu' were sold by Lal Mohammad, one of the principal accused in the Chauri Chaura case, as 'Gandhi papers' which were to be preserved and produced 'when Gandhiji asked for . . . [them]'. The receipt for donations to the Khilafat fund, which bore a superficial resemblance to a one-rupee bank note, was referred to as a 'Gandhi note' by the peasants of Gorakhpur. The editor of *Gyan Shakti*, to whom we owe this information, alleged that villagers interpreted its non-acceptance (as legal tender?) as an act of opposition to the Mahatma.[117] Whether peasants genuinely failed to recognize the difference (as officials in some Awadh districts implied),[118] or whether this was just a conscious manipulation of an ambiguous printed paper to force non-believers into acceptance, we do not know for certain. What is clear, however, is that we have in the 'Gandhi note' an index of the popular tendency to look upon the Mahatma as an alternative source of authority. We have it on local testimony that peasant volunteers proceeding to a *sabha* at Dumri on the morning of 4 February 1922 (hours before the historic clash with the police was to occur at the Chaura thana a couple of miles away), claimed that they were 'going to hold a Gandhi Mahatma Sabha' which would bring about 'Gandhi Swaraj'.[119]

The popular notion of 'Gandhiji's Swaraj' in Gorakhpur appears to have taken shape quite independently of the district leadership of

---

[116] Appeal No. 51 of 1923: King Emperor vs. Abdullah and others. Judgement of the Allahabad High Court, dated 30 April 1923, p. 9, High Court Archives, Allahabad. The evidence about Lal Mohammad in the next sentence comes from the testimony of Shikari before the Sessions Judge, p. 1.

[117] *Gyan Shakti*, Feb. 1921, p. 404.

[118] See for instance the official handbill 'Khabardar', issued by the Dy. Commr. of Rae Bareli, encl. in Jawaharlal Nehru Papers, Pt II, File 120, NMML.

[119] Evidence of Mindhai, cultivator of Mahadeva, and Birda, cultivator of Bale, Chauri Chaura Trials, pp. 512–13.

the Congress party. As the High Court judges observed, the local peasantry 'perceived of it [Swaraj] as a millenium in which taxation would be limited to the collection of small cash contributions or dues in kind from fields and threshing floors, and [in] which the cultivators would hold their lands at little more than nominal rents'.[120] During the course of the trial the district Congress and Khilafat leadership repeatedly denied having propagated any such ideas in the villages. In fact there is evidence that as early as March 1921 public proclamations about the advent of Swaraj were being made in the Gorakhpur countryside. These, as we have noted above, were denounced by the Congress paper *Swadesh*. The pro-landlord *Gyan Shakti* drew pointed attention to such occurrences as ominous signs which boded ill for all concerned:

> One night people from all the villages [!] kept awake and roamed over five villages each. That night it was impossible to get any sleep. They were shouting 'Gandhiji ki jai'. They had *dhol, tasa, jhal, majiras* (kettledrums and cymbals) with them. The din thus caused was unbearable. People were shouting, this is the drum of swaraj (*swaraj ka danka*). Swaraj has been attained. The English had taken a bet with Gandhiji that they would grant Swaraj if Gandhiji could come out of fire [unhurt]. Gandhiji took hold of the tail of a calf and went through fire. Now Swaraj has been attained. It was also announced that now only four annas or eight annas a bigha would have to be paid in rent. We have also heard that some peasants are insisting that they will not pay more than eight annas a bigha as rent.
>
> These rumours are signs of an impending clash between the peasants and the landlords. As a result of this both parties shall suffer. Sensible (*parhe-likhe*) peasants, landlords and the government should refute such rumours. Remember this! If ordinary people retain their belief in such rumours and persist in their quest for the chimerical then the attainment of Swaraj will become increasingly distant. Peasants are now refusing to obey their landlords, or work for them. This is not a good sign for the country.[121]

Quite clearly this was a miracle (Gandhi's passage through fire) consistent with the existing level of peasant consciousness and its foil in utopian hopes for a world free of rents—a far cry these from

---

[120] Judgement, Allahabad High Court, p. 9.

[121] 'Swaraj ka Danka: Char Anna Malguzari: Zamindaron ki Chinta', *Gyan Shakti*, April 1921, pp. 34–5. This rumour, which had originated in the villages of the south-eastern tahsil of Deoria, spread to the neighbouring district of north Bihar and underwent a transformation in the process. It was rumoured here that Gandhi Baba, a cow, a Brahman and an Englishman had been put to an ordeal by fire, and only the Englishman had got burned. People were to pass on this story to five other villages on pain of incurring the sin of killing five cows. Cited in Henningham, p. 100.

official Congress policy—which marked the irruption of Swaraj that night in Gorakhpur villages.[122] However, as local-level volunteer activity entered a more militant phase in late 1921, the coming of Swaraj was perceived—contrary to anything the Congress stood for at that time—in terms of the direct supplanting of the authority of the police[123] (just as the earlier notion of divine punishment for opposition to the Gandhian creed was replaced by the idea that it was for the panchayats themselves to dispense justice in such cases). Thus Sarju Kahar, the personal servant of the murdered *thanedar* of Chaura, testified that 'two or four days before the affair [he] had heard that Gandhi Mahatma's Swaraj had been established, that the Chaura thana would be abolished, and that the volunteers would set up their own thana'.[124] According to Harbans Kurmi of Mangapatti, Narayan, Baleshar and Chamru of his village said on their return from the riot that 'they had burnt and thrown away and Swaraj had come'.[125] Or as Phenku Chamar told the Sessions Judge in August 1922:

> Bipat Kahar, Sarup Bhar and Mahadeo Bhuj were coming along calling out 'Gandhi Maharaj Gandhi Maharaj' from the north, the direction of Chaura, to [the] south, the direction of Barhampur. I asked why they were calling out 'Gandhi Maharaj' and they said the thana of Chaura had been burnt and razed to the ground [by them] and the Maharaj's swaraj had come.[126]

## IX

Corresponding to this dramatic change in the manifestation of 'Gandhiji's Swaraj', there was for the peasant volunteers of Chauri Chaura a transformation in the spirit of that ubiquitous cry, 'Gandhi Maharaj ki jai', as well. We have noticed how this cry had assumed an audacious overtone during Gandhi's return journey from Gorakhpur in February 1921.[127] Within a month, as the 'Swaraj ka danka' episode suggests, the *jaikar* of Gandhi had become a militant avowal of the organized strength of peasant volunteers, a cry which mobilized

[122] The belief in an impending Swaraj was no doubt related to Gandhi's utterances on this point, though its signs were far from Gandhian.

[123] See 'Some Instances of the highhanded methods of Non-Cooperation Volunteers', encl. to Bihar Govt. letter dated, 5 Dec. 1921, Home Poll. File 327/I/1922, NAI.

[124] *Tajwiz Awwal*, Chauri Chaura Trials, p. 358.

[125] Chauri Chaura Trials, p. 525.

[126] Chauri Chaura Trials, p. 516.

[127] See pp. 19–20 above.

and struck terror in the hearts of waverers and enemies alike.[128] For the peasants of north India this had ceased in effect to be a Gandhian cry; it was now a cry with which an attack on a market or a thana was announced. 'Mahatma Gandhi ki jai' had, in this context, assumed the function of such traditional war cries as 'Jai Mahabir' or 'Bam Bam Mahadeo'. An interesting case of such a transformation is provided by the following intelligence report from Bara Banki:

> The big Mahadeo Fair near Ramnagar passed off quietly, though the extensive substitution of Gandhi ki jai for the orthodox Bam Bam Mahadeo was noticeable even when there were no government officer[s] present.[129]

The crowd of Badhiks (a so-called 'criminal tribe') that looted the Tinkonia Bazaar in Gorakhpur on 15 February 1921, did so to the cry of 'Mahatma Gandhi ki jai'. In a small fair at Auraneshwarghat in Bara Banki a dispute with *halwais* (confectioners) on 22 February 1922 led to the upsetting and looting of sweetmeat and other stalls 'to the accompaniments of shouts of *Mahatma Gandhi ki jai aur mithai le leu*'.[130]

Thus a 'jaikar' of adoration and adulation had become the rallying cry for direct action. While such action sought to justify itself by a reference to the Mahatma, the Gandhi of its rustic protagonists was not as he really was, but as they had thought him up. Though deriving their legitimacy from the supposed orders of Gandhi, peasant actions in such cases were framed in terms of what was popularly regarded to be just, fair and possible. As an official reply to the question of haat-looting in north Bihar in the winter of 1921 stated:

> The evidence in the possession of the Government leaves no doubt that the haat-looting was directly connected with the state of excitement and unrest produced by the non-co-operation agitation. The persons who started the loot first of all asked the price of rice, or cloth or vegetables or whatever the particular article might be, and when the price was mentioned, alleged that Gandhi had given the order that the price should be so much, usually a quarter of the current market rate. When the shopkeepers refused to sell at lower prices, they were abused and beaten and their shops were looted.[131]

[128] This transformation was similar to what the cry 'Sita Ram' had been undergoing in the villages of Awadh at about the same time. See Pandey, 'Peasant Revolt and Indian Nationalism', pp. 169–70.      [129] PAI, 1 March 1922.

[130] *Idem*; King Emperor vs. Badloo Badhik and others, Trial no. 25 of 1921, Judgement by the Sessions Judge, Gorakhpur, 30 April 1921.

[131] *Bihar and Orissa Legislative Council Debates*, 8 March 1921, i, p. 293. There was a rumour current in Gorakhpur villages as well, that wheat, rice and cloth would become cheaper because of the 'order of Mahatma Gandhi'. See *Gyan Shakti*, Feb. 1921, p. 405.

There was thus no single authorized version of the Mahatma to which the peasants of eastern UP and north Bihar may be said to have subscribed in 1921. Indeed their ideas about Gandhi's 'orders' and 'powers' were often at variance with those of the local Congress-Khilafat leadership and clashed with the basic tenets of Gandhism itself. The violence at Chauri Chaura was rooted in this paradox.

# Appendix I

## 'गोरखपुर का अहोभाग्य'

प्रार्थना यह है कि गोरखपुर की साधारण जनता तो केवल महात्मा जी के दर्शन को बेतरह उत्सुक है. महात्मा जी आयेंगे; अपना दर्शन देकर उसे कृतार्थ करेंगे. लोग भी अपने त्राता को, अपने सामने, भर आँख देखकर, फूले नहीं समायेंगे. परन्तु, हम पूछते हैं कि वे लोग, जो प्रत्यक्ष रूप से सरकार के साथ सहयोग कर रहे हैं . . . उनका भी ऐसे अवसर पर कुछ कर्त्तव्य है या नहीं? हृदय से आवाज़ उठती है ''बेशक''. . . . उनका कर्त्तव्यपथ निश्चित हो चुका है, वे कार्यक्षेत्र में आवें, अपने देश को गुलामी से छुटकारा दिलाने के लिए, अपनी मान-मर्यादा कायम करने के लिए और अपने को अपने देश पर न्यौछावर करने के लिए कमर कस कर तैयार हो जायें. महात्मा जी के सामने अपने घुटने टेक दें और जगदाधार जगत्नियन्ता से प्रार्थना करें कि वह उन्हें बल दे कि वो अपनी किश्ती को इस मझधार में से पार कर ले जावें. परन्तु अगर उनका हृदय डावाँडोल हो, उन्हें दुनिया की दुनियादारी अपनी ओर घसीट रही है और अगर उन्हें अपने उज्ज्वल भविष्य पर सन्देह है तो वे कृपा करके अपने हृदय पर हाथ रखकर अपने ही दिल से पूछें कि महात्मा गाँधी के प्रति उनके हृदय में कितना सम्मान है? और, अगर महात्मा गाँधी के प्रति उनके हृदय में कोई सम्मान है, तो . . . किसलिए? क्या इसलिए कि वो बहुत दुबले-पतले हैं? क्या इसलिए कि वे गाढ़े-गजी की वस्तुएँ व्यवहार में लाते हैं? नहीं, यह और इस प्रकार की कोई भी बात नहीं है. इस बात को समझने के लिए जरा महात्मा गाँधी के जीवन इतिहास की ओर नज़र दौड़ाइये, उसकी तह तक जाइये, गोते-पर-गोते लगाइये; आपको मालूम होगा कि महात्मा गाँधी का ऐसे कठिन अवसर पर हमारे बीच अवतीर्ण होना हमारे समाज और हमारे देश के लिए कितना कल्याणप्रद है. यही उपयुक्त अवसर है कि जबकि हम या तो दो बल्ले में पल्ले पार हो जायेंगे या बीच धारा में डूब कर डुबकियाँ लगाते रह जायेंगे. . . . अधिक कहना फजूल है. आगा-पीछा छोड़ो. अपने

ज़िले के पीड़ित भाइयों की सेवा करने के लिए उठ खड़े हो. गाँव-गाँव और घर-
घर में स्वराज्य का शंख फूक दो . . . . यह आन्दोलन तुम्हारे लिए अमृतबटी है.
महात्मा गाँधी तुम्हारे सामने इसे पेश कर रहे हैं. यह तुम्हारी सूझ-बूझ और
दानिशमन्दी पर मुनहसर है कि तुम इसे ग्रहण करो या छोड़ दो. कम-से-कम
महात्मा गाँधी ने तो जो बीड़ा उठाया है उसे वो पूरा करके रहेंगे, पर कहीं ऐसा
न हो कि विजय के समय तुम यह कहते नज़र आओ कि—

जिन खोजा तिन पाइयाँ गहरे पानी पैठ,
में बौरी ढूंढन गई रही किनारे बैठ.

—स्वदेश, 6 फरवरी 1921

# Appendix II

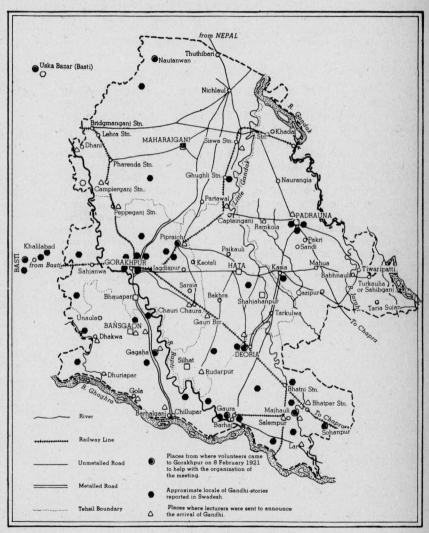

Gorakhpur District, *circa* 1909

## Notes to the Map

*Legend*

† Places where lecturers were sent to announce the arrival of Gandhi.
● Places from where volunteers came to Gorakhpur on 8 February 1921 to help with the organization of the meeting.
* Approximate locale of Gandhi-stories reported in *Swadesh*.

*Note*

This is a rough and tentative sketch map which makes no claim to be entirely accurate. Not all the unmetalled roads as they existed in 1921 have been shown. In a majority of cases it has been possible to locate the villages by checking place-names mentioned in *Swadesh* with the *Village Directory of the North-Western Provinces, xxi, Gorakhpur* (Allahabad, 1893), compiled by the Postmaster-General NWP. Where the village concerned does not appear in the district and tahsil maps, I have hypothetically situated it near the Post Office which served it. However, in spite of my best efforts I must inevitably have fallen into a degree of error in those instances where, for instance, the text does not mention either the tappa or the Post Office, especially if its name was identical with that of any other village or villages. However, it seems to me that even if the marking of villages from which a particular 'story' originated may not be cartographically accurate in all cases, a rough placement may be of some use in indicating the locale of a story and the territory generally traversed by a rumour. The geographical coverage of rumours outside Gorakhpur district has not been indicated, except by a rough marking for some of the places in Basti district.

# Appendix III

Some 'extraordinary occurrences' in Gorakhpur,
1921, other than those ostensibly related to
Mahatma Gandhi.

Motif: *Opposing the Gandhian creed*

42. 'A Koiri of mauza Tandwa forcibly brought a woman to a village and kept her in his house. Far from reprimanding and punishing him the men of the village offered their congratulations. Consequently, the harvested crops of the villagers kept at a common threshing-floor caught fire and were reduced to ashes'.

43. 'Pandit Madho Shukl of Kakarahi village (tahsil Bansgaon) continued to eat meat despite the attempts by his family to dissuade him. One day a trunk kept between two others in the house caught fire. Seeing this his wife raised an alarm and people from the village rushed to the house. Now Panditji has promised not to touch meat again'.

44. 'In Sinhanjori village (PO Kasia) hundreds of live worms emerged out of the fish fried by Shankar Kandu. Seeing this the entire village has given up meat and fish (*mans-machli*)'.

45. 'In Kurabal village shit rained in the house of a Bari (caste of domestic servants) for a whole day, and he is now living in another's house. On enquiry he has confessed to his crime (*dosh*) of slaughtering a goat'.

46. 'A gentleman from mauza Patra (PO Pipraich) writes that people of the village had given up the practice of eating meat and fish. However, on the instigation of a *karinda* some people caught fish in a shallow ditch and ate it up. Since then an epidemic has spread here; ten people have been swallowed by death (*kaal ke graas ho gaye*) in five days'.

47. 'A Muslim toddy-tapper of Padrauna was told by a Master sahab to give up this practice. One day he fell down from the tree. As a result of this incident all the Muslims are giving up toddy-tapping'.

48. 'The building of the Punjab Sugar Mill, Ghughli was being constructed. On 4 March, a few of the *memars* (construction workers) went to the bazaar of the Mahant and despite the attempt by some people to prevent them, they bought fish and drank toddy. When they sat down at night to fry the fish their huts caught fire. They had to sleep out in the open, with dew falling on them. That very night it rained and hail fell as well. In the morning the news came that their homes had also caught fire. What could they do? Crying and repenting they went back to their respective homes'.

Motif: *Boons and Miracles*

49. 'In mauza Surdahi (PO Sahjanwa), a branch has come out at one end of a dead-and-cut pipal tree. Huge crowds are gathering at this sight'.

50. 'In Padrauna on 29 April, two new springs sprouted in a well three feet above the water level. Now the source of the spring has gone down because of the rise in the water level. For the past three days large crowds have been gathering at the site'.

# V Developing Foucault

# More on Modes of Power
## and the Peasantry

### PARTHA CHATTERJEE

In an earlier article[1], I had presented a set of concepts of modes of power and forms of state organization, along with the outlines of an analytical framework, in the context of a study of peasant movements and ideologies in twentieth-century Bengal. The historical problem discussed there was the following.

There were several instances of what are called 'communal riots' between Hindus and Muslims in different parts of Bengal since the 1890s. With the launching of the Khilafat-Non-cooperation movements in 1919-20, however, the dominant mood became one of remarkable 'communal' solidarity and massive participation in the anti-colonial movements launched by the Congress. This mood was then replaced, again with astonishing suddenness, by widespread political hostility between Hindus and Muslims. From 1925-26 to the partition of the province in 1947, the principal feature of Bengal's politics was a mounting 'communal' antagonism, marked by a series of 'riots' of unprecedented spread and intensity.

There are two kinds of explanation of this phenomenon in current historiography. One may be called the 'colonialist' explanation which suggests that 'communal' identities, and hence 'communal' cleav-

---

[1] Partha Chatterjee, 'Agrarian Relations and Communalism in Bengal, 1926-1935' in Ranajit Guha (ed.), *Subaltern Studies: Writings on South Asian History and Society*, vol. I (Delhi, 1982).

ages, are inherent in the essential character of Indian society. Politicians and power-brokers, in making demands upon the colonial government or vying with one another for its favours, inevitably turn to these 'primordial loyalties' in order to gain a stamp of representative legitimacy for their claims. This therefore is the stuff of Indian politics.

The other explanation is broadly of 'nationalist' origin and asserts that the communal divide in Indian politics is wholly a creation of colonial practices. Whenever there was a nationalist consolidation of popular demands, the colonial government sought to break it up by playing up and manipulating communal issues. A 'left' variation on this nationalist theme has further argued that the real divisions in Indian society are those of class, not of communities. The colonial government on the one hand, and communalist ideologies and leaders on the other, have tried to mask the expression of what are really class issues by emphasising the communal division.

In my article, I tried to show that these explanations confuse phenomena which properly belong to two completely different domains of political beliefs and actions. In all pre-capitalist societies in a process of transition to the forms of organization of the modern state, 'politics' can only be understood in terms of the interaction of these two contrary domains. In the first domain, in which beliefs and actions are guided by popular consciousness, categories such as 'communalism' are utterly inappropriate. What may be properly called 'community' is indeed central to this consciousness, but it has no determinate form (such as that of a religious group) and consists of contradictory and ambiguous aspects. The other domain, shaped by the representative politics of the modern state, is one in which new forms of class domination emerge and consolidate themselves. It is the intersection of these two domains which becomes the main point of inquiry in the transitional process.

I constructed this framework out of the historical material provided by the course of Bengal's politics in the period 1926-35. But its scope is more general and concerns the elementary conceptualization of the general problem of politics and the state in large agrarian societies. In this paper, I elaborate on some of these general analytical implications of my framework and point out what I think are the theoretical advantages of using it.

I begin with a consideration of the recent contribution made by

Robert Brenner to the debate on the transition from feudalism to capitalism.[2]

## The Political Question in the Transition from Feudalism to Capitalism

Reviewing the contending positions in the earlier Dobb-Sweezy debate,[3] Brenner has shown with great clarity that each of the arguments in that debate was based on one form or another of economic determinism. Thus, the process of transition was explained either in terms of the dissolving effect of external trade on an otherwise static feudal economy, or the crisis of rent caused by long-term declines in productivity and by depopulation in feudal agriculture. The unacceptability of the former argument Brenner points out without too much difficulty: it is grounded in the assumption that a transition in modes of production can be explained in its essentials by developments in the sphere of exchange and circulation. Brenner shows this in the course of his discussion of Sweezy's arguments and of the more recent writings of Wallerstein.[4] The other argument, which was stated with much force by Dobb, hinges on the crucial question of the crisis of seigneurial revenues brought about as a result of the internal contradictions of feudalism and the specific resolution of that crisis. Dobb argued in terms of a single form of resolution: the breakdown of feudal relations in the countryside and the rapid emergence of a superior, i.e. capitalist, mode of production. Brenner shows that this sort of argument is in fact based on a 'determinism', viz. that the *technical* superiority of one mode of production necessarily determines its ultimate victory. It begs the whole question of the specific process of struggle between the contending forces vying for social supremacy, i.e. *the process of*

[2] Robert Brenner, 'Agrarian Class Structure and Economic Development in Pre-Industrial Europe', *Past and Present*, 70 (Feb. 1976), pp. 30-75; 'The Origins of Capitalist Development: A Critique of Neo-Smithian Marxism', *New Left Review*, 104 (July-Aug. 1977), pp. 25–92; 'Dobb on the Transition from Feudalism to Capitalism', *Cambridge Journal of Economics*, 2:2 (June 1978), pp. 121-40: mentioned hereafter as Brenner (1976), Brenner (1977) and Brenner (1978) respectively.

[3] Now available in Rodney Hilton (ed.), *The Transition from Feudalism to Capitalism* (London, 1978).

[4] Brenner (1977).

*class struggle* whose ultimate resolution describes the specific process of transition. Brenner, therefore, states the main theoretical problem of the medieval crisis in the following terms:

> . . . on the one hand . . . what was at stake were the fundamental surplus extraction relations which underpinned the ruling class's dominance; on the other hand, in the last analysis, the resolution of the crisis through the restrengthening in one form or another of feudal class relations or their dissolution would be decided in terms of the class conflict between lords and peasants, the forms of their class power and their relative strength.[5]

The seigneurial crisis of late feudalism was accompanied by a widespread decline in population all over Europe. How did the rival agrarian classes react to this crisis?

> It was the logic of the peasant to try to use his apparently improved bargaining position to get his freedom. It was the logic of the landlord to protect his position by reducing the peasant's freedom. The result simply cannot be explained in terms of demographic-economic supply and demand. It obviously came down to a question of power, indeed of force, and in fact there was intense Europe-wide lord-peasant conflict throughout the later fourteenth, fifteenth and early sixteenth centuries, almost everywhere over the same general issues: first, of course, serfdom; secondly, whether lords or peasants were to gain ultimate control over landed property, in particular the vast areas left vacant after the demographic collapse.[6]

And the outcomes were not the same everywhere. Brenner shows this by taking three specific cases: eastern Europe, western Europe and England. In each, the landlords attempted to overcome the rent crisis by increasing controls over the peasantry. In eastern Europe, controls were in fact successfully strengthened. In western Europe, peasants won freedom from serfdom, in fact obtained freehold rights over much of the land, while the aristocracy sought to reorganize its position through the medium of the absolutist state. In England, serfdom collapsed, although landlords retained control of the land. 'To account for the foregoing divergences would require an account of the differential evolution of lord-peasant class relations which lay

---

[5] Brenner (1978), p. 127. It could be argued that Brenner has been somewhat unfair to Dobb in his charge that Dobb had overlooked the class struggle aspect of the transition. The point, however, is that in spite of a masterly *empirical* presentation of this evidence, Dobb did not incorporate the class struggle as an integral part of his fundamental *theory* of the transition.

[6] Brenner (1976), p. 51.

behind the differential outcomes of class conflicts in the different European regions.' This, in turn, would require an inquiry 'into the sources of class solidarity and power of the peasantry, especially in their village communities, and of the lords, especially in their military organization and above all their state'.[7]

It is clear, therefore, that the whole question of the specific form of transition is here extricated from the bog of techno-economic determinism—depopulation, declines in productivity, dissolving impacts of external trade, etc. etc.—and posed as a problem of politics, i.e. of the class struggle.

> The element of 'indeterminacy' emerges in relation to the different character and results of these conflicts in different regions. This is not to say that such outcomes are somehow arbitrary, but rather that they tended to be bound up with certain *historically specific* patterns of development of the contending agrarian classes and their relative strength in the different European societies: their relative levels of internal solidarity, their self-consciousness and organisation, and their general political resources—especially their relationships to the non-agricultural classes (in particular, potential urban class allies) and to the state (in particular, whether or not the state developed as a 'class-like' competitor of the lords for the peasants' surplus).[8]

Brenner, in fact, goes further than this and considers historical examples of certain specific configurations of this triad, viz. landlord, peasant and the state, and the specific resolutions of the ensuing power struggles: in east Elbian Germany, west Elbian Germany, France and England. In the first case, landlords successfully increased controls because the peasant communities were weak and there were virtually no independent political institutions in the village, which in turn is attributable to the leadership of the landlords rather than of peasants in the colonization of the eastern lands. The medieval crisis therefore led to a new serfdom. In western Germany, the peasant-communal organizations of the *Gemeinde* were by the late middle ages far stronger in the economic regulation and political self-government of village life—the peasantry there was engaged in a constant struggle against the lords to perfect its common rights, such as the common lands and the common-field organization of agricultural rotation. The peasants then went on to demand reductions in rent and the right to inheritance, to replace the landlord-installed village mayors by their own elected magistrates and to choose their

[7] Brenner (1977), p. 129.
[8] Brenner (1976), p. 52.

own village priest. The lords were forced to accept the institutionalization of these rights won by the peasantry in the form of village
charters (*Weistümer*). In France, too, the peasantry resisted the
landlords and won similar rights, but the absolutist state emerged as a
contender to landlord power: it intervened on behalf of the peasantry
to reduce landlords' rents and to protect peasant proprietorship in
order to tax the peasants' surplus. Paradoxically (though not surprisingly), the state now replaced the landlords as the target of
peasant revolts. There were, in fact, similar developments in the
'mini-absolutisms' of the west German princes. In England, on the
other hand, the peasantry fought successfully against serfdom, but
the landlords responded by taking as much land as possible from the
'customary sector' and adding it on to the 'leasehold sector' where
they brought in capitalist tenants who made improvements and
cultivated by wage labour. It was the emergence of this landlord-
capitalist tenant-wage labour structure which ultimately demolished
peasant proprietorship and ushered in capitalist development in
England.

By contrasting these four specific cases, Brenner is able to suggest
that there can be more than one possible resolution of the landlord-
peasant-state tussle which is the political form of the feudal crisis.
Only under two specific conditions is the outcome directed unambiguously towards capitalist development: 'on the one hand, the
destruction of serfdom; on the other hand, the short-circuiting of the
emerging predominance of small peasant property'.[9]

But what Brenner's contribution brings out above all is the theoretical importance of locating the element of 'indeterminacy' in the
transition problem in the specific *political* form of the class struggle.
Brenner has been able to demonstrate convincingly that the path of
transition is not uniquely determined by the techno-economic terms
of evolution of a certain mode of production. The problem now is to
define the theoretical terms in which this *political* question of the
transition problem can be attacked.

The task requires new theoretical categories. It is now widely
accepted that the political structures of society (with the possible
exceptions only of the most elementary forms of social organization
in early or 'primitive' communities—but here the problems are of a
different sort) are not mere reflections of its 'economic' structures
built around the activities of social production. There are institutions,

[9] Ibid., p. 47.

and instituted processes, of power and of ideology which intervene and give the political structures a certain *relative autonomy*. But merely to state this is to stop short of posing a crucial problematic: what precisely constitutes 'relative autonomy'? Where is it located? How are we to identify and describe it in the domain of our theoretical concepts? Put in other words, what are the theoretical concepts and analytical relations which are specific to the world of the political? What Brenner has been able to suggest are certain empirical patterns among political phenomena connected with a limited number of historical examples of transition from one mode of production to another. What are the distinctive categories with the help of which specific political problems such as peasant struggles, feudal domination or the constitution of the absolutist state can be posed within a general framework of theory?

To generalize: we now possess a reasonably strong theoretical framework built around the central concept of the mode of production for the analysis of historical-material processes in human society. The mode of production has been defined[10] as an articulated combination of three elements—labourer, non-labourer and means of production—combined according to both a 'property' connection (the relations of production) and a 'real appropriation' connection (the forces of production). The problem of historical analysis is to study how the combination of these three elements changes in terms of the two connections. Now, the 'real appropriation' connection is the specific field of social production in its techno-economic aspects, for the study of which there are appropriate categories and analytical relations. What we are concerned with here are the categories and relations relevant to the analysis of the 'property' connection, i.e. the question of rights or entitlements in society, of the resultant power relationships, of law and politics, of the process of legitimation of power relations, etc. I will now attempt an elementary categorization of some of these concepts.

## The Modes of Power

Let me first repeat the definitions I had presented in the earlier essay.[11]

---

[10] Étienne Balibar, 'On the Basic Concepts of Historical Materialism', in L. Althusser and E. Balibar, *Reading Capital* (London, 1970), pp. 201-308, esp. pp. 212-16.

[11] 'Agrarian Relations and Communalism', section II.

I defined three *modes of power* which could exist, even coexist, in a particular state formation. These modes are distinguished in terms of the *basis* of specification of the 'property' connection (the relations of production) in the ordered and repeated performance of social activities, i.e. the particular pattern of allocation of rights or entitlements over material objects (sometimes extended to non-material objects such as knowledge) within a definite system of social production. The three modes of power I called the *communal*, the *feudal* and the *bourgeois* modes.

The *communal* mode of power exists where individual or sectional rights, entitlements and obligations are allocated on the authority of the entire social collectivity, i.e. the community. Here the collective is prior; individual or sectional identities are derived only by virtue of membership of the community. Institutionally, there may be various forms in which such authority could be exercised. It may consist of an assembly of all members of the community, but this is by no means a necessary institutional form. Communal authority may be exercised through a council of elders or of leading families, or even by a chief or patriarch. The point is that authority resides not in the person or even in the office; it resides only in the community as a whole. The officials or councils are no more than mere functionaries. We will see later that the communal mode of power may be said to exist even in situations where there is no definite or recognizable institutional form for the exercise of such authority.

The *feudal* mode of power is characterized fundamentally by sheer superiority of physical force, i.e. a relationship of domination. It is founded on conquest or some other means of physical subordination of a subject population. In our conception, it denotes not just the state formation which accompanies the feudal mode of production, but may in fact serve to describe political institutions corresponding to a whole range of forms of organization or production based on direct physical control over the life-processes of the producers. At one extreme, one may have production by slaves where both the life-processes of the producers as well as the labour-process itself are controlled by the master; at the other extreme, one can think of a free peasantry which is only required to make a periodic tax payment or a regular tribute to the agent of an external state; and in between there could be various degrees of serfdom, involving different degrees of control over the life-processes of the peasantry as a means of collecting a part of the social product as rent. The political domination which in all these forms of production organization is the prerequisite of rights or claims on the social product we will classify under the feudal mode of power.

In the *bourgeois* mode of power, unlike in the feudal, the domination of non-producers, i.e. capitalists, over the producers, i.e. wage-labourers, and the appropriation of surplus-value are assured not by physical control over the life-processes of the producers but by complete control over the labour-process secured by rights of property in the means of production and in the product and by the impersonal operation of the market. The necessary political conditions for the full development of capitalism as a system of social production requires, therefore, the separation of the state from the sphere of civil society, the elevation of the state into a 'neutral' institution which does not recognize real inequalities in society, making the individual the unit in political and legal transactions, conceiving of society as the result of a contract between individuals, turning all individuals irrespective of differences of race, religion, language, education or wealth into equal subjects before law. The fundamental institutional form by which the bourgeoisie sustains its political domination is that of representative government.

The rest of this essay will be concerned with an elaboration of some of the ways in which this conceptual framework can be used in the historical analysis of state formations and political processes. I will take various illustrative examples drawn from different regions of the world and different periods of history in order to emphasize the advantages as well as the difficulties of using these concepts for an understanding of the peasantry in history.

## Community and Statelessness

I avoid, for reasons of space, an explicit discussion of the formulations in Engels' classic *The Origins of the Family, Private Property and the State*.[12] The similarities and differences in approach will be evident from my arguments.

Within the domain of theory, the community is a conceptualization of the *first* instituted form of collective social authority. It is thus logically *prior* to a conceptualization of the state as a machinery of

[12] Karl Marx and Frederick Engels, *Selected Works*, vol. 3 (Moscow, 1973), pp. 191-334.

repression, as the instituted form of exploitative power relations in society. I hasten to add that this theoretical ordering does not require the support of any historicist conception of all human social groups passing through the successive stages: stateless anarchy→communal social organization→state.[13]

If one is looking for appropriate historical evidence having a bearing on this formulation (although it is worth reminding ourselves of the *logical* status of the concept of community within a theory of state formations), the community can be identified in its most *concretely expressed* form in anthropological studies of 'tribal' groups. Many such studies, particularly from sub-Saharan Africa, have revealed the existence of 'tribal' communities which apparently do not possess a state apparatus or distinctly identifiable political structures differentiated from the social group at large. The idiom of group solidarity here is often kinship, whether real, or imagined and imputed. In some of these cases, a number of local lineages are combined into a village community to comprise the smallest political segment; a number of villages united in a regional confederacy defines the tribe or people. These are usually categorized in anthropological literature as 'segmentary lineage systems' and there exists a theory about how such societies are regulated in the absence of centralized political structures or ranked and specialized holders of political authority. This explanation rests on 'the relations of local groups to one another', which, in this theory, 'are seen as a balance of power, maintained by competition between them'. Thus,

> Corporate groups may be arranged hierarchically in a series of levels; each group is significant in different circumstances and in connection with different social activities—economic, ritual and governmental. Relations at one level are competitive in one situation, but in another the formerly competitive groups merge in mutual alliance against an outside group. . . . The aggregates that emerge as units in one context are merged into larger aggregates in others, so that a segment that in one situation is independent finds that it and its former competitors are merged together as subordinate

[13] It is instructive to note the remark of an anthropologist who, in an attempt to put into a comparative framework the results of anthropological researches on tribal state organizations, has shown a similar concern to avoid this historicism. Gluckman discusses the difficulties of postulating 'a single evolutionary development for each tribal-type society into a differentiated society', but then adds: '. . . it is certain that the tribal-type antedated the differentiated society in the whole march of human history.' Max Gluckman, *Politics, Law and Ritual in Tribal Society* (Oxford, 1965), p. 81.

segments in the internal administrative organisation of a wider overall segment that includes them both. This wider segment is in turn in external competitive relations with other similar segments, and there may be an entire series of such segments.[14]

In the original formulation by Fortes and Evans-Pritchard,[15] these segments were corporate lineages, and the classic studies of such segmentary lineage systems were of the Nuer of Sudan, the Tallensi of Ghana,[16] the Tiv of northern Nigeria, the Mandari and the Dinka of southern Sudan, the Amba of Uganda, the Konkomba of Togo and the Lugbura of the Uganda-Congo region.[17] But there have also been studies of politically uncentralized societies in which there are no corporate lineages,[18] but corporate authority is vested in age-set or age-grade systems, such as among the Kikuyu and the Kamba of Kenya,[19] or in village councils as among the Kalabari, Bonny and Okrika of eastern Nigeria.[20]

[14] John Middleton and David Tait, 'Introduction' in Middleton and Tait (eds.), *Tribes Without Rulers: Studies in African Segmentary Systems* (London, 1958), pp. 1-32.

[15] M. Fortes and E. E. Evans-Pritchard, 'Introduction' in Fortes and Evans-Pritchard (eds.), *African Political Systems* (London, 1940), pp. 1-24.

[16] The studies by Evans-Pritchard and Fortes in ibid.

[17] Studies by Laura Bohannan, Jean Buxton, Geoffrey Lienhart, Edward Winter, David Tait and John Middleton in Middleton and Tait, op. cit.

[18] M. G. Smith, in an early critique of the segmentary lineage theory, pointed out its limited applicability even in the 'tribal' situation: '. . . the foundation of segmentary theory consists in a combination of two basic concepts, segmentation as a structure and process on the one hand, and political organization on the other. Where these conceptions are combined with unilineal descent groupings, segmentary lineages exist, otherwise they do not.' He pointed out that there were 'tribal' societies lacking specialized organs of administration in which the segments were not lineages, but localities or age-sets or cult-groups. Smith, of course, carried forward the argument to contend, in the manner of the 'political systems' theorists, that all political processes involved segmentation and all administrative organization involved hierarchy and that, therefore, 'the old problem of "states" and "stateless societies" is largely spurious. . . . In a real sense, therefore, the distinction . . . reduces to variability in combination and degree of explicitness in hierarchic organisation, differentiation of governmental units in terms of political and administrative functions and the variable distribution of these functions among Corporations Aggregate or Sole, organised with varying degrees of explicitness.' But a critical discussion of this last part of Smith's argument would require a long digression. M. G. Smith, 'On Segmentary Lineage Systems', *Journal of the Royal Anthropological Institute of Great Britain and Ireland*, 86:2 (July-Dec. 1956), pp. 39-80.

[19] John Middleton, *The Kikuyu and Kamba of Kenya* (London, 1953).

[20] G. I. Jones, *The Trading States of the Oil Rivers* (London, 1963).

The most interesting cases are of groups in which there exist official functionaries, such as chiefs or elders or lineage heads or priests for the performance of various administrative and other regulatory acts. There may be petty chieftains who perform routinized, often ritualized, official duties but have no special privileges. The Shilluk in Sudan have kings who are merely symbols of communal unity but have no authority.[21] And then there is the phenomenon of the 'big man' who has great personal influence because others defer to him for his personal qualities—wisdom, valour or magical powers—or because they are obliged to him in some way. Sometimes there is an institutionalized role for the stranger who acts as a mediator.[22] At other times, parallel to the institution of chiefship, there is an earth cult and there are priests who act as 'custodians of the earth': the ritual of the earth cult specifies the respective position of each structural unit with respect to the other and also symbolizes the unity of the whole community.[23] Chiefdom of a more advanced kind emerges in a larger confederation of 'tribal' groups. Here there is a ranking, because the chief or his descent group is superior to the rest.[24]

But in most of these cases where there are recognized official functionaries, there is a simultaneous institutionalization of the authority of the community as a whole, in the form of a council or even an assembly of all members which has to be summoned on occasions that require extraordinary decisions falling outside the routine competence of the functionaries. The Mandari of Sudan have hereditary chiefs, but the chief's judgements are only the expression of the views of the council of elders.[25] The Ngwato of Botswana have chiefs but 'all matters of

[21] Gluckman, op. cit., p. 130 ff.

[22] This 'becomes more significant when previously hostile tribes have had to unite against foreign domination. Then some outsider, not occupying a role of authority in established systems, arises as prophet, backed with supernatural powers, to unite the previously warring groups. This has happened in several areas of Africa: among the Nuer, among the tribes of the Cape Province of South Africa, in East and Central Africa.' Ibid., p. 102.

[23] See, for example, M. Fortes, 'The Political System of the Tallensi of the Northern Territories of the Gold Coast', in Fortes and Evans-Pritchard, op. cit. pp. 239-71.

[24] Among the Bemba, for instance, the chiefly clan is like a superior caste. Audrey I. Richards, 'The Political Systems of the Bemba Tribe—North-Eastern Rhodesia', ibid., pp. 83-120. Among the Zulus the king's family formed a superior rank; the close relatives of various chiefs were the aristocracy in the chief's tribe. Max Gluckman, 'The Kingdom of the Zulu of South Africa', ibid, pp. 25-55.

[25] Jean Buxton, 'The Mandari of the Southern Sudan', in Tait and Middleton, op. cit., pp. 67-95.

tribal policy are dealt with finally before a general assembly of the adult men in the chief's *kgotla* (council-place)'.[26]

Theoretically, it is legitimate to distinguish societies of this kind having recognized offices of authoritative functionaries, including advanced chiefdoms, from class society proper because chiefdom may still not necessarily imply an institutionalized claim on the social surplus based on political domination, i.e. the ability to coerce. Generally speaking, the distinctive features of the social organization of production in this situation are set by the low level of techniques, low productivity and the lack of any substantial quantity of social surplus. Mere subsistence and the simplest forms of social reproduction require considerable co-operation and mutual aid in productive activities and substantial communal control of consumption, sexual relations and indeed of the overall life-process itself. But perhaps the most crucial consideration which defines and shapes the form of communal political authority in stateless 'tribal' societies is the need for protection against external threat. 'The tribal superstructure', writes Sahlins, 'is a political arrangement, a pattern of alliances and enmities, its design shaped by tactical considerations. Overarching relations of clanship or regional confederacy seem most compelled by competitive threats, in connection with which large-scale economic and ritual co-operation may play the derivative role of underwriting cohesion in the face of external dangers'.[27] Thus, the need to order the internal life and labour-process of the community as well as the

[26] I. Schapera, 'The Political Organisation of the Ngwata of Bechuanaland Protectorate', in Fortes and Evans-Pritchard, op. cit., pp. 56-82

[27] Marshall D. Sahlins, *Tribesmen* (Englewood Cliffs, N. J., 1968), p. 17. Sahlins also notes 'the general propensity of tribal peoples to cloak alliances of convenience in kinship garb. Where peace is necessary or desirable, kinship is extended to effect it.' Ibid., p. 11. It is curious that in order to put this idea into a more general framework of the evolution of state institutions, Sahlins has to borrow his political theory from Hobbes. His view of this development is one from a state of 'Warre' where 'force is held in severalty' to 'Peace' where it is held in a sovereign body which has sole legitimate monopoly of force. But surely the most distinctive premise on which the Hobbesian theory is based is that of warring *individuals* and not communities already united in bonds of solidarity. The idea of individual members of society entering into a contract and passing on all coercive powers into the hands of a sovereign or sovereign body is fundamentally antithetical to the notion of communal authority. Perhaps this confusion of categories in Sahlins has to do with his attempt to generalize and elevate into a 'domestic mode of production' the Chayanovian idea of self-sufficient and jealously self-centred peasant households. Sahlins, *Stone Age Economics* (London, 1979).

requirements of evolving a viable organization of communal defence against external attack create the conditions for the institutionalization of communal authority.

### Feudal Power and Institutionalized Coercion

We can think of at least four distinct processes by which institutions of power based on force, and hence an institutionalized claim by a few on a part of the social surplus, can emerge. First, there could occur, as a process internal to the historical development of the community, a transformation of the offices of communal authority into institutions of feudal power. Thus, chiefs, warriors, priests or literati who had earlier performed as commissioners of communal power could, because of changes either in the conditions of production or in the external political environment, begin to wield coercive force on the rest of the community of producers in order to claim a part of the surplus. This, of course, is a historical process of transition for which it is impossible to set empirical thresholds or temporal datelines to demarcate the passage from stateless communal authority to feudal dominion. One historical example we could consider is provided by E. A. Thompson [28] who compares the historical accounts left by Caesar and Tacitus to show how in the first century B.C., at the time of Caesar, the German tribes ( *pagi*) had no peacetime authority, such as a chieftain, with powers over all the clans which made up a people (*civitas*), although there were war councils of tribal leaders at the time of war. By the first century A.D., however, Tacitus observed that the Germans had a permanent council of leading men to deal with matters of minor importance affecting the people as a whole, while most weighty business was decided by an assembly of warriors. But now there was also a new kind of chief whom Tacitus calls 'king' (*rex*) who was elected from within a 'royal clan'. Yet, Thompson notes that in spite of the king and 'the growing inequalities of economic power and social standing among the Germans of the first century A.D.,' the assembly of free tribesmen was still the sovereign body. In the majority of cases, the assembly's decisions 'must have been reached more or less unanimously, for there was no peaceable means by which a substantial minority of the people could have been coerced into a course of action which they strongly disapproved: there was even in Tacitus' time no public and coercive authority over and above the people themselves.'[29]

[28] E. A. Thompson, *The Early Germans* (Oxford, 1965).
[29] Ibid., pp. 44-5.

Thompson's account suggests a process by which the continuous pressure of warfare not only creates relatively permanent institutions of specialized coercive authority within a community, but also creates the *conditions* for converting these offices into seats of feudal power. The second, and more direct, method by which this could happen is, of course, the obvious one of conquest of one people by another. Where conquest is followed by direct domination by the conquering group over a subject population, and the institutionalization of exploitative relations in the formal delineation of rights, there is little problem for historical analysis. But the analysis often becomes complicated because of the complex formations one encounters in historical examples of societies in which there have been conquests, often successive waves of conquests, by other peoples. One does nonetheless find in anthropological studies examples even in politically uncentralized societies of freeborn and slave lineages, often attributable to conquest, with clearly recognized economic and ritual relations of dominance between the two categories, sometimes including direct payments in terms of labour.[30] It has also been pointed out recently that much of the conventional anthropological literature, guided by an almost obsessive concern to unravel the procedural and symbolic intricacies of the balancing mechanisms in segmentary political systems, has missed the very real exploitative relations which characterize the social formations of most extant 'tribal' peoples. Many of these relations are in fact the result of the domination imposed by conquering groups. Frankenberg, for instance, has reanalysed the political relations of the Lozi tribe, earlier studied by Gluckman, and has shown that as a result of a history of conquests, the Lozi have secured exclusive 'ownership' of the mound gardens which give them a crucial advantage in the sharing of productive resources among the peoples of Barotseland, and have thus ensured their domination over other peoples in the region.[31]

[30] Among the Bonny and Kalabari peoples of eastern Nigeria, for example, the 'tribe' is divided into freeborn and slaves, and the membership of village councils is confined only to the freeborn. G. I. Jones, op. cit. Also see Jack Goody, 'Land Tenure and Feudalism in Africa', in Z. A. Konczacki and J. M. Konczacki (eds.), *An Economic History of Tropical Africa*, vol. I (London, 1977), pp. 62-9.

[31] Ronald Frankenberg, 'Economic Anthropology or Political Economy? The Barotse Social Formation—A Case Study', in John Clammer (ed.), *The New Economic Anthropology* (London, 1978), pp. 31-60. Also see Y. Lacoste, 'General Characteristics and Fundamental Structures of Medieval North African Society', *Economy and Society*, 3:1 (February 1974), pp. 1-17; David Seddon, 'Economic Anthropology or Political Economy? Approaches to the Analysis of Pre-capitalist Formations in the Maghreb', in Clammer (ed.), op. cit., pp. 61-109.

This sort of dominance by conquest can also take the form—and this, in general terms, is the third possible form in which feudal power relations can emerge—of a simple tribute-extracting relation in which the social formation of the subject people is left largely intact, including its own internal constitution of authority which may, in fact, continue to retain a segmentary character. This, sometimes, is the form found in historical examples of large kingdoms with well-developed productive and state organizations attempting to extend their domination over more 'primitive' peoples living in peripheral regions.

And finally, of course, we have the familiar case, usually the consequence of a long and complex historical process involving a combination of 'internal' development and external political intervention over centuries, of the breakdown of segmentary forms of social organization, the evolution of more developed techno-economic forms and more complex social arrangements of production, the emergence of differentiated and institutionalized forms of extraction and distribution of the surplus, and the creation of formal institutions of coercive domination. This, properly speaking, is the typical situation in which one encounters the peasantry in history.

Now, while its seems convenient for analytical purposes to distinguish between these separate processes of the emergence and establishment of regular exploitative class relations based on sheer superiority of physical force, one would rarely find concrete historical examples of social formations in which these specific processes can be delineated with any degree of accuracy. In other words, it seems on the whole futile to attempt concrete historical analyses of either 'tribal' or peasant societies by *positing* a framework of unilineal transition from some kind of 'primitive communism' to class-divided society. A more useful approach would be to locate *all* pre-capitalist political formations in a historical process of which the central dynamic is to be found in the dialectical opposition between the communal and the feudal modes of power. Let me elaborate.

### The Oppostion Between Communal and Feudal Modes of Power in 'Transitions' to Feudalism

A common problem one comes across in the literature on political arrangements in 'tribal' societies is that of deciding when 'state institutions' have emerged. One approach to the problem is, so to speak, to postpone its solution by constructing a set of evolutionary *stages* in the process of the emergence of fully developed state institutions, and placing all societies which appeared to lack formal structures and that cannot unequivocally be designated as state formations, in one or the other of these stages. Thus, Elman Service subdivides the case studies in his book on the subject according to the 'societal levels' of band, tribe, chiefdom and 'primitive-state'.[32] Needless to say, classificatory schemes of this kind are entirely arbitrary: one can insert other stages in between any two, or lump together two or more stages and call them one. Besides, by refusing to designate as 'state' institutions all regular arrangements of exercise of class power which cannot be defined in terms of some positive criteria such as territory or legitimate monopoly of force, one naturally tends to overlook in studies of societies otherwise characterized by 'segmentary' forms of authority the process of emergence of exploitative class relations. This has, in fact, been a major argument in recent critiques of conventional anthropological methods. Fundamentally, the problem lies in the futility of trying to capture a *process* of change within a framework defined by a set of mutually exclusive positive categories.

The problem is highlighted in the work of anthropologists who, faced with incontrovertible evidence of the existence of regular processes of class domination in 'tribal' societies, have attempted to incorporate this into their conventional positivist framework. Aidan Southall, for instance, studying 'processes of domination' among the Alur people of East Africa,[33] found two contrary principles of authority—one based on kinship, i.e. authority and order within lineages and clans built upon values inculcated in the family, and then spreading outwards through the agnatic core of brothers, father and sons to embrace all kinsmen of corporate lineages or the clan section, and the other political, stemming from chiefship and delegated downwards to chieflets and the heads of corporate lineages or clan sections. The kinship authority system retained considerable responsibility for the provision of personal security and the regulation of day-to-day social relation-

[32] Elman R. Service, *Profiles in Ethnology* (New York, 1978).
[33] Aidan W, Southall, *Alur Society: A Study in Processes and Types of Domination* (Cambridge, 1953).

ships. But the society also had chiefs who not only acted as the main centres of a system for the reciprocal exchange of goods and services but also obtained fines and tributes in kind as well as in services. The system of political authority was a flexible one with much responsibility left to the heads of local groups, while the chief stepped in to reinforce their authority 'when directly called upon by them, or when violent and unresolved disorders required his intervention'.

> Alur chiefs did not enforce any rigidly defined authority within strict territorial frontiers. They relied mainly on the general influence of their ritual and supernatural authority to bring them tribute and services required to maintain themselves and the economic system of which they were the pivots, and to secure reasonable conformity to the minimal requirements of order and justice, in which the strictness of the regulations and the certainty of their enforcement diminished somewhat from the centre to the periphery of the jurisdiction. They had no military organisation to oppose against direct challenge to their political authority. But they could usually rely on the loyalty of a sufficient number of clan sections to muster an extempore force stronger than any that was likely to challenge them, and they had a miscellaneous body of dependents, closely tied to them by economic privileges, who could provide an informal body-guard.[34]

In trying to square this evidence with the conceptual framework of 'segmentary lineage systems', Southall then finds it necessary to invent the hybrid concept of the 'segmentary state'.[35] This he describes as follows:

> (1) Territorial sovereignty is recognised but limited and essentially relative, forming a series of zones in which authority is almost absolute near the centre and increasingly restricted towards the periphery, often shading off into a ritual hegemony. (2) There is centralised government, yet there are also numerous peripheral foci of administration over which the centre exercises only a limited control. (3) There is a specialised administrative staff at the centre, but is repeated on a reduced scale at all the peripheral

---

[34] Ibid., p. 237.

[35] It is interesting to note what Southall has to say about his methodological problem: 'The distinction between state and segmentary organisation is theoretically valid, and at this abstract level intermediate forms demand no separate category. But in any scheme of classification which claims empirical relevance the criteria of legitimate isolation are different, and any empirial form which has a certain frequency, stability, and structural consistency must receive due consideration. The morphologically transitional is not necessarily the empirically transitional form.' Ibid., p. 246. Positivism and empiricism go hand in hand!

foci of administration. (4) Monopoly of the use of force is successfully claimed to a limited extent and within a limited range by the central authority, but legitimate force of a more restricted order inheres at all the peripheral foci. (5) Several levels of subordinate foci may be distinguishable, organised pyramidally in relation to the central authority . . . (6) The more peripheral a subordinate authority is the more chance it has to change its allegiance from one power pyramid to another . . . [36]

It then turns out that not only a large number of African societies, but several feudal states in Europe, India and China as well, were segmentary states! All the above characteristics of a 'segmentary' distribution of power could be seen in the political organization of these ancient and medieval kingdoms:

> For, until the central authority can prove its efficacy to the average individual in terms of personal security, the individual must cling to kin or other traditional local units, and even to feudal authorities, in such a way that the distribution of power is segmentary in type.[37]

Let us overlook the rather crude psychologism of the last formulation. The important point is that after looking at the wide range of empirical evidence from 'tribal' as well as 'feudal' agrarian societies, Southall has noticed a common feature—the coexistence of two contrary principles of political authority, one based on kinship, the other on domination. He has not, of course, succeeded in locating this finding within a theory of the historical process of change in political formations. A much more remarkable anthropological study is the one by Leach on the Kachin people of upper Burma.[38] Kachin society is simultaneously segmentary and class-stratified: the lineage segmentation does not lead to 'balanced opposition' as in the theory of Fortes and Evans-Pritchard, but rather to a status ranking between superior and inferior. The way in which this happens involves a conflict between two ideal constitutions of the social order—one based on the principle of kinship and the other on the principle of rank. The *gumsa* system of ranking means a status differentiation between the chief and his followers. Ideally, it means a system of reciprocal obligations, but 'the weakness of the *gumsa* system is that the successful chief is tempted to repudiate links of kinship with his

---

[36] Ibid., pp. 248-9.
[37] Ibid., p. 261.
[38] E. R. Leach, *Political Systems of Highland Burma* (London, 1954).

followers and to treat them as if they were bond slaves (*mayam*)'.[39]
When this happens, the contrary principle of *gumlao* can be invoked
by the commoners to justify revolt against the chief. In the *gumlao*
constitution, there are no chiefs and all lineages are of the same rank.
Yet, the historical evidence seems to show that after a successful
revolt and a period of egalitarian *gumlao* regime, '*gumlao* groups . . .
seem to revert rather rapidly to class differentiation on a lineage
basis . . .'[40]

Generally speaking, then, Leach describes the political system of
the Kachin as one of oscillation between two opposed poles ideally
defined in the *gumsa* and the *gumlao*. 'A *gumsa* political state tends to
develop features which lead to rebellion, resulting, for a time, in a
*gumlao* order. But a *gumlao* community, unless it happens to be
centred around a fixed territorial centre such as a patch of irrigated
rice terraces, usually lacks the means to hold its component lineages
together in a status of equality. It will then either disintegrate altogether through fission, or else status differentiation between lineage
groups will bring the system back into the *gumsa* pattern.'[41]

Leach also identified a third ideal pattern which the *gumsa* form
tends to imitate, viz. the much more overtly 'feudal' pattern of the
Shan principalities: when the Kachin chiefs have the opportunity,
they model their behaviour on that of the Shan princes. But what is
more interesting is Leach's claim that the two contrary poles between
which the Kachin political system oscillates are not merely abstract
categories constructed by the anthropologist, but ideal types that are
recognized as such in Kachin society.[42]

Leach also points out that while certain features of Kachin society
are clearly similar to the classical segmentary type, or to Morgan's
'gentile' organization as among the Iroquois or the ancient Greeks, it
is also different in that it has a distinct class system associated with a
lineage system. In this respect, it is 'only half a step removed' from
neighbouring Shan society which resembles much more strongly
what is commonly understood as feudalism. 'The transition from
Kachin-type organisation to Shan-type organisation involves the
substitution of a straight landlord-tenant relationship for a relation-

[39] Ibid., p. 203.
[40] Ibid., p. 203.
[41] Ibid., p. 204.
[42] Ibid., pp. 285-6.

ship based either on common lineage or affinal dependence.'[43] What Leach does not point out is that the opposition between the two contrary principles of organization of power and authority is an integral aspect of political formations even in feudal society proper.

## Marx on the 'Original' Forms of Property

Let us turn to Marx's discussion in the *Grundrisse* on precapitalist formations. There are several pages here on what Marx calls the 'original forms of property and production'. The broad range of these forms Marx sets out in terms of two extremes—small, free landed property on the one hand, and 'communal landownership resting on the Oriental commune' on the other. In all the forms falling within this range, 'the worker relates to the objective conditions of his labour as to his property; this is the natural unity of labour with its material presuppositions.'

> The worker thus has an objective existence independent of labour. The individual relates to himself as proprietor, as master of the conditions of his reality. He relates to the others in the same way and—depending on whether this *presupposition* is posited as proceeding from the community or from the individual families which constitute the commune—he relates to the others as co-proprietors, as so many incarnations of the common property, or as independent proprietors like himself, independent private proprietors—beside whom the previously all-absorbing and all-predominant communal property is itself posited as a particular *ager publicus* alongside the many private landowners.[44]

Marx then gives illustrations of several of these 'original forms of property' that may occur within this range. In the first of these forms, 'an initial, naturally arisen spontaneous community appears as first presupposition'.

> Family, and the family extended as a clan, or through intermarriage between families, or combination of clans . . . . This naturally arisen clan community, or, if one will, pastoral society, is the first presupposition—the communality of blood, language, customs—for the *appropriation of the objective conditions* of their life, and of their life's reproducing and objectifying activity (activity as herdsmen, hunters, tillers etc.). The earth is the great workshop, the arsenal which furnishes both means and material of labour, as well as the seat, the *base* of the community. They relate naively to it as the *property of the community*, of the community producing

---

[43] Ibid., p. 288.

[44] Karl Marx, *Grundrisse*, tr. Martin Nicolaus (Harmondsworth, 1973), p. 471.

and reproducing itself in living labour. Each individual conducts himself only as a link, as a member of this community as *proprietor* or *possessor*. The *real appropriation* through the labour process happens under these *presuppositions*, which are not themselves the *product* of labour, but appear as its natural or *divine* presuppositions.[45]

Now, 'with the same land-relation as its foundation', this form of property can 'realize itself' in many different ways. There could be little communities existing side by side, with individual families working independently on the plots assigned to them: the only part of their labour which is kept aside is for such purely communal expenses as 'war, religion etc.' and a certain communal reserve for purposes of insurance. On the other hand, there could be a communality of labour itself, as, says Marx, in Mexico or Peru, or among the early Celts or a few clans of India. Again, communality can appear in the form of the chief of a clan, or as a council of patriarchs. That is to say, the specific organization of communal authority associated with this form of property can have various forms—relatively more despotic or relatively more democratic. It could even appear, 'as in most of the Asiatic land forms', as a comprehensive unity standing above all the little communities, a unity represented in the person of the despot who appears as the sole proprietor of the land and the little communities of producers merely as hereditary producers. Here, the surplus product, 'determined by law in consequence of the real appropriation through labour', goes as tribute to this highest entity.[46]

The second 'original' form of property Marx describes is the 'ancient' form. Here too the community is the 'first presupposition', but the difference is that the base of the community is not the countryside but the town: 'the cultivated field here appears as a *territorium* belonging to the town'. The major communal activity

---

[45] Ibid., p. 472.

[46] Ibid., pp. 472-3. It is somewhat distressing to find even in recent writings extended discussions on the 'reality' of 'communal ownership' in pre-capitalist societies. Obviously, a mercantile notion of property rights in land is irrelevant in pre-capitalist formations, and Paul Bohannan, writing about land rights in pre-colonial Africa, quite correctly dismisses such a notion as 'silly'. He also shows that it was *after* the colonial penetration that the history of landed property in Africa was written on the basis of such a definition of 'communal ownership', doubtless to suit specific colonial interests. Paul Bohannan, 'Africa's Land' in George Dalton (ed.), *Tribal and Peasant Economies* (Garden City, N. Y., 1967), pp. 51-60.

here is war, 'the great communal labour which is required either to occupy the objective conditions of being there alive, or to protect and perpetuate the occupation'. The community here is therefore 'a negative unity towards the outside'.

> The commune—as state—is, on one side, the relation of these free and equal private proprietors to one another, their bond against the outside, and is at the same time their safeguard. The commune here rests as much on the fact that its members consist of working landed proprietors, small-owning peasants, as the peasants' independence rests on their mutual relations as commune members, on protection of the *ager publicus* for communal needs and communal glory etc. Membership in the commune remains the presupposition for the appropriation of land and soil, but, as a member of the commune, the individual is a private proprietor. He relates to his private property as land and soil, but at the same time as to his being as commune member; and his own sustenance as such is likewise the sustenance of the commune, and conversely etc.[47]

The third form is the 'Germanic'. Here neither is the commune member a co-possessor of the commune property as in the Oriental form, nor is there a separation between state property and private property as in classical antiquity. Rather, the commune exists only in the actual 'coming-together' of the individual members in an assembly. The individual households here are in fact independent centres of production, and the commune and communal property appear as forms 'mediated by, i.e. as a relation of, the independent subjects to one another.'[48]

It is clear then that there can be several empirical variants of the 'original form of property'. Moreover, there is no difficulty if later historical or anthropological research persuades us to extend, amend or even reject Marx's descriptions of some of these specific historical variants, or to add new ones to his list. The fundamental theoretical criterion on which the conceptualization of the 'original form' depends is the *presupposition* of a community; all allocation of social rights, i.e. of property, proceeds from this presupposition; the objective mode of existence of the labouring individual—his relation to land and to all the conditions of his labour—is thus mediated by his existence as member of this community. Many specific variations of this objective mode of existence, and hence of the concrete forms of

[47] *Grundrisse*, p. 475.
[48] Ibid., pp. 477-84.

'communal property', are possible. The evolution of each of these would depend 'partly on the natural inclinations of the tribe, and partly on the economic conditions in which it relates as proprietor to the land and soil in reality, i.e. in which it appropriates its fruits through labour, and the latter will itself depend on climate, physical make-up of the land and soil, the physically determined mode of its exploitation, the relation with hostile tribes or neighbour tribes, and the modifications which migrations, historic experiences etc. introduce.'[49]

It is also clear now that any conceptualization of exploitative class relations, e.g. slavery or serfdom, requires as a *theoretical presupposition* the logical existence of a concept of 'communal property'. Once again, it is useful to emphasize that one does not thereby need in each specific case an *empirical* discovery of the specific form of the original property: it seems safe to assert that given existing techniques of historical research, this would be virtually impossible in a number of cases. On the other hand, by looking at *historical* situations of instituted relations of class exploitation in pre-capitalist societies in terms of the categorical opposites *community/external domination*, one obtains a perspective into the historical process in which such forms of property are embedded, and it becomes possible thereby to conceptualize the contradictory character inherent in all such instituted forms of exploitation. Marx, for instance, gives the example of one clan conquered by another:

> The fundamental condition of property resting on the clan system (into which the community originally resolves itself) . . . makes the clan conquered by another clan *propertyless* and throws it among the *inorganic conditions* of the conqueror's reproduction, to which the conquering community relates as its own. Slavery and serfdom are thus only further developments of the forms of property resting on the clan system. They necessarily modify all the latter's forms.[50]

Thus, in this particular case, community is prior; slavery or serfdom are developments on the 'original' communal forms. It is clearly possible to generalize this logical sequence of conceptualization of evolving forms of property for every other process of the imposition of exploitative relations based on the superiority of physical force. In fact, Marx himself states this quite directly:

[49] Ibid., p. 486.
[50] Ibid., p. 493.

*Property*, then, originally means—in its Asiatic, Slavonic, ancient classical, Germanic form—the relation of the working (producing or self-reproducing) subject to the conditions of his production or reproduction as his own. . . . This relation as proprietor—not as a result but as a pre-supposition of labour, i.e. of production—presupposes the individual defined as a member of a clan or community (whose property the individual himself is, up to a certain point). Slavery, bondage etc., where the worker himself appears among the natural conditions of production for a third individual or community . . . —i.e. property no longer the relation of the working individual to the objective conditions of labour—is always secondary, derived, never original, although [it is] a necessary and logical result of property founded on the community and labour in the community.[51]

## Feudal State Formations

A feudal mode of power can, therefore, be seen to operate within a specific state formation only in opposition to a conception of social authority based on the community. In all political formations in which there exists an institutionalized sphere of class domination based ultimately on the direct superiority of physical force, it is in constant battle against subordinate forces seeking to assert (perhaps reassert) an alternative mode of power and authority based on the notion of the community. The *effective limits of domination* at any point of time are thus the *resultant* at that time of this inherently contradictory process.

By looking at the question of power in feudal political formations as the opposition between *feudal jurisdiction/community*, we are thus able to conceptualize the political process of struggle in these societies in terms of the opposites *domination/resistance*.

I cannot at this stage attempt anything like a full-scale examination of the many analytical implications of this framework. Here I will only take a few illustrations, drawn mainly from European history, to show what I think are some of the advantages of using this approach and also to point out some of the major problems which will need much greater clarification than is possible at the moment.

A central question, for instance, is the one of defining 'servitude', or conversely, 'freedom', in the context of feudal relations of production. Within the theory of modes of production, servitude would, of course, be defined in terms of the specific form of the 'property' connection between the labourer and non-labourer elements in a feudal system of production. That is to say, 'property' or the conditions of labour here

[51] Ibid., pp. 495-6.

are such that while the labourer possesses the means of his labour, he himself is part of the conditions of production for the non-labourer, in this case the lord, i.e. the labourer is a part of the landlord's 'property'. This defines the labourer's servitude, and a part of his labour (or its product) is appropriated by the lord as rent, whatever the specific form of appropriation. The lord's right to rent is thus a function of his rights of 'property' in the labourer's 'person' (exclusive of course of his means of labour). That is to say, these are rights amounting to the 'appropriation of an alien will',[52] i.e. rights extending into the 'life-process' of the labourer as distinct from the 'labour-process'. (This last qualification is what distinguishes servitude from slavery, because in the latter the master's rights of property in the slave's person include his means of labour as well—the slave is 'propertyless'.) These rights, however, have their basis in a direct relation of political domination by the lord over his 'subjects'. The appropriation of rent is directly dependent on the superiority of physical force.

Thus defined, servitude cannot only have different forms, depending in one aspect on the specific form in which the surplus is appropriated as rent, but can also vary in the range of incidence as well as in intensity. Thus, the form of rent could be cash, kind or labour, or a combination of these. As a limiting case, the non-producer element could even be organized in the form of a state and the exaction of the surplus could take the form of a tax or revenue. And the quantum of rent could vary greatly. The exact form and magnitude of feudal exaction is determined as the outcome of a process of struggle between the rent-exacting classes and the subordinate peasantry: this is what determines in any given context the specific meaning of 'servitude' or 'freedom'.

In most historical examples of such struggles, the form is one of a battle over 'rights'—the determination of the respective spheres of feudal jurisdiction and peasant rights. What is interesting in the European evidence is that the sphere of peasant rights is virtually coextensive with 'communal rights'. Duby is quite definite about what a 'free peasantry' meant in early medieval Europe:

> What was meant by [freedom] was not personal independence but the fact of belonging to the 'folk' (*populus*), of being answerable to public institutions. . . . The right to bear arms, to follow the war-leader on expeditions undertaken each spring, and so to share in the eventual profits of war, all constituted the basic criteria of liberty. Freedom also implied the duty of

[52] Ibid., pp. 500-1.

assembling at regular intervals to declare the law and to do justice. Finally, it gave men a voice in the collective exploitation of patches of wasteland and in decisions on whether or not to welcome newcomers to the community of 'neighbours' (*vicini*).[53]

The extension of feudal jurisdiction and the increasing servitude of the peasantry essentially meant the erosion of institutionalized communal rights.

The most important gains made by the great estates took place at the expense, not of neighbouring estates, but of the still independent peasantry. Some peasant resistance was encountered within the nascent village community. Associations of 'neighbours' were gathering strength around the parish church and the collective possession of customary rights. It is even possible (for the class struggle may now have assumed this basic pattern) that peasants had been forming special associations to protect them from oppression by the rich.[54]

In many of the Romanized provinces, however, peasant freedom was eroded considerably. 'Nevertheless', Duby points out, 'the loss of liberty was not total',[55] and even among the most dominated serf populations, communal solidarity was kept alive in such residual institutions as communal drinking:

The humblest workers in this poverty-stricken world would indulge in merrymaking, the object of which was now and then to rekindle a sense of brotherhood and to command the goodwill of the invisible powers through communal, short-lived and joyful destruction of wealth in the midst of a universe of privation. Such were *potationes*, ritual drinking bouts of

[53] Georges Duby, *The Early Growth of the European Economy: Warriors and Peasants from the Seventh to the Twelfth Century*, tr. Howard B. Clarke (London, 1970), p. 33. Also see the excellent survey of the social forms of the medieval European peasantry in Rodney Hilton, *Bond Men Made Free* (London, 1973), pp. 25-134. It may be added here that the question of servitude or freedom should not be confused with notions of 'equality' for there was considerable inequality among the medieval European peasantry. See Rodney Hilton, 'Reasons for Inequality among Medieval Peasants', *Journal of Peasant Studies*, 5:3 (Apr. 1978), pp. 271-84.

[54] Ibid., p. 94. In the case of the Frankish kingdom, Mitteis says: 'The Frankish constitution may be defined as personal monarchy based upon folk-law. One sphere of national life remained, at least initially, outside the sphere of monarchy: the administration of justice was almost exclusively in the hands of the community, until at last royal influence began to infiltrate even this citadel of folk-law.' Heinrich Mitteis, *The State in the Middle Ages*, tr. H. F. Orton (Amsterdam, 1975), pp. 46-7.

[55] Ibid., p. 34

alcoholic beverages, aiming at one and the same time to half-open the gates of the unknowable and to reinforce group cohesion for mutual protection.[56]

Not only this. In the constant battle between feudal forces striving for greater dominance and the resistance of a subordinate peasantry waged through a wide variety of means ranging from deception to open rebellion, the balance of forces can be seen to oscillate in terms of the relative recognition of 'feudal' and 'communal' rights in the established structure of law, whether customary or codified.[57] Thus, the success of peasant resistance would often be marked by the grant of charters of liberties which would mean greater autonomy for village institutions;[58] on the other hand, increasing feudal power would mean not just a rise in the quantum of exaction but an extension of the sphere of feudal 'jurisdiction' in the matter of administering 'justice'. It is this structure of 'rights' which expressed the specific combination of the two contradictory modes of power in a given state structure. The balance was seldom stationary, and the resultant at any given moment of this struggle between the two opposing forces provided a definition of the 'degree' of servitude of the subordinate peasantry.

[56] Ibid., p. 53.

[57] In his classic study of medieval monarchy, Fritz Kern remarks: 'The medieval monarch, in a certain sense, was merely a communal head.' Thus, for a long time the monarch was chosen by kin-right. 'There is no need to deny that in most cases kin-right was supported by the overwhelmingly superior power and wealth of the royal house, and also by considerations of political expediency . . . (but) mere expediency is entirely insufficient to explain the tenacity with which folk-belief held fast to the notion of royal magic. . . .' Later, even after kin-right was transformed into hereditary right, 'this absolutism in practice never developed into absolutism in theory, and this, from our point of view, is the decisive point'. That is to say, '. . . the general conviction that the community's duty of obedience was not unconditional was deeply-rooted, and no one doubted that every member of the 'folk' had the right to resist and to take revenge if he were prejudiced in his rights by the prince. . . . This relationship . . . must not be designated simply as contract. The fundamental idea is rather that ruler and ruled alike are bound to the law; the fealty of both parties is in reality fealty to the law. . . . If, therefore, the king breaks the law, he automatically forfeits any claim to the obedience of his subjects.' Fritz Kern, *Kingship and Law in the Middle Ages*, tr. S. B. Chrimes (Oxford, 1956), pp. 6, 14, 81, 87.

[58] The most well-known set of such charters—the *Weistümer*—comes from late medieval Germany. See two recent studies on the content of these charters: David Sabean, 'German Agrarian Institutions at the Beginning of the Sixteenth Century: Upper Swabia as an Example', *Journal of Peasant Studies*, 3:1 (Oct. 1975), pp. 76-88; Heide Wunder, 'Village Community, Landlord and Political Power: Problems of Interaction in Early Modern Prussia': paper presented to the Peasants Seminar, University of London, 1978.

## The Communal Mode of Power in Feudal State Formations

Of course, since it is politics we are talking about, and politics of a sort carried out within the regularly ordered process of a relatively stable state formation, notions of authority, legitimacy, jurisdiction, resistance, rebellion, must be seen as incorporated within a unified and apparently consistent system of beliefs representing the dominant social ideology. The normal 'function' of such ideologies is always to provide legitimacy to existing structures of domination. In large and well-developed kingdoms and empires, this takes on the elaborate cultural form of a state-wise religion tying peasant communities, towns and state into a single 'great tradition'.[59] Yet, the process of legitimation itself contains within it—in myths, rituals, ceremonies, customary practices, cultural institutions, literary and aesthetic ideals, and in such values as kinship, reciprocity, paternalism, mutual trust, and so on—the signs of feudal dominium coming to terms in a relatively stable balance of forces with the world of the peasant communities. As a result, the same set of ethical norms or religious practices which justify existing relations of domination also contain, in a single dialectical unity, the justification for legitimate revolt. Let me give just one example of a phenomenon that has been noticed on numerous occasions in many different places and periods. During the revolt in Catalonia in 1640, 'rumours of strange and miraculous events spread with extraordinary speed. When the troops burnt the church of Riurdarenes, tears were seen to fall from the eyes of the Virgin in a picture of the church.' The bishop pronounced this rumour a sacrilege.

> It was only one step from excommunication by the bishop to a proclamation by the rebels that they were fighting for God and their churches. Inevitably, the episcopal censure was regarded by the insurgents as a complete vindication of their activities. It gave the rising the character of a Holy War—an idea already suggested by the miraculous tears of the Virgin and encouraged by the clergy and members of the religious orders, who told them that divine retribution was now being meted out to soldiers whom temporal justice had failed to punish.[60]

It is this inherent contradictoriness of established ideologies in feudal society which creates the possibility for these sudden inversions in signification which are so much a feature of peasant revolts. The

[59] Robert Redfield, *Peasant Society and Culture: An Anthropological Approach to Civilization* (Chicago, 1956).

[60] J. H. Elliott, *The Revolt of the Catalans: A Study in the Decline of Spain (1598-1640)* (Cambridge, 1963), pp. 426-7.

anthropologist Victor Turner has suggested that these events, and particularly the millenarian ideologies which often accompany revolts of this kind, should be seen as a kind of liminal behaviour, specifically as rituals of status reversal.[61] He argues that when society acquires a specific structure in terms of jural, political and economic positions—'differentiated, culturally structured, segmented and often hierarchical system of institutionalised positions'[62]—resistance or revolt often takes on the form of what he calls *communitas*. 'Beyond the structural lies communitas'; in contrast to segmented and hierarchical society, there is now a 'direct, immediate and total confrontation of human identities' and a belief in a model of society which is homogeneous, unstructured communitas.[63] Several features of millenarian movements have the properties of liminality, their rituals those of rites of passage: homogeneity, equality, anonymity, absence of property, reduction of all to the same status level, the wearing of uniform apparel, sexual continence (or its antithesis, sexual community), minimization of sex distinctions, abolition of rank, humility, disregard for personal appearance, unselfishness, total obedience to the prophet or leader, sacred instruction, the maximization of religious (as opposed to secular) attitudes and behaviour, suspension of kinship rights and obligations, simplicity of speech and manners, sacred folly, acceptance of pain and suffering.[64] Of course, the spontaneity and immediacy of communitas can hardly be sustained for long. Soon it returns to the domain of structure, either reverting to the old segmentations and hierarchies, or perhaps to a structure modified by the impact of the revolt. The revolt is only a moment in the historical process of domination/resistance. Its structure is to be found not in any novel reorganization of social relations, but rather, 'in Lévi-Straussian way', in 'the lurid and colourful imagery of the apocalyptic myths generated in the milieu of existential communitas'.[65] The power of the community is 'structured' in ideology: 'rules that abolish minutiae of structural differentiation in, for example, the domains of kinship, economics, and political structure

---

[61] Victor W. Turner, *The Ritual Process: Structure and Anti-structure* (London, 1969), p. 167.

[62] Ibid., p. 177.

[63] Ibid., pp. 131-2.

[64] Ibid., p. 111.

[65] Ibid., p. 153.

liberate the human structural propensity and gives it free reign in the cultural realm of myth, ritual and symbol'[66]—'an almost febrile, visionary and prophetic poetry [is] their main genre of cultural utterance'.[67]

One can, in fact, go further and note the many other possibilities which arise because of the contradictory character of ideologies legitimizing structures of domination—the many ambiguities in meaning which create possibilities for manoeuvre both by forces seeking to consolidate or extend their domination in tune with changing circumstances and by subordinate groups rising in revolt. I cite two examples, this time from a completely different historical situation. Among tribes in southern and eastern Africa with political formations made up of different types of combination of corporate kin authority and centralized state structures, there often exist two sorts of religious cults and rituals—one involving 'spirits of the household' invoked by lineage sections or segmented kin groups, and the other consisting of 'spirits of the land' invoked for the well-being of the country, defined in terms of territory, in which all, irrespective of kin linkages, take part. The history of the Mang'anja people, for instance, shows that with successive waves of migration and conquest, and the re-establishment of a political order following each of these upheavals, these cults expressing different combinations of kin solidarity and hierarchic rule have taken different forms and have been manipulated to serve different ruling interests.[68] Conversely, at the time of the 1896 uprising against white colonial rulers in southern Rhodesia, the rebel leadership of Mkwati attempted to unify in a common cause the traditionally hostile Ndebele and Shona tribesmen (the Shona were tributary tribes of Ndebele). He did this by appealing to the memories of the pre-Ndebele past and by invoking the Mlimo cult by which kinship ties are supposed to have been established among the various tribes through a woman who was made 'grandmother' of all the Matabele peoples. Mkwati, therefore, was not

---

[66] Ibid., p. 133.
[67] Ibid., p. 153.
[68] Matthew Schoffeleers, 'The History and Political Role of the M'Bona Cult among the Mang'anja', in T. O. Ranger and I. N. Kimambo (eds.), *The Historical Study of African Religions* (London, 1972), pp. 73-94. Also see I. N. Kimambo and C. K. Omari, 'The Development of Religious Thought and Centres among the Pare', in ibid., pp. 111-21.

merely using the support provided by a 'traditional' religious system. He was transforming the material provided by these religious elements 'into something more radical and revolutionary'. Mkwati's was, therefore, 'a prophetic leadership operating over and above all the restrictions implied by hierarchic order and links with the past'.

> He had no claim before the rising to be the senior Mwari cult representative. It was just before and especially during the rising that he emerged as 'the great Mlimo'. . . . When he did so it was with a revolutionary message and a revolutionary set of instructions. His followers were promised invulnerability and even immortality; they entered a new society which transcended the old. . . . When the rising became really desperate, the authority of the Mkwati and the other cult officers who had chosen the same path was elevated above that of 'traditional' political authority; *indunas* and chiefs were deposed. For however brief a period Mkwati was seeking not merely to co-ordinate but to create a 'new order'.[69]

This last example also points to another important feature of communal authority: the ability to *produce* a suitable leadership when the community needs to resist external forces of domination. Communal resistance could, of course, be carried out under the leadership of customarily recognized communal leaders and through the medium of traditional communal institutions. On the other hand, since it is the community as a whole which is the source of all authority, no one is a permanent repository of delegated powers. Hence, when the need arises, traditional leaders may suddenly be replaced or superseded by new ones who have had no previous standing in the customarily recognized arrangement of communal authority. This is a feature very common in historical examples of peasant revolts. It also makes it possible for the community to act as a community in specific instances of resistance even when there do not exist under normal circumstances any recognized institutional arrangements for the exercise of communal authority.

The structure of communal authority must be located primarily in the domain of ideology. It is possible, of course, as we have seen in some of the examples discussed above, for a given peasant community to possess specific institutional arrangements for the self-regulation of communal life when specialized state institutions are absent, or even when it operates in a vaguely and flexibly demarcated field

[69] T. O. Ranger, *Revolt in Southern Rhodesia 1896-7: A Study in African Resistance* (London, 1967), p. 214.

within a larger state structure. However, within a dialectical process defined principally in terms of domination/resistance, the institutional structures are best seen as representing a certain temporary state of equilibrium within a definite system of production and a definite arrangement of the relations of dominance/subordination. The principal dynamics *within* such a system, i.e. the class struggle *within* a specific pre-capitalist formation, must be located fundamentally in the political ('extra-economic', if you will) domain of the struggle over 'rights'. And, here, depending on the specific strategic configuration of the struggle, not only can the agents of communal authority change suddenly and spectacularly, but even the definition of the community—its boundaries—can shift. The strategic configuration may vary with changing techno-economic conditions of production or with changes in the feudal organization of power. But the conditions which make possible a specific expression of the identity and authority of a community in a specific context of struggle must be located above all in the domain of ideology.[70]

If one looks once again at the evidence on the European peasantry in the medieval age, the smallest communal unit appears to be the village, defined territorially as the agglomeration of contiguous parcels of land each of which is referred to as the *manse* or the *huba* or the hide, and each of which is occupied by an individual household.

> We understand by this an enclosure, solidly rooted to its site by a permanent barrier such as a palisade or a living hedge, carefully maintained, a protected asylum to which the entry was forbidden and the violation of which was punished by severe penalties: an island of refuge where the occupant was assumed to be the master and at whose threshold communal servitude and the demands of chiefs and lords stopped short.[71]

[70] It is worth suggesting a clarification here to a problem which often crops up in attempts to use the term 'peasantry' as an economic category for describing a certain productive organization of society. Entirely justified criticisms have been made of conceptions such as a 'peasant' or a 'domestic' mode of production. See for example, Judith Ennew, Paul Hirst and Keith Tribe, ' "Peasantry" as an Economic Category', *Journal of Peasant Studies*, 4:4 (July 1977), pp. 295-322. Yet the problem has persisted bringing within the received range of analytical categories phenomena relating to the *political* role of the peasantry in feudal or other state formations. The proposal here is to construct an explicit set of categories relating to the specification of the 'property' connection in different social formations, thus providing the analytical complement to the set of 'economic' categories describing a mode of production.

[71] Georges Duby, *Rural Economy and Country Life in the Medieval West*, tr. Cynthia Postan (London, 1968), p. 7.

However, in the European case, this territorial definition of the village as the sum of the *manses*, the arable land and the meadows, grazing grounds, forests etc., used by the community is coupled with a specific institutional arrangement:

> The unity of the *terroir* is always sanctioned and embodied by a communal body, the 'assembly of inhabitants', which abides by traditional rulings and occasionally makes new ones to ensure that where the exploitation of the land is the concern of the community it operates in the common interest. . . . What normally complicates (or perhaps simplifies) matters is that the parish 'religious' assembly often became identified in the long run with the 'agricultural' assembly of inhabitants, where concurrent debates tackled material problems to do with the church, agrarian problems to do with the *terroir* and even fiscal problems, principally those raised by the collection of royal taxation.[72]

Underlying the territorial definition, then, is a *social* conception of the group as united by ties of solidarity. In other contexts, these could take on the more explicit form of ties of kinship—real affinal connections, or imagined (perhaps fabricated) beliefs of common lineage, or lineages related to one another in specific ways that are sanctified in mythology and ritual. These bonds of affinity contain possibilities of manipulation. Thus, the boundaries of community could vary with varying contexts of collective action. The point which distinguishes the communal mode from other modes or organization of power is this: here it is *not* a perception of common interests which compels organization to achieve unity; there is rather the conviction that bonds of affinity *already exist* which then become the natural presupposition for collective action.

## The State-Lord-Peasant Triad

One important element which affects the context of communal resistance is the feudal organization of power. A specific feudal structure has its own history, encompassing movements of population, conquest and subjugation, the stabilization of complex relations of obligation and reciprocity with the subordinate population, incorporation into larger state structures, and so on. In developed kingdoms and empires, these could acquire an elaborate hierarchical structure of overlordship and vassalage. On the other hand, the

[72] Pierre Goubert, *The Ancien Régime: French Society 1600-1750*, tr. Steve Cox (London, 1973), pp. 78-9.

dominant power structure could take on the form of an overarching state bureaucracy with the complex hierarchical organization of the military-bureaucratic nobility. Political struggles in this situation can be analysed within the framework of a triad: king/state—lords/officials—peasantry. Various strategic combinations of the three elements are possible. One often finds in the history of medieval peasant revolts occasions in which the externality and distance of the monarchy can make it the ideological ally of a peasantry engaged in a struggle with local lords and officials. Thus, Elliott writes of the Catalan revolt of 1640:

> Even though more than a century of royal absenteeism had gradually weakened the patriarchal and formal ties between the king and his Catalan subjects they still looked upon him as a father who—if once the just complaints of his children were allowed to reach his ears—would promptly act to right their wrongs and remove the cause of their distresses. If the rebel bands shouted 'Death to traitors!' they also shouted, with equal enthusiasm, 'Long live the king!' The instinctive loyalty of the peasantry to a king they scarcely knew is not really very surprising.[73]

Then again, in France at the time of the *ancien régime*, the peasantry resisted the domination of all those rural patriarchs who collected 'feudal rights'. Here, writes Goubert,

(a) The king and kingship inspire loyalty and love;
(b) But there is deep-seated resentment of the financial methods of the monarchy, although it is hoped that the good king and the States-General will reform them;
(c) The majority protest against various feudal rights, or against all of them, or against the principle of them . . .
(d) There is at least equally powerful resentment, not of the principle of tithes but of the way they are collected, their unfairness, exorbitance and inconsistencies, and above all of the fact that they have been diverted from their original aim (hardly any of the *cahiers* are hostile to religion itself) . . .[74]

And yet, the events leading up to the Revolution were to culminate in popular action against the person of the king and his family. On the other hand, there are numerous instances in the history of medieval kingdoms and empires where the peasantry, especially in outlying and peripheral regions, are found resisting the encroachments of the larger kingdom in alliance with local chiefs and magnates. The

[73] Elliott, op. cit., p. 468.   [74] Goubert, op. cit., p. 11.

externality of the institution of monarchy makes its position quite ambivalent in relation to the present communities.

It is even possible to argue that there exists in peasant ideology a distinction between kings and kingship, and that a revolt against a king is not necessarily a revolt against kingship. That is to say, political struggles in feudal society, defined as a process of domination/resistance and occurring in a strategic context defined by relations within the state-landlord-peasantry triad, can be seen as a political process *within* a particular feudal state formation. As Gluckman says of rebellions in African kingdoms:

> ... societies which have a stagnant techno-economy have conflicts which can be resolved by changing the individuals occupying office or in relationship with one another, without changing the pattern of the offices or relationships. Politically, it means that a rebellion changes the king, but does not affect the kingship—nay, may even strengthen the kingship, against a tyrant who has broken its norms. Secondly, it means that the territorial sections of a kingdom struggle against the central power and each other, without disrupting the central authority.[75]

The distinction between the modes of power thus enables us to define the field of possibilities: a specific combination within the state-lord-peasant triad then becomes open to specific explanations in particular historical contexts. But thereby it also enables us to discuss the conditions which make possible the suppression, dissolution or re-appropriation of particular modes of power in the wider historical context of the transition from feudalism to capitalism.

## The Modes of Power Under Capitalism

The transition to capitalism, i.e. the historical triumph of the capitalist mode of production, also implies the rise to dominance in the state formation of a new mode of exercise of power. I have described earlier the main features of what I have called the *bourgeois* mode of power. I will not elaborate on it any further here, since, while the central attributes of the ideological conception of the state in liberal constitutional theory are well known, the actual mechanisms of the exercise of class domination in capitalist societies are a subject of considerable dispute and debate. It is not possible to stretch the implications of the framework proposed above so as to make a contribution to any of those specific debates until much further work

[75] Max Gluckman, *Order and Rebellion in Tribal Africa* (London, 1963), pp. 86-7.

is carried out into historical materials on the development of political institutions and processes in the modern period. The following comments are, therefore, entirely tentative and hypothetical.

First of all, it may be worth reconsidering the histories of the emergence of the capitalist nation-states of the world in order to delineate the specific paths by which a characteristically bourgeois mode of power gains ascendancy. It is certain that even in the most classical case of the rise to hegemony of the bourgeoisie and the complete sway of a capitalist mode of production, the evolution of *political* processes will reveal non-linearities, zigzags, disjunctures as well as continuities, representing numerous compromises with other modes of the exercise of power, and the survival and perhaps ultimate appropriation of feudal institutions, conceptions and forms of authority. One is reminded here of that rather cryptic comment by Marx in the *Grundrisse*. Talking about the *master-servant relation* in which the presupposition is that of 'the appropriation of an alien will', Marx remarks:

> … it forms a necessary ferment for the development and the decline and fall of all original relations of property and of production, just as it also expresses their limited nature. Still, it is reproduced—in mediated form— in capital, and thus likewise forms a ferment of its dissolution and is an emblem of its limitation.[76]

The identification of the specific differences in the rise of dominance of the bourgeois mode of power, and in the limits to this dominance, is central to a historical understanding of class struggles in individual capitalist countries in the phase of the rise of capitalism.

Here, a preliminary analytical tool would be the distinction between the modes of power. If one looks once again at the description given by Brenner of the difference in the transition processes in each of the European countries, one can immediately identify the main elements which describe the class struggles in this period: a feudalism in crisis, a rising bourgeoisie, the absolutist state, varying levels of organization of feudal power, varying degrees of solidarity among the peasantry. The first two elements describe what is potentially 'new' in the situation; together, they create the conditions of possibility for a transition. The specific process of transition would, however, be marked by a series of strategic configurations, shifting

[76] Marx, *Grundrisse*, p. 501.

from point to point according to the changing relative strengths and positions of each of these elements. An explicit categorization of the modes of power would, it seems to me, provide the necessary analytical complement to the task of identifying the techno-economic conditions for a transition: together, they not only provide a complete analytical encapsulation of the 'real appropriation' as well as the 'property' connections which describe a mode of production, but they also enable us to locate the element of 'indeterminacy' in the domain of the political.

The second point concerns the question of the peasantry in social formations dominated in some way or other by capitalism. It seems reasonable to argue that the establishment of bourgeois hegemony over all structures of society requires not so much the abolition of feudal institutions or feudal conceptions and symbols of authority, for these could in fact be appropriated and subsumed within a dominant bourgeois mode of exercise of power. What it requires rather i: the dissolution of the peasantry as a distinct social form of existence of productive labour, and hence the extinction of a communal mode of power. To the extent that a peasantry continues to exist as peasantry in a society dominated by a capitalism, it represents a limit to bourgeois hegemony.

This precisely is the kind of problem one encounters in countries which retain the character of large agrarian societies in the modern period of history. The usual features here are the intrusion of new extractive mechanisms into the agrarian economy, often with the active legal and armed support of a colonial political authority, leading to a systematic commercialization of agriculture and the incorporation in varying degrees of the agrarian economy into a larger capitalist world-market; the growth of a new industrial sector, usually of a limited nature in comparison with the absolute size of the economy and with varying combinations of foreign, 'comprador' and 'national' capital; the growth of new political institutions and processes based on bourgeois conceptions of law, bureaucracy and representation. The result is a differential impact on pre-capitalist structures—sometimes destroying them, sometimes modifying them to fit in with the new demands of surplus extraction and the new procedures of governance, and at other times keeping intact, perhaps bolstering, pre-existing productive systems and local organizations of power while merely establishing a suitable extractive mechanism.[77] The analytical problems which arise in the course of characterizing the relations of production or state formations which develop in these situations are numerous, and have been much debated.

The usual analytical frame in which the impact of a colonial economy on the peasantry is studied is one of differentiation—the growth of different strata within the peasantry and the progressive increase in the differences between them in terms of incomes, assets and economic viability. The problem that is often encountered, however, is that of relating this process to the political role of the peasantry in colonial (and post-colonial) societies. For here, once again, we find many asymmetries between the changing patterns of solidarity within the peasantry in their political actions and the structures of interests one would expect to find if the peasantry were seen as an amalgam of differentiated strata. Many unexpected possibilities are created here because of the combination of different modes of power—the conscious organization of group interests into larger alliances or coalitions, the continued perception of state institutions as agencies of external domination, the sudden expressions of solidarity on the presupposition that there already exist affinal bonds (which now begin to be called, in contrast with the new modes of organization of interests, 'primordial loyalties'), and the countless avenues of manipulation, mobilization and appropriation into larger structures of power that are opened up as a consequence. Talking about the innovations in the mechanisms of power in modern-day capitalist society, Michel Foucault has drawn our attention to the 'capillary form of existence' of power, 'the point where power reaches into the very grain of individuals, touches their bodies and inserts itself into their actions and attitudes, their discourses, learning processes and everyday lives. The eighteenth century invented, so to speak, a synaptic regime of power, a regime of its exercise *within* the social body, rather than *from above* it. . . . This more-or-less coherent modification in the small-scale modes of exercise of power was made possible only by a fundamental structural change. It was the instituting of this new local, capillary form of power which impelled society to

[77] For a remarkably incisive description of these differential effects in a specific region, see the study of the evolution of village communities in Wallachia and Moldavia from the thirteenth to the twentieth centuries in Henri H. Stahl, *Traditional Romanian Village Communities*, tr. Daniel Chirot and Holley Coulter Chirot (Cambridge, 1980).

eliminate certain elements such as the court and the king.[78] Foucault has sought to demonstrate the complexities of this novel regime of power in his studies of the history of mental illness, of clinical practice, of the prison, of sexuality and of the rise of the human sciences. When one looks at regimes of power in the so-called backward countries of the world today, not only does the dominance of the characteristically 'modern' modes of exercise of power seem limited and qualified by the persistence of older modes, but by the fact of their combination in a particular state formation, it seems to open up at the same time an entirely new range of possibilities for the ruling classes to exercise their domination.

[78] Michel Foucault, *Power/Knowledge*, tr. Colin Gordon, *et al.* (New York, 1980), p. 39.

# Touching the Body: Perspectives on the Indian Plague, 1896–1900*

## DAVID ARNOLD

> . . . nothing is more material, physical, corporal than the exercise of power.[1]

> What is medically desirable may be practically impossible and politically dangerous.[2]

The Indian plague epidemic which began in 1896 and claimed by 1930 more than 12 million lives[3] was so massive in scale and so fraught with political, social and demographic consequences that it could sustain many different approaches and interpretations.[4] This essay is not an attempt at a comprehensive account of India's plague

* I am grateful to Ian Catanach, Ranajit Guha and David Hardiman for their comments on an earlier draft, and to Sumit Sarkar, Gautam Bhadra and others who contributed to the discussion on the paper at the Calcutta Subaltern Studies conference in January 1986. I also wish to thank the Nuffield Foundation for a grant which enabled me to conduct research for this essay in India in January–March 1985.

[1] M. Foucault, *Power/Knowledge: Selected Interviews and Writings, 1972–1977* (Brighton, 1980), pp. 57–8.

[2] R. Harvey, Sanitary Commissioner to the Government of India, 18 April 1898, India, Home, 784, August 1898, National Archives of India, New Delhi (hereafter NAI).

[3] *Annual Report of the Public Health Commissioner with the Government of India, 1929*, (Calcutta, 1932), I, p.69. The plague epidemic was at its height between 1898 and 1908, during which time over 6 million deaths were recorded: L. F. Hirst, *The Conquest of Plague: A Study of the Evolution of Epidemiology* (London, 1953), p. 299.

[4] Among those currently working on plague in India are Ian Catanach and Michelle B. McAlpin. I am grateful to Amal Das for enabling me to see his unpublished paper on the Calcutta plague.

years. It examines only the epidemic's first, most turbulent phase, not its long, more quiescent coda. It seeks to understand the plague less as an epidemiological phenomenon than as a commentary upon the developing relationship between indigenous élites, subaltern classes and the colonial state. In these terms the plague was often of less importance than the state intervention that accompanied or preceded it. Tilak's *Mahratta* claimed with some justification in June 1897 that no measure undertaken by the British in India had 'interfered so largely and in such a systematic way with the domestic, social and religious habits of the people' as the current plague administration.[5] That the colonial government and colonial medicine attempted such forceful and far-reaching controls was indicative of the interventionist ambitions and capacity of India's mature colonial state. This was not the remote and shadowy presence British power in India is sometimes made out to be. It could (and during the early plague years commonly did) intervene directly in the lives of the people and elicit a potent response. And yet the very strength of the political and cultural backlash against the plague administration is a reminder of the practical limitations to that power and of the extent to which regulatory systems tend to be less absolute, less one-dimensional, than the writings of Foucault or Goffman would lead us to believe. Only through an awareness of the dialectical nature of such encounters is it possible to avoid assumptions of mass 'passivity' and 'fatalism'.

The plague dramatized the importance of the body—the body, that is to say, of the colonized—as a site of conflict between colonial power and indigenous politics. During the early phase of the epidemic the body had a specific medical, administrative and social significance: much of the interventionist thrust of the state was directed towards its apprehension and control, just as much of the resistance to plague measures revolved around bodily evasion or concealment. The body, however, was also profoundly symbolic of a wider and more enduring field of contention between indigenous and colonial perceptions, practices and concerns. The exercise of British power touched in many ways upon the issue of the Indian body. Moreover, as the early plague years demonstrated, the prob-

[5] *Mahratta* (Pune), 27 June 1897. Apart from the *Mahratta*, seen on microfilm at the Nehru Memorial Library, New Delhi, all the newspaper reports cited are to be found in the official selections from the vernacular press for the respective provinces, 1896–1900.

lematic was not only one of a colonial divide. It also deeply involved the growing assertion of a middle-class hegemony over the mass of the population and the equivocal responses—part resistance, part emulation—which such hegemonic aspirations evoked among the subaltern classes.

I

India's colonial state could never aspire to an absolute and exclusive control over the body of each and every one of its subjects. But there existed a latent claim that became operative in certain administrative, judicial and medical contexts. The early-nineteenth-century attempts to abolish *sati* and female infanticide were preliminary demonstrations of this arrogation of corporal power. Colonial penology is rich in other illustrations. Until well into the second half of the nineteenth century exemplary punishments were meted out against the living bodies and corpses of prominent rebels. Whipping persisted as a colonial mode of punishment and deterrence as late as the Quit India movement of 1942. Transportation, viewed with increasing disfavour in early-nineteenth-century Europe, was seized upon in India as a 'weapon of tremendous power', especially against Hindus with their fear of crossing the 'black water'.[6] Normally, however, the prison regime respected caste differences and sensibilities, seeking, for example, to devise forms of employment that would not be unduly offensive or demeaning to higher-caste convicts. And while exemplary punishments were in times of crisis and rebellion deemed necessary and legitimate, the British sought to demonstrate a superiority over pre-colonial 'barbarity' by condemning torture, mutilation and indefinite imprisonment without trial. The introduction of *habeas corpus* was one expression of this colonial concern. T.B. Macaulay conveyed the duality of British attitudes in 1835 when he called for a penal system in India that would be free from 'any circumstances shocking to humanity' and yet still 'a terror to wrong-doers'.[7]

For most of the nineteenth century colonial medicine was loath to venture where colonial penology had led. Although from early in the century attempts were made to supplant the indigenous (and

[6] *Report of the Committee on Prison Discipline* (Calcutta, 1838), p. 97.
[7] Cited in A. P. Howell, *Note on Jails and Jail Discipline in India, 1867–68* (Calcutta, 1868), p. 1.

reputedly dangerous) practice of smallpox inoculation with Jenner's cowpox vaccination, it was not until the 1870s and 1880s that this policy received legislative sanction. Even then compulsory vaccination was confined to major towns and cantonments.[8] Still more restricted and controversial was the Contagious Diseases Act of 1868, introduced to check the spread of venereal disease between Indian prostitutes and European soldiers. It was repealed in 1886.[9] As this latter example suggests, the primary responsibility of Western medicine in India until late in the century was still to minister to the health of the colonizers, not the colonized, except in so far as Indian soldiers, servants, plantation labourers and prostitutes constituted an apparent danger to European well-being. Financial as well as political constraints discouraged the colonial state from a greater degree of medical intervention.

There was, however, a substantial shift in state attitudes in the late nineteenth century. European health in India, it was increasingly argued, could only be assured through wider medical and sanitary measures. Epidemics, like the famines with which they frequently allied, were an unwelcome tax upon the profitability of empire. Sanitary reform and the curbing of epidemic smallpox and cholera in Britain created pressure for similar campaigns in India, while the advances made by Pasteur, Koch and others in the new science of bacteriology created a confidence among British medical men in India that epidemic diseases could be 'conquered' through the application of Western scientific knowledge and reason. It was at this juncture that the plague arrived in India. The first deaths occurred at Bombay in August 1896, and within three or four years the disease had spread to every province of the Indian empire. Before 1900 mainly an urban phenomenon, the epidemic was moving steadily, seemingly remorselessly, into the countryside. The urban focus of the disease in the early years was reflected in the greater intensity of plague operations in the towns and cities. This in turn partly explains the urban character of much of the early resistance to plague measures, though it had also been remarked in earlier decades that vaccination too often encountered greater opposition in the towns than in the rural areas.[10]

[8] D. Arnold, 'Smallpox and Colonial Medicine in India' (forthcoming).

[9] K. Ballhatchet, *Race, Sex and Class under the Raj: Imperial Attitudes and Policies and their Critics, 1793–1905* (London, 1980).

[10] E.g. *Returns of Vaccination for the North-Western Provinces, 1872–73*

After a brief period of medical uncertainty and administrative hesitancy, the provincial government in Bombay, backed by the Government of India, introduced measures which, in the words of W.C. Rand, Pune's Plague Commissioner, were 'perhaps the most drastic that had ever been taken in British India to stamp out an epidemic.'[11] On 6 October 1896 the Bombay government sanctioned a programme for the disinfection and destruction of infected property under the Bombay Municipal Act of 1888. Four months later the Epidemic Diseases Act gave the government the power to detain and segregate plague suspects, to destroy property, inspect, disinfect, evacuate and even demolish dwellings suspected of harbouring the plague, to prohibit fairs and pilgrimages, to examine road and rail travellers—in short, to do almost anything medical and official opinion believed to be necessary for the suppression of the disease.[12] In Bombay, Pune, Karachi and Calcutta responsibility for health and sanitation was taken away from municipal councils and entrusted to small committees of European doctors and civil servants. In practice, even if not in theory, Indian opinion was brushed aside. Caste and religion were afforded scant recognition except as obstacles to the implementation of the necessary sanitary programme. The proclamation issued by Bombay's Municipal Commissioner on 6 October 1896 announced that all plague cases would be hospitalized, by force if necessary. It was not explained that relatives would be permitted to visit the sick nor that caste was to be respected in the hospital arrangements. A directive from the city's Surgeon-General in December 1896 stated that while caste 'prejudices' would be observed as far as possible, they could not be allowed to stand in the way of essential sanitary and medical measures.[13] Never before had the medical profession in British India commanded such public power and exercised it with such administrative arrogance.

Behind the urgent and far-reaching nature of these measures lay several considerations. Plague, although present in some parts of

---

(Allahabad, 1873), pp. 29–30; *Report on Vaccination throughout the Bombay Presidency and Sind for the Year 1861* (Bombay, 1862), p. 2.

[11] *Supplement to the Account of Plague Administration in the Bombay Presidency from September 1896 till May 1897* (no publication details), p. 3.

[12] M. E. Couchman, *Account of the Plague Administration in the Bombay Presidency from September 1896 till May 1897* (Bombay, 1897), pp. 3, 32.

[13] Ibid., p. 3.

India during the nineteenth century, was seen in 1896 as an invading disease which had to be checked before it could establish itself. Appearing first in Bombay (probably as a result of importation from Hong Kong), the plague challenged the prosperity of one of British India's premier ports and administrative centres. Apart from the threat to Bombay's own commerce and industry, the economic pressure for prompt action was increased by the possibility of an European embargo on Indian trade unless the epidemic was quickly brought under control. But no less powerful was the medical pressure from experts in Britain and India who argued that the disease could be stopped from spreading if only the appropriate measures were promptly and thoroughly implemented.

At this stage, too, the etiology of the plague was not fully understood. The role of rats in its transmission was still generally thought secondary to that of man: the part played by rats' fleas was not finally established until 1908.[14] The human body—and the clothes, bedding and habitations associated with it—was thought to be the disease's principal vector. The perceived centrality of the human body was further emphasized by the difficulty at first experienced in identifying the disease. A physical examination was made to try to find the characteristic buboes or swellings; in dubious cases post mortems were used to search for internal evidence. The body was thus both the presumed vector of the disease and the bearer of its diagnostical signs. It followed that anti-plague measures concentrated upon the interception, examination and confinement of the body. This entailed a form of direct medical intervention that swept aside the rival or preferential claims of relatives and friends, *vaids* and *hakims* (Hindu and Muslim medical practitioners respectively), religious and caste leaders. The body, as in the West, was treated as a secular object, not as sacred territory, as an individual entity, not as an element integral to a wider community. The body, moreover, was exposed not just to the 'gaze' of Western medicine but also to its physical touch, an intrusion of the greatest concern to a society in which touch connoted possession or pollution.

## II

The Foucauldian analogy between the prison and the hospital, between penology and medicine, was most evident in the recourse to

[14] Hirst, *Conquest of Plague*, pp. 172–4.

hospitalization and segregation. In the colonial perception India's social and physical environment was seen as injurious to bodily and moral well-being, constituting both the cause and the context of crime and disease. Reform or cure could, it was believed, best be effected by removing the individual from his customary environment and placing him within a 'rational' and orderly prison or hospital regime. In penology this attitude gave rise not only to the prison but also to the reformatories for former *thugs* and to the settlements for 'criminal tribes'. In medicine there was a preference for hospitals over dispensaries in the belief that the former offered better opportunities for isolation, observation and control.

In India, too, climatic and miasmatic theories of disease causation persisted longer than in Europe, perhaps from the strength of Western antipathy to India's physical and social environment. The accounts of the plague compiled by Brigadier-General Gatacre as chairman of Bombay's plague committee in 1897, and by R. Nathan for the Government of India in 1898, placed particular emphasis upon the 'insanitary and filthy conditions' to be found in Indian towns and villages as 'predisposing causes' of the disease. Removal to the sanitized and orderly world of the plague hospital and segregation camp was thus seen as essential for the effective containment and treatment of the disease. Gatacre went so far as to claim that during an epidemic the plague hospital was one of the safest places to be. The disease did not appear to him normally to be contagious except in conditions of 'overcrowding, destitution, deficient cubic space, ventilation and sunlight.'[15] The instructions issued to Gatacre by Lord Sandhurst as Governor of Bombay in March 1897 listed as priorities the discovery of all plague cases, the treatment of all plague cases in hospital, and the segregation of all suspected cases, as far as possible, it was added, respecting 'native usages.'[16]

Although European medical theory and practice were gaining acceptance, especially among the Western-educated middle class, there was general repugnance at the ways in which the policy of segregation and hospitalization was carried out. 'Rightly or wrongly', wrote the *Gujarati* of Bombay on 18 October 1896, 'the feeling of the Native community is strongly against segregation.' It argued

[15] W. F. Gatacre, *Report on the Bubonic Plague in Bombay, 1896–97* (Bombay, 1897), pp. 50–1; R. Nathan, *Plague in Northern India, 1896, 1897* (Simla, 1898), I, pp. 71–90.

[16] *Mahratta*, 14 March. 1897.

that social customs, religious sentiments and 'the strong ties of affection' were all against it. 'The very idea', the paper explained, 'of tearing off one's dear relative from those affectionately devoted to him and of his departing the world without the usual religious ministrations is revolting to the mind of the Native community.' In petitions as well as in newspaper editorials and correspondence columns the same basic view was frequently repeated. Indian values and sentiments were contrasted with the 'indifference and callousness' of Western medicine and the colonial administration.[17] In trying to explain the unpopularity of hospitals the *Mahratta* of 21 November 1897 pointed, among other things, to the difficulty patients had in keeping in touch with their families. The sick man was nursed, the paper maintained, not by caring relatives and friends but by people who were 'at best mere strangers, invariably callous and patent mercenaries'. In Western eyes a sanitized and healing environment, the hospital was to many Indians (not least to the higher castes) a place of pollution, contaminated by blood and faeces, inimical to caste, religion and *purdah*. The *Kesari* of 6 April 1897 carried in illustration of such antipathies the story of a Brahmin who had had to live on milk while in hospital because the food had been polluted by a Sudra's touch. The *Mahratta* six weeks later, on 23 May 1897, complained that caste observances were being violated in Pune's general hospital and protested against the impending closure of the city's Hindu Plague Hospital, where, it said, caste was scrupulously respected.

In Bombay, as later in other major cities, the government tried, once it began to realize the strength of public opposition to hospitalization, to meet such objections and fears by encouraging the setting up of special caste or community hospitals. By early 1898 there were more than thirty such institutions in Bombay. Along with other concessions (such as the right of patients to be treated by their own vaids and hakims), this did much (at least among the middle classes) to overcome the deep suspicion of hospitals and hospital treatment.[18]

Although opposition to segregation and hospitalization was commonly expressed in the idiom of male pollution and deprivation, it

[17] *Gujarati*, 18 April. 1897.
[18] J. M. Campbell, *Report of the Bombay Plague Committee on the Plague in Bombay, 1st July 1897 to 30th April 1898* (Bombay, 1898), pp. 60, 137f.

was the seizure of women and their removal to camps and hospitals that provoked some of the fiercest resistance. Nearly a thousand mill-hands attacked Bombay's Arthur Road hospital on 29 October 1896 after a woman worker had been taken there as a suspected plague sufferer.[19] On 9 March 1898 Julaha Muslim weavers in the city forcibly prevented the removal to hospital of a twelve-year-old girl after a hakim had been refused permission to see her.[20] At Kanpur on 11 April 1900 an attack on the local segregation camp, involving mainly the city's Chamars, mill-hands and butchers, was partly inspired by reports and rumours of women being detained there against their will.[21]

Opposition to Western medical intervention was strong, too, among those Indians who saw the plague as a form of divine punishment, as a visitation against which the use of Western medicine was bound to be either impious or ineffective. 'We will not go to hospital', declared one young Muslim in Bombay in December 1896, 'Our Musjid is our hospital.'[22] Others, encouraged by the apparent failure of Western medicine to stem the disease's advance, looked to the indigenous systems, Ayurveda and Unani, for humoral explanations and appropriate therapies. According to the vaid Kaviraj Vijayratna Sen, plague had been known to ancient Ayurveda as *bradna* and was caused by 'eating phlegm-producing and indigestible food, inhaling damp air and sleeping on damp beds.'[23] A writer in Allahabad's *Prayag Samachar* on 15 May 1900 attributed the disease to excessive consumption of salt, acids, bitters and heating foods. An anonymous poster which appeared in Delhi in February 1898 at the height of the plague scare in the city vigorously defended the use of Unani medicines but stopped short of claiming a cure for the plague.[24]

The physical examination of travellers and the residents of plague-struck towns and cities was no less a cause of alarm and

[19] Couchman, *Account of the Plague Administration*, pp. 11–12; *Prabhakar* (Bombay), 30 October. 1896; *Kaiser-e-Hind* (Bombay), 1 Nov. 1896.

[20] Campbell, *Report of the Bombay Plague Committee*, pp. 23–4; *Vartahar* (Bombay), 23 March. 1898.

[21] India, Home (Public), 291–302, June 1900, NAI; *Hindustan* (Kalakankar), 15 April. 1900.

[22] Gatacre, *Report on the Bubonic Plague*, p. 14.

[23] *Bangavasi* (Calcutta), 10 Oct. 1896.

[24] Home (Sanitary), 555, May 1898, NAI.

opposition. Because most of the doctors were male as well as white, their touch was considered either polluting or tantamount to sexual molestation, especially when it involved the examination of women's necks, armpits and thighs. Sholapur's *Kalpataru* protested on 24 October 1897 that 'Native feeling' was 'most touchy' on this issue. 'Native ladies', it claimed, 'will prefer death to the humiliation of having their groins examined by male doctors who are utter strangers to them'. Another Marathi paper, *Gurakhi* of Bombay, angrily denounced the examination of women passengers at Kalyan railway station. 'That a female should be publicly asked by a male stranger to remove the end of her sari (from the upper half of her body)', wrote the paper on 19 February 1897, 'is most insulting and likely to lead to loss of life.' Passengers travelling to Calcutta via Khana Junction had to survive a similar ordeal. Forced to alight from the train, they were divided by sex and made to wait to be inspected in full public view by a European doctor. It was only after an outcry in the press had shown the strength of Indian feeling that screens were provided and a few women doctors found to assist in the examinations. But the basic antipathy remained. As Moradabad's *Nizam-ul-Mulk* put it on 16 April 1900, 'The very sight of plague doctors at the railway station curdles the blood of passengers.'[25] Public examinations on the streets of Pune as much as the frequent house searches fed mounting indignation in the city and helped provoke the assassination of Rand, the Plague Commissioner, on 22 June 1897 [26] The hero of Sarat Chandra Chattopadhyay's *Srikanta* recorded his humiliation at having to stand in line with coolies to be examined by the white 'Dogdari of plague' before being allowed to embark for Rangoon. So roughly did the doctor handle the more sensitive parts of his body that, the author said, even a wooden doll would have cried out in protest.[27]

[25] The scale (and dubious efficacy) of the plague measures can be seen from the fact that in 1896–7 1.8 million rail travellers were inspected, of whom 40,000 were detained, but a mere 6 proved to be suffering from the disease: Hirst, *Conquest of Plague*, p. 115.

[26] *Dnyan Prakash* (Pune), 19 April. 1897; *Sudharak* (Pune), 10 May 1897; Damodhar Chapekar's 'confession', 8 October 1897, Home (Public), 240, November. 1897, NAI. Some houses in Pune were searched as many as eleven times between 13 March and 19 May 1897: in all 218,124 house searches were made, leading to the discovery of 338 plague cases and 64 corpses. *Supplement to the Account of Plague Administration*, p. 9.

[27] Sarat Chandra Chattopadyay, *Sukrata* (Calcutta, 1918), in *Collected Works*, II, pp. 17–18. I am indebted to Gautam Bhadra for this reference.

The treatment of Indians as 'mere beasts', with all the racial contempt it implied, was made still more offensive by the use of British
troops in Pune (and on a much smaller scale in Bombay) to enforce
plague measures.[28] Inevitably, this invited comparisons with military conquest and occupation. The citizens of Pune saw the recourse
to soldiers as a crude attempt by the Bombay administration to in-
timidate its opponents. But the use of these 'white bulls' had a
further connotation. In recent years British soldiers had been involved in a series of racial incidents in India—women had been
molested and raped, villagers had been beaten up, even shot at, by
soldiers on hunting expeditions. One one pretext or another the soldiers received only negligible punishments in the courts, a travesty
of justice the Indian press bitterly resented.[29] The use of a thousand
British soldiers to conduct house searches in Pune seemed either an
act of gross insensitivity or a deliberate provocation. Reports of sexual harassment, insults and abuse on the part of British troops soon
began to circulate in the city.[30] It did not escape comment that when
white men or women were attacked Europeans took a very different
attitude. *Moda Vritt*, a Marathi paper, wondered on 15 July 1897
how Indians could be expected to feel grief at the deaths of Rand
and Lieutenant Ayerst, assassinated a month earlier at Pune, when
Europeans went unpunished for 'taking the lives of helpless Natives
under the impression that they are monkeys, crows and bears.'[31]

Nor was the living body alone subjected to insults and indignities. The examination and disposal of corpses figured prominently
in early plague policy. According to the Bengal plague committee in
a memorandum of mid 1897 a 'plague corpse is a focus of infection',
especially when the victim died outside a hospital. It followed,
therefore, that 'All religious rites and ceremonies should . . . be cur-
tailed as much as possible.'[32] The Secretary of State for India, under

[28] *Vartahar* (Bombay), 10 January 1898.

[29] E. g. *Indian Spectator* (Bombay), 9 May 1897; *Bombay Samachar*, 12 May 1897;
*Indu Prakash* (Bombay), 10 February 1898; *Hitavadi* (Calcutta), 13 May 1898;
*Rahbar* (Moradabad), 16 April 1899.

[30] *Dnyan Prakash*, 15 March 1897; *Kesari*, 6 April 1897. Rand, by contrast, found
it 'a matter of great satisfaction' that 'no credible complaint that the modesty of
woman had been intentionally insulted had ever been made either to the Plague
Committee or to the soldiers' own officers': *Supplement to the Account of Plague
Administration*, p. 34.

[31] See also *Kesari*, 2 February 1898, for a similar sentiment.

[32] Bengal, Municipal (Medical), 89, February 1898, West Bengal State Archives,
Calcutta (hereafter WBSA).

the influence of medical opinion in Britain, urged that a systematic policy of corpse inspection be instituted as the best way of countering deficient plague registration and as a check to the spread of the disease.[33] Opinion in India was more divided. The civil administration was well aware of the sensitivity of the issue and that corpse inspection was, as the Viceroy, Lord Elgin, noted in August 1897, 'likely to produce great irritation' among Indians of all classes.[34] This was amply and widely demonstrated. In October 1896 a European doctor in Calcutta caused great excitement by insisting on examining (and taking a sample of blood from) the body of a zenana woman who had apparently died of mumps, but whom he suspected might have been suffering from plague. 'If this is not highhandedness', commented *Hitavadi* on 30 October, 'nothing is'. In the Bombay presidency it was decreed that bodies could not be buried or cremated until they had been inspected by a qualified (and hence almost invariably European) doctor to ascertain whether plague had been the cause of death. With scores of deaths occurring daily in towns and cities and few doctors available, this might entail a delay of many hours before funeral rights could be proceeded with. The *Mahratta* on 6 June 1897 complained that twelve or even twenty-four hours might elapse before permission could be obtained, adding that the 'detention of dead bodies in houses for such a long time is condemned both by religion and the science of sanitation'. A European witness to the Indian Plague Commission of 1898–9 pointed out that one of the principal objections to corpse inspection was that it 'delayed the disposal of the body, and, in consequence, nobody living in the same muhulla could eat or drink until the body had been removed.'[35] The delay was often felt to be more irksome than the inspection itself.[36]

The carrying out of post-mortems on suspected plague victims was also widely resented. The practice was stopped at Jawalpur,

[33] Secretary of State to Government Bombay, 24 August 1897, India, Home (Sanitary), 142, September 1897 NAI. One British expert, W.S. Reade, in urging that corpse inspection be adopted as the 'sheet-anchor' of plague detection, said he could see nothing in it to 'hurt the caste or susceptibilities of the various races of India': Bengal, Municipal (Medical), 2 February 1898, WBSA.

[34] Elgin to Governor, Bombay, 26 August 1897, India, Home (Sanitary), 143, September 1897, NAI.

[35] Evidence of E.F.L. Winter, ICS, 'The Indian Plague Commission, 1898–99', *Parliamentary Papers*, xxxi, 1900, p. 49.

[36] Campbell, *Report of the Bombay Plague Committee*, p. 61.

near Hardwar in the North-Western Provinces, after an attack on the plague camp there on 30 March 1898 had drawn officials' attention to the strength of public feeling against it.[37] In Calcutta when one of the Doms employed to cut up bodies for dissection himself died of plague, fellow Doms 'absolutely refused to let their friend be cut up. They came down in considerable numbers and carried him off to the burning-ghat' to be cremated.[38] Interference with customary funeral rites and practices—which in the Bombay presidency in 1897–8 included the closure of overcrowded cemeteries and a requirement that plague corpses be wrapped in a sheet soaked in perchloride of lime or covered with quicklime—gave rise to several demonstrations of defiance. At the town of Rander in Surat district on 9 March 1897 an order from the Assistant Collector directing that a plague corpse be taken to a mosque on the outskirts of town with no more than fifteen mourners in attendance was openly defied. Some three thousand Muslims carried the body in procession to the central mosque for the final prayers to be said over it.[39]

The search for plague cases and corpses in Bombay and Pune was not only met, at times, by outright resistance, but also, more commonly, by evasion and concealment. The sick, whether suffering from plague or any other disease that might be casually mistaken for it, were smuggled out to areas free of search parties, or were hidden in lofts, inside cupboards, under furniture or in secret rooms. Plagues corpses were buried clandestinely, sometimes within house or compound. The British were dismayed that even a 'Westernized' community like the Parsis should resort to such evasions and deceptions.[40]

The colonial assault on the body was not, to be sure, the only cause of opposition to the government's anti-plague measures. There was concern, too, for the loss of property and possessions, destroyed or pilfered during the plague operations. For the poor

[37] Sanitary Department, resolution, North-Western Provinces, 27 April 1898, India, Home (Sanitary), 521, May 1898, NAI.

[38] J.N. Cook, 'Report on Plague in Calcutta', 31 August 1898, in *Report of the Epidemics of Plague in Calcutta during the Years 1898–99, 1899–1900 and up to 30 June 1900* (Calcutta, 1900), p. 8.

[39] *Praja Pokar* (Surat), 10 March 1897; *Deshi Mitra* (Surat), 11 March 1897.

[40] *Supplement to the Account of Plague Administration*, p. 7; Gatacre, *Report on the Bubonic Plague*, pp. 179–80; Campbell, *Report of the Bombay Plague Committee*, p. 56.

hospitalization and segregation meant the loss of wages, possibly of a job. Merchants were resentful of the restrictions placed upon their movements as well as at the destruction of their grain stores and other assets.[41] But above all else it was the actual, threatened or imagined assault on the body that aroused the greatest anger and fear in the early plague years and was the commonest cause of evasion and defiance.

## III

So far in this essay little attempt has been made to distinguish between the attitudes and responses of different sections of the Indian population. To some extent this seems appropriate. The British at first made little distinction in their plague policy between one class and another. Equally, much initial criticism of the plague administration was voiced on behalf of 'the Native community' and in defence of 'Native feelings'. If one turns, however, to a consideration of the rumours thrown up by the plague and, more commonly, by the state measures deployed against it, one becomes aware of a significant divergence of outlook between the middle classes and the subordinate population.

Rumour flourished in the atmosphere of fear and uncertainty generated by the plague and the colonial medical intervention against it. There are, though, many difficulties in the way of trying to interpret the plague rumours as a species of popular discourse. As they have come down to us the rumours are far from being an uncontaminated source. The transition from the oral to the written form inevitably involves selection and distortion. Plague rumours were often written down and printed—in the press, in official reports, in memoirs—specifically in order to show the absurdity, the ignorance and the irrationality of the masses, to demonstrate, as one paper put it, that 'King Mob' was 'impervious to reason.'[42] The wilder the rumour the better it suited this purpose. In the press rumours were often merely alluded to or given in only crude and summary form on the assumption that their nature and substance was already familiar to readers. Nor, of course, is it safe to assume

[41] *Vartanidhi* (Pune), 3 March 1897; *Mahratta*, 28 March 1897; Champion (Bombay), 21 March 1897; *Ahmedabad Times*, 11 April 1897; *Indian Spectator*, 20 May 1898.
[42] *Hindustan* (Kalakankar), 26 April 1900.

that rumours were an unalloyed product of the subaltern classes and circulated exclusively among them. In his report on the Calcutta plague J. N. Cook, the city's Health Officer, noted rather despairingly in 1898 that it was 'extraordinary how natives occupying a respectable position gave credence to the wildest and most improbable stories.'[43] It would be rash, too, altogether to disregard as colonial or middle-class prejudice the suggestion made, especially at the time of the Calcutta plague disturbances of May 1898, that some rumours were 'set in circulation by badmashes with the object of frightening people and getting an opportunity of looting them.'[44] Vaids and hakims were also thought to have a likely interest in spreading alarming reports about Western medicine, inoculation and hospitals.[45] But, for all these caveats, the rumours appear to take us appreciably closer to popular perceptions and responses than most other available sources.

One striking feature of the plague rumours, in seeming contrast to many other examples of this form of popular discourse in India, was their secularity.[46] It is true that reports sometimes made reference to 'absurd rumours' that 'the intention of Government was to interfere with the religion and caste of the people', and 'to destroy caste and religious observances, with the ultimate design of forcing Christianity on the natives of India.'[47] At the time of the Kanpur riot in April 1900 it was said that 'the wildest rumours of impending danger to Hindu and Musalman alike' were in circulation.[48] But the overwhelming concern of the majority of recorded rumours was with an assault on the body, whether by poisoning, dissection, or other means. The principal themes of the rumours appear as follows:

[43] Cook, 'Report on Plague in Calcutta', p. 25.

[44] *Civil and Military News* (Ludhiana), 18 May 1898; *Hitavadi* (Calcutta), 6 May 1898; Magistrate, Howrah, to Commissioner, Burdwan, 5 May 1898, Bengal, Judicial (Police), 14–16, August 1898, WBSA.

[45] Deputy Commissioner to Commissioner, Delhi, 5 March 1898, India, Home (Sanitary), 550, May 1898, NAI.

[46] For a seminal discussion of this and other aspects of rumour in India, see R. Guha, *Elementary Aspects of Peasant Insurgency in Colonial India* (Delhi, 1983), pp. 251–77.

[47] India, Home (Sanitary) (Plague), 16 July 1900, in Sanitary Despatches to London, 14, 26 July 1900, India Office Records, London (hereafter IOR).

[48] General Administration Department resolution, North-Western Provinces, 15 May 1900, India, Home (Public), 298, June 1900, NAI.

1. *Poisoning*: Commonest of all rumours were those relating to
the deliberate poisoning of Indians by doctors, hospital staff and
other colonial agencies. One of the first reports to this effect was
carried by the *Mahratta* on 1 November 1896 in connection with
Bombay city. The *Kesari* of 16 February 1897 also referred to
rumours of the 'systematic poisoning' of hospital patients. A fuller
and more elaborate version was given in the *Poona Vaibhar* on 21
February 1897. 'In some villages', it reported,

> the people have come to think that the Sarkar, finding its subjects un-
> manageable, is devising means to reduce their number. They say that it
> mixes poison in opium. They even hesitate to accept the dole of bread
> distributed in the famine camps under the belief that poison is mixed
> with the bread. They think that the hospitals are now under the manage-
> ment of new doctors who put poison into the medicines.

In other versions it was the village well or the municipal water supply that had been poisoned: such rumours were widespread in northern India in 1900. In its issue of 26 April 1900 the *Hindustan* of
Kalakankar referred to rumours 'to the effect that plague patients
are poisoned by doctors, that the water-works supply has been
poisoned by Government to kill the people, and that six bags of
snakes and other worms had been ground [up] and dissolved in the
water-pipe at Cawnpore to bring on plague among consumers'.
Earlier, during the first months of the epidemic, there was a rumour
in Bombay that snake venom had been put into the water supply to
cause plague.[49]

2. *Cutting up the Body: Extracting 'Momiai'*: A second cluster of
rumours concerned the cutting up of bodies, again especially in hospitals. A correspondent of the *Mahratta* on 20 December 1896
claimed that 'All natives have an idea that they are taken to hospital
and killed in order that the doctors may cut them up.' The paper's
editor agreed that hospitals were seen by some Indians as 'so many
slaughter-houses for the benefit of human vivisectionists'. Writing
in the aftermath of the mill-hands' attack on the Arthur Road hospital in Bombay the *Kaiser-e-Hind* on 1 November 1896 explained
that the workers believed there was 'something diabolical about the
hospital which claimed so many victims'. In their eyes the hospital
was 'the very incarnation of the Devil, and the Devil was to be exor-
cised at all costs'. The purpose behind hospitalization was some-

[49] Hirst, *Conquest of Plague*, p. 21.

times seen as the extraction of the vital oil or balm known as *momiai*.[50] Enthoven attributed the flight of thousands of mill workers from Bombay in the closing months of 1896 to the fear that 'officials were seizing men and boys with the intention of hanging them head downwards over a slow fire and preparing a medicine drawn from the head.'[51] According to Lely residents of the town of Bulsar in Gujarat would not pass along the road in front of the local hospital in the early days of the plague because it was 'universally believed, or at any rate said, that an oil mill was under every bed to grind the patient into ointment for use on European patients in Bombay.'[52] An Urdu paper, *Jami-ul-Ulum* of Moradabad, carried a similar story on 14 April 1900: 'a small quantity of blood', according to the 'ignorant natives' of Kanpur, was being sought to prepare momiai for soldiers wounded in the Boer War in South Africa. The 'illiterate Dubalas' (or Dublas, a tribal community) of Udvada in Surat district were said by the *Gujarat Mitra* on 14 March 1897 to believe that the livers of patients in the local segregation ward were sent to Bombay as a protection against the plague there. And a boatman near Bilimora told Maconochie that the insection shed at the nearby railway station contained a 'big machine' which squeezed oil from passengers' bodies: this was sent to Bombay where it was 'put into other people, and then they get plague too.'[53]

[50] Crooke linked momiai with the Arabic *mumiya*, an embalmed body (hence the English 'mummy') and *mum*, meaning 'wax'. In India the term connoted a magical balm thought to cure wounds and make the user invulnerable. 'The popular idea is that in order to prepare Momiai, a boy, the fatter and blacker the better, is caught, a small hole is bored in the top of his head, and he is hung up by the heels over a slow fire. The juice or essence of the body dripping from his head produces seven drops of this precious substance. It is believed that a European gentleman, the Momiai Saheb, enjoys a monopoly granted by the government of enticing away suitable boys for this nefarious manufacture.' Crooke adds: 'Surgeons are naturally exposed to the suspicion of being engaged in the trade, and some years ago all the coolies in one of the hill stations struck work when an anatomist set up a private dissecting room.' W. Crooke, *Religion and Folklore of Northern India* (London, 3rd edn., 1926), pp. 111–12. I am extremely grateful to David Hardiman for drawing my attention to this reference and those from Enthoven, Lely and Maconochie cited below.

[51] R.E. Enthoven, preface to ibid., p. 2.

[52] F. S. P. Lely, *Suggestions for the Better Governing of India* (London, 1906), p. 29.

[53] E. Maconochie, *Life in the Indian Civil Service* (London, 1926), p. 83. The author identifies this story as a misunderstanding of Haffkine's anti-plague inoculation rather than a momiai tale.

3. *Seizing and Searching*: Rumours of this class partly overlap with those in the two previous categories. They concern the powers said to have been entrusted to doctors, police, soldiers and sanitary officials. In some instances they are barely exaggerated versions of the authority actually conferred by the state upon such people. On 1 November 1896 the *Indian Spectator* reported that in Bombay it was rumoured that the police could despatch anyone they chose to hospital, from which they would never emerge alive. A common rumour, not without some foundation in reality, was that perfectly healthy men and women were seized and sent to hospitals and segregation camps. It was sometimes said that the plague did not exist at all but had been invented to enable low paid government servants to plunder the people at will, or that doctors were deliberately spreading the plague (by poisoning wells and other means) to improve their business. At the time of the Calcutta disturbances of May 1898 the police were rumoured to carry bottles of poison which they held to the noses of their victims unless bribed to desist.[54]

4. *Inoculation*: The introduction of Haffkine's anti-plague inoculation in 1897–8 sparked off many rumours concerning its nature, purpose and effects. Despite government denials rumours were rife that inoculation would be (or had already been) made compulsory. This was a cause of attacks on Europeans and on Indians suspected of being inoculators, notably in Calcutta in May 1898, when an Austrian sailor drowned trying to escape from his pursuers.[55] Inoculation, it was said, caused 'instantaneous death' or brought impotency and sterility.[56] Inoculation rumours current in the Punjab in 1901–2 included that—

[54] *Tohfah-i-Hind* (Bijnor), 20 April 1900; E. Wilkinson, *Report on Plague in the Punjab from October 1st 1901 to September 30th 1902* (Lahore, 1904), p. 71; Cook, 'Report on Plague in Calcutta , p. 14.

[55] *Bangavasi* (Calcutta), 14 May 1898; Cook, 'Report on Plague in Calcutta', pp. 14, 23–5. The sudden appearance of a European accompanied by two policemen at a fair in Banaras in May 1899 caused immediate speculation that he was an inoculator and there was 'a general stampede': *Prayag Samachar* (Allahabad), 8 May 1899.

[56] *Aftab-i-Punjab*(Lahore), 9 May 1898; Wilkinson, *Report on Plague in the Punjab*, p. 28; Maconochie, *Life in the ICS*, p. 208. In this and in the political backlash created there are interesting parallels between the British plague administration of 1896–1900 and the vasectomy campaign which contributed to Mrs Gandhi's downfall in 1977.

the needle was a yard long; you died immediately after the operation; you survived the operation six months and then collapsed; men lost their virility and women became sterile; the Deputy Commissioner himself underwent the operation and expired half an hour afterwards in great agony; and other like nonsense.[57]

When inoculations were performed on Europeans or on prominent Indians without apparent adverse effects it was said that only rose-water had been used: the real poison was reserved for lesser Indians.[58]

5. *Collapse or Weakness of British Rule*: A rumour of this kind gave rise to a riot at the village of Chakalashi in the Kaira district of Gujarat. According to the *Mahratta* of 23 January 1898 a local 'fanatic' told the people that British rule was over. In Lely's version of the story it was believed that 'the British Empire had fallen in the country south of the Mahi, and that the plague cordon which had been drawn along that river was really for the purpose of preventing the news from getting through to the north'. By this account 'a new kingdom was proclaimed and preparations made for selecting a Raja', until the police intervened and bloodshed followed.[59] A related plague rumour, touching in another way upon the weakness of British power in India and circulating in northern India in 1900, was to the effect that the British were spreading the plague deliberately in order to discourage the Russians from invading India. This rumour might be linked to others current at the time about Russian advances into Afghanistan and Kashmir.[60] It was said in Calcutta in 1898 that in order to save British India (from what is not clear) the Viceroy had met a yogi in a remote part of the Himalayas 'and made a compact with him to sacrifice 2 lakhs of lives to the Goddess Kali'. The British were suspected of trying to keep this bargain by distributing poisonous white powders and black pills and by giving lethal inoculations.[61]

[57] Wilkinson, *Report on Plague in the Punjab*, p. 28.

[58] Cook, 'Report on Plague in Calcutta', p. 25. For further discussion of plague rumours, especially those relating to inoculation, see I. J. Catanach, 'Plague and the Indian Village, 1896–1914', in P. Robb (ed.), *Rural India: Land, Power and Society under British Rule* (London, 1983), pp. 224–6.

[59] Lely, *Suggestions*, p. 29.

[60] India, Home (Sanitary) (Plague), 16 July 1900, Sanitary Despatches to London, 14, 26 July 1900, IOR.

[61] Cook, 'Report on Plague in Calcutta', p. 23. Cf. Wilkinson, *Report on Plague in the Punjab*, p. 71: 'The most general idea was that Government had found from the

6. *General Catastrophe*: A final collection of rumours, or in some cases authored predictions (which thus go beyond the realm of true rumour), concerned a spate of imminent disasters and calamities, of which the plague and famine then sweeping India were only the precursors. An earthquake confidently predicted in Delhi in January 1898 fuelled alarm over the anticipated imposition of draconian anti-plague measures.[62] The month of Kartik in the Sambat year 1956 (November 1899) was widely expected to initiate an age of affliction and catastrophe for India and the world.[63]

What significance can we see in these plague rumours? They are evidence first of all of how extensively the epidemic was discussed among the Indian population and the widespread fear and suspicion with which the state's plague measures were viewed. 'The word plague', wrote the *Hindustan* on 8 April 1899, 'is even in the mouths of children.' On the eve of the Kanpur riot the 'plague administration, especially the segregation of the sick, became the common subject of conversation among the better classes of the city' in the first week of April 1900, and from them 'anxiety gradually extended down to the masses of the people.'[64] When Sir John Woodburn, the Lieutenant–Governor of Bengal, held a meeting with doctors at the Eden Hospital to discuss the likelihood of an outbreak of plague in Calcutta, rumour rapidly spread. By noon the same day, 28 April 1898,

> the excitement in the town was intense. In business houses and in bazaars, streets and bustees the question was discussed, had the dreaded Bombay plague come at last, were their houses going to be forcibly entered, and their wives and daughters torn away by British soldiers, was quarantine to be established, and were they all to be forcibly inoculated?[65]

In a situation where the government was generally disinclined to ex-

---

Census and from the occurrence of recent famines, that the population was too large and consequently had given a sort of contract to the doctors to kill off so many lakhs.'

[62] India, Home (Sanitary), 543–50, May 1898, NAI, *Patiala Akhbar*, 21 January 1898.

[63] *Prayag Samachar*, 20 April 1899; *Liberal* (Azamgarh), 24 September 1899; *Oudh Akhbar* (Lucknow), 30 October 1899.

[64] General Administration Department resolution, North-Western Provinces, 15 May 1900, India, Home (Public), 298, June 1900, NAI.

[65] Cook, 'Report on Plague in Calcutta', p. 10.

plain its intentions and take the people into its confidence, rumour had something of a predictive quality. It was an attempt to anticipate and explain what the government was up to, and people took the action—flight, resistance, evasion—that seemed in consequence appropriate. In Bombay in late 1896, as in Calcutta in April-May 1898, thousands of people fled not just to avoid the plague but also to escape the measures which it was believed the government intended to visit upon them. Rumour informed action.

Turning to the content of the rumours it is possible to discern two basic preoccupations. There was, first of all, a deep suspicion of the nature and methods of Western medicine. This was not new. For much of the nineteenth century hospitals and such practices as surgery, post-mortems and vaccination had given rise to widespread fear and opposition. Some of the rumours concerning vaccination directly parallel the inoculation rumours of the early plague years. But such doubts and fears were given fresh intensity by the unprecedented scale of medical intervention in 1896–1900, and by the coercive and comprehensive nature of the measures which seemed to threaten the life or the body of almost every Indian. Some of the rumours were garbled accounts of an unfamiliar medical technology—the needles a yard long, the poisoning and dissecting hospitals. Perhaps the rumours about snakes in the water supply even had their origin in some health officer's well-intentioned attempt to explain water-borne parasites and diseases. But with growing familiarity with Western medicine (something which the sheer scale of medical intervention against the plague helped to bring about) and as the coercive aspects of plague policy were diminished (largely in response to popular protest and resistance) inoculation and hospitals lost much of their former terror. As fear abated the rumours it had occasioned also began to die away.

But it was not only the nature and novelty of Western medical technology that sent rumour flying. The plague and still more the state measures deployed against it were seen to have a deeper meaning or purpose and to reflect the underlying character and intentions of British rule. In this 'effort after meaning', rumour pasted together into a kind of collage aspects of the current crisis—plague, hospitalization, segregation, inoculation—with other disturbing or significant items of news and recent events—the famines, talk of overpopulation and growing political opposition to British rule, Russian advances, even the South African War. To outsiders it appeared that these fragments were completely unrelated and were brought together in an entirely random and nonsensical way. And yet at the level of popular discourse this association of ideas provided a partially coherent pattern of explanation. It seemed to explain what was otherwise difficult to account for: why, in particular, were Europeans apparently immune to the disease unless they had some part in its propagation? Underlying almost all the rumours was an assumption of British self-interest and spite, a readiness to victimize and sacrifice Indians for the preservation of British power. As one newspaper pointed out,[66] the rumours leant no support to the idea of the Raj as *ma-bap*, a notion conventionally attributed to popular perceptions of state power and one which the British had claimed in justification for their own rule. Even the Viceroy, by popular report, was willing to kill off 200,000 of the inhabitants of Calcutta so that British power could be maintained. Here was no kindly tsar, no benevolent white queen, to whom an oppressed people could appeal against the tyranny of their overlords. European power appeared as a monolith, undivided in its malevolence. This was an understanding of British power which the coercive character of the early plague measures—and the rough handling which lower-class Indians generally received from soldiers, doctors and officials—must have done much to nurture. It seemed perfectly credible, not some extravagant fantasy, that the British should poison wells, give lethal injections or grind out momiai, such was their apparent contempt for the sentiments, the lives, the bodies of their Indian subjects.

We can venture one stage further in identifying rumour as a form of popular discourse. Some of the rumours voiced a suspicion not only of the British but also of those Indians who appeared to be their agents and allies. The Indian rajas and notables who assisted the British in their plague operations or allowed themselves to be inoculated were seen as accomplices in the evil conspiracy to poison, pollute and plunder the people. In Calcutta in May 1898 Indian 'topi-wallahs' became targets of popular violence and were attacked on suspicion of being inoculators or plague doctors.[67] From long experience, too, the subordinate classes had reason to expect the worst of the Indian policemen entrusted with enforcing plague reg-

---

[66] *Poona Vaibhar*, 21 February 1897.

[67] Magistrate, Howrah, to Commissioner, Burdwan, 5 May 1898, Bengal, Judicial (Police), 14 August 1898, WBSA; Cook, 'Report on Plague in Calcutta', pp. 23–5.

ulations. Given their 'deadly enmity to the tyrannical police',[68] it was not surprising that workers, like the Bombay mill-hands of October 1896, believed that the plague administration had been set up to allow the police to pillage and murder the people. While it was mainly an image of British cruelty and self-interest that the plague rumours projected, they suggested that there were Indians, too, who shared in the rulers' selfish or malevolent intentions.

## IV

Plague provided a pretext for a second colonial assault—on the growing political assertiveness of the Indian middle classes. This was most evident in relation to the municipalities of Bombay, Calcutta and Pune. Plague reached Pune towards the end of 1896 at a time when the provincial administration, headed by Lord Sandhurst, was already bent on humbling the Poona Sarvajanik Sabha and the city's Brahmins for their persistent criticism of British policies. The plague was used as a convenient excuse to strike back at Tilak's militancy: his Sivaji and Ganapati festivals were banned in 1897 as part of the plague restrictions and he was imprisoned for his alleged part in provoking or plotting the assassination of W.C. Rand, the city's unpopular Plague Commissioner.[69] But the government's counter-

---

[68] *Kaiser-e-Hind* (Bombay), 1 November 1896. Before leaving plague rumour, it is worth noting that plague, like smallpox, cholera and other epidemic diseases, in time acquired its own deity: see L.S.S. O'Malley, *Census of India, 1911, Volume V, Bengal, Bihar, Orissa, and Sikkim, Part I: Report* (Calcutta, 1913), p. 228; H. Whitehead, *The Village Gods of South India* (2nd edition, Calcutta, 1921), p. 21 and photographs facing pp. 76–7. It is significant, however, that the initial response, especially in northern India in 1898–1900, where plague measures often preceded or came close on the heels of the epidemic, was to hold the British rather than a disease goddess responsible or to see British medical intervention as the phenomenon that challenged explanation. Despite the mortality caused, the plague goddess appears never to have assumed the ritual importance and permanence of Sitala or Olabibi, deities of smallpox and cholera respectively.

[69] The part played by events in Pune in 1896–7 in the emergence of Tilak as a Maharashtrian and nationalist leader have been too frequently, if often uncritically, described to need detailed comment here. See, in particular, R.I. Cashman, *The Myth of the Lokamanya: Tilak and Mass Politics in Maharashtra* (Berkeley, 1975), esp. p. 113; S.L. Karandikar, *Lokmanya Bal Gangadhar Tilak: The Hercules and Prometheus of Modern India* (Pune, n.d.), pp. 134–70; T.V. Parvate, *Bal Gangadhar Tilak: A Narrative and Interpretive Review of his Life, Career and Contemporary Events* (Ahmedabad, 1958), pp. 82–91; D.V. Tahmankar, *Lokamanya Tilak: Father of Indian Unrest and Maker of Modern India* (London, 1956), pp. 73–4. Most of

thrust was also directed against the Pune municipal council, which was seen by British eyes to be Brahmin dominated, politically suspect and administratively incompetent.

The issue of the Pune municipality went back to 1885. Lord Reay, the governor of the day, had decided to meet the demands of the Poona Sarvajanik Sabha by liberalizing the proposed nature of the municipal council: its membership was raised from twenty to thirty, of which only ten councillors were to be government nominated, and the council was to elect its own president. It was argued that this 'experiment' was justified by the spirit of Lord Ripon's local self-government reforms and by the 'large and intelligent class of educated native gentlemen' to be found in Pune.[70] By 1898, however, European bureaucrats had decided that the experiment of a decade earlier was a 'conspicuous failure' and welcomed the crisis created by the plague as an opportunity for its partial reversal.[71] The attack on the Pune municipal council was symptomatic of a wider assault on the abilities and ambitions of the 'native gentlemen' whom the British increasingly viewed as the greatest threat to their supremacy in India.

In his report on plague operations in the city, compiled shortly before his death in June 1897, Rand went out of his way to denounce the Indian municipal councillors. They had, he said, done little to check the epidemic on its first appearance at Pune, had shown want of resolution in enforcing segregation and hospitalization against popular hostility, and had appointed a young Brahmin as the city health officer who was 'quite unfit for the place.'[72] Armed with exceptional powers under the Epidemic Diseases Act, Rand virtually ignored the municipal council and set up his own three-man committee to run plague operations in the city. His use of European troops to enforce the plague measures was a calculated affront to Pune's Indian élite. In Rand's own words the soldiers

---

these accounts belong to the 'élite mobilization' school. They do little to probe Tilak's highly ambiguous attitudes towards the 'masses' and Western medical ideas and practice, nor do they suggest the extent to which men like Tilak were *responding* to popular unrest rather than mobilizing it.

[70] General Department. resolution, Bombay, 26 June 1885, vol. 91, no. 332, 1885, Maharashtra State Archives, Bombay (hereafter MSA).

[71] J.K. Spence, Commissioner, Central Division, to H.E.M. James, 11 August 1898, Bombay, General, vol. 70, no. 813, 1898, MSA.

[72] *Supplement to the Account of the Plague Administration*, pp. 7, 12–14.

were 'disciplined', 'honest', and could be 'relied on to be thorough': 'no native agency', he averred, was either available 'or could be relied on if it were'. His only use for 'native gentlemen' was as 'interpreters' to accompany the military search parties and explain their purpose to the horrified inmates.[73] That few middle-class Indians would come forward to take up such a demeaning and unpopular task was seen by the Plague Commissioner as further evidence of the unsuitability of 'native agency'. It followed, too, that sanitation in the city would have to remain under European control 'for some time to come' if the gains which Rand believed had been made under his guidance were not to be frittered away by Indian incompetence. It was conveniently overlooked that the municipal councillors's earlier initiatives to combat the plague had been blocked or ignored by the provincial government.[74] Rand's arguments, backed by other civil servants and sanitary officers, became the basis for a revision of the municipal council in 1898, when the number of nominated councillors was raised from ten to eighteen in order to strengthen official and European control.[75] The plague crisis in Pune (as in Calcutta) was thus seized upon by the British as evidence of Indians' incapacity to manage their own affairs and as an argument for the indefinite continuance of British administrative responsibility.[76]

But while racial contempt and political retaliation help to explain the severity of the early plague measures, in Pune especially, the political factor also acted, paradoxically, as a major constraint on British policy and forced a significant modification of the state's anti-plague strategy. By late 1897 and early 1898 the colonial administration faced a double crisis. Despite intensive plague operations the epidemic had continued to spread and was now reaching Bengal, the North-Western Provinces, Punjab and Hyderabad. In addition, there was mounting evidence of the unpopularity of the plague mea-

[73] Ibid., pp. 3, 7.

[74] *The Administration Report of Poona City Municipality for 1896–97* (no publication details), p. 25. See, too, the reports and memoranda of the Health Officer and President of the Municipal Council for January 1897 in the Poona Municipal Correspondence Book, 1896–7, Municipal Archives, Pune.

[75] R.A. Lamb, Collector, Pune, to J.K. Spence, Commissioner, Central Division, 18 June 1897, and memoranda by Spence, 21 June 1897, and C. Ollivant, 19 September 1898, Bombay, General, vol. 70, no. 908, 1898, MSA.

[76] C. Furedy, 'Lord Curzon and the Reform of the Calcutta Corporation 1899: A case study in Imperial Decision-Making', *South Asia*, n.s. 1:1 (1978) pp. 77–8, 81.

sures and public determination to resist them. The riot in Bombay city in October 1896 was followed by a second in March 1898 and by a number of smaller incidents. Elsewhere in the province there were several disturbances, including one at Sinnar in Nasik district in January 1898. Further afield there was rioting against house-searches, segregation and hospitalization at Jawalpur in March 1898, at Garhshankar in Punjab in April, in Calcutta in May, and at Sri-rangapatnam near Mysore in November. Further incidents occurred in a number of provinces over the following two years, and even where there was no actual riot 'passive resistance', as in rural Bihar, made the implementation of plague measures extremely diffi-cult.[77] Deputations of leading citizens, municipal councillors and caste and religious leaders urged the government to show grea-ter sensitivity to Indian sentiment and custom, warning of even more opposition and bloodshed if their pleas were not heeded.[78] Anonymous placards and petitions appearing in Delhi in February 1898 drew ominous comparisons with the events of 1857.[79] If, administrators began to reason, the plague measures could provoke such resistance in Bombay and Bengal, what would happen when they were enforced against the Muslims and the 'martial races' of northern India?[80]

[77] In addition to sources already cited, see India, Home (Sanitary), 177–82, December 1898, NAI; Home (Sanitary), 720–4, January 1899, NAI; Home (Sanitary), 13–14 April 1900, NAI; G. Hutcheson, *Report on Plague and Plague Operations in the Central Provinces from September 1896 to 31st March 1899* (Nagpur, 1899), pp. 3–5.

[78] E.g. at Pune on 2 April 1897 (*Mahratta*, 4 April 1897) and Bombay in March 1897 (*Muslim Herald*, 24 March 1897). See also the Muslim petition to the Lieutenant-Governor of Bengal at about the same time, in Bengal, Municipal (Medical), 88, February 1898, WBSA.

[79] 'People are very much dissatisfied at the issue of notice with regard to the arrangements proposed to be made if bubonic plague breaks out. These would ruin their good name, respect and religion. Is that civilization? We caution Government to excuse us and not to adopt the procedure. We are quite prepared to sacrifice our lives for our religion and respect. We are ready to die. The notice will call emotion equal to that of 1857 Mutiny': anonymous notice posted in Delhi in February 1898, India, Home (Sanitary), 553, May 1898, NAI.

[80] Elgin, minute, 14 June 1897, Home (Sanitary), 483–90, July 1897, NAI. For the British another worrying sign was the joining together of Hindus and Muslims to oppose the proposed plague measures in northern India: Deputy Commissioner to Commissioner, Delhi, 5 March 1898, India, Home (Sanitary), 550, May 1898, NAI; Agent, Rajputana, to Private Secretary to the Viceroy, 21 May 1898, India, Home, 777–813, KW v, August 1898, NAI.

In a letter to the Viceroy, Lord Elgin, on 29 April 1898, Sir A.P. MacDonnell, the Lieutenant-Governor of the North-Western Provinces, summed up many of these fears and reservations. He claimed that 'success', by which he meant 'not only the suppression of the disease, but the prevention of the spirit of discontent', could only be attained by 'working through the people themselves'. There had, he said, to be a compromise. The Muslims of the province would not put up with 'constant domiciliary visits, or the forcible removal of their sick to hospitals'. Defective isolation and segregation and the consequent spread of disease might follow from a partial abandonment of these measures, he conceded, but 'in the present state of public feeling in the country I consider the danger of popular discontent and tumult to be a more serious evil than even the prolongation of the disease'.[81] The Government of India was increasingly of the same mind. As one viceregal adviser put it: 'political must prevail over sanitary considerations';[82] or, in the words of the government's own Sanitary Commissioner, Dr R. Harvey, 'What is medically desirable may be practically impossible and politically dangerous.'[83]

MacDonnell's letter also drew attention to other factors which militated against attempts to impose plague measures as rigorously and as comprehensively as they had been in Bombay and Pune. One was the enormous cost involved, especially now that plague had spread beyond its initial foothold in Bombay and was moving from the cities into the countryside. Another was that the extensive use of police and medical subordinates was creating enormous opportunities for extortion and harassment. 'This corruption', MacDonnell pointed out, 'was perhaps more oppressive to, and more resented by, the people than even the discomforts of isolation and segregation.'[84] The distrust of 'native agency' extended to Indian subordinates as well, but the Pune alternative of employing British troops was clearly impractical and undesirable over India as a whole.

In addition, the civil administration and many of its leading medical advisers were beginning by 1898 to doubt that there were any easy or rapid medical solutions to the plague epidemic. The

[81] MacDonnell to Elgin, 29 April 1898, ibid., KW II.
[82] C.M. Rivaz, 24 April 1898, ibid., KW I.
[83] Harvey to Government of India, 18 April 1898, India, Home, 784, ibid.
[84] MacDonnell to Elgin, 29 April 1898, ibid., KW II.

best that could be hoped for was the gradual containment of the disease and for this to be possible co-operation had to take the place of coercion. Although, for example, Waldemar Haffkine urged that inoculation be made the mainstay of the government's plague policy, the Government of India on the advice of Harvey, its Sanitary Commissioner, firmly rejected the idea. There were many reasons why Haffkine did not receive a more sympathetic hearing from the colonial medical establishment—he was a Russian, a bacteriologist and a Jew—but the main objection was that fear of compulsory inoculation had already provoked rioting in Calcutta in May 1898 and could only be introduced slowly and on a voluntary basis alongside other medical and sanitary measures. 'The question', Harvey insisted, was 'not one of theory, but of practical administrative experience.'[85]

As a consequence of the resistance encountered and as a result of the reappraisal of its political priorities and administrative limitations, the Government of India made in 1898–9 a series of compromises and concessions in its plague policy. The most central was the recognition that the use of force was likely to be counterproductive, provoking either outright opposition or forms of evasion that negated sanitary and medical measures. The more coercive and unpopular aspects of plague administration  house and body searches, compulsory segregation and hospitalization, corpse inspections and the use of troops—were accordingly abandoned or greatly modified. One consequence of this shift away from compulsion was a greater reliance upon measures which the people were willing to take up voluntarily and upon agencies (the hitherto despised vaids and hakims) whom they trusted. The temporary evacuation of villages was one method followed with some success; another was the cleansing of houses in ways that conformed to customary Indian beliefs and practices rather than Western medical dogmas.[86] While

---

[85] Harvey added: 'it is idle to dream of an alien Government successfully imposing universal inoculation on the people of India'. Harvey, note, 5 July 1898, India, Home (Sanitary), 766–71, August 1898, NAI. For an interestingly sympathetic account of Haffkine in India, see E. Lutzker, 'Waldemar Mordecai Haffkine', *Haffkine Institute Platinum Jubilee Commemoration Volume, 1899–1974* (Bombay, n.d.), pp. 11–19.

[86] Secretary, Government of Bengal, to Secretary, Home, Government of India, 9 March 1900, India, Home (Sanitary), 13, April 1900, NAI; Wilkinson, *Report on Plague in the Punjab*, pp. 6–7, 27.

vigorously denying any intention to make inoculation compulsory, doctors and administrators made every effort to persuade the people to take up immunization voluntarily. In Punjab, especially, many thousands of inoculations were being performed annually by the early 1900s.[87]

A further important change was the great reliance now placed upon 'leading men' who could use their influence to persuade others to adopt suitable plague measures. Through the plague the British rediscovered the political and administrative value of 'indirect rule, and the utility of the hierarchical principle in India . Some concessions had already been made along these lines in Bombay city under Gatacre: the riot of March 1898 was a further stimulus. Instead of sending out its own search parties the government chose 'persons possessing personal influence over the inhabitants of their sections' of the city to report cases of plague and to encourage the adoption of approved preventive and remedial measures.[88] The same idea was being applied in other parts of India in the early months of 1898. In Delhi, for example, during the plague scare of February 1898 the administration enlisted the help of Hakim Abdul Majid Khan ('perhaps the most influential man in the city') to reassure the public and quell the excitement and alarm.[89] The technique was not infallible: some 'leaders' declined to lead or lacked the influence the British attributed to them. In Jawalpur, at Kanpur and among some communities in Bombay city the administration failed to discover any men with a controlling influence at all.[90] But the Punjab *Plague Manual* of 1909 conveniently summed up the essence of the new policy developed after 1898 in two basic precepts. The first 'cardinal principle' was that there 'must be . . . no pressure or compulsion, in any shape or form . . . brought to bear on the people'. The second stated that the 'co-operation of the people and the active assistance

[87] E. Wilkinson, *Report on Plague and Inoculation in the Punjab from October 1st 1902 to September 30th 1903* (Lahore, 1904), pp. 7, 48, 60—this despite the deaths of nineteen people at Malkowal in Punjab in November 1902 from tetanus as a result of inoculation with a contaminated needle: ibid., pp. 45–6.

[88] Campbell, *Report of the Bombay Plague Committee*, p. 24.

[89] Commissioner, Delhi, to Junior Secretary, Punjab, 7 March 1898, India, Home (Sanitary), 549, May 1898, NAI.

[90] Minute, 1 April 1898, A.P. MacDonnell, Lieutenant-Governor, North-Western Provinces, India, Home (Sanitary), 173, April 1898, NAI; MacDonnell to Viceroy, 16 April 1900, India, Home (Public), 293, June 1900, NAI; Campbell, *Report of the Bombay Plague Committee*, pp. 54–5.

of their leaders is . . . not merely a political desideratum, but an absolute necessity.'[91] The British had retreated a long way from Rand's deployment of European troops and his disdain for 'native agency'. Moreover, the change in policy appeared to bring results. The return of the plague to Calcutta in February–April 1899 was not met with compulsion or the threat of obligatory hospitalization and inoculation. The new approach, according to the municipal administration report, 'resulted in a great change in the attitude of the people'. Unlike the 'great opposition' experienced during the first outbreak in May 1898, 'practically nothing of the kind was encountered during the second and far more serious epidemic' the following year.[92]

## V

The plague crisis of 1896–1900 dramatically highlighted the ambiguous attitudes of the Indian middle classes, especially the Western-educated professionals, who saw themselves as both the articulators and educators of Indian opinion. In part their criticism of the plague administration was a riposte to the political thrust that lay behind the severity of Rand's regime in Pune and the supercession of municipal authority in several cities. The blatant contempt shown towards 'native gentlemen' and the state's recourse to raw coercion was roundly condemned. The imposition of a punitive police force on Pune following Rand's assassination (and before responsibility for the murder had been established) stirred *Kesari* to remark on 13 July 1897 that the 'policy of governing by making a parade now and then of the physical power' of the government was 'unjust'. 'To govern is not to unsheath the sword and to threaten the people with death and destruction at every moment.'

But it would be erroneous to see the response of the middle classes to the plague crisis merely in terms of opposition to colonial autocracy on the one hand and a defence of Indian custom and tradition on the other. The latter was an attitude more common among the merchant and moneylending classes, the Banias and Marwaris especially, who were not only among the principal victims of

[91] *Punjab Plague Manual, 1909* (Lahore, 1909), p. 1. Note too the highly favourable references to indigenous medical practitioners on pp. 10, 16.

[92] *Administration Report of the Commissioners of Calcutta for 1898–99* (Calcutta, 1899), i, p. 13.

**the disease** in its early years[93] but who were also among the strongest·opponents of segregation and inoculation (as, indeed, they were of vaccination).[94] Among the professionals, however, the response was a more complicated one. Tilak's position is particularly interesting in this regard and can be taken as broadly representative of his class. The Maharashtrian leader was strongly opposed to the autocratic manner in which Rand tried to implement plague measures in Pune. He took particular objection to the use of British troops and the contempt shown towards the municipality and the city's Indian élite. He did not dispute the need for anti-plague measures, but only the way in which they were being carried out. He even gave an initial, if cautious, welcome to the Epidemic Diseases Act, which some of the Bengali papers saw from the outset as a potentially tyrannical piece of legislation.[95] Like many other newspaper editors and politicians, Tilak saw it as his responsibility to educate the public in Western medical and scientific ideas and to refute the wilder rumours about the nature and purposes of hospitalization and segregation. One of his papers even carried a sympathetic account of the career and findings of the French bacteriologist Yersin, who had studied the plague bacillus during the 1894 epidemic in Hong Kong.[96] At the same time, however, Tilak's Hindu nationalism caused him to distance himself somewhat from the Western medical tradition, to be critical of what he saw as its practical limitations in the context of Indian society and culture, and to view with favour the revival of Ayurveda. In reviewing a recent book on Ayurvedic medicine in the *Mahratta* on 7 March 1897, Tilak speculated that the indigenous tradition, might be no less valid than the Western one and he called for a 'judicious combination of the two systems.'[97]

[93] Hirst, *Conquest of Plague*, pp. 265–6, 311–14; Wilkinson, *Report on Plague in the Punjab*, pp. 29–30, 45. In some parts of the Deccan the association was so evident that plague was known as the 'Marwadi sickness': Campbell, *Report of the Bombay Plague Committee*, p. 52.

[94] *Administration Report . . . Calcutta, 1898–9*, pp. 39–40.

[95] *Mahratta*, 14 February 1897; cf. *Hitavadi* (Calcutta), 12 February 1897.

[96] *Mahratta*, 14 March 1897. 'It is true that the masses look upon plague as a providential visitation and have little faith in the efficacy of methods suggested by sanitary science. But because the masses are ignorant it is a mistake to suppose that the leaders and specially the educated classes do not appreciate the usefulness of modern sanitary measures': ibid., 28 March 1897.

[97] Gandhi, Sumit Sarkar has pointed out, was exceptional among India's nationalist leaders in rejecting Western medicine and scientific rationality.

But for Tilak and those who thought like him the medical and sanitary issues were secondary to the question of leadership. In an editorial in the *Mahratta* on 11 April 1897, entitled 'Do the Educated Lead the People?', he returned to a theme on which he had already commented frequently in recent months. He strongly condemned those members of Pune's élite who, for all their patriotic professions, had fled the city at the first signs of plague. It was, he insisted, their duty to help the poor who were the main sufferers of the disease by securing for them adequate and appropriate medical attention and educating them out of their worst 'prejudices' and 'superstitions'. It was the responsibility of the 'educated people', too, to protect the 'common people' from the excesses of an oppressive state, and through their intercession force it to respect the commonalty's legitimate needs and apprehensions. But for Tilak leadership had a further and highly important meaning—compelling the state to recognize that, as an alien regime, it could not hope to exert direct authority (except in the crudest form of armed might) over the mass of the people. To be effective, British medical intervention (and the wider administrative system of which it was part) must first acknowledge the authority of Indian leaders and seek to work through their mediation and assistance.

This was, of course, precisely what Rand and Sandhurst had at first tried to demonstrate they did not need—that India's 'leaders' were selfish, self-appointed men with no effective or legitimate hold over the masses. But it was also the policy the British administration was forced to adopt as a result of popular resistance and middle-class protest, in 1898–9. Even in Pune, where Rand's assassination had at first made the provincial government more assertive than ever, it soon came to be accepted that inviting the co-operation of local leaders was preferable to mass resistance and the unchecked spread of the plague. In September 1897 the city's plague regulations were amended so that the British soldier accompanying each search party remained outside while two Indian soldiers went inside the house to look for possible plague cases under the direction of an Indian volunteer. This was a small concession—if only because military might was still in evidence and the case for some European agency had not been abandoned—but it was hailed by the *Kesari* as providing 'a fine opportunity' for the leaders to show that 'Natives are as capable of managing these things as Europeans and that they do possess the organizing and administrative tact.'[98] The *Mahratta* of 26 November 1897 also praised the new regulations as consistent with Indian 'self-respect' and welcomed them as giving a chance to show that 'the excesses in the last plague campaign', which had eventuated in Rand's assassination, had been 'entirely due to Native help and sympathy being despised'.

What is striking in all this is that there emerged an area of convergence and compatibility between the respective positions of the colonial state and the Indian middle classes. Despite their political rivalry the British had in large measure been forced to concede the claim of the Indian middle classes that access to the body of people could only effectively be gained through their mediation as 'native leaders'. Attempting to enlist the support and influence of princes, zamindars, officials and other Indians credited with power and authority over the mass of the population had, in fact, been one of the tactics long since employed to encourage the adoption of vaccination. But in the context of the plague in the 1890s it represented a significant climb-down from the self-confidence and the arrogant disregard for Indian sentiment and Indian agency which had characterized the colonial administration and the medical establishment at the start of the epidemic. Moreover, although the term 'native leaders' was capable of many interpretations including 'traditional' figures like zamindars, caste heads and religious authorities, it in practice gave recognition to the novel ambitions of the professional middle class to be accepted as leaders by the colonial state.

In claiming to speak for the best interests and for the physical well-being of the masses, for the body (in both a literal and a metaphorical sense) of the people, the middle classes were making a clear demonstration of their broader hegemonic aspirations. But there was also a powerful contradiction within this bid for middle-class political and cultural ascendancy. While contending that British rule in India could only be effective in so far as it relied upon

---

[98] *Kesari*, 28 September 1897. In January 1898, while he was held in Byculla jail, Bombay, the British put Tilak's leadership (and his ambivalence towards Western medicine) to the test by asking him if he would be inoculated as an example to the other prisoners. Despite Tilak's publicly stated reservations about Haffkine's inoculation, he apparently agreed, but was then too ill for the operation to be performed. The prisoners were inoculated regardless. Karandikar, *Tilak*, p. 160.

middle-class assistance and mediation, the middle classes were also revealing a narrower class interest of their own which emphasized their distance from the masses, their imperfect ascendancy over them, and the continuing possibility of class-operation with British rule as well as political and racial antagonism against it. For example, one of the reasons why the middle classes protested so vehemently over house searches, compulsory hospitalization and the inspection of rail passengers was precisely that these measures treated Indians as an undifferentiated whole, without acknowledging differences of caste and class. On 13 October 1897 the *Phoenix* newspaper of Karachi objected to the way in which 'respectable Native gentlemen' were being detained for inspection' at railway stations while 'third-rate Europeans and Indo-Europeans [Eurasians] 'were being 'exempted from all restriction'. The Bombay press was similarly indignant in January 1898 that Indian judges, solicitors and other 'Native gentlemen of position' were being subjected to the same humiliating treatment at Victoria Terminus as third-class passengers.[99] Perhaps, too, the hero of *Sukrata* was as much incensed at having to stand in line with illiterate, low-caste coolies as he was by the physical abuse he received from the European doctor. There was resentment, therefore, at the privileged position afforded to the European body and at the failure to recognize a similarly favoured status for the body of the Indian élite. In this area, too, the British were forced to make concessions. Although the bulk of the rioting and the physical resistance had come from the peasants, labourers and urban workers, it was the middle classes who reaped the greatest benefits from the violence and obstruction. Segregation and the examination of travellers became frankly discriminatory along class as well as racial lines. First-class Indian passengers were granted the same exemption as Europeans and only those in the third class were subjected to the full treatment of public searches. The *bhadralok* of Calcutta were allowed to segregate their sick within their own houses and gardens while the poor were still likely to be despatched to the nearest hospital or segregation camp.[100]

There was also real contempt, and at times indignation and fear, in middle-class attitudes to popular ideas and responses during the

[99] *Gurakhi* (Bombay), 8 January 1898: *Kaiser-e-Hind*, 16 January 1898.
[100] Municipal and Medical Department resolution. Bengal, 8 February 1898, India, Home (Sanitary), 482, March 1898, NAI; Viceroy to Secretary of State, 25 August 1898, India, Home, 809, August 1898, NAI.

plague crisis. It is necessary here to enter a note of caution for news-paper editors could not show too great a sympathy for rioters and resisters without themselves being branded 'seditious' and risking prosecution under the press laws. Sometimes their reporting of pla-gue riots, though framed in the language of condemnation, thinly disguised a delight at British discomfiture and the unpopularity of colonial rule. Hence the *Mahratta* of 23 January 1898, in discussing the Chakalashi episode, remarked that this 'silly affair' was none the less 'very significant' in showing 'unmistakably . . . that British rule has no hold on the minds of the masses'. But, contrary to what offi-cialdom and the Anglo-Indian press might maintain, it was obvious that the many riots and disturbances which arose from the early pla-gue administration were autonomous subaltern movements without middle-class direction or instigation. One possible exception to this was the riots at Kanpur in April 1900 when Marwari merchants, fearful of the way in which plague measures were beginning to effect their own community, appear to have played a part in whip-ping up popular opposition.[101] But the contemptuous language sho-wered upon 'ignorant rustics' and the 'superstitious' beliefs of peasants and mill-hands, the criticism of their 'filthy habits', and the contrast repeatedly drawn between the 'intelligent' and 'educated classes' on the one hand and the 'foolish and illiterate' peasants on the other, cannot have been intended for the censor's eye alone.[102] This attitude became even more pronounced when, as in Calcutta in May 1898, the 'topi-wallahs' themselves had been the targets of popular violence. The editor of the paper *Hitavadi*, hitherto one of the most outspoken critics of colonial plague policies, angrily de-cried the actions of the 'budmashes' whom he believed had been re-sponsible for the attacks. 'No one', he fumed, 'has the right to kick up a row and create a disturbance.'[103] The followers of Ramakrishna were more restrained in their disapproval but they issued a state-ment calling for calm and urging the people not to be misled by '*canards* or bazaar gossip'.[104] The desire to lead and to educate the

[101] MacDonnell to Secretary, Home, Government of India, 17 April 1900, India, Home (Public), 294, June 1900, NAI.

[102] *Kaiser-e-Hind* (Bombay), 1 November 1896; *Kalpataru* (Sholapur), 3 March 1897; *Indian Spectator* (Bombay), 7 March 1897; *Gurakhi* (Bombay), 4 February 1898; *Dhureen* (Belgaum), 9 March 1898.

[103] *Hitavadi*, 13 May 1898.

[104] *Basumati* (Calcutta), 12 May 1898.

'rough people'[105] was in part grounded in a fear of their violence and 'irrationality'.

The early years of the Indian plague epidemic thus provide an important illustration of the complex interplay of coercion and co-operation, resistance and hegemony, class and race in the colonial situation. The initial phase of the anti-plague measures demonstrated the strength and political opportunism of the colonial state and its willingness to put state power at the disposal of Western medicine. The force of the Indian reaction resulted in a reassertion of political over sanitary considerations and the shift to a policy of accommodation directed primarily at winning over middle-class support and co-operation. Coercion was tempered with consent. Subaltern resistance played an important part in wresting these concessions from the colonial state, but middle-class hegemony was the greatest beneficiary. While the initial conflict over the plague administration opened up a significant racial and political division between rulers and ruled, it also revealed the importance of an increasingly assertive, if as yet unconsolidated, middle-class ascendancy over the Indian masses. In the short term the subaltern classes in the towns and countryside were disposed to view the middle classes with suspicion and as allies of the British. In the longer term, however, emulation of higher-caste, middle-class ways was a significant factor in persuading the 'common people' to overcome their doubts about Western medicine and to show a greater acceptance of hospitals and inoculation than during the early plague years.

[105] *Mahratta*, 5 March 1898.

# Glossary

| | |
|---|---|
| *Adivasi* | Autochthonous population; member of an Indian tribe |
| *Arkati* | A recruiter of labour for plantations, roadworks, railways, etc. |
| *Arzi* | Petition |
| *Asahyog* | Non-cooperation |
| *Ashraf* | Well-born; a person of rank; Muslim gentleman |
| *Avatar* | Incarnation |
| *Ayurveda* | Traditional Indian system of medicine |
| *Bahi-khata* | Account book |
| *Bajra* | A kind of Indian millet |
| *Bania* | Merchant |
| *Barati* | A member of a wedding party |
| *Begar* | Forced labour |
| *Bedakhali* | Ejectment; eviction from land held as tenant/subtenant |
| *Bharat* | Younger brother of the Hindu mythical hero Rama. Bharat is the indigenous name for India. |
| *Bhaiyachara* | 'Brotherhood'; a form of tenure in which estates are held by the descendants of a common stock and the shares and responsibility for government demand are fixed in proportion to the actual area occupied by each share. |
| *Bidroha* | Rebellion; uprising |

| | |
|---|---|
| *Biswadar* | Holder of a share or shares in a co-parcenary village; a sub-proprietory tenure holder under a chief proprietor |
| *Bohra* | A community of Muslim merchants |
| *Brahmchari* | A Hindu celibate; technically, a novice |
| *Budmash* | Hooligan; a rascal |
| *Bustee* | Locality |
| *Chaddar* | Sheet; a piece of cloth |
| *Chait* | The last month in the Indian calendar roughly corresponding to March-April |
| *Chamar* | A low-caste Hindu often engaged in leather work |
| *Charkha* | Spinning wheel |
| *Chauk* | A raised platform, usually situated in crossroads; squares |
| *Chowrassee* | A subdivision of a district or pargana comprised of originally eighty-four villages, although usually reduced to a much smaller number |
| *Daira* | A musical instrument |
| *Dal* | Pulse; all species of lentils |
| *Darshan* | Ritualized viewing of an image of a god or a god-like person |
| *Dhaphili* | A musical instrument |
| *Dharmpodeshak* | Religious preacher |
| *Dhing (tribal)* | Rebellion; uprising |
| *Diku (tribal)* | Foreigner; alien; outsider |
| *Dom* | An untouchable caste who dispose of dead bodies |
| *Dooly* | An improvised palanquin |
| *Facir* | A religious (esp. Muslim) mendicant; ascetic |

| | |
|---|---|
| *Ganatantrik* | From 'Ganatantra' (a republic); republican |
| *Ghazi* | A soldier who fights for Islam against the infidels |
| *Ghee* | Clarified butter |
| *Gur* | Unrefined raw sugar; molasses |
| *Haat* | A periodic village market |
| *Hakim* | From 'hukm' (order); master, used colloquially for district and tahsil (q.v.) officials |
| *Halwas-puri* | Sweetmeat and special bread prepared for festive occasions |
| *Hissadar* | A share holder; a co-parcener in a village |
| *Hool (tribal)* | Rebellion: uprising |
| *Hukumnamah* | An official (civil or religious) order |
| *Jai* | Victory |
| *Jai Mahavir* | Victory or glory to the Hindu god Shiva |
| *Jaikar* | Shouting 'Jai': Long live . . . |
| *Jama* | Assessed revenue; total land revenue levied on an estate |
| *Jat* | A major Hindu agricultural caste in northwest India |
| *Jowar* | A kind of Indian millet |
| *Julaha* | Weaver; caste of Muslim weavers |
| *Kanhaiya* | Popular name of the Hindu god Krishna |
| *Karahi* | A cooking pan (a wok) |
| *Khaddar* | From 'Khadi'; fabric made of hand-spun yarn and used mostly for wear as a sign of commitment to the nationalist cause |
| *Khap* | Clan area |
| *Khera* | A deserted village; a village from which a number of subordinate hamlets have grown in the neighborhood |

| | |
|---|---|
| *Kisan; Krishak* | Cultivator; farmer; peasant |
| *Kist* | Installment of revenue or rental |
| *Kothi* | Establishment; usually branch agency of mercantile concern or Zamindar's house (q.v.) |
| *Kshatriya* | A Hindu upper caste of warriors |
| *Lakh* | A hundred thousand |
| *Lathi* | A wooden or bamboo pole; a club |
| *Lumbardar* | A village headman with whom the revenue engagement has been usually done |
| *Ma-baap* | 'Mother and father'; often used to represent the relation between the peasants and superordinate elite authorities as one between children and parents |
| *Maafi* | Land exempt from payment of revenue |
| *Mahajan* | 'Greatman'; a substantial merchant moneylender |
| *Mahal* | Area often taken as a unit of revenue |
| *Mahratta* | A native of Maharashtra, a state in western India |
| *Malik* | 'Lord'; proprietor; a cultivator possessing hereditary rights |
| *Marsia* | Shi'ite lamentations in verse commemorating the death of prophet Mohammed's grandson |
| *Masjid* | Mosque |
| *Maulvi* | Muslim religious scholar or teacher |
| *Mazar* | Muslim grave |
| *Mela* | Fair |
| *Minnat* | A pledge made to a deity in anticipation of a specific piece of good luck |
| *Morcha* | Barricade |
| *Mukka* | Maize |

| | |
|---|---|
| *Muqaddam* | Village headman |
| *Murti* | Image; specifically religious icon |
| *Naib Tahsildar* | An influential officer in the subdivisional revenue administration; deputy tahsildar |
| *Nazrana* | Premium paid by tenant/subtenant for admission or re-admission to a holding; generally a form of illegally extracted dues. |
| *Nilhe Saheb* | Indigo planter |
| *Paltan* | From (platoon); a squad of soldiers |
| *Panch* | One or all of the five members of a local council |
| *Panchali* | A form of Hindu devotional folk music |
| *Parja* | *See* Praja |
| *Pargana* | A subdivision within a tahsil (q.v.) |
| *Pattah* | A document or deed specifying the conditions under which a cultivator or undertenant holds his land |
| *Pattidar* | Holder of share in a co-parcenary village estate |
| *Paschimbanga* | West Bengal |
| *Peer (tribal)* | A subdivision resembling a pargana in singhbhum; a tribal area in modern Bihar state |
| *Pir; peer* | A Muslim saint; a holy man; chief of a religious sect |
| *Pradesh* | Region |
| *Praja* | 'Subject'; used primarily to mean tenant cultivators, connoting their relationship of dependence on their landlords |
| *Prasad* | Food ritually offered to Hindu dieties for subsequent distribution to the devotees |
| *Puja* | Worship |

| | |
|---|---|
| *Qasbah* | Small country town; 'urban' manufacturing, marketing or administrative centre |
| *Qazi* | Judge trained in Islamic law; interpreter of Islamic law and injunctions |
| *Raees* | Rich |
| *Raiyat; Ryot; Ryut* | Officially recognized tenant; peasant |
| *Ramlila* | A folk festival which celebrates the career of the Hindu mythical hero Rama by dramatizing principal episodes |
| *Rangmahal* | A luxurious palace |
| *Rasad* | A grain levy traditionally imposed by the state or federal chiefs to provide for troops on the march or for hunting expeditions |
| *Sabha* | Meeting; organisation |
| *Sadhu* | A Hindu holy man; ascetic; mendicant |
| *Sahib* | A term of respect for persons of rank and Europeans |
| *Sahukar* | Moneylender |
| *Salim Chisti and Sheikh Burhan* | Renowned sufi saints |
| *Samgram* | Battle |
| *Samskar* | A sanctifying or purificatory Hindu ritual |
| *Sarkar* | Government; regime |
| *Sati* | An Indian widow who burns herself on her husband's pyre; the custom of doing this |
| *Seth* | A rich trader or banker |
| *Sewa* | Service |
| *Shariat* | Quranic laws governing both secular and religious matters |

| | |
|---|---|
| *Shivalaya* | A small temple of the god Shiva used for ritual worship |
| *Shuhda* | A rogue |
| *Sir* | Land cultivated by the Zamindar (q.v.) themselves with labourers or tenants-at-will as their own exclusive share |
| *Sivaji* | Maratha ruler of late sixteenth century |
| *Sontal* | A tribe of central and eastern India |
| *Sowar* | Rider |
| *Subahdar* | Chief of a Subdah or province |
| *Saggar; Suggar* | Small cart used in singhbhum |
| *Suraee* | Inn |
| *Sri Ramachandraji* | Rama, the mythical Hindu hero |
| *Swaraj* | Self-rule; the word used in nationalist idiom for Indian independence |
| *Taga* | A dominant land-owning caste in northwestern India |
| *Tahsil* | A subdivision within a district |
| *Talwar* | Sword |
| *Tapasya* | Austere endeavor to achieve an end |
| *Tappa* | An administrative division smaller than a tahsil (subdivision) |
| *Tazia* | Replica of the mausoleum of the prophet Mohammed's grandson carried in procession during Muharram, the annual commemoration of his death |
| *Tel-sindur* | Oil and vermilion used in Hindu rituals |
| *Thakur* | Member of a dominant landed caste in eastern U.P. |

| | |
|---|---|
| *Thakurdwara* | Temple |
| *Thana* | Police station |
| *Thanadar* | Officer in charge of a police station |
| *Thok; Thoke* | A share or portion of land in co-parcenary village; maximal lineage |
| *Thug* | A member of a religious fraternity that murdered by strangling or poisoning, especially in central and western India in the nineteenth century |
| *Topiwallah* | 'Person with a cap'; in nationalist idiom, a sympathizer or member of the Indian National Congress |
| *Ulema* | Scholars well-versed in Islamic law and theology |
| *Ulgulan* | Rebellion; uprising |
| *Unani* | 'Greek' (Ionian); the Islamic system of medicine |
| *Urdu* | A language of Arabic, Persian and Hindustani origin particularly used by the Muslims of India |
| *Vaid* | Native doctor |
| *Vratakatha* | Folk ballad or narrative recited on certain Hindu ritual occasions |
| *Zamindar* | Superior land-right holder; landlord |